GOVERNING GLOBAL FINANCE

Global Finance Series

Edited by
Michele Fratianni, Indiana University, U.S.A., John J. Kirton, University of Toronto, Canada, and Paolo Savona, LUISS University, Italy

The intensifying globalisation of the twenty-first century has brought a myriad of new managerial and political challenges for governing international finance. The return of synchronous global slowdown, mounting developed country debt, and new economy volatility have overturned established economic certainties. Proliferating financial crises, transnational terrorism, currency consolidation, and increasing demands that international finance should better serve public goods such as social and environmental security have all arisen to compound the problem.

The new public and private international institutions that are emerging to govern global finance have only just begun to comprehend and respond to this new world. Embracing international financial flows and foreign direct investment, in both the private and public sector dimensions, this series focusses on the challenges and opportunities faced by firms, national governments, and international institutions, and their roles in creating a new system of global finance.

Related titles in the G8 and Global Governance series

New Directions in Global Economic Governance
John J. Kirton and George M. von Furstenberg, eds.
ISBN 0 7546 1698 3

Guiding Global Order
John J. Kirton, Joseph P. Daniels and Andreas Freytag, eds.
ISBN 0 7546 1502 2

Shaping a New International Financial System
Karl Kaiser, John J. Kirton and Joseph P. Daniels, eds.
ISBN 0 7546 1412 3

The G8's Role in the New Millennium
Michael R. Hodges, John J. Kirton and Joseph P. Daniels, eds.
ISBN 1 84014 774 1

Governing Global Finance

New challenges, G7 and IMF contributions

Edited by

MICHELE FRATIANNI
Indiana University

PAOLO SAVONA
LUISS University

JOHN J. KIRTON
University of Toronto

Ashgate

Published by
Ashgate Publishing Limited
Gower House
Croft Road
Aldershot
Hampshire GU11 3HR
England

Ashgate Publishing Company
131 Main Street
Burlington, VT 05401-5600 USA

Ashgate website: http://www.ashgate.com

British Library Cataloguing in Publication Data
Governing global finance : new challenges, G7 and IMF
    contributions. - (Global finance)
    1. Group of Eight (Organization) 2. International Monetary
    Fund 3. International economic relations 4. Globalization
    I. Fratianni, Michele II. Savona, Paolo, 1936- III. Kirton,
    John J.
    337.1

Library of Congress Control Number: 2002103340

ISBN 0 7546 0880 8

Printed and bound in Great Britain by MPG Books Ltd, Bodmin, Cornwall

Contents

DOCUMENTARY APPENDICES

List of Tables

List of Figures

List of Contributors

Sir Nicholas Bayne, KCMG, is a Fellow at the International Trade Policy Unit of the London School of Economics and Political Science. As a British diplomat, he was High Commissioner to Canada from 1992 to 1996, Economic Director at the Foreign and Commonwealth Office from 1988 to 1992, and Ambassador to the Organisation for Economic Co-operation and Development from 1985 to 1988. He has published numerous articles and books, including *Hanging In There* (Ashgate, 2000); he is co-author, with Robert Putnam, of *Hanging Together: Co-operation and Conflict in the Seven Power Summits* (Harvard University Press, 1987), and, with Stephen Woolcock, of *Economic Diplomacy* (Ashgate, forthcoming). Sir Nicholas also contributed to *New Directions in Global Economic Governance: Managing Globalisation in the Twenty-First Century* (Ashgate, 2001) and *New Directions in Global Political Governance: The G8 and International Order in the Twenty-First Century* (Ashgate, in press).

Michele Fratianni is the W. George Pinnell Professor and Chair of Business Economics and Public Policy at the Kelley School of Business at Indiana University in Bloomington, Indiana. He has taught also at the Catholic University of Louvain, the Università Cattolica of Milan, the Università Sapienza of Rome, Marquette University, and the Frei Universität of Berlin. He has served as economic advisor to the European Commission in Brussels, and senior staff economist with the U.S. President's Council of Economic Advisers. Recipient of the Medal of the President of the Italian Republic for scientific achievements, he has also received the Pio Manzú Center Gold Medal, the Scanno prize in economics, and the St. Vincent prize in economics. He is Managing Editor of *Open Economies Review* and is a widely published author of many articles and books, including *Storia Monetaria d'Italia (The Monetary History of Italy*, Etas, 2001). He is co-editor, with Paolo Savona and Dominick Salvatore, of *Ideas for the Future of the International Monetary System* (Kluwer Academic Publishers, 1999).

Andreas Freytag is Senior Economist and Managing Director of the Institute for Economic Policy in Cologne, and has been a Visiting Scholar at the Faculty of Economics and Politics at Cambridge University. He has published widely on international economic relations and globalisation, and is currently working on the political economy of international monetary policy. He is co-editor, with John J. Kirton and Joseph P. Daniels, of *Guiding Global Order: G8 Governance in the Twenty-First Century* (Ashgate, 2001).

Giorgio Gomel is currently Head of International Relations at the Bank of Italy in Rome. He holds a degree from the University of Torino, Italy, and an M.Phil. from Columbia University in New York. He has taught or lectured at a number of U.S. and Italian universities. For many years he has been an economist and director in the Research Department of the Bank of Italy. In the mid 1980s he served as Advisor to the Italian Executive Director of the International Monetary Fund. He has been a member of several committees and groups, both at the European and the international levels. He has published essays in academic journals on international economic policy co-ordination, financial crises, external debt and country risk, and international migration.

Diana Juricevic is currently enrolled in a combined J.D./M.A. (Economics) programme at the University of Toronto Faculty of Law. She is a senior research analyst with the University of Toronto G8 Research Group, contributing editor to the *Attaché International Affairs Journal*, and assistant editor of the University of Toronto *Faculty of Law Review*.

John J. Kirton is Director of the G8 Research Group, Associate Professor of Political Science, Research Associate of the Centre for International Studies, and Fellow of Trinity College at the University of Toronto. He has advised the Canadian government on G7 participation and international trade and sustainable development, and has written widely on G7/8 summitry. He is co-author of *Environmental Regulations and Corporate Strategy: A NAFTA Perspective* (Oxford University Press, 1999) and co-editor of *The G8's Role in the New Millennium* (Ashgate, 1999), *Shaping a New International Financial System: Challenges of Governance in a Globalizing World* (Ashgate, 2000), *Guiding Global Order: G8 Governance in the Twenty-First Century* (Ashgate, 2001), and *New Directions in Global Economic Governance: Managing Globalization in the Twenty-First Century* (Ashgate, 2001). Professor Kirton is Principal Investigator of 'Securing Canada's Environmental Community Through International Regime Reform' (the EnviReform project).

Takashi Kiuchi is Economic Advisor of the Shinsei Bank Ltd. in Tokyo. He has been a guest scholar at the Brookings Institution, and a member of the Faculty of Economics at Yokohama National University. He served as an advisor on governmental committees on numerous occasions and authored many articles and scholarly works, including 'The Asian Crisis and Its Implications' in *Shaping a New International Financial System: Challenges of Governance in a Globalizing World*, edited by Karl Kaiser, John J. Kirton and Joseph P. Daniels (Ashgate, 2000).

Ella Kokotsis is the Communications Co-ordinator at the Independent Electricity Market Operator and is Director of Analytical Studies for the University of Toronto G8 Research Group. She served on the National Round Table on the Environment and the Economy's Task Force on Foreign Policy and Sustainability in preparation for the 1995 G7 Halifax Summit, and has prepared commissioned policy papers for the Canadian Centre for Foreign Policy Development at the Department of Foreign Affairs and International Trade. Author of *Keeping International Commitments: Compliance, Credibility, and the G7, 1988–1995* (Garland, 1999), Dr. Kokotsis holds a Ph.D. in International Relations from the University of Toronto.

Alina Kudina is a doctoral student at Templeton College at the University of Oxford. Before coming to Oxford, she worked for the Harvard Institute for International Development, doing macroeconomic modelling and policy analysis. Her master's thesis was devoted to the motives for foreign direct investment in Ukraine. She was also one of the major contributors to the International Bank for Reconstruction and Development's project on the interests and capacity of foreign investors in Ukraine.

John C. Pattison is Senior Vice-President of Regulatory and Corporate Affairs at the Canadian Imperial Bank of Commerce in Toronto. His activities involve managing regulatory activities on a global basis. He is a former faculty member of the School of Business Administration at the University of Western Ontario. His books and articles have been published in Canada, the United States, Switzerland, Germany, Italy, the Netherlands, and the United Kingdom. In 1998, the Government of France conferred on him the honour of Chevalier de la Légion d'Honneur.

Alan M. Rugman holds the L. Leslie Waters Chair in International Business at the Kelly School of Business at Indiana University in Bloomington, Indiana, and is Thames Water Fellow in Strategic Management at Templeton College at the University of Oxford. Author of *The End of Globalization* (McGraw-Hill Ryerson, 2001), he has published widely, including 'From Globalisation to Regionalism: The Foreign Direct Investment Dimension of International Finance' in *Shaping a New International Financial System: Challenges of Governance in a Globalising World*, edited by Karl Kaiser, John J. Kirton, and Joseph P. Daniels (Ashgate, 2000).

Dominick Salvatore is Distinguished Professor of Economics and Department Chair at Fordham University in New York. He is a Fellow of the New York Academy of Sciences and Chair of its economics section. He served as President of the International Trade and Finance Association in 1994/95 and is a Research Fellow at the Institute for European Affairs at the Vienna University of Economics and Business. He has published extensively in the field of international trade and finance, including 'The Euro Versus the Dollar' in *Global Economy Quarterly* (January/March 2000), 'Forecasting Financial Crises in Emerging Market Economies' in *Open Economies*

Review (co-written with Derrick Reagle, July 2000), 'The Euro, the European Central Bank, and the International Monetary System' in *Annals of the American Academy of Political and Social Science* (February 2002), and 'How Will the Euro Affect the Dollar?' in *Eastern Economic Journal* (February 2002).

Paolo Savona is Professor of Political Economy at LUISS-Guido Carli University in Rome. A graduate of the University of Cagliari, he is also chair of Impregilo Group and of Consorzio Venezia Nuova, deputy chair of the Aspen Institute Italia and an editorialist for the *Corriere della Serra*, Italy's leading newspaper. Professor Savona is co-editor of the *Open Economics Review*, and author of, among other publications, *The New Architecture of the International Monetary System* (Kluwer Academic Publishers, 2000). Formerly the Minister of Trade and Industry in the 50th Italian government, he has served in a wide variety of positions, including researcher in the special studies section of the Board of Governors of the Federal Reserve System in Washington DC, director of the financial market section of the research department of the Banca d'Italia, and secretary general for economic planning in the Ministry of Budget and Planning in Rome.

George M. von Furstenberg, for many years a titled Professor of Economics at Indiana University, is the inaugural holder of the Robert Bendheim Chair in Economic and Financial Policy at Fordham University. His academic pursuits have alternated with work as Division Chief at the International Monetary Fund from 1978 to 1983 and at agencies of the Government of the United States, such as the Department of Housing and Urban Development (1967–68), the President's Council of Economic Advisers (Senior Economist, 1973–76), and the Department of State (1989–90). In Washington, he has also been a resident fellow, economist, or advisor at the Brookings Institution and the American Enterprise Institute. His interests are consequently oriented toward policy, broad and international, with core subjects of macroeconomic theory and international finance. Professor von Furstenberg's book projects include regulation and supervision of financial institutions in the countries participating in the North American Free Trade Agreement and learning from the world's best central bankers. He is co-editor, with John J. Kirton, of *New Directions in Global Economic Governance: Managing Globalisation in the Twenty-First Century* (Ashgate, 2001), and a contributor to *Shaping a New International Financial System*, edited by Karl Kaiser, John J. Kirton, and Joseph P. Daniels (Ashgate, 2000), and *Guiding Global Order: G8 Governance in the Twenty-First Century*, edited by John J. Kirton, Joseph P. Daniels, and Andreas Freytag (Ashgate, 2001). Professor von Furstenberg joined the G8 Research Group and its Professional Advisory Council in 1999. In 2000, he was president of the North American Economics and Finance Association, focussing on integration processes in the western hemisphere.

Preface and Acknowledgements

This book is the first in Ashgate Publishing's new Global Finance series. It continues a tradition, begun in 1998 with the G8 and Global Governance series, of using the annual G8 Summit as a catalyst for edited volumes that explore the central themes in the emerging dynamic of global governance. The current volume is the fourth occasion from the two series that takes a close look at the field of international finance. The continuing and compounding need for the global community to combat financial crises, generate global growth, confront deeper structural issues, and create a new international financial architecture in an era of intense globalisation has inspired both this volume and the new series that it inaugurates.

The first book dealing with international finance was *The G8's Role in the New Millennium*, produced on the basis of the 1998 Birmingham G8 Summit. It examined the contribution of the G7/8 as it began a new era with Russia as a virtually full member, with a rapidly expanding array of ministerial level institutions, and with a new, highly domestic agenda that included financial supervision, employment, and financial abuse. The 1999 Cologne Summit, taking place as the 1997–99 global financial crisis was coming to an end, inspired *Shaping a New International Financial System*. This book took an economic and political-economy approach to the central issues confronting the global economic community at that time. The 2000 Okinawa Summit led to *New Directions in Global Economic Governance*. It examined international finance in its global and Asian dimensions, the international trade system in the wake of the failed attempt at Seattle in December 1999 to launch a new Millennium Round of multilateral trade negotiations, and the new digital economy that is transforming national societies and the international system alike.

The current volume, based on the work of the G7 leading up to and at the 2001 Genoa Summit, expands the existing explorations in several ways. First, it takes up the urgent and new challenge of how to generate global growth amidst the unprecedented combination of a sharp simultaneous slowdowns in all three G7 regions, the simultaneous eruption of financial crisis in two major emerging economies in two key regions, and the collapse of many of the leading-edge 'new economy' sectors and firms. Second, it addresses the ongoing effort to construct a new international financial architecture to produce stability, growth, and equity in a rapidly globalising era. Here its emphasis is on the new generation of issues in the architectural effort, notably designing mechanisms to prevent crises and reform the multilateral development banks. Third, it looks at the deeper, structural issues upon which the smooth functioning of the global financial system and the construction of an effective new system of global financial governance ultimately depends. It examines in particular the issues of currency consolidation and 'dollarization', the impact of derivatives on world monetary growth and international financial volatility and stability, and the relationship of foreign direct investment, mergers and acquisitions, trade liberalisation, and ecological concerns on the international financial system. In all cases, it assesses the performance and potential of the G7, the International Monetary Fund (IMF), and the international institutions centred on each, in addressing these new challenges.

To explore these new issues, the Associazione Guido Carli and the G8 Research Group mounted a conference on 'Assembling a New International Financial Architecture: The Deeper Challenges'. The conference was held at LUISS University in Rome on 17 July 2001, in the immediate lead-up to the 2001 Italian-hosted Genoa G7/8 Summit. It assembled a dozen scholars, practitioners, and policy makers from all G7 regions to present papers in an intense, day-long interchange with a similar number of expert colleagues based in Europe, North America, and Asia. Taking place just after the G7 finance ministers met in Rome on 7 July to prepare their reports to leaders, and occurring immediately before the leaders themselves gathered in Genoa on 20 July to consider these reports and related issues, the conference offered a timely opportunity to deepen the analysis and widen the array of options available to the G7 leaders. It also outlined an agenda for intensified analytical work and policy analysis in the year leading up to the Canadian-hosted Summit at Kananaskis, Alberta, on 26–27 June 2002. To continue this work, the Associazione Guido Carli and the G8 Research Group have established the Research Group on Global Financial Governance as an ongoing contribution to the scholarly and policy analysis of these vital issues.

This volume synthesises the results of three ongoing research programmes. The first is the work of the Associazione Guido Carli on the international monetary system. That work has generated two major edited volumes: *Ideas for the Future of the International Monetary System,* edited by Michele Fratianni, Dominick Salvatore, and Paolo Savona (Kluwer Academic Publishers, 1998), and *The New Architecture of the International Monetary System,* edited by Paolo Savona (Kluwer Academic Publishers, 2000). The contributions of Paolo Savona, Michele Fratianni, and Dominick Salvatore in this current volume reflect their work in that programme. The second research programme is the G8 Research Group's ongoing exploration of international finance, in which John Kirton, Nicholas Bayne, George von Furstenberg, Alan Rugman, Takashi Kiuchi, and Andreas Freytag have been involved. The third is the University of Toronto's Centre for International Studies' project on 'Securing Canada's Environmental Community Through International Regime Reform' (the EnviReform project), financed by the Social Science and Humanities Research Council of Canada, through its strategic grant programme on 'Globalisation and Social Cohesion in Canada'. John Kirton and Alan Rugman are involved in this project.

Governing Global Finance draws its contributors from all of the G8's constituent regions of North America, Europe, and Japan, and most of its member countries. Those contributors come from the disciplines of economics, the international political economy field of political science, and management studies, and from leading universities in the United States, Italy, Britain, Germany, Canada, and Japan. Many of the authors have experience at senior levels within many of the core governmental and intergovernmental institutions at work in managing and governing the international economy, or have served in senior advisory capacities. With this wide variety of perspectives, analytical approaches, and judgements, the collection combines the insights of scholars and practitioners familiar with Italy, with those in North America, and other leading G7 countries, who draw on a rich assortment of theoretical traditions, interpretative frameworks, and concluding convictions. Yet all share a basic belief that fundamental changes are underway in the international financial system, that the existing arrangements for global financial governance are still struggling to identify and address them adequately, and that the G7 plays an important role in meeting these new challenges in a rapidly globalising age.

This volume was prepared before the terrorist attacks on the United States of 11 September, and the Argentinean default in late December 2001, both the world's largest in their respective categories, gave new severity and urgency to the issues addressed within it. Although the introductory chapter has been revised and extended to take more direct account of these developments, no attempt has been made to reconstruct the individual contributed chapters in the light of these events. Indeed, the emphasis of this volume on underlying structural issues has given its contributions a value beyond the disruptions of short term, or even decade-defining developments. In many cases, the analyses here have anticipated, and had their relevance reinforced by, the shocks of the last half of 2001. In the introductory chapter, however, the editors have placed the analyses in this volume more directly in the context of the events of 11 September and December, and of the forthcoming Kananaskis Summit that will be called upon to respond.

Acknowledgements

In producing this volume, we have enjoyed the exceptional support of those who contributed in many different ways. Our first debt is to Antonio Fazio, Governor of the Bank of Italy, who as Chairman of the Associazione Guido Carli provided the funding that made our conference possible, and who supported his senior officials in participating in our event. We are also grateful to David Dodge, Governor of the Bank of Canada, his senior advisor John Murray, and Canada's Associate Deputy Minister of Finance, Jonathan Fried, who offered support and practical advice along the way. We also owe much to Canada's outstanding Ambassador to Italy, Robert Fowler, to Giuliano Amato, President of the Council of Ministers of the Italian Republic, and to Francesco Olivieri, Valerio Astraldi, Roberto Toscano, and their colleagues on Italy's G8 team. We further appreciate the willingness to take a major role in our project by several members of the G8 Research Group's Professional Advisory Council: Nicholas Bayne, George von Furstenberg, Alan Rugman, and Takashi Kiuchi. Other members of the Council, Pierre Jacquet, Norbert Walter, and Curzio Giannini also provided useful support.

We are also most grateful to Mario Arcelli, rector of LUISS University, and his colleagues for providing the splendid facilities in which our conference took place. In Rome and Milan, Laura Neri, Chiara Oldani, and Sabrina Canossi were a model of tireless efficiency and co-operation in making the many physical arrangements required for our venture. In Toronto, we owe a special word of thanks to Madeline Koch, the Managing Editor of the G8 Research Group, whose managerial and editorial skills were essential in helping organise the conference and ensuring that initial thoughts and rough drafts were transformed into a polished integrated book. More broadly, we note with deep appreciation the indispensable contribution of Gina Stephens, Co-ordinator of the G8 Research Group, of Sandra Larmour, the Director of Development of the G8 Research Group, of Michael Rollason of RBC Dominion Securities, of Jason Wong of the Government of Ontario, and of Shinichiro Uda, Director of the G8 Research Group's office in Japan.

At the University of Toronto, we are grateful to President Robert Birgineau, Vice-President Heather Munroe Bloom, Patrick Gutteridge, Judy Noordermeer, and their colleagues for their full co-operation in assisting the G8 Research Group with arrangements for President Amato's visit on 29 March 2001. We also acknowledge the continuing support of our colleagues at the Centre for International Studies: its director, Professor Louis Pauly, who oversees our research activities, and Professor Peter Hajnal, who assumed the vital task of securing the anonymous referees who reviewed our draft manuscript and who collectively approved it for publication. We owe much to the comments of our referees, whose often trenchant but always supportive comments have been taken fully into account. At Trinity College, we acknowledge the critical support of provost Tom Delworth, bursar Geoffrey Seaborn, who manages the G8 Research Group's accounts, head librarian Linda Corman, who oversees the development of the G8 Research Library Collection, and Professor Robert Bothwell, Co-ordinator of the International Relations Program. At the Department of Political Science, Professor Robert Vipond, the Chair, and professors Ronald Deibert and Lawrence LeDuc have provided encouragement. At the University of Toronto Library, chief librarian Carole Moore, internet director Sián Miekle, and project manager Marc Lalonde have been indispensable.

As always, we reserve a special word of thanks for Kirstin Howgate, and her colleagues at Ashgate, for recognising the virtue of producing this volume and for working so effectively to ensure the smooth adoption and speedy publication of the manuscript. Finally, we acknowledge the understanding, patience, and support of our families as we laboured to convert raw drafts into published text. We are also indebted to the alumni of the G8 Research Group and our students at universities throughout the G7. They provided a constant source of inspiration and constructive criticism as we pursued our work. It is to this next generation of scholars on global financial governance that we dedicate this book.

Michele Fratianni, Paolo Savona, and John Kirton, February 2002

List of Abbreviations

ADRs	American depository receipts
AMF	Asian monetary fund
APEC	Asia-Pacific Economic Cooperation
ASEAN	Association of South-East Asian Nations
BIS	Bank for International Settlements
CAP	Common Agricultural Policy
CBA	currency board arrangement
CCL	contingent credit line
CDF	Comprehensive Development Framework
CPI	consumer price index
DAC	Development Assistance Committee
ECB	European Central Bank
EEA	European Economic Area
EMS	European Monetary System
EMU	European Monetary Union
EVO	Evaluation Office
FAO	Food and Agriculture Organization
FATF	Financial Action Task Force
FDI	foreign direct investment
FILP	Fiscal Investment and Loan Program
FIUs	financial intelligence units
FSAL	Financial Sector Adjustment Loan
FSAP	Financial Sector Assessment Program
FSF	Financial Stability Forum
FSSA	Financial System Stability Assessment
FTAA	Free Trade Agreement of the Americas
G5	Group of Five
G10	Group of Ten
G20	Group of 20
G22	Group of 22
GAB	General Arrangements to Borrow
GATS	General Agreement on Trade in Services
GATT	General Agreement on Tariffs and Trade
GDP	gross domestic product
GDRs	global despository receipts
GPGs	global public goods
HIPCs	heavily indebted poor countries
HLIs	highly leveraged institutions

IAIS	International Association of Insurance Supervisors
ICT	information and communications technology
IDA	International Development Association
IDG	International Development Goals
IFIs	international financial institutions
IMF	International Monetary Fund
IMFC	International Monetary and Financial Committee
IOSCO	International Organization of Securities Commissions
IT	information technology
LDCs	less developed countries
LDP	Liberal Democratic Party (Japan)
LIBOR	London Interbank Offered Rate
LOLR	lender of last resort
LTCM	Long-Term Capital Management
MAI	Multilateral Agreement on Investment
MDB	multilateral development bank
MEC	marginal efficiency of capital
MFN	most-favoured nation
MIC	middle income countries
MNC	multinational corporation
MPIs	macro prudential indicators
NAFTA	North American Free Trade Agreement
NATO	North Atlantic Treaty Organization
NCCTs	nonco-operative countries and territories
NDFs	nondeliverable foreign exchange forwards
NEPAD	New Plan for African Development
NGO	nongovernmental organisation
OCR	ordinary capital resources
ODA	official development assistance
OECD	Organisation for Economic Co-operation and Development
OFC	offshore financial centre
OPEC	Organisation of Petroleum Exporting Countries
PPI	producer price index
PRSPs	poverty reduction strategy papers
RDBs	regional development banks
ROSCs	reports on observance of codes and standard
SDDS	Special Data Dissemination Standards
SDRs	special drawing rights
SSD	sample standard deviation
UNCTAD	United Nations Conference on Trade and Development
UNSCR	United Nations Security Council Resolution
WB	World Bank
WHO	World Health Organization
WTO	World Trade Organization

Chapter 1

Introduction, Summary, and Conclusions

Michele Fratianni, Paolo Savona, and John J. Kirton

The New Assault on Economic Globalisation

There is a wide 'disconnect' between the proclamations and activity of so-called civil society at international events such as the 2001 Genoa G7/8 Summit and the interests of the poor countries that this civil society claims to represent. While civil society aggregates an assortment of different groups with often conflicting agendas — from debt relief to solidarity and religious groups, from José Bové's antipathy for imported foods to the destructive Black Block — one common and unifying denominator is a belief that the world would be a better place if markets were less globalised or, alternatively, if the world was to re-nationalise the economy. This is exactly the opposite of what an undergraduate student learns in a course in international economics. Why is there such a divide? Who is wrong?

In the textbook version, international trade promotes comparative advantage and fosters an environment of innovation and economic growth. Not everyone, of course, gains from international trade and finance. The protected industry at home suffers from the reduction or elimination of trade impediments. Workers in the protected industry likewise lose from a more open economic environment. In a democratic society, the losing groups voice their interests and often obtain relief from national governments. The compensation of the losers by the winners is an ongoing process and part of the bargain, or 'compensation pact', that is necessary to reach a more liberal world economy. Underlying that bargain is the evidence or belief that the gains from open trade and finance outweigh the losses (Collier and Dollar 2001). Those who gain have enough surplus to compensate those who lose from a more liberal economic order. Clearly, no country will agree to a more liberal order unless it perceives that the gains from open trade and finance outweigh the losses. What could go wrong in this process?

Several possibilities spring to mind. The first is a miscalculation of the benefits and costs of a more open trade and finance regime, for instance, of how a more open regime affects poverty in a society. These miscalculations could be rectified by reopening the compensation pact between losers and gainers within a nation. Democratic societies tend to respond to these issues and are inclined to renegotiate the compensation pact. Nondemocratic societies may be obtuse to these issues; for example, corrupt political leaders who capture the bulk of the benefits of an open trade and finance regime may have no incentive to redress a deteriorating income distribution. Here, the appropriate protest of civil society is to promote more democracy in poor developing countries.

The second problem may result from external shocks to the economy, such as from contagious financial crises as with that of 1997–99 or from an unexpected increase in world interest rates that, together with slower global growth, raise the foreign debt burden of emerging economies and poor developing countries alike. The debt burden may become unsustainable, leading debtors — such as, most recently, Argentina — to seek a reprieve from creditors. If such a reprieve does not occur, the indebted country will suffer and so will the creditors. Debt relief is a legitimate response to an unexpected shock. Creditors acquiesce to debt relief when they realise that without it total debt repudiation may occur. Here, civil society appears to have good grounds in focussing on the debt of the poorest, whose enduring internal economic difficulties can be compounded by new external shocks. The debt burdens of some poor countries are excessive, a fact recognised by G7/8 summits in their treatment of the debt of the poorest since the G7 met in Toronto in 1988.

The third, and the most important, problem is that international trade and finance do not constitute a level playing field. The industrialised countries have struck a deal that captures most of the net benefits; developing countries are not allowed to exploit their comparative advantage fully. Industrialised countries, in their effort to protect domestic losers from a more open trade and finance environment, have erected barriers against imports from the developing countries. Labour-intensive agricultural products and textiles are not given full access to the markets of the industrial countries. The Common Agricultural Policy (CAP) of the European Union protects EU farmers against imports. The same is true in Japan. In the United States, agriculture is much less protected. The textile industry is the other large protected sector in the rich countries, especially in the United States and the EU.[1] Furthermore, the industrial countries, in particular again the United States and those in the EU, are champions in using antidumping measures to restrict imports.

Here, the appropriate protest of civil society is to ask the rich countries to open their economic borders fully. Developing countries have an interest in broadening the degree of globalisation, not in reducing it. The right slogan is 'more trade, finance, foreign direct investment (FDI), and some debt relief'; it is not 'debt relief without trade and finance from abroad'.

Why then, with developing countries themselves having adopted this logic so fully over the past two decades, is there such a divide between the request of civil society for less globalisation and the lessons from theory and history? One answer is that some of the groups represented under the umbrella of civil society are misinformed or use international meetings to promote their narrowly defined interests, or attend those meetings because of the inebriation from the 'sport of risk'. For those who enjoy risk, the meetings of the International Monetary Fund (IMF) and the G7/8 summits are no different than an open-air concert or a football match where the spectator may get a thrill from the expectation that the event may become ugly. However, the majority of civil society appears to have strong convictions and a spirit of generosity.

Where is their protest actually directed? While it is dangerous to generalise, media accounts of the protesters' profiles reveal a longing for an egalitarian world. In the 1960s, such protest was directed at national authorities and domestic institutions to correct actual and perceived income inequalities within the sovereign state. Today, the protest is directed at international organisations and intergovernmental institutions such as the G7/8 to correct inequalities among nation-states. The motivation is the same; the targets have changed. The antiglobal civil society not only uses the internet to organise itself, but also proposes a globalised form of income equalisation.

Nowhere has this egalitarian instinct been more intense than the face of the dominant institutions for governing global finance. To be sure, the death of the Multilateral Agreement on Investment (MAI) at the Organisation for Economic Co-operation and Development (OECD) in 1997 and the delay in the launch of a Millennium Round of multilateral trade negotiations at the Seattle ministerial meeting of the World Trade Organization (WTO) in 1999 showed that dissatisfaction among civil society and developing countries was sufficiently deep to stop further liberalisation in the field of FDI and, for a time, trade (Hodges, Kirton, and Daniels 1999). But it was in the field of finance, with the devastating Asian-turned-global financial crisis of 1997–99, that the costs of unrestrained economic globalisation were brought home to so many around the world. The initial response within the G7 was go beyond the institutionalised routines and resources of the IMF to stop the crisis and contain the costs for those in the developing countries and developed world alike (Kaiser, Kirton, and Daniels 2000). The subsequent reaction, peaking just as the IMF and G7 finance ministers meetings began to attract violent protests in 1999, was to assemble a new international financial architecture that would govern the intensely globalised world of finance effectively and devise more socially sensitive ways to protect the losers in this process (Kirton, Daniels, and Freytag 2001a; Kirton and von Furstenberg 2001; Savona 2000; Fratianni, Salvatore, and Savona 1999). At the same time, responding to pressures from some G7 governments and their civil society nongovernmental organisations (NGOs), there was a renewed, more aggressive move to relieve the debt of the poorest.

Much has been accomplished in this process. However, the following years have seen a proliferation of violent protests to now deadly levels, the outbreak in 2001 of new financial crises in Turkey and Argentina, and the simultaneous economic slowdown in all three G7 regions and much of the global economy. It is clear that finding an effective and legitimate system for governing global finance in an intensely globalising world remains an outstanding and compelling challenge.

Global Governance

In devising such a system, what role should be played by national governments, by broad multilateral organisations such as the United Nations or the IMF, and by exclusive compact bodies such as the G7 or G20? It is now generally accepted that international co-operation is a necessary supplement and a sometimes superior alternative to independent national policies in an interdependent world: the actions of one country often have effects beyond its borders. This raises critical questions: How does one bring about such international co-operation? Who is to govern it? Civil society would appear to prefer an institution that represents all countries, such as the UN, over the more exclusive G7 summits. But the UN is ineffective because of its size and the heterogeneity of the membership; on many vital issues, it is no more than a talking shop. In contrast, the G7 is a sufficiently small and homogeneous group that it can reach significant solutions. The accusation that the G7 is an exclusive club is true in a formal sense, but not in substance. If the G7 were to transform itself into an all-inclusive institution, it would lose whatever effectiveness it has.

It is important to separate romantic notions of international co-operation from the hard facts of how agreements are reached among sovereign states. One such fact is that economic and political power in the world is distributed asymmetrically: Costa Rica does not count as much as the United States. International organisations that ignore this principle distort reality and become ineffective. The economics of international co-operation are rooted in the economics of oligopoly and not in the economics of perfect competition (Fratianni and Pattison 2001). Power asymmetry was very high immediately after World War II. The U.S. was the dominant nation in the world, producing more than half of the world's output. This environment was conducive to extensive international co-operation led by the U.S., which was willing to bear a disproportionate cost. A whole range of co-operative activities, from the Marshall Plan to the design and support of the Bretton Woods international financial institutions, was the direct result of U.S. leadership. Over time, the U.S. share of the world output fell as other countries grew more rapidly than the U.S. Other countries emerged as big players — those in Western Europe, Japan, Canada, China, and Brazil — and these now have a larger stake in the global economy (Kirton 1999, 58–59). The United States, on its own, has diminished supply-side incentives to lead with the same vigour it did immediately after World War II. In today's world, the incentive structure suggests collegial leadership, not hegemony. The G7 is one answer to the requirement for collegial leadership. To be sure, the United States can have a stronger voice than the other members; the United States is recognized as *primus inter pares*. As the distribution of economic and world power continues to change, the G7 may have to consider altering its membership. New large members bring benefits and costs to the club. On the cost side, the increased difficulty of reaching agreements within the club must be considered.

The fact that an institution has a small membership does not mean that it ignores the interests of nonmembers. The G7/8 Summit in Cologne is a good case in point:

> ... the 1999 Cologne Summit marked a major escalation of the demand for the more effective influence and direct inclusion of civil society in the emerging centres of global governance. ... the creation of the new G20, and subsequent calls by the 1999 G8 chair Gerhard Schroeder and the 2000 chair, Japanese prime minister Keizo Obuchi, for China to participate in the G8 Summit demonstrated a broadening effort to expand the G7/8's inclusiveness and representativeness, and thus the legitimacy of the global order it guided (Kirton, Daniels, and Freytag 2001b, 2).

Effective governance cannot be divorced from the legitimacy of the institution that makes decisions. For many, legitimacy means representation. A more representative institution is more legitimate than a less representative one. But this refers back to the starting point: namely, that all-inclusive institutions are ineffective. The tradeoff between effectiveness and representation is at the heart of global governance. Those who call for greater representation must accept the inevitable consequence of more laborious governance and a lower quality of output from international co-operation.

The Approach

Governing Global Finance deals with the critical issues that such governance structures do and will confront. It is an analysis of the new generation of challenges posed by a rapidly globalising world economy for the creation and operation of an international financial system that is efficient, equitable, and legitimate in the minds of all those it affects. This volume continues the recent concern with finding workable mechanisms to combat crises, to prevent contagion, to limit citizens' liability through their public sector for misjudgements made by private market participants, and to ensure that public funds flow in ways effective for those most in need. But it focusses on three new challenges brought by the twenty-first century.

First, it takes up the urgent new challenge of how to generate global growth amidst the unprecedented combination of the collapse of many of the leading-edge new economy sectors and firms, the sharp simultaneous slowdown in 2001 of all three G7 regions, and the eruption of financial crisis in two major emerging economies — Turkey and Argentina — in two key regions.

Second, it addresses the ongoing effort to construct a new international financial architecture to produce stability, growth, and equity in this more challenging macroeconomic and systemic environment. Here it emphasises the new generation of issues in the architectural effort, notably the design of mechanisms to prevent crises and reform the multilateral development banks (MDBs).

Third, it examines the deeper, structural issues that may ultimately determine the smooth functioning of the global financial system, and the construction of an effective new system of global financial governance. It explores more specifically the issues of currency consolidation in general and dollarization in particular, and considers the impact of derivatives on world monetary growth and on international financial volatility and stability; it also looks at the relationship of FDI, mergers and acquisitions, trade liberalisation, and ecological concerns to the international financial system.

In all three cases, *Governing Global Finance* assesses the performance and potential of the IMF, the G7, and the world's leading governments, beginning with the United States, in addressing these new challenges. It evaluates their success against both the economic logic of the market and the political values shared by governments as public sector institutions, and by their citizens.

To conduct this examination, the book combines the contributions of experts based in all of the G8's constituent regions of North America, Europe, and Asia, and in most of its member countries. The contributors come from the disciplines of economics, the international political economy field of political science, and management studies, and from leading universities in the United States, Italy, Britain, Germany, Canada, and Japan, as well as from central banking. Many of the authors have experience at senior levels of core governmental and intergovernmental institutions involved in managing and governing the international economy, or have advised such institutions. Others have a wealth of practical experience in private sector finance. They thus offer a wide variety of perspectives, analytical approaches, and judgements, drawing from a rich assortment of theoretical traditions, interpretative frameworks, and observational vantage points. Yet all share a basic belief that fundamental changes are underway in the international financial system, that the existing arrangements for global financial governance are still struggling to identify and address them adequately, and that the G7 institutions and member governments have an important role in meeting these new challenges.

The Contributions

Part I, 'Governing Global Finance: The G7's Contribution' examines the monetary and financial issues that have been central to the G7's operation since its 1975 creation and that remain vital in the increasingly interdependent world of the twenty-first century: co-ordination of monetary policy, exchange rates, and financial regulation.

This examination begins in Chapter 2, with Nicholas Bayne's 'Reforming the International Financial Architecture: The G7 Summit's Successes and Shortcomings'. Bayne considers the record of the G7 summits in dealing with the 'dark side' of globalisation, namely the fragility of integrated financial systems, the abuses of the financial system, and the widening income disparities between rich and poor countries.

His scoring function uses five criteria: leadership, effectiveness, durability, acceptability, and consistency.

According to Bayne, in dealing with global finance, the summits have scored better on leadership, effectiveness, and consistency than on durability and acceptability. The fact that the three issues under discussion reappear year after year is symptomatic of solutions with short shelf lives. Acceptability or legitimacy of the G7 summits is also problematic:

> In the 1970s and 1980s, the G7 members could be sure that whatever they decided would be accepted without question. Now, as globalisation advances, the summits must satisfy a much wider and more critical circle of other governments and nonstate actors (p. 28).

Bayne's historical assessment of the summits underscores the importance of the G7 members resolving their internal differences, before worrying whether their solutions will be accepted by the wider international community. It is unrealistic to expect that the latter will accept all of the proposed solutions. However, the legitimacy of summit proclamations is enhanced if G7 countries themselves shows determination in implementing them.

At Genoa, the top agenda item was poverty reduction, going beyond debt relief. The summiteers accepted the notion that poor countries remain poor even if debts are forgiven. To grow out of poverty, these countries need aid for education and health care and open access to the markets of industrialised and middle-income developing countries. Despite the disappointment voiced by those groups of civil society pushing for complete debt forgiveness, Genoa can be considered a success. Had it not been for the seven heads of governments, debt relief for the poorest would not have moved forward. In fact, in Bayne's view, the leaders went beyond the proposals of their finance ministers and scored high on acceptability.

In Chapter 3, 'Consensus and Coherence in G7 Financial Governance', John Kirton explores the internal dynamics of the G7 summits, in particular the process through which consensus is reached. At Genoa, there were three new leaders, with a philosophy different from that of the older members of the group. With newcomers President George W. Bush of the United States, Prime Minister Junichiro Koizumi of Japan, and Prime Minister Silvio Berlusconi of Italy, it was natural that:

> the new right leaders and resulting ideological divisions raised the question of whether the G7 could create the consensus needed to provide effective leadership for global financial governance in the new era (p. 46).

At Genoa, the new turned out to mix with the old very well. The 'new right-wing leaders' underwent a rapid socialisation process and the G8 was able to reach consensus on several important points, namely poverty reduction in Africa, global economic growth, financial crisis prevention in Argentina and Turkey, IMF reform, and the launch of a new trade round. On the subject of Argentina and Turkey, the summiteers endorsed the IMF programmes and the adjustment policies taken by the two countries. Argentina, furthermore, received an implicit commitment for an additional rescue package. Delivered in August, the package staved off major economic hardship and gave the country another chance to reform itself. On the new trade round, the U.S. and the EU agreed to put aside their differences and present a common position to the developing countries so that a new trade round could be launched, as it was, by WTO ministers in Doha in November. Under pressure from civil society, the leaders further pledged that the trade round would be consistent with sustainable development.

The main challenges to the summits now, concludes Kirton, are not internal and ideological but external and epistemic. Despite the ability to reach a consensus, Genoa did not make a significant advance in the design of a comprehensive, forward-looking international financial architecture. Yet the G7 is the appropriate forum where such a design can be constructed and launched. To produce it, future summits need to work with the private sector and nongovernmental experts and organisations.

Part II, 'Generating Growth in the Global Economy', examines economic policies that can foster economic growth throughout the world. In Chapter 4, 'The G7's Contribution to Global Economic Growth: An Agenda', Andreas Freytag argues that the G7 countries should pursue policies and structural reforms that promote economic growth at home. This selfish agenda will have positive effects elsewhere in the world through trade and finance linkages among nations. Good policies tend to foster competition. But competition does not equal *laissez faire*. Competition works best when it is constrained by rules. Here, the G7 countries as a group can contribute to world economic growth by setting basic global rules, such as avoiding beggar-thy-neighbour competitive devaluations, avoiding unfair trade practices such as socially or environmentally motivated protectionism, and promoting a more liberal international trade regime.

Aid through international trade, Freytag argues, promotes more economic prosperity than aid through debt relief. Although the latter can be justified when the affected economies are hit by adverse external shocks, a sustained policy of debt relief encourages moral hazard behaviour. If countries know that their external debt will be forgiven, they have no incentive to avoid incurring more debt in the future. Hence, summits should make debt relief a one-time-only event. Debt relief should not be confused with foreign aid.

Freytag concludes with an encouragement to study the summits with the principles and methods of public choice:

> The G7 governments are regularly under pressure to deliver politically appealing results, which do not take into account long-term growth necessities. As Nicholas Bayne (2000; 2001b) has shown, the acceptability of the summits' outcome is an important criterion for

G7 governments' efforts in economic policy making. Acceptability, however, can easily become a euphemism for pleasing rent-seeking groups. One must make sure that this criterion will not overrun all other criteria in judging the summits, in particular in assessing the efficiency and the potential for developing the policies they produce and endorse (p. 83).

In Chapter 5, 'Japan, Asia, and the Rebuilding of the Financial Sector', Takashi Kiuchi investigates two interrelated issues: the nature and implications for the Japanese economy of Prime Minister Koizumi's reform package and the Japanese position on the design of a durable international financial architecture. The Japanese economy is still struggling and remains the weakest of the largest three economic areas of the world. Koizumi's strategy is to focus primarily on structural reforms, with a special emphasis on a public sector viewed as very bureaucratic and stifling efficiency and innovation in the private sector. The reform package is expected to include the privatisation of public and semi-public institutions operating under the sprawling Fiscal Investment and Loan Program. On the issue of banks' nonperforming loans, Koizumi appears less decisive. At the moment, writes Kiuchi,

> money is abundant. Most of the banks are weary of the continuous inflow of deposits, but their efforts to steer their depositors toward other savings instruments are proving unsuccessful. In fact, only a small fraction of applicants for new loans are creditworthy. Thus, the lending spread is exceptionally thin by international standards, and no sign of improvement is in sight. Money is chasing borrowers with good prospects, but cannot find very many (p. 91).

With regard to the international financial architecture, Japanese thinking has been heavily influenced by the events of the 1997–99 Asian financial crisis. Japanese authorities considered that crisis to be caused by capital account considerations. They seriously doubted the IMF's ability to provide the necessary liquidity. Consequently, they wanted to expand significantly the resources of the IMF and create a new organisation that would directly target Asia. The resource issue was further driven by a belief that financial contagion is a serious problem and can be stopped only through massive injections of liquidity. The quick response of the summiteers to Turkey and Argentina appears to accept the Japanese viewpoint. Otherwise, Japan is satisfied with the progress of the international financial architecture achieved since the Cologne Summit in 1999.

Part III, 'Assembling a New International Financial Architecture', deals with the motivations for a new international financial architecture and the possible configurations of such a structure. In Chapter 6, 'Problems and Reforms of the International Monetary System', Dominick Salvatore examines two key problems of the present international financial regime: excessive exchange rate volatility and misalignment and international financial crises in emerging markets. On the first issue, exchange rate misalignment is a much more serious problem than volatility. Unlike short-term fluctuations of exchange rates that can be hedged at little cost or blunted through currency diversification, persistent deviations of the exchange rate from its long-run equilibrium — involving primarily the three big economic areas of the United States, 'Euroland', and Japan — impose significant costs to the economy in the form of unemployment, overcapacity, bankruptcy, and, ultimately, protectionism. The present international monetary system has failed to produce a mechanism whereby countries with large and durable current account imbalances can institute policies to correct such imbalances; in essence, the system has failed in the co-ordination of national economic policies. Salvatore concludes that while hard policy co-ordination is not feasible among the three major economic areas, soft co-ordination has happened in the past and can be revived. In addition, through its annual review of the economy, the IMF can exert pressure on countries with misaligned exchange rates. Benign neglect does not work; appeals to a single world currency, on the other hand, are utopian.

There have been six international financial crises since the mid 1990s: Mexico (1994–95), Southeast Asia (1997–99), Russia (1998), Brazil (1999), Turkey (2001), and Argentina (1999–2002). Integrated capital markets permit owners of funds to move in and out of crisis-afflicted countries quickly. When domestic policies, weaknesses in the domestic financial system, or external shocks appear inconsistent with the maintenance of the existing exchange rate regime, capital flows out of the country and precipitates a crisis; the crisis in one country may spill over to other countries that are financially sound. The community of international organisations, under the leadership of the G7/8, has reacted with a barrage of new instruments and policies to blunt if not eliminate the crises: increased transparency in international financial transactions, strengthening banking and financial systems through the adoption of standards, promoting greater private sector involvement, and providing emergency liquidity. Salvatore, while applauding these initiatives, concludes that

> even if all the reforms under consideration were adopted, they would not eliminate all future financial crises. All that can hoped for is that these reforms would reduce the frequency and severity of future financial crises. In short, some international financial instability and crises may be the inevitable result of liberalised financial markets and the cost that must be paid in return for the benefits that liberalised financial markets provide to industrial and emerging market economies alike (p. 114).

In Chapter 7, 'One Region, One Money: The Need for New Directions in Monetary Policies', George von Furstenberg analyses the causes of the declining usefulness of the national currencies of small open economies. He concludes that currency consolidation in the world would enhance international financial stability. In essence, an excess of national monetary sovereignty contributes to international financial crises. E-commerce, regional economic integration, and global liberalisation are three factors responsible for undermining the monopoly of currencies in small open economies. Technology and integration have raised the degree of currency substitution and currencies of small open economies are now uncompetitive in relation to the currencies of large and stable economies. While there is no viable alternative to letting the three major currencies of the world — the U.S. dollar, the euro, and the yen — float against one another,

> for the smaller countries in each region, the questions raised by financial liberalisation are quite different. For them, maintaining separate currencies, and, consequently, exchange rates, became less desirable when exchange rates became a growing source of shocks to the economy and its finances (p. 118).

Currency consolidation can either be hard, once-and-for-all, and fully credible, or it can be soft and less credible, with the adopting country leaving an opening for a return to the national currency. The currency board, even when the domestic currency is linked to its natural key currency, is an example of the latter. A hard, and thus fully credible, currency consolidation takes place by the country either adopting a large currency as its own, as in the case of Ecuador with the U.S. dollar, or negotiating a monetary union with other countries, as in the case of the European Monetary Union with the euro. In the first instance, the decision is virtually unilateral and the adopting country has no formal say in the conduct of monetary policy of the adopted currency. In the multilaterally negotiated monetary union, the country has a voice in setting common monetary policy. Clearly, the multilateral solution is more complicated and almost requires the pre-existence of a regional trade agreement; the history of the EU is a good lesson in this regard. Von Furstenberg laments the failure of international financial institutions and the G7 summits to recognise the 'needless pain and suffering caused by small countries hanging on to a separate currency that is being eroded by market forces and to recommend multilateral alternatives' (p. 128).

In Chapter 8, 'International Standards, Crisis Management, and Lenders of Last Resort in the International Financial Architecture', Michele Fratianni and John C. Pattison consider two related issues: emergency official lending and financial crisis management, and their link with financial standards. On the first topic, the authors note that there is no pure international counterpart to the domestic lender of last resort, although the IMF has acted as such in a limited way. According to the Meltzer Commission, the IMF should be transformed into a *de jure* international lender of last resort and provide emergency assistance almost exclusively to countries that meet specific standards. Such pre-qualification, in contrast with *ex post* conditionality lending, would solve the moral hazard problem.

There are weaknesses in both pre-qualification and *ex post* conditionality. With the former, the disbursing agency may lend either too much to the qualifiers or too little to the nonqualifiers, creating either moral hazard or welfare losses. With the latter, the

IMF runs the risk of being too generous or too restrictive with the conditions attached to its lending. Another difficulty with *ex post* conditionality is that the adjustment policy pursued by the borrowing country is more difficult to monitor than pre-existing states of nature.

Regardless of the model adopted, official international emergency lending needs tightening: it is now done with much less diligence and care than private sector loans receive. Often, international agencies have been lenders of last resort in terms of credit more than in terms of liquidity; that is, they have lent on conditions materially inferior to those of private lenders. Such practices distort incentives and create dependency. Consider how often Turkey has gone to the money well of the IMF.

Given the constraints in creating a true international lender of last resort, more attention should be paid to strengthening the crisis management capability of the IMF or the Bank for International Settlements (BIS). As Fratianni and Pattison put it:

> The job description of a crisis manager would include due diligence, choice of applicable law, setting an interest rate to clear the market on a risk-adjusted basis, as well as acting as agent for the group of lending institutions co-ordinating the credit conditions of the loan, loan covenants, collateral where applicable, and monitoring. As an agent, the crisis manager would determine appropriate covenants to secure the assets, monitor conditions applying to the loan, such as any collateral, and assess the actions of the borrower to ensure agreement and compliance with loan covenants. As an interest-rate setter, the crisis manager would ask the five most important domestic LOLR [lender of last resort] providers in the world — the U.S. Federal Reserve, the European Central Bank, the Bank of Japan, the Bank of England, and the Swiss National Bank — whether they would be willing to satisfy the loan request at, say, the London Interbank Offered Rate (LIBOR) plus two percentage points. If that request was not fully met at that rate, the penalty rate would then move up, say, to LIBOR plus three, and so on (p. 156).

Part IV, 'The Need for New Directions', includes three chapters. In the first, 'Crisis Prevention and the Role of IMF Conditionality,' Giorgio Gomel considers the issue at the centre of the debate over a new international financial architecture, particularly with the advent of the Bush administration in the U.S. He suggests that the issue of crisis prevention has come to the fore as a result of concerns in the late 1990s about the adequacy of official reserves to react to crises in globalised markets, and the moral hazard that such crisis response could create. Moreover, the crisis of the 1990s took the IMF well beyond traditional macroeconomic conditionality into microeconomic measures, market operating rules, and prudential supervision. This pointed to the need for 'ex ante conditionality' as the centrepiece of a crisis prevention strategy in which many actors, including the IMF, had important roles to play.

Gomel argues that the solution to the difficult challenge of crisis prevention lies in combining firm *ex ante* limits to official financial support with the possibility of debtor countries resorting to standstills. Thus, the IMF in its crisis prevention and management role must rely on structural conditionality: 'Structural conditionality is not a capricious addition to the IMF's policy toolkit, but stems from the many challenges that the organisation has been required to address since the 1980s' (p. 169). Indeed, it is essential to realizing the long-term considerations in IMF programmes.

Gomel also challenges some of the currently fashionable views on the need to reduce the core areas of the IMF's activities and ensure ownership of its programmes by recipients. A review of the evidence, he suggests, shows that neither solutions are necessary to the success enjoyed by the IMF in the recent past. More broadly, the current emphasis on the 'soft law' approach, seen in the work of the new Financial Stability Forum, also requires the hard-law contribution of the IMF if it is to be effective in the realms of standards, governance, and incentives.

In Chapter 10, 'On Some Unresolved Problems of Monetary Theory and Policy', Paolo Savona sets the goal of reconciling globalisation with monetary policies. Central to his argument is the proposition that financial innovation, in general, and derivatives, in particular, have eroded the ability of monetary authorities to control the money stock (Hale 2001). It is thus not surprising that the various monetary aggregates, such as M2 or M3, have lost significance in current monetary management. The resulting environment

> has brought about the paradox identified by Keynes (before modern derivatives even existed), namely the paradox of liquidity: everyone feels liquid but the system itself is not. And the consequence of the paradox is that the central banks, when faced by systemic crises brought on by excessive speculation, become lenders of last resort, responding on demand to the market's need for a monetary base. The example of Long-Term Capital Management in the U.S. is a textbook case (p. 181).

Financial innovation, concludes Savona, has made the stock of world money largely endogenous and tends to expropriate national monetary sovereignty. It is time to examine a new framework and practice of monetary control rather than proceed by strengthening only the existing two pillars of the international financial architecture: better order at home and better surveillance.

In Chapter 11, 'Britain, Europe, and North America', Alan M. Rugman and Alina Kudina raise the question of whether the United Kingdom should join the European Monetary Union, sacrifice national monetary sovereignty, and integrate with the EU, not only economically and monetarily but also politically. They conclude that the United Kingdom should not. The reason is that Britain's economic interdependence with North America is as great as its interdependence with the EU. While it is true that the United Kingdom trades more goods and services with the EU than with North America, the opposite is true with regard to FDI. Different measures of integration yield conflicting conclusions in regard to which the country should ally itself with.

One wonders, however, how important trade and FDI are in the minds of the 70 percent of British voters who oppose UK membership in the European Monetary Union. The conflicting evidence on relative shares of international trade and FDI may mimic the dual allegiance of British voters, without being a cause of it. Rugman and Kudina write:

> The current Blairite one-dimensional focus on European integration presents major political and social pitfalls for the UK. While most British trade is with the EU, only a minor amount of both inward and outward FDI stocks is with the EU; as much, or more, is with North America. As a consequence, Britain needs to revert to balanced economic diplomacy within a triad/regional world economic system (p. 194).

In sum, the analyses contained in this volume offer a diverse and interdisciplinary array of judgements on the key issues of guiding global financial governance at the start of the twenty-first century. Assessments of global order and the role of the G7/8 in it differ, not only among economists and political scientists, but also among scholars within the same discipline. The disagreements enrich the scholarly and policy debate. Yet all the contributors share the common faith that the G7/8 is the central institution for guiding global financial order. They do so directly — through explicit endorsement of the proclamations and new guidelines taken at summits — and, indirectly, by asking it to influence the decisions taken by all-inclusive international organisations such as the IMF.

Conclusions

Judging from television coverage and newspaper headlines, the 2001 Genoa Summit will be remembered for urban guerrillas and the death of an Italian anarchist assaulting a security officer. Indeed, the orgy of protest, violence, damage, injury, and death in the streets of Genoa made the Summit, infamously, one of the top ten news stories of the year. Journalists, commentators, and a few unnerved politicians reacted to the spectacle by calling for a radical change in the format of the summits, if not for their outright elimination. Was Genoa a failure, as these calls assume? According to Nicholas Bayne, the most respected summit analyst, Genoa was typical of the strengths and weaknesses of the G7/8 annual meetings. Genoa focussed on poor countries and promised to increase the emphasis on socially sustainable globalisation, the themes of the last two summits at Cologne and Okinawa (Bayne 2001a). Genoa made material progress on the Global Fund to Fight AIDS, Tuberculosis, and Malaria and launched the Genoa Plan for Africa. While the sums pledged were a disappointment to civil society, the focus on poverty reduction and conflict prevention signalled that the G8 was receptive to addressing the negative aspects of globalisation.

Some caution, however, is in order on the long-term ability of industrialised countries to incorporate social objectives into global governance. Public choice considerations suggest that governments do not take decisions without going through a political calculus of the benefits and costs of their actions. Against the benefit of foreign aid for the poorest countries there is the cost of higher taxes or the value of foregone programmes for the voting public in the donor countries. Aid has an immediate benefit for the recipient countries' poor — who, however, do not vote in the donor countries — and a long-term benefit, through more international trade and fewer conflicts, for the voting population in the donor countries. The donor countries' taxpayers or pressure groups with programmes that are being crowded out by more foreign aid feel the cost of more foreign aid immediately. If solidarity was dominant, one would see more foreign aid; one does not. In fact, foreign aid is less grounded in solidarity than in the national interests of the donor countries.

As noted above, debt relief — a form of foreign aid — is justified if the borrower is in trouble through no fault of its own, for example, as a result of external shocks. But it is difficult to differentiate excessive foreign debt stemming from external and unavoidable causes from inappropriate (and avoidable) domestic policies. If domestic policies are primarily responsible for the unsustainable foreign debt, then debt relief may encourage more of the same behaviour in the future. Thus, even if there is agreement on the amount of foreign aid to be given, the manner in which this aid is disbursed matters. As the old saying goes, it is better to teach a hungry person how to fish than simply to hand over a fish. Lasting poverty reduction flows from productivity-based output increases. Debt relief may raise income in one or two years, but if the resources freed from debt repayments are not used to increase domestic productivity, poverty will return. Aid that raises health and education standards is superior to unconditional debt relief. Opening market access in the industrial and middle income countries is more potent than debt relief. The G7/8 leaders are aware of this and have taken actions in this direction. However, a word of caution is again in order.

Agricultural protectionism in the EU and Japan and textile protectionism in the EU and the United States do not exist in a vacuum. Politicians who vote for these barriers are aware of the collateral damage of such policies, both for more efficient foreign producers and for domestic consumers, but they find it in their interest to support the claims of domestic producers. While protectionism is not economically optimal, it survives because of the political intermediation process. Lashing out at protectionism is tantamount to lashing out at democracy. One cannot suppress the political weight of European farmers, who are the pillars of the CAP. The success of the new trade round, launched at Doha in November 2001, will not depend on ignoring the voice of voting rent seekers, but on the ability of domestic politics to 'bribe' them into accepting the agreement. The big players in the new trade are the EU, Japan, the United States, and Canada on one side and the middle-income countries on the other side. The poor countries, in reality, do not matter, because their trade share in world exports is inconsequential. Nonetheless, that does not mean that they should be ignored. The big players are obliged to open their markets to the exporters of the poor countries and thus give concrete meaning to the slogan of socially sustainable globalisation.

Genoa did not make significant breakthroughs on the new international financial architecture. While the G7/8 leaders supported the IMF's existing programmes in Turkey and Argentina and signalled some willingness to extend more support to Argentina, they remained silent on the causes of financial instability and any possible remedies (see Appendix B). The conservative nature of the recommendations may indicate the leaders' satisfaction with the progress achieved so far, their ignorance of the causes of financial instability, their knowledge of the causes but also of the impracticality of the solutions, and the lack of consensus on the content of a new architecture within the G7 club.

Of these possibilities, perhaps the most likely is that the leaders, given the absence of contagious global crises from mid 1999 through 2002, were reasonably happy with progress achieved thus far and were waiting for implementation to bear its fruits. The G7 may take heart in the reform process undertaken by the IMF, the surveillance and implementation of standards and codes, efforts to reduce moral hazard by private lenders — for example, through rescheduling and write-downs — and its (negative) position on the Tobin tax on financial transactions. Yet financial stability, as Argentina's December 2001 debt moratorium shows, does not appear to be around the corner.

It is fair to say that complete financial stability is not a realistic goal in a world of deregulated financial markets and liberal capital flows. Targets should be reachable. The relevant question is whether an alternative monetary regime could lower financial instability without inhibiting the efficiency of competitive financial markets and the mobility of capital. Should the G7 recognise the futility of many small currencies competing with well-established currencies of large economic areas and call for currency consolidation, as von Furstenberg advocates? Or should the G7 acknowledge the pernicious consequences of derivatives on money supply management and capital flows, as Savona advocates?

Drastic solutions require firm shared beliefs; the G7 does not have them. But even if it had, what could it do with regard to the above diagnoses? For example, the G7 could endorse the currency consolidation proposal; the IMF, by reflection, would also do so and recommend it to small open economies. Ultimately, the decision would fall on the authorities of the country in question. Would that country act unilaterally and adopt the 'relevant' foreign currency, be it the U.S. dollar, the euro, or the yen? Or would it search for partners to form a monetary union? The first strategy can be implemented quickly but imposes political costs, not only of loss of national identity but also loss of representation in the conduct of monetary policy. Could politicians in Argentina sell a complete dollarization plan without obtaining representation either on the Board of

Governors of the Federal Reserve System or creating a new 13th Federal Reserve district? Would U.S. politicians acquiesce to Argentinean representation in the Federal Reserve System? The monetary union alternative to unilateral adoption of a foreign currency is more attractive on the grounds of tax (that is, seigniorage) and legitimacy, but it takes time. Perhaps this is the natural evolution of the system. Perhaps the G7 could encourage countries to think about the evolution in earnest.

Grading the Genoa G7's Governance of Global Finance

Judgements about how well the G7 leaders did at Genoa in governing global finance and related economic fields come from many quarters, evaluative methods, and judgemental vantage points. But all share a sense that the G7's performance at Genoa, while adequate, left much to be desired in a fast-changing and fully transforming world.

Expert Assessments

Perhaps the most generous overall evaluation comes from Nicholas Bayne. He judges that Genoa as a whole launched some important initiatives that, if implemented, may make it one of the most influential summits ever (see Appendix A). But these initiatives tended not to come in the economic or finance field. Bayne considers the G7's strongly worded passage on a new WTO round to be one of the most important results of the Summit. But its message on the global economy seemed too optimistic, its statement on Argentina and Turkey guarded, its message on MDBs paternalistic and noncommittal, and its statement on tax havens very weak.

George von Furstenberg shares the view that Genoa took little decisive action on the finance front, even if he is more approving of parts of such complacency (see Appendix B). According to him, G7 leaders wisely resisted any temptation to fine-tune macroeconomic levers to combat the mild growth recession that faced them, concentrating instead on pressing for structural reform in Europe and above all Japan. They also prudently made no new major moves on debt relief for the poorest. But the leaders failed to break needed new ground in the analysis of the causes of financial instability of the Argentina-Turkey sort, or of measures to prevent them, or of the appropriate exchange rate system and number of currencies required in the new world.

Issue Evaluations

Similarly lukewarm are the evaluations of those in the G8 Research Group who monitor individual issues. Microeconomic issues received a B, as a result of the neglect of the need to implement changes in markets within G7 countries other than Japan. Debt relief for the poorest was awarded a B−, due to the absence of any Cologne-like initiative on deeper, faster, or broader debt relief, even though real concern with the issue continued. Again, the G7 was seen to do better in trade, as its stronger performance than in past years, even with critical omissions, brought it a B+.

The Significant Commitments Score

The most systematic way of determining how productive the Genoa G7 leaders were in governing global finance comes from the results of the study of significant commitments produced by the G8 Research Group. This study, based on methodologies developed by Eleonore Kokotsis and Diana Juricevic, identifies the number of discrete, concrete, future-oriented and measurable collective decisions or commitments made publicly by the leaders in their concluding communiqués. It assesses each commitment according to significance, based on the identification of a goal, implementing measures, and target date, and by the timeliness, novelty, and wide scope of the substantive measure. The multiplication of the number of commitments by the significance of each produces an overall indication of the G7's performance in individual issues areas and broader policy domains. The ten commitments identified by this method in the G7 communiqué at Genoa (with their significance scores in brackets) are listed in Appendix C. This performance of the G7 at Genoa in generating significant commitments in the economic domain can be assessed by comparing with available data on the G7 (and G8, with Russia) at Okinawa the previous year, Naples 1994 (the previous occasion when Italy hosted the G7) and selected earlier years. The results are listed in Appendix D.

This analysis suggests that the G7 leaders at Genoa proved to be a little less productive than their colleagues at Okinawa, judged by the number and range of identifiable, specific, future-oriented commitments issued in the communiqué. The document issued by the G7 leaders at Genoa offered ten commitments. Of these, one referred to the issue of world economy, two to trade, four to strengthening the international financial system, one to financial abuse, and two to heavily indebted poor countries (HIPCs). This contrasts with the twelve commitments identified in the Okinawa G7 communiqué, which contained four identifiable commitments on HIPCs, three on international financial architecture, three on the global financial system, and two on nuclear safety.

Weighting these commitments by their significance yields a similar conclusion. The G7's Genoa commitments received an overall significance score of 40 percent, slightly below Okinawa's 43 percent in 2000. In the specific field of the international financial system, however, the score was almost equal. Genoa's lower scores on HIPCs and financial abuse brought its overall G7 significance score down.

There are several reasons why the G7 did slightly less well at Genoa than it did at Okinawa the year before. One is the memory of the Asia-turned-global financial crisis of 1997–99, still fresh in 2000 at Okinawa in the heart of Asia but much diminished by the European summit of 2001. Yet the second shock of Argentina and Turkey, in the Americas and Asia, and the major challenge in Japan should have been enough to bring some of it back (Kirton 2001). A second reason is the large number of new leaders participating at Genoa, with diminished inherited memory of the old programme or attachment to an old agenda. Yet the presence of former finance minister and G7 veteran Jean Chrétien of Canada, as well as Italian host Silvio Berlusconi (host in 1994) and Germany's Gerhard Schroeder, with their background in business, should have been an assist.

There were thus a number of factors, within the control of leaders, that made this slightly weaker performance a somewhat self-constructed and therefore correctable affair. One factor was the choice of theme and of the major items on the agenda. Here Genoa's focus on poverty reduction in Africa and multilateral trade came at the expense of finance issues. The imminence of the WTO ministerial meeting in Doha on 9–13 November 2001 and the growing dissent on the streets about the logic and legitimacy of trade liberalisation exerted an understandable diversion (Ullrich 2001, see Appendix A). More immediately, the G7 decision to meet with several African leaders and heads of UN organisations, and the consequent need to take some time at the G7 meeting to prepare for this outreach dialogue, directly reduced the time available for a close look at the field of finance. When news of the fatality on the streets came, the leaders' understandable desire to consider it consumed even more scarce time.

A second factor was the decision to give themselves so little overall time — to remain confined to the 1998 formula of allowing only an afternoon for a economic dialogue among the G7 leaders immediately before the G8 Summit began. Although the leaders arrived fresh for this event, they came focussed on the entire G8 event and its big deliverables to come. This formula also left them with little freedom to extend their G7 session if the agenda so warranted, or to conduct an economic and financial dialogue with outside stakeholders possessing considerable expertise. Indeed, the outside stakeholders who came to Genoa to present the fruits of their labour based on one of Okinawa's major achievements — the Dot Force — were left to do it, largely unnoticed, on their own.

A third factor was another legacy effect of the 1998 Birmingham formula, namely the decision to separate the finance ministers from their leaders, with the latter meeting more than two weeks earlier in Rome. With ongoing crises in Argentina and Turkey and fast-moving events elsewhere, and with the new leaders at Genoa inexperienced in finance, the temporal and geographical gap had its costs.

This combination of too much distraction, too little time, and too much delegation together took its toll. The G7/8 has properly become much more than an economic summit; it is indeed a comprehensive integrated flexible forum for global governance. Yet it remains an economic summit as well. The overall challenges of global governance in the twenty-first century, as they did at Rambouillet in 1975, demand the attention of the G7 leaders to the economic and finance core.

Opportunities for Canada's 2002 Kananaskis Summit

There thus remained much to be done in the field of finance as the G7/8 leaders prepared for their next summit in Kananaskis on 26–27 June 2002. That summit was committed to extend the Genoa formula by including the leaders of major African and developing countries and international organisations, not merely in a pre-Summit outreach meeting but as part of the regular G8 meeting itself. But in both its process and agenda, the Kananaskis Summit was affected by the legacies of the proliferation of violent protest and terrorist threats at Genoa, the September 2001 terrorist attacks in the United States, and the financial crisis that erupted in Argentina at the end of 2001. As host, Canada's Jean Chrétien sought to deliver a summit that solved the Genoa protest problem, strengthened its work on poverty reduction in Africa, and was inspired in both process and substance by the model of Canada's first G7 Summit at Montebello in 1981.

The adjustments that Chrétien sought for the Kananaskis Summit should allow the more experienced group of G7 and G8 leaders to deal in more depth and with more personal engagement on the core issues of international finance and global economic growth as a whole. Although they would still take time to meet with outside leaders, and will do so without their attending finance ministers, the isolated rustic retreat-like setting of Kananaskis meant small delegations, maximum informal dialogue among leaders alone, minimum pomp and circumstance, most of the media kept far away, and less time spent worrying about the precise wording of a pre-scripted communiqué.

As Canada assumed the chair at the start of 2002, it also sought a summit that will focus heavily on three themes: generating global growth, reducing poverty in Africa, and combating terrorism. It desired outcomes centred on three core messages: The first is that medium-term prospects for growth in the G7/8 and the global community are good but may require productivity-enhancing structural policies to sustain growth, perhaps with alternative approaches for different regions and countries. The second is that the world must go beyond the old philosophy of development to ensure that recipients, civil society, and private sector actors all participate fully in the process. The third is that G8 and its global commitments on combating terrorism must be fully implemented, made comprehensive, and backed by the capacity building required to ensure their effectiveness.

On the theme of generating growth, Canada aimed to emphasise that, beyond Japan, the fundamentals were sound for good medium-term growth. Thus, building on the 1999 and 2000 summits, more attention must be paid to productivity, especially as the cost of terrorism was now being priced into the G7 economic systems. The expenditures generated by 11 September and all national policies should be scrutinised for their contribution to productivity, which has the potential to raise growth levels on a permanent basis. An emphasis on productivity could help resolve the existing debate between Europe and the United States over whether fiscal integrity or fiscal stimulus is most needed to boost growth, and would ensure that North American stimulus was a positive contribution to recovery. The success of the WTO ministers at Doha in launching a new round of multilateral trade liberalisation would be welcomed as an important element in productivity-based global economic growth, although the Kananaskis leaders would not try to reap an early harvest from or give direction to the WTO process newly underway.

On poverty reduction in Africa, Canada took seriously the proclamation of African leaders in their New Plan for African Development (NEPAD) that they represented a new generation with a new domestic commitments and approach to development. The challenge was for the G8 and Africa to agree on a new paradigm and find the real resources to make it work. Here one possibility was to work through the international financial institutions so that the IMF and World Bank, in their poverty reduction strategy plan reviews, invite recipient countries and their citizens to take ownership, to review lending conditionality so as to restrict the costly paper and personnel burden imposed on developing country capacity, and to review the programme for HIPCs. It also meant more emphasis on aid effectiveness and on recipients' responsibilities, emphasising good governance through the rule of law, civil society participation, social policy, sustainable development, an educated workforce, and a sound banking sector.

Canada recognised the need to raise new resources to finance development, both by enhancing the levels of traditional official development assistance (ODA) and by instituting innovative global mechanisms. The latter required a close look at British finance minister Gordon Brown's proposal for a US$50 billion trust fund, a Tobin tax, a new allocation of special drawing rights (SDRs), a carbon tax, an air travel tax, an armaments tax, or a return to the 1960s Lester B. Pearson–like targets. Canada's strategy was to move in a cumulating and integrated fashion from March's United Nations Conference on Financing for Development in Monterrey, Mexico, through the Kananaskis Summit to the 'Rio+10' World Summit on Sustainable Development in Johannesburg in September 2002.

In financing development, in principle Canada favoured President George Bush's Genoa idea of simply having the International Development Association (IDA) give money as grants rather than long-term concessional loans. As IDA funds went to the least credit-worthy countries, which repaid little of them and where the donors then wrote off the loans, it seemed logical to admit that the human infrastructure, education, and some other public goods required by the poorest countries should be financed by grants. An all-grant mechanism would be affordable. However, the idea was strongly resisted by the Europeans. The prospective result was a compromise that yielded a significantly larger portion of IDA funding given in pure grant form.

Another element was to continue, through the G7 process, Canada's longstanding effort to construct a regime for private sector participation in response to financial crises, as part of a new financial architecture. Here it could now build on the November 2001 G20 agreement to have G20 deputies conduct a detailed operational study of such issues as how to immunise countries from domestic lawsuits in the face of an international 'standstill' mechanism, and which would serve as the neutral arbiter in making a standstill mechanism work. The the world's largest ever debt moratorium and subsequent default by Argentina in December 2001 infused the Canadian thrust with more momentum and broader support.

The final theme of combating terrorism included pressing implementation of the G20-generated Action Plan on Terrorist Financing. Here the host's strategy was to follow the G7-G20-IMF support-building cadence to make the new regime fully global, devoid of holes, and brought into effective action by the use of the sticks of sanctions and the carrots of ODA, technical assistance, and human assistance to developing countries.

Taken together, these three thrusts represented one of the more ambitious agendas put forward by a summit host, and a trilogy with three components that each contained innovations in the field of finance. As the June 2002 Kananaskis Summit approached, it remained to be seen whether international crisis would erupt to deflect the summiteers' attention, and whether Prime Minister Jean Chrétien could mobilise the energy and enthusiasm to secure from all his summit partners the consensus needed to put his far reaching plan into effect.

Note

1 In August 2001, the *Financial Times* reported that 30 members of the House of Representatives would not back a new fast-track trade negotiating authority unless the domestic textile industry was adequately protected (Alden 2001).

References

Alden, Edward (2001). 'Textile Industry Threat to Bush'. *Financial Times*, 6 August, p. 2.

Bayne, Nicholas (2000). 'The G7 Summit's Contribution: Past, Present, and Prospective'. In K. Kaiser, J. J. Kirton and J. P. Daniels, eds., *Shaping a New International Financial System: Challenges of Governance in a Globalizing World*, pp. 19–35. Ashgate, Aldershot.

Bayne, Nicholas (2001a). 'The G7 and Multilateral Trade Liberalisation: Past Performance, Future Challenges'. In J. J. Kirton and G. M. von Furstenberg, eds., *New Directions in Global Economic Governance: Managing Globalisation in the Twenty-First Century*, pp. 23–38. Ashgate, Aldershot.

Bayne, Nicholas (2001b). 'Managing Globalisation and the New Economy: The Contribution of the G8 Summit'. In J. J. Kirton and G. M. von Furstenberg, eds., *New Directions in Global Economic Governance: Managing Globalisation in the Twenty-First Century*, pp. 171–188. Ashgate, Aldershot.

Collier, Paul and David Dollar (2001). *Globalization, Growth, and Poverty: Building an Inclusive World Economy*. World Bank and Oxford University Press, Washington DC and New York.

Fratianni, Michele and John C. Pattison (2001). 'International Organisations in a World of Regional Trade Agreements: Lessons from Club Theory'. *World Economy* vol. 24, no. 3 (March), pp. 333–358.

Fratianni, Michele, Dominick Salvatore, and Paolo Savona, eds. (1999). *Ideas for the Future of the International Monetary System*. Kluwer Academic Publishers, Boston.

Hale, David (2001). 'Have Hedge Funds Become an Agent of Monetary Policy?'. Zurich Financial Services, 13 June.

Hodges, Michael R., John J. Kirton, and Joseph P. Daniels, eds. (1999). *The G8's Role in the New Millennium*. Ashgate, Aldershot.

Kaiser, Karl, John J. Kirton, and Joseph P. Daniels, eds. (2000). *Shaping a New International Financial System: Challenges of Governance in a Globalizing World*. Ashgate, Aldershot.

Kirton, John J. (1999). 'Explaining G8 Effectiveness'. In J. J. Kirton and J. P. Daniels, eds., *The G8's Role in the New Millennium*, pp. 45–68. Ashgate, Aldershot.

Kirton, John J. (2001). 'Generating Genuine Global Governance: Prospects for the Genoa G8 Summit'. <www.g7.utoronto.ca/g7/evaluations/2001genoa/prospects_kirton.html> (February 2002).

Kirton, John J., Joseph P. Daniels, and Andreas Freytag, eds. (2001a). *Guiding Global Order: G8 Governance in the Twenty-First Century*. Ashgate, Aldershot.

Kirton, John J., Joseph P. Daniels, and Andreas Freytag (2001b). 'Introduction'. In J. J. Kirton, J. P. Daniels and A. Freytag, eds., *Guiding Global Order: G8 Governance in the Twenty-First Century*, pp. 1–18. Ashgate, Aldershot.

Kirton, John J. and George M. von Furstenberg, eds. (2001). *New Directions in Global Economic Governance: Managing Globalisation in the Twenty-First Century*. Ashgate, Aldershot.

Savona, Paolo, ed. (2000). *The New Architecture of the International Monetary System*. Kluwer Academic Publishers, Boston.

Ullrich, Heidi K. (2001). 'Stimulating Trade Liberalisation after Seattle: G7/8 Leadership in Global Governance'. In J. J. Kirton and G. M. von Furstenberg, eds., *New Directions in Global Economic Governance: Creating International Order for the Twenty-First Century*, pp. 219–240. Ashgate, Aldershot.

PART I
GOVERNING GLOBAL FINANCE:
THE G7'S CONTRIBUTION

Chapter 2

Reforming the International Financial Architecture: The G7 Summit's Successes and Shortcomings

Nicholas Bayne

This chapter reviews the occasions during the 1990s and early 2000s when the G7 summits have contributed to the design of the world's financial and monetary system. From this review of recent G7 performance, it draws some lessons on how the summit can best contribute to international financial reform in conditions of advancing globalisation. The chapter speaks of the G7 throughout, rather than the G8, since the Russians play no part in these financial discussions. It is an updated and amended version of an analysis produced in 1999, omitting most of the evidence from the summits of the 1970s and 1980s, which featured in the earlier inquiry, while adding new material.[1] It takes account of the impact of the terrorist attacks of 11 September 2001 on this activity, although of course these were not foreseen at the Genoa G8 Summit in July.

Three areas of summit activity are examined, all spread over a number of years but remaining active subjects on the G7 agenda. These are

- *Debt relief for the poorest.* This has been active from Toronto 1988 onward, especially at Lyon 1996 and Cologne 1999.
- *The speculative financial crisis.* The most important summits were Halifax 1995, Birmingham 1998, and Cologne 1999.
- *Abuses of the financial system.* These abuses, especially money laundering, were first featured at Paris 1989 and returned to the summits at Okinawa 2000 and Genoa 2001.

Two earlier subjects of summit attention — the legitimisation of floating rates, at Rambouillet 1975, and the commercial bank debt crisis, active from Versailles 1982 to Paris 1989 — were examined at length in the original analysis. But since they are receding into the past and can now be considered closed, these historical episodes receive only brief treatment here.

In each of the chosen topics, the summit's achievements are judged against a range of criteria:

- *Leadership.* Did the summit succeed in stimulating agreement, resolving differences, and reaching solutions that could not be achieved at lower levels?
- *Effectiveness.* Did the summit exercise its talent for reconciling domestic and external pressures?

- *Durability.* Did the agreement reached at the summit provide a lasting solution to the problem?
- *Acceptability.* Was the agreement reached among the G7 leaders readily accepted by the wider international community?
- *Consistency.* Did the summit's decisions on international financial issues fit in well with the policies adopted on other subjects?

The judgements against these criteria form the basis for the overall conclusions. But excluding the earlier episodes from the inquiry reveals how the weight of the different criteria has changed. The durability criterion has become harder to meet; none of the three topics can be regarded as finally resolved so that they can be taken off the agenda. The acceptability criterion has likewise become more demanding. In the 1970s and 1980s, the G7 members could be sure that whatever they decided would be accepted without question. Now, as globalisation advances, the summits must satisfy a much wider and more critical circle of other governments and nonstate actors.

Subject to these modifications, the lessons from the summit's performance in the 1990s and early 2000s are summarised below.

First, the G7 leaders must use the summit as a means to resolve disagreements among them that have persisted at lower levels. This is what the summit is for.

Second, the issues must have maximum advance preparation, in order to limit the issues for resolution at the summit. If the leaders are confronted with too many problems, they will temporise or fudge. That will allow damaging differences among the G7 to persist.

Third, the summits must keep up the pressure to ensure that whatever they agree is properly carried out. Commitments that are not fulfilled or are allowed to drag on undermine the authority of the summits. On the other hand, durable action on key issues allows the G7 leaders to revive and redirect their action in times of crisis, as with money laundering after 11 September.

Fourth, the G7 leaders must take a lead — that is expected of them — but they must not expect others to follow blindly. They must explain their proposals persuasively, responding to the concerns of others, especially poor and vulnerable countries. They must also justify their policies before the wider public, who are growing suspicious about who gains and who loses from globalisation. Wherever possible, they should associate private business and civil society with their work.

Fifth, they must integrate their policies on financial reform with their other economic recommendations. If not, this lack of consistency will undermine all their efforts, both in finance and elsewhere. The Genoa Summit of 2001 recognised this by seeking to correct the earlier neglect of international trade and going beyond debt relief to address other aspects of development, especially health and the problems of Africa. Reforms of the financial architecture must also serve all countries, not just those that carry weight in the system.

The Historical Episodes:
Floating Rates and the Commercial Bank Debt Crisis

The first summit of all, at Rambouillet in 1975, reached agreement that the International Monetary Fund (IMF) should permit floating exchange rates as a legitimate currency regime, as opposed to a temporary expedient in times of crisis. France had hitherto resisted this. But at Rambouillet French president Valéry Giscard d'Estaing agreed to legitimise floating, in return for undertakings from the United States and the others to intervene to counter short-term currency fluctuations. This agreement was based on meticulous advance preparation between U.S. and French officials. The IMF rapidly introduced amendments to its articles that embodied the Rambouillet agreement.[2]

The Rambouillet episode scores highly against the criteria. The summit showed *leadership* in resolving the persistent dispute between France and the U.S., in ways acceptable to the others. The Summit proved *effective,* because of the meticulous advance preparation. The Rambouillet agreement was *durable* where it was incorporated into the IMF's Articles and applied world-wide. This was readily *acceptable* to the wider membership of the IMF and created no problem of *consistency.* However, the informal arrangement on countering short-term fluctuations did not prove *durable*, because the G7 countries adopted economic policies that were *inconsistent* with currency stability.

The Versailles Summit of 1982 ignored the signs of an imminent debt crisis among developing countries. The crisis broke in August of that year, with major debtors threatening to default on their borrowings from commercial banks. Default on this scale threatened a systemic collapse. But the summits gave the crisis very little attention, as the Reagan administration only once brought debt issues to the summit, at London in 1984. Under U.S. president George Bush and treasury secretary Nicholas Brady, however, things changed at once. The 'Brady Plan' introduced the radical concept of debt reduction. When the IMF meetings in spring 1989 could not agree on it, Bush and Brady raised the issue to summit level. The Brady Plan was endorsed by the Paris Summit of July 1989 and accepted at the IMF annual meeting in September. The long-standing debt crisis was effectively resolved.[3]

The summit's record here is less favourable. The summits from 1982 to 1988 score badly, while only Paris 1989 scores well. For a long time, the summits showed no *leadership,* so that the crisis dragged on for seven years. But in 1989 the leaders' authority ensured acceptance of the radical new concept of debt reduction. Likewise, the summits were largely *ineffective,* up to 1989, in reconciling the domestic pressures from the creditor banks with the external requirements of the debtor countries. A *durable* solution only emerged with the Brady Plan in 1989. Once that was in place, the problem went definitively off the agenda. Debt reduction had been rejected by the IMF in early 1989, but became *acceptable* after endorsement by the summit.

The *inconsistency* of G7 policies contributed to the debt crisis. The G7 had encouraged the recycling of oil producers' surpluses to oil importers. But this was undermined by the world recession, provoked by the G7's tight economic policies.

Debt Relief for the Poorest:
From Toronto 1988 to Lyon 1996 and Cologne 1999

The first current episode concerns the summit initiatives on debt relief for low-income countries, which go back to the Toronto Summit of 1988 but remain active up to the present. The record here, despite some weaknesses, is much better than on middle-income debt. The G7 leaders have realised that effective arrangements for very poor countries are a neglected part of the international financial system and need to be integrated into any reforms.

Both middle-income and low-income countries accumulated large stocks of debt as a result of the oil crises. The debts owed to commercial banks by middle-income countries were so large that they threatened the system in the 1980s. The debts owed to governments by poor countries were much smaller in total and thus nonthreatening, but they were a much heavier burden to the countries concerned. As the crisis eased for middle-income countries, the G7 summit came to recognise the special problems of the poorest.[4]

The first initiative, agreed at Toronto in 1988, offered relief on debt owed to governments by poor countries following IMF programmes. The Toronto terms were fairly modest. But once the Brady Plan had been accepted, debt reduction could be given to poor countries, too. Thus, more generous terms were endorsed at the London III Summit in 1991 and again at Naples in 1994. The Lyon Summit of 1996 expanded these into the heavily indebted poor countries (HIPC) programme. This provided further relief not only on debt owed to governments but also on debt to the IMF, World Bank, and other such institutions. A large proportion of poor countries' debt was owed to these bodies. Hitherto the institutions had refused debt relief for fear of weakening their credit rating. But they now agreed to set aside funds, from their own resources and from bilateral donors, to service these debts. Forty-one poor countries, mainly in Africa, were eligible to benefit from the programme.

Though the HIPC programme was intended to be more generous than what went before, its drawbacks were soon revealed. Poor countries had to endure IMF discipline for a very long time — usually six years — before benefiting from debt relief. The amounts of relief, once received, often proved insignificant. The financing of the scheme was not assured, in part because of dissent over the use of IMF gold for this purpose.[5]

British prime minister Tony Blair wanted debt relief to be a major subject at Birmingham 1998. But despite pressure from articulate public opinion, led by the Jubilee 2000 campaign, the leaders could only agree on modest changes. A year later, however, Cologne 1999 produced a complete overhaul, thanks to a change of policy by the new German government.[6] The amount of debt relief on offer was doubled and the qualifying period was halved. Poverty reduction strategies were introduced to ensure that the money saved was well used, especially on education and health care, and to involve civil society from debtor countries. The financing commitments were less clear at the Summit, but they were tightened up at the annual meeting of the IMF and World Bank in September 1999. That meeting agreed on a scheme to make use of IMF gold and produced the necessary voluntary commitments.

At Cologne, the G7 leaders had agreed to forgive up to 90 percent of their government debt to poor countries, and more, if needed. They set a target of getting debt relief agreed for three quarters of the 41 eligible countries by the end of 2000.[7] By the time of the Okinawa Summit in July 2000, all the G7 governments were in fact offering 100 percent relief on their own debts. But only nine countries had reached an agreement on relief programmes, largely because of the time taken to prepare the new poverty reduction strategies required by the Cologne reforms. This slow progress dismayed Jubilee 2000, and the summit itself could do little about it.[8] But thereafter the pace quickened, so that by the Genoa Summit of 2001, 23 countries had agreed on debt relief programmes. A few other eligible countries decided not to bid for debt relief, preferring to service their debts and keep their credit record. Most of the countries still outside the programme were hampered by war or civil conflict.

The main topic for Genoa 2001 was poverty reduction, going beyond debt relief. This recognised that poor countries remain poor, even when their debts are forgiven, and need help in areas such as trade access, health care, and education. Genoa also continued to work on unfinished business in the HIPC programme. This included making the best use of resources saved by debt relief, helping countries in conflict to get into the programme, ensuring debt relief led to a 'lasting exit' from unsustainable debt burdens, and getting other creditors to match what the G7 had done. But there was no improvement of the terms of debt relief itself. Campaigners for complete debt forgiveness or for the reduction of IMF/World Bank debt (such as Drop the Debt, the successor to Jubilee 2000) were clearly disappointed.

The review of the summit's performance against the criteria on this issue yields a broadly positive judgement.

The summit has consistently shown *leadership* since it took up this issue. It is clear that if the heads of government themselves had not pushed for action on debt relief for the poorest, nothing would have happened at all. The initial proposals were not adequate for the scale of the problem. But the G7 leaders were not content with a single initiative. They remained engaged and kept coming back to improve it, often going further than their finance ministers were prepared to go.

The summit did have problems of *effectiveness* in reconciling domestic and external pressures. These measures to help the poorest were not provoked by any systemic crisis or major threats to the G7's economic interests; they were driven by a clear ethical motivation. For a long time, this was not strong enough to ensure agreement among the G7 on sufficiently generous terms of debt relief or adequate financing. But from Cologne onward, these problems were eased, thanks to the change of government in Germany in 1998 and the voting of adequate funds by the U.S. Congress in 2000.

The summit likewise found it hard to agree on a *durable* debt relief programme. Every year or so the leaders had to come back and adapt it. But this reflected their determination to come up with a programme that would really achieve its objectives. Even now future modifications are necessary, for example to bring more help to countries emerging from conflict.

Successive debt relief programmes emerging from the summits had no real difficulty in winning acceptance internationally, from other governments. Each programme was endorsed by the full membership of the IMF and World Bank and any problems arose within the G7 itself.[9] More recently, the summit also faced the test of *acceptability* from the charities and other nongovernment organisations (NGOs) that made up the Jubilee 2000 campaign for complete debt forgiveness. The campaigners recognised the advance made by the G7 leaders at Cologne, but hoped that it would lead to even more generous relief. Drop the Debt wanted the IMF and World Bank to forgive their debts outright. The absence of movement on this subject at both Okinawa and Genoa frustrated the campaigners.

The judgement on *consistency* shows poor performance in the 1990s but some improvement in the 2000s. Debt relief was for many years about the only area where the G7 summits directly addressed the problems of the poorest countries. In other fields of concern to these countries, notably aid policy and trade access, the summits of the 1990s did much less. But in preparing for Okinawa 2000 and especially for Genoa 2001, the G7 realised that a wider involvement in development issues was essential to complement debt relief. This was reflected in the decisions at the 2001 Summit on the new Global Fund to Fight AIDS, Tuberculosis, and Malaria and the Genoa Plan for Africa.

The Speculative Financial Crisis:
Halifax 1995, Birmingham 1998, and Cologne 1999

The second current episode concerns the search for new international financial architecture. This was provoked by the crisis that broke out in three Asian countries just a few days after the Denver Summit of 1997 and took 18 months to bring under control.

The crisis did not, in fact, begin in 1997. It was a revival, in a more acute form, of the troubles that overwhelmed Mexico at the turn of 1994 and 1995. Like the subsequent upheavals, the Mexican crisis was marked by the collapse of exchange rates, the haemorrhage of volatile capital, and rapid contagion both around the region and further afield. It was checked by an exceptional IMF-led programme, on the record scale of US$50 billion, early in 1995. This Mexican programme provoked sharp disagreement between the U.S. and the Europeans. The 1995 Halifax Summit restored harmony among the leaders, who agreed on a series of reforms for the IMF and World Bank as a response to the experience of Mexico.

At Halifax, the G7 leaders agreed a four-point plan, which was rapidly adopted by the IMF and World Bank. The four elements were 1) stronger IMF surveillance for all countries, based on better data; 2) a new emergency financing mechanism, backed by extra funds; 3) better co-operation between regulators of financial institutions; and 4) exploring procedures for countries comparable to insolvency for firms.[10]

At Halifax, French president Jacques Chirac, in a striking image, denounced international speculators as the AIDS virus of the world economy. The Halifax measures were intended to deter further outbreaks of the disease. Instead, they only provided a period of remission, before the crisis broke out worse than before. This was because the implementation of the Halifax programme was tardy and incomplete. To take the four elements in reverse order: the G10 declared 'insolvency' impractical for countries, the G7 finance ministers reported only limited progress on regulations to Lyon 1996 and Denver 1997, the funds for the new mechanism were committed far too slowly, and stricter surveillance was left as the only defence. Surveillance on its own was not enough, as countries in difficulty had every incentive to conceal unwelcome data.[11]

As a result, the work on reform — on the new financial architecture — had to start again in the light of what happened in Asia. This differed from the Mexican crisis not only in its scale — US$112 billion had to be mobilised for Thailand, Korea, and Indonesia — but also because it was caused more by the errors of the private sector than by government. The IMF's traditional remedies attracted wide criticism.[12] In early 1998, the G7 finance ministers assembled a package of reforms, which were endorsed by Birmingham 1998. But they were overtaken by renewed crisis in Russia (only months after the first G8 Summit) and in Brazil. A much more extensive range of measures was prepared for Cologne 1999. The leaders endorsed them once again, preparing the way for implementation by the IMF and World Bank.

The Cologne measures built on the Halifax programme and greatly expanded it. Surveillance was strengthened by new standards for data as well as by codes of conduct prescribing greater transparency in monetary, fiscal, and social policies. Co-operation among regulators was promoted by the new Financial Stability Forum (FSF), which brings together the G7 and the IMF with the Bank for International Settlements (BIS), and the International Association of Insurance Supervisors (IAIS) and the International Organization of Securities Commissions (IOSCO). The Halifax emergency mechanism was fully funded, while a new IMF contingent credit line (CCL) was intended to help countries following responsible policies to resist financial contagion. There were elaborate provisions for involving the private sector in financial rescue operations. The work of the G7 and IMF was reinforced by a new G20, associating 'systemically significant' developing and ex-communist countries with the preparation of reforms.[13]

Although none of these measures was really radical, taken together they amounted to an extensive overhaul of the machinery for preventing and responding to financial crises. For two years after they were agreed upon, the financial system remained calm. But without the pressure of crisis conditions, implementation of the measures slowed down and some of the more difficult issues, such as involving the private sector in financial rescues, remained unsettled. There was a sense that the reform process was incomplete, so that new ideas kept surfacing, especially from the United States.[14]

The summits at Okinawa 2000 and Genoa 2001 were not called upon to do much more than endorse work in progress among their finance ministers. But the slowdown in the U.S. economy in 2001, coupled with persistent weakness in Japan, began to impose visible strains on the system. Countries that had recovered rapidly from the Asian crisis, because of strong American demand for their exports, began to suffer as this demand fell away.

These problems were aggravated by the terrorist attacks of 11 September 2001, which damaged growth world-wide and severely affected certain groups of countries, for example those dependent on tourism. The Genoa Summit also showed some concern for the deepening problems of Argentina (see Appendix K).[15] International action, in fact, could not save Argentina from financial collapse and default. But there has been little contagion from the crisis, which has revived the search for an 'insolvency' regime for countries.

On this topic, the summits from Halifax to the present get a mixed but generally favourable assessment, as follows.

The 1995 Halifax Summit demonstrated *leadership*. Although the rescue of Mexico had been contentious, the Summit restored G7 harmony in the pursuit of IMF reform. At Birmingham 1998 and Cologne 1999, the heads of government also provided leadership in that they provided the focus for their finance ministers' work, ensuring that agreement was reached and giving it the necessary authority. The conclusions on financial architecture were key achievements of these two summits. However, the leaders contributed nothing on their own account, in contrast to their personal involvement with debt relief. At Okinawa 2000 and Genoa 2001, this topic no longer had such high priority.

All three summits were *effective* in reconciling domestic and external pressures. The key was thorough and detailed preparation, carried through by the G7 finance ministers and their officials.

The Halifax reforms were manifestly not *durable*. This was because of slow and incomplete implementation, without sufficient pressure from Lyon 1996 and Denver 1997 to get things done. After the crisis broke out again in Asia, the Birmingham and Cologne summits were concerned not to make the same mistake. But once calm returned, implementation again tended to slacken off. So far the new architecture has proved robust and durable enough to withstand the strains caused by the slowing U.S. and Japanese economies, together with the shock of the terrorist attacks; while it could not save Argentina, it deterred contagion. But further tests lie ahead.

All the reform proposals emerging from the summits have proved widely *acceptable* to the IMF and World Bank. The G7 did not leave this to chance, but took care to involve other parts of the membership in the reform process. This was chiefly done through the G22, which was launched by the U.S. in 1998 and brought in some of the key Asian countries. The G20, forecast at Cologne 1999 and confirmed at the next IMF annual meeting, has put this wider consultation on a permanent footing and is proving very valuable (see Appendix N).[16]

The judgement on *consistency* is less positive. Although the summits of the late 1990s had good reasons for focussing on financial architecture, this led them to neglect other parts of the international economic system, notably the trade regime.[17] This was not properly corrected until Genoa 2001. The summits of the early 2000s — Okinawa and Genoa — increasingly turned their attention to the problems of developing countries, especially the poorest. But it was unclear whether the new architecture served the interests of all countries or only the G7 members and those like them.

Abuses of the Financial System:
Paris 1989, Okinawa 2000, and Genoa 2001

Abuse is the third area where the summits have intervened in the financial system, embracing concerns about money laundering, offshore financial centres (OFCs), and harmful tax competition. The involvement of the leaders has been much less direct than in areas of debt relief and financial architecture. But it has become an active issue over the last two years and has gained special prominence since the terrorist attacks. It is therefore suitable for judgement against the criteria.

The summit's involvement in money laundering grew out of its concern to check the growth of drug trafficking in the late 1980s. The Paris Summit of 1989, in an unusual joint initiative by France and the United States, created the Financial Action Task Force (FATF) to limit access to the financial system for drug traffickers (and other criminals) and to make it easier to track down and seize the proceeds of crime.[18] The authority of the G7 leaders gave this initiative enough impetus to bring in other countries alongside the G7 and to find a home for the FATF alongside the OECD, although it remains independent. Within a year, the FATF members drew up a complete set of countermeasures against money laundering, embodied in the FATF Forty Recommendations. The FATF spent the whole of the 1990s ensuring that its 28 members observed these recommendations and seeking to persuade other countries to adopt them.[19]

By 2000, the FATF decided the time had come to identify publicly countries that were open to money laundering and that had financial systems that gave too many opportunities to criminals. In June 2000, it published a list of 15 such 'nonco-operative' jurisdictions. In July, the G7 finance ministers, meeting at Fukuoka, commended this action and added that countries that did not mend their ways would be vulnerable to countermeasures. This in turn was endorsed by the G7 leaders at Okinawa, even though Russia was on the list.

The G7 leaders at Okinawa endorsed two other parallel recommendations from their finance ministers. The first was to encourage the FSF in its work on improving regulation in OFCs, especially those identified as not meeting international regulatory standards. The second was linked to the work of the Organisation for Economic Co-operation and Development (OECD) on harmful tax practices; the OECD had again identified a list of tax havens which were called upon to mend their ways.[20]

All three topics, which identified lists of countries that failed to meet certain standards, returned to the G7 finance ministers and thus to the G7 leaders in 2001, but the results were not uniform. The work on OFCs was proceeding steadily and without great controversy. The OECD's action in identifying tax havens, however, provoked strong adverse reactions. Many of the countries targeted complained that the OECD had neither consulted them properly nor explained what they were expected to do to correct matters.[21] They argued that the OECD members, being mainly high-tax countries, were trying to impose standards on poorer countries that were trying to become competitive.[22] In addition, the new U.S. administration would not agree that the OECD should tell other countries at what level to set their taxes, although the U.S. remained concerned about tax evasion. In consequence, the approach endorsed by the G7 in 2001 was much less demanding than it had been a year before, focussing more on information exchange than prescription.

On money laundering, there was clear progress between Okinawa and Genoa, in that four jurisdictions had so mended their ways that they could be taken off the list and eight others had shown improvement. Only three, including Russia, were at risk of countermeasures and six new countries, including Hungary and Egypt, were added to the list. The G7's work on money laundering, however, proved its greatest worth later in 2001, after the terrorist attacks. Action against the financial networks used by al Qaeda and similar groups soon emerged as the only economic weapon with direct impact on the terrorists and was given priority in the early statements by G7 finance ministers (see Appendices L and M).[23] The FATF was given a new mandate to attack terrorist finances, and G7 and other FATF countries overhauled their money laundering legislation for this purpose — often revealing shortcomings in their earlier measures in the process.

The judgement on the summit's performance varies according to the topic addressed, as described below.

Money laundering is a good example of summit *leadership*. The original initiative got enough impetus from the leaders in 1989 that it did not need summit attention for ten years. It returned in 2000–01 when the FATF needed summit authority for a more aggressive policy; this proved of unexpected value after 11 September. With OFCs and tax havens, however, the leaders did no more than endorse current action by finance ministers, which hardly needed summit attention.

With money laundering, the domestic measures taken by FATF members, including the G7, provided a reasonably good basis for *efficient* international intervention. After 11 September, it was easy to mobilise further action, as well as to correct earlier inadequacies. The same applies to OFCs, but is less true of the OECD's action on tax havens.

The action on money laundering has had slow but *durable* effects, and has been easily adapted for use against terrorists. With OFCs, however, it is too early to say. With tax havens, the G7 has already had to go into reverse to some degree.

In all three areas, the actions taken are unwelcome to those countries identified on the list. But raising standards of regulation in OFCs is seen as part of the new financial architecture, which is generally *acceptable*. The FATF has given plenty of warning and opportunity for amendment to target countries. Action against money laundering already carries wide *acceptability*, while the recent actions against terrorist finances have gained remarkable world-wide support. In contrast, the OECD's action against tax havens is perceived to be hasty and unfair, so that it is resisted not only by the countries concerned, but also by developing countries more generally.

As regards OFCs and money laundering, the G7 actions are *consistent* with the summit's wider campaigns to strengthen the financial architecture and the fight against international crime, the drugs trade, and now terrorism. But some aspects of the OECD's action on tax havens seem *inconsistent* with G7 efforts elsewhere to encourage developing countries to make the most of whatever competitive advantages they have.

Lessons from the Summit Record

It is now possible to draw some lessons from the summit record in handling issues concerned with the international financial system in the 1990s and early 2000s. These conclusions look at their performance under the five criteria.

Leadership

The heads of government must use the summit as the occasion to resolve disagreements among them that have persisted at lower levels. That is the underlying rationale for summits. The achievement of Halifax 1995 demonstrates this; so do the summits from Toronto 1988 onward that dealt with debt relief for the poorest. In particular, Cologne 1999 was able to make progress that had not been possible at Birmingham 1989. Alternatively, the heads of state and government can ensure that their finance ministers come to agreement, as happened before Birmingham and Cologne with financial architecture.

Effectiveness

The issues coming to the summit must have maximum advance preparation in order to limit the items requiring resolution at the summit itself. The most effective summits of this period clearly demonstrate this. Without proper preparation, the leaders will be confronted with too many problems and they will stall or vacillate. This leads to disagreements persisting among the G7 countries, which can undo any apparent consensus at the summit. This was the main weakness of the G7's work on debt relief for the poorest, so that it required constant reference back to the summit itself.

Durability

The main lesson to be drawn from the recent summit record — on how to make its agreements durable — is that proper implementation is essential. The summits must keep up the pressure to ensure that whatever they agree upon is properly carried out. The record on money laundering is a good example of what should happen, as it enabled action to be rapidly mobilised against terrorist finance. The leaders have also kept up the pressure on debt relief.

In contrast, commitments that are not fulfilled, or are allowed to drag on, undermine the authority of the summits.[24] This was the mistake made after Halifax, which left the world vulnerable to the Asian financial crisis. So the most important task for the summits of the 2000s in the financial field will be to ensure that the decisions of earlier summits are being thoroughly implemented.

Acceptability

The demands made on the summit under this criterion have grown over the years. It is expected that the G7 must give a lead from the summit. But the leaders must not expect others simply to follow. They must set a good example of international behaviour — no one will respect new rules if the G7 leaders themselves do not do so. They must explain their proposals persuasively within the global institutions, such as the IMF, responding to the concerns of others, especially poor and vulnerable countries. On all these points, the G7 action in supporting the OECD campaign against tax havens was open to criticism. In contrast, the new G20 forum is very helpful in associating major developing countries with the process of reforming the financial architecture.

The G7 must also respond to a wider public. There is increasing doubt and suspicion about who gains and who loses from globalisation. Charities and other NGOs, grouped under the banner of 'civil society', are keen to correct what they see as the dangers of globalisation, for example, for the poorest countries. The summit leaders must be ready to explain and defend their decisions before this audience too. Wherever possible, private business and civil society should be involved in the implementation of G7 decisions. This is working well with the poverty reduction strategies linked to the HIPC programme. Involving private lenders in financial rescues has proved more difficult, though; since Genoa, Argentina's default has provided a new stimulus.

Consistency

The analysis suggests that *consistency* is the hardest criterion for the summit to satisfy. None of the episodes examined in this chapter shows a wholly satisfactory record. The summits' attention to debt relief during the 1990s contrasted with how little the G7 was otherwise doing to help the poorest countries. Those summits that gave close attention to financial matters neglected international trade. The G7 paid a heavy price for this neglect, which contributed to the spectacular failure of the WTO ministerial at Seattle to launch a new round of trade negotiations in December 1999.

The 2000 Okinawa Summit showed a first recognition of these underlying inconsistencies. It extended the G7's attention to other problems faced by the poorest countries, focussing on health, education, and the digital divide. But it could not go far in resolving differences over trade so close to the U.S. presidential election. Genoa 2001 was able to build on these foundations. Its main economic theme was how to go beyond debt relief to address the wider problem of world poverty. It launched the Global Fund to Fight AIDS, Tuberculosis, and Malaria and the Genoa Plan for Africa, based on a partnership between G8 and African leaders. On trade, the close rapport achieved between Pascal Lamy and Robert Zoellick, the EU and U.S. trade negotiators, enabled the leaders to take a firm position on a new WTO trade round and how to launch it. While Genoa's conclusions on trade were fairly general, so as to avoid any appearance of dictating to the rest of the WTO membership, they no longer concealed unresolved differences among the G7. This contributed to the successful launch of a new round at Doha in November 2001.

The G7's work on developing and applying the new financial architecture must also be integrated into this concern for the poorest countries. The new architecture must respond to the needs of all countries, even the poorest and smallest, not just to advanced economies like the G7's or even the 'systemically significant' countries that sit on the G20. Some parts of the new system look very complex. For example, the new rules for capital adequacy worked out by the BIS have proved so difficult technically that their implementation has been delayed a year ('Basel Postponed' 2001). This extra time should be used to make them more accessible to small and poor countries. In other areas, there is a suspicion that the large countries are imposing their will on others. The clearest example here is the OECD's crusade against tax havens, condemned by some of the targeted countries as an attempt by large advanced economies with high tax rates to inhibit the legitimate policies of smaller ones.

Conclusion

At their summits since Birmingham 1998, the G7 leaders have been directly responding to anxieties about what is perceived as the dark side of globalisation. Measures to make the financial system stronger and more equitable address three of these anxieties directly: about financial panic, where the herd instincts of the market penalise prudent and imprudent alike; about world poverty, where low-income countries fall ever further behind; and about international crime, where globalisation seems to help the criminal as much as the honest citizen. The summits have shown leadership in these areas and have produced some effective, durable, and acceptable results. The value of the work on money laundering became manifest after the terrorist attacks of 11 September. But more needs to be done, especially to integrate the G7's financial proposals into a wider economic and social context.

After the violent riots associated with the Genoa Summit and the launch of the international campaign against the terrorist attacks of 11 September, the G7's record is under close scrutiny. The summit will not get everything right. Problems only come up to the summit when they have defied settlement lower down. Many of them are too deep-seated to be resolved at a single session. Mistakes of judgement may be forgiven, provided the G7 leaders persevere in trying to do better. But the G7's reputation will not survive persistent disagreement among themselves or failure to implement what they have agreed.

Notes

1   This chapter is an amended version of Bayne (2000a), incorporating new material on abuses of the financial system and the results of Okinawa 2000 and Genoa 2001.
2   An account of the Rambouillet monetary agreement is provided by Putnam and Bayne (1987, 38–41).
3   Jacques Attali (1995), President François Mitterrand's sherpa, covers the 1989 Paris Summit in detail in his memoirs. For the Brady Plan at Paris 1989, see also Bayne (2000b, 64).
4   Huw Evans (1999) gives an insider's account of how the summits came to focus on debt relief for the poorest and how agreements were reached.
5   A pre-Birmingham critique of the inadequacy of the HIPC programme was produced by Christian Aid, the leading charity in the Jubilee 2000 campaign (Lockwood et al. 1998). Bayne (1998) describes the disappointing outcome of the Birmingham Summit on this issue. Criticism continued right up to the Cologne Summit in 1999; see Holman and Peel (1999).
6   The German change was signalled in an article by Chancellor Gerhard Schroeder (1999) in the *Financial Times*.
7   For an assessment of the Cologne Debt Initiative, see Bayne (2000b, 182–185); see also Dluhosch (2001).
8   The outcome of the Okinawa Summit on debt relief is analysed in Bayne (2001b).
9   This process was helped by the practice of Britain and Canada seeking prior support for their debt relief proposals from the finance ministers of the Commonwealth — see Bayne (1998).

10 An account of the monetary reforms agreed at Halifax are in Bayne (2000b, 118–124). See also Cooper (1995) for proposals offered in advance.

11 Initial assessments of the Halifax programme had been generally satisfied with the progress and did not expect a new crisis to break out. See Kenen (1996), which has an introduction by Lawrence Summers, then Deputy Secretary of the U.S. Treasury.

12 Stanley Fischer (1997), Deputy Managing Director of the IMF, replied to attacks by Martin Wolf (1997) and Jeffrey Sachs (1997) in the *Financial Times*. See also the exchange of articles in *Foreign Affairs* by Martin Feldstein (1998) and Fischer (1998). Michel Camdessus and James Wolfensohn (1998), in a volume prepared for the Birmingham Summit, give a joint defence on behalf of both the IMF and the World Bank. Stephen Haggard (2000) provides a more extended analysis of the Asian crisis.

13 In general, the summits favoured cautious, piecemeal measures, such as those advocated in Eichengreen (1999), rather than radical changes. An assessment of the work by the Birmingham and Cologne summits on new financial architecture is in Bayne (2000b, 171–178).

14 An American commission chaired by Allan Meltzer (2000) produced a report in early 2000 that called for the IMF to lend only to countries meeting strict conditions in advance and for the World Bank to provide grants not loans. Paul O'Neill, the new U.S. Treasury Secretary in the administration of President George W. Bush, seemed attracted by some of these ideas. On his recommendation, Bush made a speech on the eve of the Genoa Summit arguing that the World Bank should give grants, not loans, to poor countries. But this idea was not endorsed by the rest of the G7.

15 The G7 leaders at Genoa appeared to have promised further help to Argentina, if its problems persisted, but this is not made clear in their published document. See Blitz and Fidler (2001).

16 For a full analysis of the role of the G20, see Kirton (2001).

17 The adverse consequences of the summit neglecting trade are argued vigorously in Bayne (2000a; 2001a).

18 For the foundation of the FATF, see Bayne (2000b, 66).

19 On the activities of the FATF in the 1990s and 2000s, see the Organisation for Economic Co-operation and Development (OECD) (2001b).

20 For a full analysis of the work under all three headings, see Wechsler (2001).

21 On the OECD's work on harmful tax practices, see OECD (2001a).

22 Many of the tax havens targeted by the OECD are members of the Commonwealth. As a result, the Commonwealth has been active in a mediatory role. For an analysis, see Persaud (2001).

23 Action against terrorist finances was the main point of substance in the first G7 statement, on 25 September 2001 (see Appendix L), and the first item in the statement issued after the finance ministers met on 6 October (see Appendix M). Wechsler (2001, 47) had already drawn attention to Osama bin Laden's use of clandestine financial networks.

24 See Kokotsis and Daniels (1999) and Kokotsis (1999) for assessments of the general summit record of compliance with commitments. The subsequent assessment of Okinawa 2000 shows an exceptionally high level of compliance.

References

Attali, Jacques (1995). *Verbatim III*. Fayard, Paris.

'Basel Postponed'(2001). *Economist*, 30 June, pp. 83–84.

Bayne, Nicholas (1998). 'Britain, the G8, and the Commonwealth: Lessons of the Birmingham Summit'. *Round Table* vol. 348, no. 445–457.

Bayne, Nicholas (2000a). 'The G7 Summit's Contribution: Past, Present, and Prospective'. In K. Kaiser, J. J. Kirton and J. P. Daniels, eds., *Shaping a New International Financial System: Challenges of Governance in a Globalizing World*, pp. 19–35. Ashgate, Aldershot.

Bayne, Nicholas (2000b). *Hanging in There: The G7 and G8 Summit in Maturity and Renewal*. Ashgate, Aldershot.

Bayne, Nicholas (2001a). 'The G7 and Multilateral Trade Liberalisation: Past Performance, Future Challenges'. In J. J. Kirton and G. M. von Furstenberg, eds., *New Directions in Global Economic Governance: Managing Globalisation in the Twenty-First Century*, pp. 23–38. Ashgate, Aldershot.

Bayne, Nicholas (2001b). 'Managing Globalisation and the New Economy: The Contribution of the G8 Summit'. In J. J. Kirton and G. M. von Furstenberg, eds., *New Directions in Global Economic Governance: Managing Globalisation in the Twenty-First Century*, pp. 171–188. Ashgate, Aldershot.

Blitz, James and Stephen Fidler (2001). 'G7 Leaders Seem Upbeat on Economy'. *Financial Times*, 21 July.

Camdessus, Michel and James D. Wolfensohn (1998). 'The Bretton Woods Institutions: Responding to the Asian Crisis'. In M. Fraser, ed., *The G8 and the World Economy*. Strategems Publishing Ltd., London.

Cooper, Richard N. (1995). 'Reform of Multilateral Financial Institutions'. In S. Ostry and G. R. Winham, eds., *The Halifax G7 Summit: Issues on the Table*. Centre for Policy Studies, Dalhousie University, Halifax.

Dluhosch, Barbara (2001). 'The G7 and the Debt of the Poorest'. In J. J. Kirton, J. P. Daniels and A. Freytag, eds., *Guiding Global Order: G8 Governance in the Twenty-First Century*, pp. 79–92. Ashgate, Aldershot.

Eichengreen, Barry J. (1999). *Toward a New International Financial Architecture: A Practical Post-Asia Agenda*. Institute for International Economics, Washington DC.

Evans, H. P. (1999). 'Debt Relief for the Poorest Countries: Why Did It Take So Long?' *Development Policy Review* vol. 17, no. 3, pp. 267–279.

Feldstein, Martin (1998). 'Refocusing the IMF'. *Foreign Affairs* vol. 77, no. 2, pp. 20–33.

Fischer, Stanley (1997). 'IMF: The Right Stuff'. *Financial Times*, 16 December.

Fischer, Stanley (1998). 'In Defense of the IMF'. *Foreign Affairs* vol. 77, no. 4, pp. 103–106.

Haggard, Stephen (2000). *The Political Economy of the Asian Financial Crisis*. Institute for International Economics, Washington DC.

Holman, Michael and Quentin Peel (1999). 'Too Much to Bear'. *Financial Times*, 12 June.

Kenen, Peter B. (1996). *From Halifax to Lyon: What Has Been Done about Crisis Management?* Essays in International Finance, No. 200. Princeton University Press, Princeton.

Kirton, John J. (2001). 'The G20: Representativeness, Effectiveness, and Leadership in Global Governance'. In J. J. Kirton, J. P. Daniels and A. Freytag, eds., *Guiding Global Order: G8 Governance in the Twenty-First Century*, pp. 143–172. Ashgate, Aldershot.

Kokotsis, Eleanore (1999). *Keeping International Commitments: Compliance, Credibility, and the G7, 1988–1995*. Garland, New York.

Kokotsis, Ella and Joseph P. Daniels (1999). 'G8 Summits and Compliance'. In M. R. Hodges, J. J. Kirton and J. P. Daniels, eds., *The G8's Role in the New Millennium*, pp. 75–91. Ashgate, Aldershot.

Lockwood, Matthew, Emma Donlon, Karen Joyner, et al. (1998). 'Forever in Your Debt? Eight Poor Nations and the G8'. Christian Aid, London. <www.christian-aid.org.uk/indepth/9805fore/forever1.htm> (February 2002).

Meltzer, Allan H. (2000). *Report of the International Financial Institutions Advisory Commission*. United States Congress, Washington DC. <www.house.gov/jec.imf/meltzer.htm> (January 2002).

Organisation for Economic Co-operation and Development (2001a). 'Harmful Tax Practices'. <www.oecd.org/daf/fa/harm_tax/harmtax.htm> (February 2002).

Organisation for Economic Co-operation and Development (2001b). 'More about the FATF & Its Work'. <www.oecd.org/fatf/AboutFATF_en.htm> (February 2002).

Persaud, Randall B. (2001). 'OECD Curbs on Offshore Financial Centres: A Major Issue for Small States'. *Round Table* vol. 359 (April 2001), pp. 199–211.

Putnam, Robert and Nicholas Bayne (1987). *Hanging Together: Co-Operation and Conflict in the Seven-Power Summit*. 2nd ed. Sage Publications, London.

Sachs, Jeffrey (1997). 'Power Unto Itself'. *Financial Times*, 10 December.

Schroeder, Gerhard (1999). 'Germany's Helping Hand'. *Financial Times*, 21 January.

Wechsler, William F. (2001). 'Follow the Money'. *Foreign Affairs* vol. 80, no. 4, pp. 40–57.

Wolf, Martin (1997). 'Same Old IMF Medicine'. *Financial Times*, 8 December.

Chapter 3

Consensus and Coherence
in G7 Financial Governance

John J. Kirton[1]

Since 1975, the G7 major industrial democracies, operating at both the leaders' and ministerial levels, have played a central role in shaping the international financial system and managing it to contain systemic crises and sustain global growth (Bayne 2000a, 2000b; Putnam and Bayne 1987; Funabashi 1987). As the age of intensified globalisation took hold during the second half of the 1990s, bringing with it a series of financial crises that culminated in the great Asian-turned-global crisis of 1997–99, the G7 played an ever more central and ultimately successful role in crisis response, global macroeconomic management, and financial system reconstruction (Hodges, Kirton, and Daniels 1999; Kaiser, Kirton, and Daniels 2000; Kirton, Daniels, and Freytag 2001a). It did so largely by working through the International Monetary Fund (IMF) and through newer bodies such as the International Monetary and Financial Committee (IMFC) and the G20, and by operating as a concert within which a process of mutual adjustment and a sense of collective responsibility prevailed (Kirton 2001a, 2001b). At the dawn of the twenty-first century, the G7 appeared to have put a new, effective edifice for global financial governance firmly in place (Kirton 2001b; Bayne 2001; Kirton and von Furstenberg 2001).

The year 2001, however, brought two severe challenges to this new structure, and to the comfortable conclusion that the G7 had adapted well to the intensely interconnected, fully global financial system of the new era. The first challenge, an internal one, came from the sharp rightward shift within major G7 governments as new political leaders took office in 2001. The shift began in the United States with the election of President George W. Bush. His treasury secretary Paul O'Neill began by questioning the very value of the G7 finance ministers forum, of G7 governments' provision of national 'second lines of defence' to combat foreign financial crises, of much of what the IMF and multilateral development banks (MDBs) had recently done (including support for a democratising Russia), and of the G7's success in fighting financial abuse through the Financial Action Task Force (FATF). The spring brought a new Japanese prime minister, Junichiro Koizumi, whose bold promise to end an era of massive fiscal deficits and financial relief for ailing banks and to undertake genuine structural reform appeared to repudiate the patronage-reinforced Keynesian orthodoxy that had long prevailed.[2] Elsewhere, the election of the government of Silvio Berlusconi in Italy in May 2001, following that of Vladimir Putin as Russia's president at the outset of 2000, seemed to confirm the sharp rightward shift.

To be sure, the re-election of the centrist governments of Tony Blair's Labour Party in Britain in June 2001, following that of Jean Chrétien's Liberals in Canada the previous year, promised a liberal loyal opposition lodged in two of the G7's smaller countries. However, the U.S.-led 'new right' coalition seemed to have the weight to dominate the much reduced 'third way' caucus of old. Even if it could not, within a G7 where Germany's 'Red-Green' coalition and France's statist leadership remained, the new divide and resulting paralysis could more easily allow the market-driven forces much loved by the Bush administration to prevail. Taken together, the new right leaders and resulting ideological divisions raised the question of whether the G7 could create the consensus needed to provide effective leadership for global financial governance in the new era.

The second, external, challenge arose from a series of assaults from the markets. Financial crises erupted in Argentina and Turkey, with their effects threatening to spread to other countries and regions and raising the fear of rampant, devastating global contagion once again. Driven by a sharp downturn in the internet-based new economy, by rising oil prices and by increasing inflation, the United States, followed soon by Japan and Europe, entered a period of sharply slower growth, suggesting a serious, synchronous global slowdown that would render more difficult the tasks of crisis response, global growth management, poverty reduction, and debt relief for the poorest. Moreover, the international financial system itself seemed to need a new generation of reforms, if not to mobilise more money for crisis response, then to strengthen private sector responsibility, sharpen the IMF's focus, reinvent it as a crisis prevention institution, improve its relationship with a reformed array of MDBs, and address such new globalisation issues as the impact of derivatives and the process of dollarization (Fratianni, Salvatore, and Savona 1999; Hale 2001; von Furstenberg 2000, 2001).

Together these events evoked the spectre of a return to an alleged tendency, identified in the mid 1990s, for the G7 to retreat to impotent inactivity in the face of globalised markets its members felt they could no longer control (Bergsten and Henning 1996). They even suggested that the world's major governments in the G7 had in fact been rendered relatively powerless by a world of rampant globalisation and by the prevailing neoliberal Washington consensus and the 'constitutional' confines it brought, and that recent efforts to counter with a socially sensitive approach to global governance were for naught (Gill 1993; Cerny 1995; Birdsall and de la Torre 2001; Kirton, Daniels, and Freytag 2001b). Most broadly, they raised the question of whether national governments, even acting together through the old IMF or newer G7/8, and recent offshoots such as the IMFC, the G20, and the Financial Stability Forum (FSF), could offer a coherent governance response to the pressure of the market in an intensely globalising age.

In the face of these severe tests from a new U.S.-led market-friendly leadership and a fragile global economy, however, during the first half of 2001 the G7 proved able to arrive at a solid consensus within its ranks and to begin to devise a more coherent collective approach to global financial governance outside. With the United States setting aside its initial ideological convictions and complaints, the G7 quickly mobilised through the IMF the large sums required to stabilise Turkey and Argentina, and, with them, Brazil, Europe, the North Atlantic Treaty Organization (NATO), the democratic Americas, and emerging markets as a whole. It moved to combat slowing growth in the global economy, not only by continuing its longstanding emphasis on structural reform, but also by returning, under U.S. leadership, to the 'locomotive' theory. This theory had flourished in the interventionist 1970s and had led to some of the G7's greatest successes (Putnam and Bayne 1987), before being discarded by the new neoliberal non-interventionist 'Ronald-Thatcherism' brought by the 1980s. Within the international financial institutions (IFIs), the new U.S. administration provided an added impetus to the private sector participation and 'back to the basics' focus long promoted by others, including IMF managing director Horst Köhler. The Bush administration also continued to support the contingent credit line (CCL) facility invented by the Clinton administration, promoted MDB reform in the direction of social and equity concerns, took up the prevailing consensus on debt relief for the poorest, and rapidly accepted much of the French-led approach to money laundering and financial abuse. As the Genoa 2001 G7 Summit ended, it was clear that the G7 had met its first challenge of internal consensus, as the new U.S. administration adjusted to the prevailing G7 consensus incorporating social concerns. It was much less clear, however, that the G7 was meeting its external challenge of providing coherent, effective global financial governance for a global economy suffering an increasingly severe and synchronous slowdown. What appeared adequate in July in Genoa was exposed as too little too late when the unforeseen 11 September terrorist assault sent the U.S. economy and some of its allies into a real recession, and again when the December debt repayment moratorium by Argentina revealed that the time bought by G7-inspired support was not effectively employed.

This rapid restoration of the G7's consensus within the club in the face of a sharp initial policy assault from a new U.S. administration, and the G7's slower effort to provide coherent leadership to an outside world increasingly afflicted by severe market challenges, is explained well by the features of an extended version of the concert equality model of G7/8 governance (Kirton 1999, 1993, 1989). During 2001, despite the rise in the value of the U.S. dollar to its highest trade-weighted level in 15 years, the G7-leading plunge in U.S. gross domestic product (GDP) led even initially inward-looking U.S. leaders to drop the American arrogance that had flourished at the 1997 Denver Summit, recognise that they needed stimulative help from their G7 partners and revive the Carter-like collective locomotive approach (Kirton 2001c).[3] The relatively strong currencies and growth of the G8's smaller members — Canada,

Britain, and Russia — assisted this awakening, at a time when integrated production in the North American Free Trade Agreement (NAFTA) area, the tightly wired financial markets that join London to New York, and an emerging energy 'crisis' appropriately focussed the U.S. administration. The intensifying intra-G7 and global intervulnerability bred by globalisation was recognised by a slowing Germany, which had initially been tempted to assume that its Euro-fortress, growing more rapidly than America, could survive without help from the United States. The prospect of contagious intervulnerability, combined with the common purpose of support for democratic and market principles, induced the U.S. to put aside its doubts about large, bureaucratic international organisations and have the IMF give financial support to a democratic, secular, NATO ally and western-oriented Turkey and to a democratic Argentina vital for the realisation of a Bush vision of a western hemisphere in which free trade and its freedoms flourished.[4] Finally, the newly elected leader in the U.S., as in G7 host Italy, was familiar with and committed to the G7/8 system and its strengthening, even as the narrowest of political victories for the U.S. presidency and a divided Congress constrained ideologically driven American unilateralism. Moreover, the leaders and finance ministers in liberal Britain and Canada had both been recently re-elected with massive majorities, came from parliamentary systems, and were the longest serving G7/8 veterans in their positions. Compared to the past great G7/8 political transitions — the 'Ronald-Thatcher' conservative era of the 1980s, and the Clinton-Chrétien-Blair-Schroeder 'third way' of the 1990s — the G7/8 institution easily socialised the Bush-led conservatives into continuing a systematically responsible, and socially sensitive consensus approach.

This process, however, took time, especially as there were no evident external crises or recognisable second shocks in the first half of 2000 to hasten the internal socialisation, learning, and adjustment process and to inspire the G7 to act more aggressively and creatively *vis-à-vis* the external world. Moreover, although the U.S. Federal Reserve System began steep and sustained interest rate cuts at the outset of January, it was only in the late autumn that the United States government officially declared that its economy had been in recession since March, and through the year there was much hope that the massive monetary stimulus would have the desired effect. The G7 has no particular capacity beyond that of its member governments to predict and prevent future events, even those as familiar as the workings of the business cycle before the new economy had set in. Most importantly, concerts are inherently conservative forms of global governance, much better at preserving the *status quo* in response to threats and at slowly infusing new principles, norms, and rules than at preventing crisis or proactively dictating a new order in the short term. Indeed, even at the start of 2002, there was still a strong possibility that the recession in some G7 countries in 2001 would be unusually short and mild, and that the Argentinean moratorium would have few severe systemic consequences.

This chapter explores the cadence and dynamics of the G7's internal socialisation, learning, and adjustment process, the adequacy of the results of its policy in the face of more difficult market forces, and the utility of the concert equality model in explaining the G7's internal and external performance. It first offers an analytic framework for assessing internal 'consensus' and external 'coherence', and develops an extended concert equality model as an explanation. It then empirically examines the response of the G7 and the IMF to the challenges of financial crisis, global growth, international financial architecture, and related issues during the first half of 2001. Here it explores in turn the work of the G7 at its stand-alone February meeting in Palermo, the activity of the G7 and IMFC at their April meetings in Washington, the core issues concerning reform of the IMF, the behaviour of the G7 at its pre-Summit meeting in Rome on 7 July, and the G7's performance on its finance and related economic agenda at and immediately after the Genoa Summit itself. It ends with an assessment of how well the extended concert equality model accounts not only for the internal G7 consensus that was its initial focus for the model, but also for the external coherence of the G7's global governance in a rapidly globalising age.

Consensus, Coherence, and Concert Equality: An Analytic Framework

The Concept of Consensus

Assessing and explaining the G7's performance in global financial governance requires an analytic framework for identifying the degree of internal consensus and external coherence achieved, and a parsimonious causal model that accounts for both phenomena. Despite ongoing doubts as to its accuracy as a descriptive model of G7 performance (Franchini-Sherifis and Astraldi 2001, 162), the concert equality model, first developed by Kirton (1989; 1993) continues to offer a suitable framework for identifying and explaining the internal consensus achieved by the G7/8 generally, and, in its refined version, in the particular field of global finance in a globalising era (Kirton 2000, 2001b).[5] The current challenge is to develop an analytical framework to assess the G7's external performance in governing a globalised system, and in extending the concert equality model to explain G7 performance in this regard.

Following the concert equality model, the G7's internal performance can be assessed according to the degree of 'consensus' it achieves within the group among its members. Consensus is defined in traditional terms as the ability of G7 leaders and ministers to reach agreement in their deliberative, directional, and decisional roles (mutual enlightenment, reinforcement, adjustment, and co-ordination) (Putnam and Bayne 1987; Kirton 1989). Over its 26 years, the G7 has, as virtually all observers agree, exhibited a wide variation in the degree of consensus it has achieved.

The Concept of Coherence

Externally, the G7's collective performance in providing effective global governance can be assessed according to the concept of 'coherence'. Coherence can be conceived of as the provision of a credible, internally consistent, complete, and thus effective system of global governance, in response to the demands produced by the global system at any time. Although coherence in this context has multiple meanings, four are important to the analysis here.

The first component is clarity — the provision by implied or threatened collective action of a credible, clear commitment with sufficient detail to serve as a reference point, moral suasion, or deterrent threat for outside actors, who thus respond to G7 commitments in the intended way, *even in the absence of further implementing action by G7 governments*. Clarity includes credibility, as the soft law embodied in G7/8 statements offers a convincing medium-term expression of determination and self-binding, while avoiding generality, ambiguity, or obsolescence in the face of fast-moving circumstances that the principles, norms, and rules entrenched in the formal charters of ratified intergovernmental treaties suffer from (cf. Simmons 2000). This process is seen in the G7's successful action at the height of the 1997 Korean financial crisis (Kirton 2000), in its constant attempt to provide messages of macroeconomic confidence, in its directional role of defining new principles, and in the ongoing sensitivity of foreign exchange markets to G7 statements regarding currencies. It explains the paradox that G7 members' compliance with G7 economic and energy commitments is slightly higher when measured by welfare outcomes achieved than by G7 government instruments employed (von Furstenberg and Daniels 1992). In short, the G7 can get what it wants merely by identifying its preferred action, without having to take implementing action itself.

The second component is compliance — the G7's governments' faithful adherence to their collective consensus through 'first-order' implementing actions designed to fulfil their commitments (Kokotsis 1999). Here an extensive body of evidence points to widespread variation across time, members, and issue areas in the extent of member governments' efforts to implement their G7/8 commitments (von Furstenberg and Daniels 1992; Kokotsis 1999). It also points to a pattern of increasing compliance, even by the largest and most initially unfaithful — the U.S. and France — as the globalising 1990s unfolded.

The third component is consistency — the G7 countries maintaining their G7 identity externally and operating as a group within all international organisations (such as the IMF) and forums (such as the G20 and the FSF) to which its members belong, in order to forward this intra-G7 consensus. In this respect, G7 members are not constrained by the particular regimes embedded in these other institutions, but use these institutions as delivery vehicles or as legitimating mechanisms to forward the G7 consensus within a broader group.

The fourth component is comprehensiveness — the provision of effective intergovernmental or 'private authority' institutions to address the full range of global challenges, either by reforming existing international institutions, helping create new ones, or establishing G7/8 bodies to meet these new governance needs. Comprehensiveness can be assessed in four ways: spatially, according to the full set of global regions included; functionally, according to the range of issue areas dealt with; temporally, according to the crisis prevention to post-crisis restoration conducted; or vertically, according to the degree of domestic intrusiveness sought and obtained. Its full realisation takes maximum advantage of the G7's unique character, as a flexible, leaders-delivered forum with an unlimited mandate and agenda, for linking issues in creative ways to create large general welfare-enhancing package deals or new directions for the global community as a whole.

These four components of coherence may be conceived of as a spectrum, requiring progressively greater investment by G7/8 members and representing ever greater degrees of the provision of G7/8 global governance. It should be noted that although internal consensus is logically necessary for the G7/8 collectively to provide coherence in global governance externally, complete internal consensus can co-exist with a complete absence of external coherence. Indeed, the 'false new consensus model' of Fred Bergsten and Randall Henning argues precisely that G7 members are in complete agreement that they are now powerless to take any effective action aimed at governing globalised financial markets (Bergsten and Henning 1996; Kirton 1989). Thus, the concert equality model developed and shown to account for intra-G7 consensus may not, in its inherited form, be adequate for explaining the G7's external coherence. An extended version is required to explain the additional dimension of the G7's external performance.

Explaining Consensus and Coherence through the Concert Equality Model

The concert equality model explains internal consensus by predicting, in contrast to the competing 'American leadership' model (Putnam and Bayne 1987), the creation of collective G7/8 agreement through a process of fluid coalition diplomacy in which any member will lead, any member will support and oppose, and even the most powerful country will eventually adjust. Such a process arises from five factors: the predominance without and equality within of members' capabilities, constricted participation, crisis-activated intervulnerability, the commonality of democratic values, and political control by popularly elected leaders.

The logic of the concert equality model can be extended to account for the G7's external performance in providing coherent global governance. Here several components of the model yield direct hypotheses of varying strength and scope.

First, the greater the collective predominance of G7/8 members in relevant capabilities, the greater the coherence of G7/8 global governance will be. Predominance will induce outside actors to accept the G7/8's reference and deterrence points as those likely to prevail. They will provide the resources for compliance. They will produce the sense of responsibility and resources that generate consistency, by making it more likely that G7/8 members will exert dominant influence and have formal management responsibilities within broader multilateral organisations. Such resources and responsibility will also induce comprehensiveness, as this collective hegemon has the resources and incentive to pioneer governance arrangements of extensive and domestically deep reach.

Moreover, internally equal or equalising capabilities make it likely that markets and outside actors will respond to collective G7/8 consensus, rather than that of the leading United States alone. Moreover, such equality, by offering each member a credible threat of retaliation for any member's defection, increases the prospects of compliance in general, consistency in particular, and of the collective provision of more comprehensive governance arrangements (Kirton 1993).

Second, constricted participation is likely to have a negative impact on coherence in all its dimensions. A small self-contained G7/8, while more easily able to generate internal consensus, will lack the immediate awareness of outside problems and conditions, the direct infusion of information and expertise, the intimate knowledge by outsiders of what the G7/8 consensus actually is, and the sense of political inclusion and legitimacy to assist its consensus in prevailing among outside actors. It will also reduce the incentive for the G7/8 to take up problems of the outside world or global system beyond the G7/8, as opposed to those directly affecting its members inside. Compliance, consistency, and comprehensiveness will likely be slower, more costly, and more likely to generate resistance than would be the case if more actors were more closely involved from the outset in the formation of the G7/8 consensus. Thus constricted participation within a self-contained G7, while powerfully promoting internal consensus by K-group logic (Snidal 1985), erodes external coherence with equal force.

Third, intervulnerability activated by crisis has both a negative and a positive relationship with coherence. Crisis within the G7/8 creates an inward-looking preoccupation that detracts from an outward-looking vocation to provide global governance. Yet crises within that have their origins in conditions without — the essential feature of the era of intensifying globalisation, as the Asian-turned-global financial crisis of 1997–99 indicated — force the G7/8 to look outward, to respond to external crises, and, ultimately, to attempt to prevent crises at their distant global source. Finally, as G7/8 countries become 'intervulnerable' with the outside world, as well as with one another, their incentive and experience in providing coherent global governance grow.

Fourth, the common purpose of democracy at the core of the G7/8 as a modern democratic concert provides a similar incentive to take up the task of global governance. As the G7/8's internal challenge of democracy (the 'crisis of governability', and spread of communism in western Europe) always had external sources, its attention was necessarily externally oriented from the outset.[6] When the internal challenge was met by the second half of the 1980s, it could reorient its attention to completing the democratic revolution in the Soviet Union and addressing severe human rights violations in South Africa and China and in the developing world as a whole. This core comprehensive collective concern with the principle of democracy, as a priority over marketisation, gives the G7/8 a powerful general incentive to provide governance on behalf of democratic polities and principles everywhere, including as a constraint on the unbridled market processes unleashed by globalisation. It follows that the G7/8 will act to provide coherent global governance in those situations in which democracy, the rule of law, human rights, and good governance are most severely and immediately threatened. By extension, the spread of open democratic polities dedicated to human rights globally increases the responsiveness of publics to the G7/8 consensus and the legitimacy accorded to its actions, when these are consistent with democratic principles and practices (including transparency and accountability).

Finally, political control by popularly democratic leaders has a direct positive impact on the provision of coherent global governance. G7/8 leaders with a large measure of popularity and electoral freedom at home have a margin of political capital that enables them to address distant global problems, especially of a long-term, structural, or emerging nature. By extension, should such leaders have a similar popular appeal in countries beyond the G7/8, they will be looked to for leadership, and their proposed solutions will secure a responsiveness and legitimacy and, therefore, impact, even should outside national governments and intervening international organisations resist.[7]

The G7 Finance Ministers at Palermo, 17 February 2001

The G7's first effort to generate consensus and coherence in the face of its new internal and external challenges in 2001 came at its initial ministerial meeting, held in Palermo, Italy, in February. The Palermo meeting was the first for the Italian 2001 G7/8 chair, and the first for the new United States administration and its newly named treasury secretary, Paul O'Neill. Prospects for progress at the meeting appeared low. Italy was led by the centre-left coalition government of Giuliano Amato that, polls showed, was likely to be voted out of office in the general election of 13 May 2001, as did happen. The Bush administration was not yet fully installed in Washington, in large part due to the delay in the Florida recount. As a result, the U.S. treasury team was still busy making and securing Senate approval for its senior appointments. Indeed, some members needed special approval from Congress prior to their formal approval, even to make the trans-Atlantic trip. Even as they were flying to Europe, they were preoccupied by the prospect of a sharply slowing U.S. economy, a decline that had been drastically signalled by the stunning mid-meeting interest rate cut by Federal Reserve chairman Alan Greenspan at the outset of January.

Even so, the prospective market challenge had not yet emerged with full force. Despite the Greenspan surprise and the advent of much slower U.S. growth in the fourth quarter of 2000, U.S. stock markets and their new-economy component were still at elevated levels, several economic indicators were promising, and there was faith that Greenspan's action alone would restore any needed confidence. Moreover, in distant Europe, as well as in neighbouring Canada, there was a belief that — even in an age of globalisation — indigenous factors such as solid national growth, new tax cuts, and low inflation could allow these G7 partners, with their national houses in order, and the global economy economy as well, to escape any U.S. economic downturn.

The political assault from the new U.S. administration was much more acute. Just before leaving for Palermo, O'Neill had publicly expressed scepticism about the very value of the G7 intergovernmental forum. Perhaps reflecting his background in the private sector as chief executive officer of Alcoa, he implied that the forum would have to prove itself to the U.S. if he were to return to participate in it. O'Neill stated that he was going to Palermo to listen, suggesting that U.S. leadership or even an open discussion of the new administration's priorities would be lacking. He and his associates had been harsh critics of the G7-led IMF bailout of Russia and of financial support to beleaguered emerging economies during the 1997–99 financial crisis, and were great believers in private sector capital, free market forces, and low taxes in the U.S. and abroad; there was thus little prospect for an instant meeting of the minds with G7 colleagues who were still mostly from the centre left. There was also the possibility that the G7 forum itself might fail to pass muster in the eyes of the U.S. and thus slip into ineffectiveness, as other international caucus groups had.

As it turned out, the G7 at Palermo passed O'Neill's test. Equally important, the U.S. Treasury Secretary passed the test implicitly given by his G7 colleagues. He left Palermo issuing reassuring words about the value of the forum. The ministers had had a good exchange on a wide range of issues, including developments in the world economy, exchange rates, emerging market economies, Russia, debt relief for the highly indebted poor countries (HIPCs), development beyond debt relief, strengthening the international financial architecture, reform of the multilateral development banks, and financial abuse and the FATF. The agenda had reflected in a balanced fashion new U.S. priorities such as MDB reform, those of common concern such as development beyond HIPC, and those for which other G7 partners were in the lead, such as financial abuse. Discussion of these issues at the meeting had avoided any sharp divisions between the new U.S. team and its partners. Some of the new U.S. initiatives had been approved and recommended to the IMF for further work.

Externally, the concluding communiqué and the individual ministers sounded a encouraging note of harmonious, short-term optimism about the state of, and prospects for, the global economy (see Appendix E). In addition to such market clarity, the meeting provided consistent agenda-setting guidance to the IFIs about the blend of new priorities and continuing emphasis they should focus efforts on.

Given its prospects, as a deliberative, 'get-acquainted' meeting Palermo thus proved to be a strong intra-G7 success. However, in view of global economic conditions and market uncertainties, as an exercise in forward-looking, preventive global economic management, it did much less well. Despite its short-term injection of optimism, the world was soon faced with the outbreak of new financial crises in Turkey and Argentina, and a sharp slowdown in growth in the U.S., Europe, and Japan. U.S. listening had not yet yielded to learning about new ways to govern a global financial system coming under threat. The slowness of the G7's response, as well as its flexibility and capacity for rapid reaction in the face of clear crisis, was evident on 19 March, when the G7 issued an unusual special statement supporting Turkey's economic reform programme and its support by the IMF and World Bank (see Appendix F).

The G7 and International Monetary and Financial Committee at Washington, April 2001

Ten weeks later in Washington, the finance ministers in the G7 and the IMFC faced much the same agenda, but with new external pressure arising from a far more formidable set of market threats. At Washington, the challenge from U.S. political change was considerably reduced. Whereas U.S. passivity at Palermo could be attributed to the fact that the meeting was held at a moment too early for the new U.S. team to impose its agenda and approach, in April in Washington the U.S. was the host of the G7 meeting. O'Neill was nonetheless still largely silent, listening, and, as it turned out, learning. There were a few early indications of what the new U.S. attitudes and approaches might be. One was a shift away from large IFI and government financing packages and toward crisis prevention and private sector involvement. Another was a new U.S. coolness to prosecuting countries that offered lower taxes in their national 'havens'. Yet apart from the Undersecretary for International Affairs, John Taylor, who had just been confirmed, very few of O'Neill's officials were in place. The U.S. 'listening and learning' approach continued through the discussions and decisions on the four urgent matters that dominated the G7's Washington agenda.

Global Growth Prospects

The first such matter was concern about global growth prospects. The mood had changed dramatically since January. There was now a real, well-recognised, and ever deepening slowdown in the U.S. and Japan remained moribund. In a previously resilient Europe, growth was falling off. Many speakers at both the G7 and IMFC meetings doggedly called attention to such remaining bright spots as low unemployment, moderate inflation, sound fiscal positions, and the manoeuvring room that surplus governments with a tax-cutting or spending disposition had. This brave burst of confidence was the tone reflected in the communiqué (see Appendix G). But in the meetings themselves, there was clear anxiety among the ministers and central bank governors about G7 and global growth prospects for 2001. The sober consensus within thus yielded hopeful clarity without in the form of a clear message of confidence. The latter came with no compliant action in terms of new measures to generate global growth.

Turkey, Argentina, and the Emerging Market Economies

A second anxiety, particularly for the G7 but also for the IMFC, related to the newly precarious situation of the emerging market economies. By April, both Turkey and Argentina had dropped into the danger zone, leading the bond markets and sovereign debt markets in emerging economies to plunge. This prospective successive shock — the threat of another contagious meltdown, so soon after the 1997–99 crisis cadence — was uppermost in the minds of G7 and IMFC ministers as they sought to stabilise the situation in these two critical countries. As in Thailand, Indonesia, Korea, Russia (on the first occasion), and Brazil in 1997–99, the G7 had the IMF again ride to the rescue. But in this first twenty-first century instalment, it did so in what it saw as a more flexible and country-specific manner. The G7 ministers applauded the IMF for its new-found desire to tailor its rescue programmes to individual country cases and specific circumstances. They suggested that this was the right way forward, especially as the two current crisis cases were quite different.[8]

This G7 consensus reflected the ease with which the Bush administration adjusted to the prospective successive shock and resulting new vulnerability from abroad. The administration was by then developing a new, more conservative, international economic policy approach, particularly to the role of the IMF and crisis resolution. Yet the U.S. proved to be highly pragmatic in its response to individual crises such as Turkey and Argentina, with their immediate threats to the economies of neighbouring Europe and North America, and their status as stable secular democratic polities central to core U.S. and G7 foreign policy interests. Although U.S. instincts were for the IMF to provide a small financial assistance package rather than a large one to each country, the U.S. examined each case on its merits. At the IMF executive board's discussion of the Turkey package, instead of vetoing the proposed measures, the U.S. submitted a measured statement that identified the pros and cons, and on balance, offered support.

A second novel element of the G7-guided IMF crisis response was the emphasis on private sector participation. In a memorable German phrase first used by Helmut Kohl in regard to Russia and now borrowed by IMF managing director and former G7 sherpa Horst Köhler, IMF money was to be 'help for self-help'. The desire was for 'forced haircuts', to send the message that if private investors made a mistake, they would pay and not be bailed out by the public sector funds of the IMF. Köhler was adamant that there would be no public bailouts for bad investment decisions, that the private sector must be responsible for its actions, and that there would be winners and losers alike. Private sector responsibility thus became a key conviction of both the IMF and G7, if one easier to proclaim as a principle and create a consensus on than to put into practice in crisis situations in the immediate future.

This new emphasis and emerging consensus were consistent with the much more pointed priority on private sector involvement in the new U.S. approach. The crusade for affirming this principle within the G8 had long been led by Canada, Britain, and Germany, and, more recently, by the IMF's Köhler. The U.S. under Bill Clinton, Robert Rubin, and Larry Summers had resisted, preferring the flexibility to bail out (mostly New York) investors should the economic or political need arise (Kirton 2000). While this change in the U.S. position helped give this principle a much sharper emphasis, it was a case of the U.S. adjusting to an emerging G7 consensus, rather than a new initiative led by the U.S.

A third element of the new approach to emerging market rescues was the clear statement that these IMF packages were really the last chance for Argentina and Turkey. If either failed, no more money would be forthcoming, even if risk premiums were to continue to rise across developing countries. Yet the IMF was cautiously optimistic that these programmes would work, given the massive amount of money leveraged and the catalytic role of the IMF acting on other lenders. The IMF had given the recipients' reform programmes a veneer of respectability, in order to help sell the programme to markets and to their own societies. The IMF judged Argentina's finance minister Domingo Cavallo to have done very well with his debt swap, and Turkey's economy minister Kemal Dervis to have put his career on the line as a sign of his commitment to the success of his reform programme. The belief that the programmes must succeed was one that G7 finance ministers agreed to inject into the G7 leaders' discussions at Genoa.

In these packages, the new U.S. administration could claim that no national monies were used in a second line of defence, and that the recipient governments were forced to undertake the harsh but needed domestic reform programme before rather than after the IMF money arrived. But the IMF-only approach referred to a channel rather than to the origins or amount of the money. In the IMF, the U.S. and its G7 partners still committed the largest funds and commanded the largest share of votes. Moreover, the rescue packages were the largest ever for the IMF, as measured as a percentage of the quota share and thus borrowing rights of the recipient governments. Ultimately, the fulfilment of the conditions was a matter of timing, tactics, and optics rather than any fundamental change.[9] The real test for change would only come if Turkey's reformed programme failed and Bush was prepared to do nothing while his NATO ally, a partner in the war against Iraq, and the secular bastion against Islamic fundamentalism at the crossroads of the Middle East descended into chaos. The G7 had thus produced an adequate short-term compromise that combined clear and forceful threats to resistant political actors within Turkey and Argentina to accept the IMF's detailed conditions, with consistent action within the IMF to raise the necessary funds, and the option of a residual role for G7 leaders if required.

Crisis Prevention

At the G7 and IMFC meetings in April, there was a very clear, new consensus on the importance of crisis prevention and on the integrally related issue of the role and reform of the IMF. The IMF, always a crisis resolver, was now, through evident and consistent U.S.-led G7 consensus and action, directed to reinvent itself as a crisis preventer. The new G7 emphasis on crisis prevention immediately spawned a great deal of new work in the IMF, as G7 proposals, codified in the communiqué, were injected into its work programmes. With the agreement of the G7 and the entire membership, the IMF was now charged with detecting and preventing financial crises. The key instrument was surveillance, in keeping with the mandate in the IMF Articles of Agreement to conduct firm surveillance over exchange rates and the global economy. The IMF would thus enter countries to provide objective and clear advice, work with the local finance ministry, and develop and publish indicators of risk, such as macro prudential indicators (MPIs), as a main instrument of crisis prevention. It would develop data on leading indicators of crisis in a country. It would further conduct 'stress tests' on national financial systems.[10]

The G7 and IMF, in the spirit of the new emphasis on conflict prevention, also placed a premium on the use of standards and codes that they had been developing over the previous few years. This longstanding initiative of Britain and Canada had been supported by Japan and Germany. The U.S. now became a full convert to their use as an intergovernmentally encoded and legitimated instrument for providing clarity to market actors. The IMF would develop reports on the observance of standards and codes (ROSCs), as the most effective way of mobilising peer pressure. This would lead, it calculated, to the diffusion of best practices from one country to another, across a wide range of areas, including money laundering and fiscal, monetary, and banking policy and supervision (Porter 2001). Clarity, IMF-centred consistency, and comprehensive monitoring (across the international and domestic financial domains, if not the full economic or related ecological and political domains) were thus at the core of this new G7 consensus.

Also reinforced was the move toward greater transparency. Britain and Canada had strongly pushed the principle of transparency, and had now secured the support of the U.S. The new emphasis was on as much public reporting as possible, designed to make the IMF the most transparent international organisation ever. The result was a sea change that represented perhaps the most striking transformation at the IMF over the previous five years. This complete change in culture and mentality was cemented in the attitudes of a new generation of staffers at the IMF. The G7-led consensus on the need for market clarity, operating consistently though an institutional transformation of the IMF, was quickly brought into effect.

The Role and Reform of the IMF

With the G7's approval, the IMF also continued its move to reform its lending instruments and streamline conditionality (Kirton 2001b). It would reduce the number of lending instruments, raise the interest rates for using them and lower the time they could be used before countries would have to return to the private sector and abide by market principles. In doing so, the G7 declared that the IMF was not a development institution. In this case, the outcome reflected the views of the U.S. Meltzer Commission report (Meltzer 2000), and represented a reduction in the comprehensiveness of the global governance provided by the IMF.

One issue that aroused considerable controversy at the G7 meeting, but was not mentioned in the communiqué, was the issue of streamlining conditionality. Germany, France, and Japan pushed hard on this issue. The U.S., along with Canada, Britain, and Italy, stood opposed. They argued that lending and conditions should ensure the success of the reform programme, and that the IMF would get its lent money back. They pointed to the fact that Article 1 of the IMF Articles of Agreement directed the institution to lend with appropriate safeguards. The IMF responded by offering concepts, with a view to inviting comments, assessing responses, and discussing them at its board.

At Washington, the G7 also addressed broader issues of IMF reform, as part of its ongoing effort to assemble a new international financial architecture. It did so with some satisfaction that, thanks in large part to G7 efforts, the IMF was a very different institution than it had been five years ago. There was a broad consensus internationally that the IMF should focus on three core tasks. These were promoting macroeconomic and financial stability as a precondition of sustained economic growth, fostering the stability and integrity of the international monetary and financial system as a global public good, and helping members develop a sound financial sector to protect against risk and mobilise finance and to take advantage of the opportunities of globalising financial markets. The IMF would thus move out of the realm of structural policy, unless it had a direct bearing on the macroeconomic situation. The IMF would also modernise its financial instruments, so that it would no longer compete with private lenders, but rather would shepherd countries toward private instruments. It would thus institute sharp surveillance of how it spent.

As part of the reform package, a reluctant G7 and IMF acknowledged that the financial institution would have to have accept what many regarded as an unworkable and counterproductive CCL, even if was now revamped. Even with the new Bush administration, the U.S. remained as enamoured of the instrument as it had been under the Clinton administration, and was eager to have emerging market countries ask for one. The U.S. saw CCLs as a precautionary part of the new crisis prevention emphasis.

If a country was following good policies and wanted access to a line of credit, the IMF would review the request and have US$10 to $15 billion instantly accessible should the need arise. Bipartisan U.S. hegemony thus forced a reluctant G7 and IMF to accept the CCL as a legitimate lending instrument. But even in a world awash in financial instability, a hegemonic U.S. under Bush still proved unable to have a single country request a CCL — even neighbouring Mexico — thanks in large part to the conditions placed by the G7 on its use within the IMF. The U.S. victory thus remained stillborn (Kirton 2001a, 2001b). The G7 was able to use the rules of the IMF to give life to the real consensus within, rather than a U.S.-dictated one.

There was further interest in focussing the IMF on what it did best and having countries take ownership of their reform programmes. To cultivate national ownership, the IMF considered incorporating civil society, and providing a menu of options rather than one Washington consensus (Birdsall and de la Torre 2001). The goal was to secure public input and come to the fall meetings of the G7 and IMF with a formal proposal on how to proceed.

The IMF also sought to become a centre of excellence on the financial sector. It thus began work on early warning, indicators of vulnerability, and incremental strategies to see just where the tipping points might be, given that market psychology was key. Transparency remained very important, in part because it reduced the propensity for crisis and thus reinforced the IMF's crisis prevention agenda.

The final issue the IMF had to face was financial abuse. The French, with high taxes that its citizens were eager to avoid, had long been incensed about the abuse of the financial system from money laundering, tax havens, and offshore financial centres. They mobilised the international community, and took the FATF's 40 recommendations out from the obscure margins of the Organisation for Economic Co-operation and Development (OECD) and put them onto centre stage of the G7 agenda and action. With France pushing hard, all G7 members bought in and involved the IMF, despite its aversion to assume the new role of 'tax police'.

Nonetheless, when O'Neill entered office he threatened to reverse the long-standing supportive U.S. policy on this issue. O'Neill asked why the Bush administration should protect high-tax countries abroad, when it was dramatically lowering taxes at home. His instinctive preference was that France should reduce its taxes, too, rather than persecute America's small Caribbean neighbours such as Antigua and Barbuda for having low tax rates. Yet he readily acquiesced in the G7 and FATF's decision to place three countries on a public list, with a timetable, for instituting reforms or facing sanctions if they did not.[11] At the same time, the ongoing struggle over competing approaches continued on the road to Genoa. As much of the money in these havens came from OECD countries, there was a strong argument for dealing with the problem at the source, rather than only by sanctioning the very small and poor recipients of the funds flows.

The HIPC Initiative

At both the G7 and IMFC meetings, there was broad satisfaction with the initiative for HIPCs. Indeed, there were discussions of a post-HIPC era that would go beyond reducing the nominal value of the debt. Britain was the leader, having been the most vocal on this issue over the past few years. Yet the centre-left government of Italy, as host of the G7 Summit, readily adopted the theme as a centrepiece of its preparations for Genoa (Amato 2001).

Under the influence of civil society organizations and Britain, the G7 challenged the IMF, and World Bank with the question: 'How do we keep the HIPC recipient countries out of debt rather than have them move into a new destructive cycle of borrowing and default'? This issue of longer-term debt sustainability was added, cautiously, to the agenda of the Genoa G7 gathering. Here the G7 was slated to approve tracking poverty-related expenditures on the poor in HIPC countries to see where the recipient governments spent their debt relief, and the quality of their poverty reduction strategy papers (PRSPs). The IMF would encourage the governments to discuss their PRSPs with their societies, as they had seldom done before, and would not support those countries that did not do so.

A further G7 demand was that recipient countries improve the environment so as to improve productivity, attract investment, and consequently reduce poverty. This was the one initiative from Paul O'Neill, who otherwise remained silent. His views may have reflected those of his new deputy, John Taylor, who stressed the need for better trade opportunities for the less developed countries (LDCs).

The G7 Finance Ministers at Rome, 7 July 2001

By the time G7 finance ministers met again, ten weeks later in Rome, the internal U.S. political assault had further diminished, even as the external market challenge had again intensified. Although U.S. indicators remained mixed, it was clear that major interest rate cuts by the Federal Reserve, the prospect of a soon-to-arrive US$1.35 trillion tax cut and lower energy prices had not brought a quick U.S. recovery, nor would they bring it about soon. Moreover, Japan, with negative growth in the first quarter and almost certainly negative growth in the second, had slipped back toward, or even into, recession for the third time in a decade — before its new Prime Minister's strategy of tough bank writeoffs and deficit cutting had begun. Led by Germany, followed by France, Europe showed signs of serious slippage, to the point where some respected forecasters suggested that a recession might be in store there, too. Even more ominously, the ravages experienced by U.S. new-economy companies had finally come to Europe, bringing massive decreases in corporate earnings, in employment, and in share prices. The euro followed suit, dropping to near historic lows against the U.S. dollar.

The first consequence of this common downward movement was a plea by the U.S. Treasury Secretary for help from his G7 partners. It came in the form of a revival of the locomotive theory that had flourished during the initial years of the G7 in the 1970s but died in the following years. Clearly recognising the responsibility of the U.S. and the G7 to ensure growth in the global economy as a whole, O'Neill argued that the U.S. had acted to meet this objective through its own interest rate and tax cuts. It was now time for Europe to do the same, led by the European Central Bank (ECB) that had until then steadfastly refused to lower interest rates even as European growth fell. On the eve of the Rome meeting, O'Neill's plea earned a harsh retort from French finance minister Laurent Fabius, who blamed the global slowdown squarely on the United States. With a negative U.S. jobs report and news of major new layoffs in Europe in the days before the Rome meeting opened, the mood was grim.

During and after the meeting, however, the prevailing spirit was one of hanging together rather than falling apart over who was to blame. All G7 finance ministers, following the briefing notes thoughtfully provided by the Italian hosts, proclaimed that all countries and continents must do their part to strengthen growth. Led by O'Neill's promise that the U.S. was bound to return to 2 percent growth in the fourth quarter and 3 percent in the first quarter of the following year (compared to 1.2 percent in the first quarter of 2001), all sounded a note of cautious optimism. The only discordant voice, which proved prescient, came from the British Chancellor of the Exchequer, Gordon Brown, who mused that conditions might get worse before they improved. On all other items of their agenda, the public mood of G7 solidarity and confidence completely predominated. In a move toward consistency and comprehensiveness, while concentrating on preparing three reports for their leaders for Genoa on the IFIs, financial abuse, and 'Beyond Debt Relief', the G7 finance ministers took two concrete steps (see Appendices H and I). They asked independent experts to explore structural reforms in each of their countries, and they called for a new round of multilateral trade liberalisation to begin.

Yet just as the G7 succeeded in forging consensus from its internal political challenge, an external economic one threatened to spin out of control. Immediately after the meeting, reports of an impasse between Turkey and the IMF and of provincial resistance leading Argentina to miss its deficit-cutting targets led markets in emerging economies to plummet. More ominously, those in Eastern Europe, led by Poland, began to catch the contagion.

The G7's Performance at Genoa, 20–22 July 2001

The prospects of a simultaneous, severe drop in growth within all G7 regions and of two financial crises in their consequential neighbours persisted as G7 leaders met in Genoa on 20 July 2001. Despite the demands of those on the streets for a socially oriented Genoa Summit, led by a spending assault on HIV/AIDS, there was clear need to address several urgent hard core financial and economic issues (see Appendix B).

During their afternoon meeting, the G7 leaders dealt with global economic growth and poverty reduction in Africa, the latter in preparation for the 'outreach event' with Kofi Annan and African leaders that would take place immediately afterward. Their statement, however, also dealt with other issues, such as trade, which they subsequently discussed 'at eight' (see Appendix A). Despite the drain on their time and attention from the scheduled African outreach event, and from the news of a fatality among the violent protesters, over the course of the three-day Summit the G7 was able to reach consensus on several difficult issues. At best, that consensus constituted only an adequately coherent response to an Argentina that was to receive another IMF financial transfusion in August and to a G7 economy that was to plummet into real recession in all three regions in the wake of the 11 September terrorist attacks.

Global Growth Prospects

The first difficult issue was the continuing concern with global growth prospects. By 20 July, the U.S. slowdown had become entrenched. The U.S. had dropped from 5 percent growth to less than 1 percent, constituting an enormous decline that became more psychologically consequential with each passing month. Rising unemployment and drops in the stock markets threatened to have a real economic effect throughout middle America, as Americans held off on large purchases and became concerned about credit card debt. The return of 1970s-style stagflation in Europe was also a concern, particularly in view of its potentially heavy political effects in elections in France and Germany in the coming year.

In their statement, the G7 leaders maintained the mood of optimism previously struck by their finance ministers. But they also signalled that they would remain vigilant and ready to act to 'ensure' that their economies performed up to their potential (see Appendix J). Indeed, they sent their sherpas back to inject more action-oriented language into their draft communiqué in order to communicate their vigilance effectively and to indicate to astute observers what actions they would take should conditions deteriorate. An effort at greater clarity and credibility, now with the full authority of the leaders themselves, was thus made.

Emerging Market Situation

At the time of the Genoa Summit, Turkey and especially Argentina remained on the critical list. The G7 faced a major potential problem in other emerging markets, notably stagnating Brazil, until these two major G20 countries, afflicted simultaneously in two separate regions, returned to sustained growth. In a passage added by the leaders themselves, the G7 statement firmly endorsed the existing steps the IMF and the afflicted countries themselves had taken, in part to reassure markets and to signal resistant forces within the two countries that they would find no support from abroad. Moreover, both host Silvio Berlusconi and France's Jacques Chirac publicly noted that the G7 would respond to the letter sent to the G7 leaders from Argentinean president Fernando de la Rua, and would offer more help if it were required (Bayne 2001). In a notable contrast to the Mexican 1994–95 crisis (Kirton 1995), it was thus clear that the G7's European members, recognising their global responsibilities (as well as the interests of fellow EU member Spain), were prepared to join with their North American ones to provide the support required to rescue Argentina.

Here the G7 acted with considerable clarity, compliance, and consistency. Within a month, a reluctant O'Neill joined the G7 consensus and had the IMF offer a new, conditional US$8 billion support package on 21 August. The package came following a round of consultations among Köhler and G7 finance ministers and officials, and immediately following a G7 statement of support issued on 19 August (see Appendix K). The IMF, urged on by the G7 and the U.S., further produced a new US$15 billion standby credit, operating until December 2002, for beleaguered Brazil, to help it stave off contagion from its neighbour's financial woes. The G7-inspired action gave Argentina another five months to address its domestic fiscal problem, and gave global markets time to analyse and distinguish the particular Argentinean problem from the very different conditions in emerging markets as a whole. The Argentineans misused their new lease on financial life by failing to meet fiscal targets in the autumn, leading the IMF to suspend disbursements and the Argentineans to counter with the world's largest ever debt repayment moratorium and then default. Nonetheless, the G7 actions did succeed in protecting the emerging market financial system, as 2002 opened with other emerging markets little affected by contagion from the Argentinean move. The G7 through the IMF had been unable to induce Argentineans to rescue themselves, but it did save the global financial system as a whole from the consequences of the Argentinean failure.

G7 leaders also touched on other pivotal cases, including the condition of Russia. While doing well in the short term as rising energy prices boosted GDP, Russia continued to have long-term structural problems, especially in regard to taxation, corporate governance, and widespread corruption. It also suffered from capital flight of US$20 billion a year, sums that the G7 and IMF were no longer willing to finance. President Vladimir Putin felt strongly about stopping this outflow. His attitude indicated that the consensus on core economic subjects was rapidly expanding from G7 to G8.[12]

New Trade Round

The G7 leaders at Genoa, following their finance ministers in Rome, importantly supported the launch of a new trade round by pledging to remain 'personally and jointly involved' to ensure a successful launch (see Appendix J). Setting aside longstanding differences between the U.S. and EU, they moved a considerable way toward adopting a common approach to take to the World Trade Organization (WTO) meeting at Doha, and one that offered enough to developing countries to keep the prospects for a quick launch alive. The IMF agreed to mobilise developing countries to realise that liberalisation was key, and to help deliver capacity-building support to enable developing countries to enter newly opened industrial country markets.

In making this move, the G7 consciously sought to provide clarity. G7 members judged that markets would calculate that the prospect of multilateral trade liberalisation would stimulate growth, and that this calculation would stimulate confidence and thus growth in the short term. They thus moved more comprehensively to recognise and act on the link between trade liberalisation and macroeconomic stimulus. Here they were again inspired by the unprecedented combination of a simultaneous growth slowdown in all G7 regions and two major financial crises in Europe and the Americas erupting at once.

Moreover, in keeping with the new Cologne consensus on socially sustainable globalisation and as a result of civil society pressure, the G7 leaders also pledged that such trade liberalisation would be done in ways that ensured it supported sustainable development (Kirton, Daniels, and Freytag 2001a).[13] This move toward comprehensiveness was one of the most far reaching ever made in the trade-environment field by the G7, taken in an area where the institutions of the WTO and UN system had manifestly failed. However, the link between finance and the environment that had been forged at the finance ministers meetings of the Asia-Pacific Economic Cooperation (APEC) countries at Canada's Kananaskis in 1998 and at the Montreal G20 meeting in October 2000 remained to be drawn.

As the WTO November ministerial meetings at Doha concluded, it was clear that the G7 leaders had complied with their Genoa commitment. The WTO launched a new round of multilateral trade liberalisation negotiations, and did so in a way that, relative to past WTO performance, went a long way to drawing the trade-environment link.

Ongoing Reform of the IMF

G7 leaders also took stock of the continuing reform of the IMF. There was widespread satisfaction, verging on complacency, with the work to date. On the core issues of MDB reform, the U.S. received very little of its core demand, made public by Bush just before the Genoa Summit, that the World Bank shift from giving loans to grants and focus those grants on education and health. The G7 promised merely to 'explore' the issue and to do so in the context of a 'meaningful replenishment' of the International Development Association (IDA). The G7 expected, by the end of July, to receive public input on these issues as well as indications of IMF staff views at the most senior levels. Several new senior-level appointments at the IMF would set the direction, and there would be progress on crisis prevention and early indicators. With the direction provided by the G7 at Genoa, the IMF was expected to deliver by the fall.

Conclusion

At the Genoa G7 meeting in 2001, one of the greatest internal dramas was whether the collective harmony reached easily among the new and old G7 incumbents at the ministerial level would flourish as fully as it did among the heads of state and government themselves. Despite his inexperience in international and financial affairs, George W. Bush gave firm evidence that such harmony did thrive. This was no small success, for it was rare to have so many relative newcomers, from such different parts of the political spectrum, arrive at the G7/8 table all at once. In addition, having the government change in the host country so close to a summit was rare. Moreover, although Silvio Berlusconi had hosted Italy's last G7 Summit at Naples in 1994, it had taken some time for him to assemble a cabinet in the lead-up to Genoa.

The G7 at Genoa thus proved to be successful, at both the ministerial and leaders levels, in rapidly socialising new right-wing leaders into the forum, and in arriving through mutual adjustment at consensus of a deliberative, directional, and decisional sort. Indeed, in their concluding communiqué, the G7 leaders made ten specific commitments, only a slight drop from the twelve in their statement at Okinawa the year before. Moreover, these commitments were of considerable ambition and significance, receiving a score of +40 percent compared to the +43 percent for those the previous year (Kirton, Kokotsis, and Juricevic 2001a; see Appendix D).

Nonetheless, the G7's achievements in providing coherent global financial governance were much less pronounced, if arguably adequate to the challenges the market mounted during the first seven months of 2001. The G7 provided sufficient clarity, although with several iterations, to avert or delay acute financial crises in Turkey and Argentina, and to provide consumers in G7 countries (other than a deeply troubled Japan) with the minimum levels of reassurance required to maintain their spending levels in the face of sharply slowing overall growth. Moreover, the G7 displayed a level of compliance at the leaders level much greater than average, as the economic commitments made at Okinawa were complied with an unusually high +78 percent of the time. This compares with an average score for the period beween 1996 and 2001 of +39 percent (Kirton, Kokotsis, and Juricevic 2001b).[14] Consistency was also much in evidence, as the G7 consensus on assistance to Turkey and Argentina, the new priorities on crisis prevention and MDB reform, and the old consensus on financial abuse easily prevailed in a much reoriented and somewhat reconstructed IMF. Despite some advances in fields such as MDB reform and the forging of links between trade and finance and trade and the environment, there were few signs of the fuller comprehensiveness required by a globalising international financial system, which other fora, such as the G20 with its 'Montreal consensus', had already moved to address (Kirton 2001a).

The G7's recent and prospective shortcomings are not primarily internal and ideological but external and epistemic in nature. The G7 has coped easily with the challenge of absorbing a new rightward-oriented U.S. administration, with a leader and treasury secretary with little experience in international economic affairs, even as it simultaneously had to socialise similarly predisposed and configured new governments in number-two Japan, host Italy, and always relevant Russia. Despite this internal consensus, however, the G7 has been less successful in meeting the external market challenge through innovative new approaches or actions to govern an international financial system in the process of profound change. To be sure, there has been some progress, as with the new emphasis on crisis prevention and the move to develop strategies for a post-HIPC era. Moreover, some of the old ways, as in the rescue packages for Turkey and Argentina, were arguably necessary to avert larger disasters. But some of the continuities, notably the bipartisan Clinton-Bush love affair with the CCL, are poorly tailored to meet systemic needs. Some issues, notably exchange rate management, have been deferred. Others have not been taken up at all. These include the potential inflationary impact and instability caused by the proliferating use of derivatives, the need to manage and facilitate the intensifying processes of currency consolidation and dollarization, the need to offer a rules-based liberalisation for the ballooning foreign direct investment (FDI) that is widely seen as a superior substitute for portfolio investment in the emerging markets and developing world, and the advantages of a common approach to competition policy to regulate the massive merger and acquisition activity that can dominate FDI flows. A further task, in keeping with the G7's Cologne consensus, the G20's Montreal consensus, and the 1998 APEC finance ministers conclusion, is to establish links between finance and the environment, beyond environmentally responsible export finance, that protect the ecological and natural resource capital of crisis-ridden countries, reduce fiscally and ecologically wasteful subsidies, mobilise national and IFI instruments to promote sustainable development, and account for ecological capital in the ongoing surveillance activity of the IFIs. There remain real questions as to whether the IMF, at the heart of the old international financial architecture, or newer forums, such as the IMFC, the G20, and the FSF, can adapt quickly enough to such challenges without decisive G7 leadership.

It is thus clear, that the world must look not to the old, even reinvented IMF but to the G7 as the central forum for leadership in governing global finance in a globalising era. As the concert equality models explains, as an international institution the G7 is certainly up to the task of socialising internally large and potentially ideologically outlying member states into new collective concepts of their interests and even identities and inducing collective commitments, statements of clarity, compliance, consistency, and comprehensiveness. Yet the paradox is that concerts such as the G7 are a particularly conservative form of international institution, much better at satisficing to avoid disaster and maintain the existing order than operating in optimising fashion to pioneer new principles and processes in response to a rapidly changing world. The ultimate challenge for the G7/8 beyond Genoa is to find a formula to reach beyond the constraints of its deep structure as a concert and to create, conceptually and concretely, the new international financial architecture that a globalised world now needs.

In doing so, it could well begin with one innovation in process, the absence of which may help explain the G7's sluggish response to the fast-moving external market challenge in recent years. This refers not to its lack of the much-discussed legitimacy and representativeness, for the recent creation and effective performance of the G20 and the FSF have gone far in meeting the need for horizontal outreach in the governmental world. Indeed, in the ultimate indicator of legitimacy, as de la Rua's letter to G7 leaders at Genoa in 2001 showed — as had Gorbachev's letter at Paris in 1989 — it is to the G7 that consequential outsiders direct their pleas for help when crisis comes.

Rather, what the G7 itself lacks, even more strikingly within a G7/8 system that has recently done so much to engage civil society actors, is vertical outreach with relevant private sector actors and nongovernmental experts and organisations. The G7 finance ministers' call at Rome for a group of experts to assess structural impediments to growth within the G7 is a useful first step, but it neglects the new global agenda generated by globalised markets, and the precedents set by the G8's Dot Force and Renewable Energy Task Force. Especially in view of the critique advanced by advocacy groups of the current governance of global finance (Naiman 2001), the time has come, in the spirit of crisis prevention, for the G7 to create a new multistakeholder group to help it identify, research, and address in advance the new generation of challenges that the globalised markets of the twenty-first century are likely to bring.

Notes

1   The author thanks those colleagues who provided comments on earlier versions of this chapter given at a conference on 'Assembling a New International Financial Architecture: The Deeper Issues', at LUISS University, Rome, 17 July 2001, and at a panel on 'Competing Sources of Authority in the Governance of Global Finance' at the 2001 ISA Conference, Asian Pacific Region, 27 July 2001, Hong Kong.

2   Although Japanese Liberal Democratic Party governments are difficult to position on a broad right-left ideological spectrum (Kirton 1989), the Koizumi government's abandonment of the traditional Keynesian approach of fiscal and monetary policy stimulus and reliance on structural

reforms such as deregulation and privatisation (most notably of the postal saving system) indicates a classic shift to the right in economic policy. More broadly, Koizumi's declared intention to visit a traditional war shrine and to introduce textbooks glossing over Japan's World War II atrocities also suggest a rightward shift in the political sphere.

3 Because the slowdown in G7 economies, combined with emerging markets financial crises, led to slower growth in the non-G7 world (except China), the G7 maintained its predominant capability in the system as a whole. Going into the G7 Genoa Summit, U.S. GDP was known to have plunged from 5 percent in 2000 to 1.2 percent in the first quarter of 2001 (Kirton 2001c). Immediately after, the U.S. reported growth in the second quarter of 2001 of just 0.7 percent, while revising the figures for the first quarter and for 2000 to 4.1 percent (and those for 1999 from 4.2 percent to 4.1 percent and for 1998 from 4.4 percent to 4.3 percent). In contrast, GDP growth for Canada, the G7's smallest economy, was 4.4 percent in 2000, 5.1 percent in 1999, and 3.9 percent in 1998.

4 As intervulnerability is most potent when activated by a 'second shock', the eruption of crises in Turkey and Argentina readily reawakened memories of the Russian and Brazilian 1998 cases that, unlike the Asian crises of 1997 (involving Thailand, Indonesia, and Korea) immediately and severely threatened the U.S. liquidity system with the collapse of Long-Term Capital Management (LTCM) (Kirton 2000). The simultaneous eruption of two crises in two regions from two leading emerging markets and G20 members made for a more rapid and robust response. Moreover, the U.S. had two major democratic projects (Kosovo-Macedonia-NATO and the Summit of the Americas/Free Trade Agreement of the Americas) in these regions.

5 Those suggesting that the G7/8 is best understood and explained as a modern international concert include Wallace (1984), Lewis (1991–92), Odom (1995), Schwegmann (2001).

6 The globalising era has brought a new internal 'crisis of governability', with the eruption of major violent protests for the first time at the Genoa G7/8 Summit in 2001.

7 The popular appeal of G7/8 leaders among citizens of other G7/8 countries induces consensus rather than coherence.

8 The two situations were most notable in the exchange rate regime, as Argentina was a currency-based adjustment. Turkey had a crawling peg that the IMF was encouraging Turkey to float, anchored in a monetary-based quasi-inflation target.

9 The conditions imposed on Turkey, including appointments to board seats on a state-owned telecommunications company, were highly detailed and domestically intrusive, in sharp contrast to the new policy emphasis on restricting conditionality to macroeconomic basics.

10 In such an instance, it might ask how an economic downturn would affect a bank's portfolios and whether this could be the start of a crisis, or about the levels of nonperforming loans or of short-term debt, or about the composition of the debt and whether there is a bias toward a single currency.

11 At the time, the U.S. was losing an estimated minimum of US$70 billion in tax revenue a year due to assets hidden offshore. By July, O'Neill outlined an approach to Congress that would pursue those who used offshore tax havens to escape U.S. taxes, but opposed international efforts to dictate to other countries how they should structure their tax systems.

12 Further evidence came from Russia's failure to press its case for Paris Club relief of its Soviet-era debt, and from its financial contribution to the new Global Fund to Fight AIDS, Tuberculosis, and Malaria.

13 The passage read: 'The WTO should continue to respond to the legitimate expectations of civil society, and ensure that the new Round supports sustainable development' (see Appendix J, para. 8).

14 No data are available on commitments or compliance for G7 work at the finance ministers level.

References

Amato, Giuliano (2001). 'The Challenges of Global Governance'. *Politica Internazionale* vol. 29 (January-April), pp. 31–35.

Bayne, Nicholas (2000a). 'The G7 Summit's Contribution: Past, Present, and Prospective'. In K. Kaiser, J. J. Kirton and J. P. Daniels, eds., *Shaping a New International Financial System: Challenges of Governance in a Globalizing World*, pp. 19–35. Ashgate, Aldershot.

Bayne, Nicholas (2000b). *Hanging in There: The G7 and G8 Summit in Maturity and Renewal*. Ashgate, Aldershot.

Bayne, Nicholas (2001). 'Managing Globalisation and the New Economy: The Contribution of the G8 Summit'. In J. J. Kirton and G. M. von Furstenberg, eds., *New Directions in Global Economic Governance: Managing Globalisation in the Twenty-First Century*, pp. 171–188. Ashgate, Aldershot.

Bergsten, C. Fred and C. Randall Henning (1996). *Global Economic Leadership and the Group of Seven*. Institute for International Economics, Washington DC.

Birdsall, Nancy and Augusta de la Torre (2001). 'Washington Contentious'. *Politica Internazionale* vol. 29 (January-April), pp. 97–104.

Cerny, Philip G. (1995). 'Globalization and the Changing Logic of Collective Action'. *International Organisation* vol. 49, no. 4, pp. 595–625.

Franchini-Sherifis, Rosella and Valerio Astraldi (2001). *The G7/G8: From Rambouillet to Genoa*. Franco Angelo, Milan.

Fratianni, Michele, Dominick Salvatore, and Paolo Savona, eds. (1999). *Ideas for the Future of the International Monetary System*. Kluwer Academic Publishers, Boston.

Funabashi, Yoichi (1987). *Managing the Dollar: From the Plaza to the Louvre*. Institute for International Economics, Washington DC.

Gill, Stephen, ed. (1993). *Gramsci, Historical Materialism, and International Relations*. Cambridge University Press, Cambridge.

Hale, David (2001). 'Have Hedge Funds Become an Agent of Monetary Policy?'. Zurich Financial Services, 13 June.

Hodges, Michael R., John J. Kirton, and Joseph P. Daniels, eds. (1999). *The G8's Role in the New Millennium*. Ashgate, Aldershot.

Kaiser, Karl, John J. Kirton, and Joseph P. Daniels, eds. (2000). *Shaping a New International Financial System: Challenges of Governance in a Globalizing World*. Ashgate, Aldershot.

Kirton, John J. (1989). 'The Seven Power Summit as an International Concert'. Paper presented at the International Studies Association annual meeting, April. London.

Kirton, John J. (1993). 'The Seven Power Summits as a New Security Institution'. In D. Dewitt, D. Haglund and J. J. Kirton, eds., *Building a New Global Order: Emerging Trends in International Security*, pp. 335–357. Oxford University Press, Toronto.

Kirton, John J. (1995). 'The Diplomacy of Concert: Canada, the G7 and the Halifax Summit'. *Canadian Foreign Policy* vol. 3, no. 1 (Spring), pp. 63–80.

Kirton, John J. (1999). 'Explaining G8 Effectiveness'. In J. J. Kirton and J. P. Daniels, eds., *The G8's Role in the New Millennium*, pp. 45–68. Ashgate, Aldershot.

Kirton, John J. (2000). 'The Dynamics of G7 Leadership in Crisis Response and System Reconstruction'. In K. Kaiser, J. J. Kirton and J. P. Daniels, eds., *Shaping a New International Financial System: Challenges of Governance in a Globalizing World*, pp. 65–94. Ashgate, Aldershot.

Kirton, John J. (2001a). 'The G20: Representativeness, Effectiveness, and Leadership in Global Governance'. In J. J. Kirton, J. P. Daniels and A. Freytag, eds., *Guiding Global Order: G8 Governance in the Twenty-First Century*, pp. 143–172. Ashgate, Aldershot.

Kirton, John J. (2001b). 'Guiding Global Economic Governance: The G20, the G7, and the International Monetary Fund at Century's Dawn'. In J. J. Kirton, J. P. Daniels and A. Freytag, eds., *Guiding Global Order: G7 Governance in the Twenty-First Century*, pp. 143–167. Ashgate, Aldershot.

Kirton, John J. (2001c). 'Prospects for the 2001 Genoa G7/G8 Summit'. 15 July, <www.g7.utoronto.ca/g7/evaluations/2001genoa/prospects_kirton.html> (February 2002).

Kirton, John J., Joseph P. Daniels, and Andreas Freytag, eds. (2001a). *Guiding Global Order: G8 Governance in the Twenty-First Century*. Ashgate, Aldershot.

Kirton, John J., Joseph P. Daniels, and Andreas Freytag (2001b). 'Introduction'. In J. J. Kirton, J. P. Daniels and A. Freytag, eds., *Guiding Global Order: G8 Governance in the Twenty-First Century*, pp. 1–18. Ashgate, Aldershot.

Kirton, John J., Eleanore Kokotsis, and Diana Juricevic (2001a). 'G7/G8 Commitments and Their Significance'. 22 July, <www.g7.utoronto.ca/g7/evaluations/2001genoa/genoa_commitments_sum.html> (February 2002).

Kirton, John J., Eleanore Kokotsis, and Diana Juricevic (2001b). 'Promises Made, Promises Kept: Commitment and Compliance at the Okinawa 2000 G7/G8 Summit'. Paper prepared for Canada's Department of Foreign Affairs and International Trade.

Kirton, John J. and George M. von Furstenberg, eds. (2001). *New Directions in Global Economic Governance: Managing Globalisation in the Twenty-First Century*. Ashgate, Aldershot.

Kokotsis, Eleanore (1999). *Keeping International Commitments: Compliance, Credibility, and the G7, 1988–1995*. Garland, New York.

Lewis, Flora (1991–92). 'The G7 1/2 Directorate'. *Foreign Policy* vol. 85, pp. 25–40.

Meltzer, Allan H. (2000). *Report of the International Financial Institutions Advisory Commission*. United States Congress, Washington DC. <www.house.gov/jec.imf/meltzer.htm> (February 2002).

Naiman, Robert (2001). 'The "Errors" of the International Financial Institutions'. *Politica Internazionale* vol. 29 (January-April), pp. 83–90.

Odom, William (1995). 'How to Create a True World Order'. *Orbis* vol. 39, no. 2, pp. 155–172.

Porter, Tony (2001). 'The Politics of International Financial Standards and Codes'. Paper prepared for the International Studies Association meeting, 26 July. Hong Kong.

Putnam, Robert and Nicholas Bayne (1987). *Hanging Together: Co-operation and Conflict in the Seven-Power Summit*. 2nd ed. Sage Publications, London.

Schwegmann, Christoph (2001). 'Modern Concert Diplomacy: The Contact Group and the G7/8 in Crisis Management'. In J. J. Kirton, J. P. Daniels and A. Freytag, eds., *Guiding Global Order: G8 Governance in the Twenty-First Century*. Ashgate, Aldershot.

Simmons, Beth (2000). 'The Legalization of International Monetary Affairs'. J. Goldstein, M. Kahler, R. O. Keohane, A. M. Slaughter, eds., 'Legalization and World Politics,' special issue. *International Organization* vol. 46, pp. 391–425.

Snidal, Duncan (1985). 'The Limits of Hegemonic Stability Theory'. *International Organisation* vol. 39, no. 4 (Autumn), pp. 579–614.

von Furstenberg, George M. (2000). 'Transparentising the Global Money Business'. In K. Kaiser, J. J. Kirton and J. P. Daniels, eds., *Shaping a New International Financial System: Challenges of Governance in a Globalizing World*, pp. 97–111. Ashgate, Aldershot.

von Furstenberg, George M. (2001). 'Assembling a New Financial Architecture: The G7's 2001 Role and Response'. Paper presented at the conference on Assembling a New International Financial Architecture: The Deeper Challenges, LUISS University, 17 July. Rome.

von Furstenberg, George M. and Joseph P. Daniels (1992). 'Economic Summit Declarations, 1975–1989: Examining the Written Record of International Cooperation'. *Princeton Studies in International Finance*, no. 72.

Wallace, William (1984). 'Political Issues at the Summits: A New Concert of Powers?' In C. Merlini, ed., *Economic Summits and Western Decisionmaking*. St. Martin's Press, London.

PART II
GENERATING GROWTH
IN THE GLOBAL ECONOMY

PART II

GENERATIVE GROWTH OF THE LOCAL ECONOMY

Chapter 4

The G7's Contribution to Global Economic Growth: An Agenda

Andreas Freytag[1]

For some time, many in academia and — more frequently — in politics have expressed high-flying hopes that a new economy lies before us (Kirton and von Furstenberg 2001). Yet since mid 2001, the forecasts have become increasingly pessimistic. The short-term growth perspectives in industrialised economies have diminished and stock prices in North American and Europe (notably the U.S. NASDAQ and the New Market in Germany) have fallen significantly. Does this imply that the new economy did not exist at all, or merely that its time has passed?

To answer this question, it is important to understand what is meant by the phrase 'new economy'. There is, in fact, no clear, single definition. Rather, it is one of those concepts that many are uncertain about. Some breezily say that the old economy represents things that hurt when dropped on one's feet, whereas the new economy contains all those things that do not. This definition focusses on a certain industry, namely the information technology (IT) sector (Lawton 2001; Mastroeni 2001). This sector indeed encompasses a broad area, as one can see when looking at the variety of firms represented by the NASDAQ. However, this definition has flaws. A new technological development or a new industry does not in itself constitute the new economy. Too many new economies of this kind have emerged and lost their importance over the past century. Instead of being called the new economy, this concept should rather be called the 'next economy'.

Interpreting the new economy as a new path of macroeconomic development (Freytag 2000; Stiroh 1999), rather than as a new industry, seems to be a more promising approach. Such a perspective can offer economic policy options. Here, the phrase 'new economy' implies simply that the economy grows more rapidly and with lower inflation rates than before — developments that are possibly associated with less volatile business cycles. This definition requires a qualitative shift for a new economy to exist.

How does a new economy thus defined emerge? At least three factors contribute to such a development: information technologies, globalisation, and appropriate economic policy. The latter two factors are especially important to the analysis in this chapter, which addresses two questions: first, whether growth — in particular, growth in the new economy — is a global phenomenon that demands global action if it is to be fostered and, second, what possible contribution can the G7 make to foster such growth in a global context.

This analysis suggests that there is indeed much serious work for the G7 to do. The need for and nature of that work are identified through an exploration, in turn, of the new economy in the context of globalisation, the global and local dimensions of growth, and the G7's past contribution to global growth. It suggests that the G7's most important contribution to global economic growth comes through a solid, growth-oriented domestic economic policy. The G7 countries should thus focus on policies that are directed to improving their own economic performance within the G7 club. These policies include new measures for structural reform, trade liberalisation globally and among the G7 member countries, stability-oriented monetary policy, and the like. With such actions, growth potentials elsewhere are raised as markets are opened, purchasing power, and, consequently, demand in G7 countries are increased and competition is spurred. If the G7 countries focus on these internal fundamentals, the prospects of a realising the benefits of a genuinely new economy are bright — despite the latest downturn of the business cycle. The G7 and the global community can still make good use of the powerful combination of an appropriate economic policy, global competitive effects, and IT.

Information Technology, Globalisation, and the New Economy

Two key external factors can contribute to the new economy, that is, to sustained higher rates of non-inflationary economic growth world-wide. These are information technology and globalisation. Information technology and its applications, such as electronic commerce, can be defined as ubiquitous technologies (German Council of Economic Advisors 2000, 182), as they are applied by all sectors of the economy. As a consequence, one can hope that the general application of these technologies will increase productivity and flexibility in all sectors. There is thus a potential for increasing rates of economic growth.

The second factor — globalisation — is strongly correlated with the emergence of information technology. It is a process fuelled by new technological developments and political action, mainly within an international framework. The interesting feature of globalisation, compared to the older concept of internationalisation, is that globalisation implies the increasing interaction of individuals around the world. Today, it is easily possible for individuals to communicate with one another all over the world without asking anyone for permission. Some products, namely digital products such as music, books (or other written texts), and financial services can be traded online with very few or no barriers. Thus, globalisation and IT offer an enormous potential for mutually beneficial trade and exchange. Recent research by developmental economists has also displayed the potential of new IT for leapfrogging the development process in poorer countries (see, for example, Hiemenz 2001).

However, in addition to creating these enormous economic opportunities, globalisation combined with IT exerts heavy pressure on all factors of production and demands an adjustment both in the industrialised and in the industrialising worlds. Increasing competition drives some domestic firms into bankruptcy, resulting in job losses. In particular, the entry of the developing and transition countries into the international division of labour enhances competition in labour-intensive goods. Consequently, less-skilled labour in industrialised countries faces fiercer competition and the prospect of falling real wages. If north-south trade intensifies, there will indeed be greater wage pressure on low-skill jobs in the developed world.

Yet, the division of labour between industrialised and developing countries has another new facet. In addition to traditional trade in so-called Heckscher-Ohlin goods — trade depending on differences in factor endowment — there is the possibility of an increasing share of trade in IT applications. In the industrialised countries, this places even more pressure on the factors of production. Much is at stake, but much more is to be gained. Therefore, economic policy directed at supporting economic growth is becoming increasingly difficult.

To benefit from these new opportunities, the developing countries must create the foundations for the new economy. First, they must create a stable micro- and macroeconomic environment — what the Germans refer to as a *Konstanz der Wirtschaftspolitik*. This enables individuals to make long-term dispositions and commitments. This is an old but ever-present challenge, to which only a few countries all over the world have found a satisfying solution. Second, to make better use of IT, a certain infrastructure, consisting of adequate human and real capital, is required. The G8 has shown its willingness to support the developing countries in facilitating the increasing use of IT, as well as in the rule-setting process, by formulating a declaration of purpose called the Okinawa Charter on Global Information Society.[2]

Growth: A Global or a Local Phenomenon?

Economic growth is a long-term phenomenon, and depends on supply side factors. It can be observed globally, so that a rate of global economic growth can be calculated. Thus, some argue that in a globalised world, economic problems should be solved globally. Yet growth is primarily a local affair. It is influenced by local policies and affects local actors. Due to global competition, however, interdependencies exist among different localities.

According to Herbert Giersch (1979), economic growth takes place in time and in space. For a time, a Schumpeterian framework can be chosen, which explicitly focusses on disequilibrium, dynamic competition, spontaneity, and so on. With regard to the dimension of space, Johan Heinrich von Thünen's concentric circles around one centre are relevant. In the centre, there are scale economies in the supply of both public and private goods, as well as congestion costs. The more distant a spot lies from the centre, the fewer economic activities emerge and the lower the income is. In Giersch's interpretation, the world consists of several income cones. The centre is the top of the cone, as the income per capita there is the highest. It declines depending on the distance from the centre. An empirical example of an income cone is the Ruhr area in North Rhine Westphalia in the 1960s. With the Ruhr at the centre, per capita income declined in all directions on the European continent.

Among the many causes of economic growth, human capital plays a major role, as do investments in real capital stock. Human capital enables the individuals in the centre to create knowledge, new products, and new production methods. Both forms of capital are scarce in the global context. Their scarcity differs among countries and regions. At the centre, they are accumulated and, therefore, less scarce than on the periphery. Nevertheless, the periphery can attract human and real capital, because it has a higher marginal efficiency of capital (MEC). In other words, the differences in MEC between equally distant locations are, generally speaking, caused by local economic policy differences. These differences are relevant both on the micro level and the macro level. The policy instruments that are employed to diminish scarcity in human capital and physical capital include regulations, fiscal policy, monetary policy, trade policy, education policy, and so forth. In other words, to create the foundation for the new economy, economic policy must allow for a quick and flexible response to new challenges on the markets for goods and services. Schumpeterian behaviour must be allowed for and should promise a good return.

If local economic policy has flaws, the income cone is dented and the income per capita is lower than is possible. The location does not attract enough capital (both human and real) to fill the gap. Local (or national) economic policy, therefore, is economic policy in a competitive environment. Locations compete for scarce mobile production factors in order to enhance the employment opportunities of the interregional immobile factors. The more capital they attract, the better the prospects of individual localities for employment and growth. As a consequence, economic policy is a process of trial and error comparable to the Schumpetarian process of creative destruction. A government always has to fear that its competitors will find new tools to attract more capital than before and drive it out of its own country.

Although growth rates in different regimes are increasingly interdependent through global competition, global growth in itself is a statistical artefact. It is the weighted aggregate of all the local growth that is occurring around the globe. As such, it is not a meaningful concept for economic policy. It makes no sense to aim at a certain global rate of economic growth. In addition, given the competitive nature of economic policy, a globally installed growth policy is economically senseless. To summarise, economic growth is not a global challenge demanding global answers. Nevertheless, it does make sense to look for an adequate policy for the world to prepare itself properly for the new economy and to foster economic growth globally, in the sense of 'everywhere on this planet'. Apart from the contribution of national governments in economic policy, there may thus be a role for the G7. What can the G7 do to enhance growth on a global scale?

The G7's Contribution to Global Growth

Competition is not the same thing as *laissez-faire*. It requires rules. Otherwise, there may be cartels and collusive behaviour. This holds for enterprises as well as for governments. The G7 is a powerful institution, able to wield enormous influence on how rules are set, perceived, and enforced. It should therefore be very careful and responsible when setting the global rules for economic policy. From a normative economic perspective, the options for the G7 to contribute to world-wide economic growth can take two directions.[3]

First, the G7 should refrain from all those measures and actions likely to reduce global growth by offering individuals and governments the wrong incentives. Among these measures, several actions stand out: avoiding beggar-thy-neighbour policies on foreign exchange markets, avoiding unfair trade practices such as antidumping tariffs, and avoiding socially or environmentally motivated protectionism. Second, the G7 can take steps to facilitate growth directly and actively at home. Such steps include domestic structural reforms, stable monetary policy, encouraging the World Trade Organization (WTO) to liberalise international trade further, and fostering reform of the core international organisations. The economic rationale for these suggestions follows, starting with the first suggestions of what to avoid.

Currently, a beggar-thy-neighbour policy does not appear to be considered as a serious policy option among G7 members. However, the downturn in the business cycle, observed since the end of 2000, may tempt governments to break the rules and promote domestic economic activity by manipulating the exchange rate toward their major trading partners. In particular, a further slowdown in the U.S. could cause friction between the U.S. and the European Union because of the undervalued euro. Unfortunately, neither the U.S. Federal Reserve System nor the European Central Bank (ECB) is responsible for exchange-rate policy (Theuringer 2001).

A beggar-thy-neighbour policy can be dangerous for three reasons. First, it creates bilateral tensions and domestic distortions. The G7 countries themselves lose by it. Second, other countries also may lose due to international spillovers. Third, it may reduce international discipline and thus have a negative image effect. Other countries may feel embarrassed and react by, for example, raising trade barriers. The international economic climate may then seriously suffer. What was meant to be a beggar-thy-neighbour policy could result in what the literature refers to as a 'beggar-thyself' policy.

In 1999, the G7 agreed to support the debt relief scheme for the 41 poorest countries — the so-called highly indebted poor countries (HIPCs), a list established by the International Monetary Fund (IMF) and the World Bank (see also International Monetary Fund 2001, and; Bayne 2001b). The initiative was a response to strong public pressure and does not seem to have caused an increase in development in the supported countries thus far. There are only a few arguments in favour of debt reduction schemes (see Dluhosch 2001, 85–86), but one very important and empirically valid argument against it: moral hazard. The countries subject to former debt reduction plans did not make the appropriate use of the aid. Rather, they became subject to the next round of indebtedness as they did not change their economic policy and focus on growth. The reason for this behaviour was that there was no credible commitment by the donor countries to a policy that there would be no further help for those recipients abusing the relief. This pattern is sustainable, whereas further assistance through ever more debt relief is not. Thus, the G7 should make clear that it is no longer willing to relieve debt in the future.[4]

This leads to a much more promising and fruitful approach: aid by trade. Time and again, industrialised countries have tried to prevent competition from developing countries by imposing new trade barriers against the latter. In particular, antidumping measures have gained much importance in recent years. The EU and the U.S. use this instrument widely. Apart from domestic distortions caused by antidumping legislation, such as a cartellisation of domestic markets (Messerlin 1990), this policy impedes development in the less developed countries (LDCs). A G7 initiative to abolish antidumping legislation gradually, as well as safeguard clauses aiming at abandoning Articles VI and XIX of the General Agreement on Tariffs and Trade (GATT), would be most valuable. At the WTO meeting in Doha in 2001, it was put on the agenda for the next round of negotiations.

By the same token, newer efforts to introduce social and environmental clauses into the multilateral trade framework must be judged critically from a development point of view. In the first place, they can be seen as a trial to impose the G7's preferences on developing countries. There are good reasons to suppose that social and environmental protection are superior goods emerging with higher per-capita income. There are also good reasons for a positive link among trade, growth, and social as well as environmental protection. In other words, to prevent trade for the sake of social and environmental protection is a contradiction in terms.[5] Thus, one cannot rules out the argument that claims to help the poor with social and environmental clauses are little more than veiled calls for protection (Curzon-Price 2000).

These are the most important policy measures for the G7 to avoid. If the G7 countries mansage to refrain from them and to reverse the discussion about trade policy, they would not only help the poor, but would also foster domestic economic growth. In addition, there are several positive steps to be taken by the G7 to spur domestic economic growth. And if growth rates in G7 countries rise, the amount of available capital to be invested in the periphery also increases.

The first such positive step is structural reform. In most G7 countries, the economy is heavily in need of structural reforms. This need has been emphasised by economists as well as by international organisations, including the European Commission, that analyse economic policies in G7 countries. For instance, in Germany the design of the labour market calls for an adjustment to lower long-term unemployment and to allow for more competition. However, instead of taking into account the necessities of a globalised world, the German government has pushed through a reform of the industry constitution law, which tends to increase the already strong corporatist elements in the labour market. There are plenty of other examples, in particular in continental Europe as well as in Japan (Kiuchi 2001).

Such reforms — after an adjustment period that makes them politically unattractive as employment will probably even decrease and the fiscal problems even rise in the short run — will not only foster economic growth in the respective countries. They will also lead to higher demand for goods from the developing world in G7 countries and to higher human and physical capital accumulation in the centre. Even more importantly, they may function as a blueprint and encourage developing countries to copy them.

A second task for G7 countries is to maintain monetary stability. In the last decade, inflation has been at a historically low level, which has benefited the G7 countries as well as helped with the disinflation processes in developing and transitional countries. A number of the such countries fixed their currency to the U.S. dollar or the Deutschmark (now euro) via a nominal anchor or currency board or have even dollarized (euroized). Most were able to import stability. There can be no doubt, as the empirical evidence shows, that stability is positively correlated with economic growth. In other words, inflation is costly in terms of growth rates (Barro 1995). Therefore, the G7 must stay on the stability track. This course does not exclude considering new problems of monetary policy in the age of globalisation along the way, as discussed by Paolo Savona (2001).

A third active policy programme is directed at further trade liberalisation. Such liberalisation includes serious compliance with the results of the Uruguay Round, through the reduction of agricultural protection as well as the complete abandonment of the barriers to trade in textiles and apparel imposed by the Multifibre Agreement. It also contains an initiative to start a new round of multilateral trade liberalisation in the next few years, one that takes into account the wishes of developing and transitional countries even more than the previous Uruguay Round did. In particular, the G7 should make clear that social and environmental conditionality clauses fostering protectionism in trade agreements are not a suitable means to foster development.[6]

One way to move further in trade liberalisation is to liberalise internally, that is, to open up markets and tear down trade barriers within the G7 among its member countries.[7] This move, floated earlier under the label of a plurilateral 'super-GATT', can indeed be an economically meaningful alternative to the slow pace and partial results of broad multilateral trade liberalisation negotiations. It would solve some very important trade conflicts of the past (and the present), namely those between the EU and the U.S.[8] These two WTO members have by far more trouble with each other than with developing countries. If such an endeavour works, it probably would bolster the credibility of the recently initiated trade liberalisation round. However, it would be extremely difficult politically to liberalise the G7's internal trade further, as the experience with the new transatlantic agenda in the mid 1990s makes clear (see Donges, Freytag, and Zimmermann 1997; Gardner and Stefanova 2001).

There is another problem related to internal liberalisation. There may be not only trade creation taking place within such plurilateral or regional arrangements, but trade diversion and trade deflection as well. This is especially the case when an economically powerful group such as the G7 dismantles internal trade barriers. This outcome could counter all efforts to foster development in the developing and transition countries. The world beyond the G7 might also feel that the G7 wants no further integration with it. This sentiment would certainly put the multilateral trading order at risk. One way to avoid this scenario is 'open regionalism', meaning that the regional free trade agreement — the G7 in this case — applies most-favoured nation (MFN) status to all WTO members unilaterally (Bergsten 1997). Here the experience of the nineteenth century is very valuable, as it shows the potential of unilateral free trade for world-wide liberalisation and, subsequently, for economic growth. However, whether this proposal is easy to push through politically is subject to serious doubt.

Fourthly and finally, the G7 should play an active role in the process of reforming the IMF and the World Bank (Kaiser, Kirton, and Daniels 2000; Savona 2000). This proposal is not meant to provide any detailed plans on how to organise these institutions in the future. There have already been many suggestions in this regard, the most ambitious being the recommendations by the Meltzer Commission (Fratianni and Pattison 2001).

Conclusion

Although economic growth takes place locally and depends on local (national) economic policy, there is much potential for the G7 to enhance it on a global level. This does not, however, imply the need for — and value of — activist, discretionary global macroeconomic policy co-ordination and *ad hoc* measures, such as the politically attractive but economically useless debt reduction scheme for countries still poor and performing poorly. Rather, there is good reason for such an activist policy on a global scale to diminish growth, because it depresses policy competition.

The G7 primarily contributes to global economic growth through a solid, growth-oriented domestic economic policy. The G7 countries should thus be completely selfish in the sense that their policies are directed to improving the economic performance within their own countries. These policies include measures for structural reform, trade liberalisation, stability-oriented monetary policy, and so on. As a side effect, growth potential elsewhere is increased as markets are opened, purchasing power, and, therefore, demand in G7 countries are increased and competition is spurred. If the G7 countries do their homework, the prospects of a new economy, as defined above, are bright — despite the latest downturn of the business cycle. The world still can make good use of the combination of appropriate economic policy, global competitive effects, and IT.

The economic analysis seems to be straightforward. Within academia, there is widespread agreement about the general direction, if not the details, of the economic policy that the G7 ought to take at the beginning of the twenty-first century. However, political economy reasoning shows clearly where the difficulties lie in transferring appropriate theoretical policy suggestions into practical politics. The G7 governments are regularly under pressure to deliver politically appealing results, which do not take into account long-term growth necessities. As Nicholas Bayne (2000; 2001a) has shown, the acceptability of the summits' outcome is an important criterion for G7 governments' efforts in economic policy making. Acceptability, however, can easily become a euphemism for pleasing rent-seeking groups. One must make sure that this criterion will not overrun all other criteria in judging the summits, in particular in assessing the efficiency and the potential for developing the policies they produce and endorse. It thus seems appropriate that both theorists and practitioners pay more attention to the political economy of the G7 in the coming years.

Notes

1 The author gratefully acknowledges helpful comments from Peter Tillman.
2 For a critical analysis of the Okinawa Charter, see Freytag and Mai (2001). See also the charter itself (G8 2000). In the meantime, the Dot Force created at the Okinawa Summit delivered its first results in May 2001 (G8 2001).
3 Because economic growth is a long-term phenomenon, there is no discussion here of short-term policy measures to be taken by the G7 in case of emergencies such as floodings, earthquakes, and the like. This section focusses only on measures that have an effect on long-term economic growth.
4 Needless to say, the G8 must still comply with its 1999 commitments.
5 This does not rule out preventing child labour and other forms of exploitation where possible. However, it would be naive or unfair not to point out the opportunity costs (Solow 2000).
6 As mentioned above, conditionality clauses are unlikely even to meet the objectives they aim at.
7 The author is grateful to John Kirton for raising this question.
8 The EU as a whole would likely be part of the agreement.

References

Barro, Robert J. (1995). 'Inflation and Economic Growth'. *Bank of England Quarterly Bulletin* vol. 35, pp. 166–175.

Bayne, Nicholas (2000). 'The G7 Summit's Contribution: Past, Present, and Prospective'. In K. Kaiser, J. J. Kirton and J. P. Daniels, eds., *Shaping a New International Financial System: Challenges of Governance in a Globalizing World*, pp. 19–35. Ashgate, Aldershot.

Bayne, Nicholas (2001a). 'Managing Globalisation and the New Economy: The Contribution of the G8 Summit'. In J. J. Kirton and G. M. von Furstenberg, eds., *New Directions in Global Economic Governance: Managing Globalisation in the Twenty-First Century*, pp. 171–188. Ashgate, Aldershot.

Bayne, Nicholas (2001b). 'Reforming the International Financial Architecture: The G7 Summit's Success and Shortcomings'. Paper presented at the conference on Assembling a New International Financial Architecture: The Deeper Challenges, LUISS University, 17 July. Rome.

Bergsten, C. Fred (1997). 'Open Regionalism'. *World Economy* vol. 20, pp. 545–565.

Curzon-Price, Victoria (2000). 'Seattle Virus: A Mutant Form of Protection'. In K. R. Leube, ed., *Vordenker einer neuen Wirtschaftspolitik, Festschrift für Christian Watrin*, pp. 43–53. Frankfurter Allgemeine Buch, Frankfurt.

Dluhosch, Barbara (2001). 'The G7 and the Debt of the Poorest'. In J. J. Kirton, J. P. Daniels and A. Freytag, eds., *Guiding Global Order: G8 Governance in the Twenty-First Century*, pp. 79–92. Ashgate, Aldershot.

Donges, Juergen B., Andreas Freytag, and Ralf Zimmermann (1997). 'TAFTA: Assuring Its Compatability with Global Free Trade'. *The World Economy* vol. 20, pp. 597–583.

Fratianni, Michele and John C. Pattison (2001). 'International Lender of Last Resort: A Concept in Search of a Meaning'. Paper presented at the conference on Assembling a New International Financial Architecture: The Deeper Challenges, LUISS University, 17 July. Rome.

Freytag, Andreas (2000). 'Was ist wirklich neu an der New Economy?' *Zeitschrift für Wirtschaftspolitik* vol. 49, pp. 303–312.

Freytag, Andreas and Stefan Mai (2001). 'Does E-Commerce Demand International Policy Co-ordination? Some Reflections on the Okinawa Charter on the Global Information Society'. Paper presented at the Annual Public Choice Society Meeting, 9–11 March. San Antonio.

G8 (2000). 'Okinawa Charter on Global Information Society'. Okinawa, 22 July. <www.library.utoronto.ca/g7/summit/2000okinawa/gis.htm> (February 2002).

G8 (2001). 'Digital Opportunities for All: Meeting the Challenge. Report of the Digital Opportunity Task Force (Dot Force) Including a Proposal for a Genoa Plan of Action'. 11 May, Genoa. <www.g7.utoronto.ca/g7/summit/2001genoa/dotforce1.html> (February 2002).

Gardner, Hall and Radoslava Stefanova, eds. (2001). *The New Transatlantic Agenda: Facing the Challenges of Global Governance*. Ashgate, Aldershot.

German Council of Economic Advisors (2000). 'Chancen auf einen höheren Wachstumspfad'. Annual Report 2000/2001, Metzler-Poeschel, Stuttgart.

Giersch, Herbert (1979). 'Aspects of Growth, Structural Change, and Employment: A Schumpeterian Perspective'. *Weltwirtschaftliches Archiv* vol. 115, pp. 629–652.

Hiemenz, Ulrich (2001). 'Internet, E-Commerce, and Asian Development'. Mimeo. Organisation for Economic Co-operation and Development, Paris.

International Monetary Fund (2001). 'Debt Relief under the Heavily Indebted Poor Countries (Hipc) Initiative. A Factsheet'. <www.imf.org/external/np/exr/facts/hipc.htm> (February 2002).

Kaiser, Karl, John J. Kirton, and Joseph P. Daniels, eds. (2000). *Shaping a New International Financial System: Challenges of Governance in a Globalizing World*. Ashgate, Aldershot.

Kirton, John J. and George M. von Furstenberg, eds. (2001). *New Directions in Global Economic Governance: Managing Globalisation in the Twenty-First Century*. Ashgate, Aldershot.

Kiuchi, Takashi (2001). 'Japan, Asia and the Rebuilding of Financial Sector'. Paper presented at the conference on Assembling a New International Financial Architecture: The Deeper Challenges, LUISS University, 17 July. Rome.

Lawton, Thomas (2001). 'The New Global Electronic Economy: The Contribution of the G8 Summit'. In J. J. Kirton and G. M. von Furstenberg, eds., *New Directions in Global Economic Governance: Managing Globalisation in the Twenty-First Century*, pp. 39–60. Ashgate, Aldershot.

Mastroeni, Michele (2001). 'Creating Rules for the Global Information Economy: The United States and G8 Leadership'. In J. J. Kirton and G. M. von Furstenberg, eds., *New Directions in Global Economic Governance: Managing Globalisation in the Twenty-First Century*, pp. 61–74. Ashgate, Aldershot.

Messerlin, Patrick (1990). 'Anti-Dumping Regulations or Pro-Cartel Laws'. *The World Economy* vol. 13, pp. 465–492.

Savona, Paolo, ed. (2000). *The New Architecture of the International Monetary System*. Kluwer Academic Publishers, Boston.

Savona, Paolo (2001). 'On Some Unresolved Problems of Monetary Theory and Policy'. Paper presented at the conference on Assembling a New International Financial Architecture: The Deeper Challenges, LUISS University, 17 July. Rome.

Solow, Robert (2000). 'Umweltpolitik und internationaler Handel'. Otto-von-Guericke Lecture, Otto-von-Guericke-Universität, 24 May. Magdeburg.

Stiroh, Kevin J. (1999). 'Is There a New Economy?' *Challenge* vol. 82, no. 4, pp. 82–101.

Theuringer, Martin (2001). 'International Macroeconomic Policy Co-operation in the Era of the Euro'. In J. J. Kirton, J. P. Daniels and A. Freytag, eds., *Guiding Global Order: G8 Governance in the Twenty-First Century*, pp. 173–187. Ashgate, Aldershot.

Chapter 5

Japan, Asia, and the Rebuilding of the Financial Sector

Takashi Kiuchi

The global economy seems to be entering a new challenging phase. For the first time in almost a decade, the U.S. economy has slowed down considerably. The impact has been felt everywhere in the rest of the world. One key question in the Asian region is whether its major economy, Japan, will be able to sustain its own recovery, which appears to be less tenable than Europe.

This question cannot be addressed without properly assessing the new political leadership in Japan. A relatively unknown Junichiro Koizumi became the nation's 87th prime minister in late April 2001, immediately after his surprise victory in the ruling Liberal Democratic Party (LDP) presidential election. On every occasion since then, he has eloquently put forward his slogan of 'change the LDP, and change the nation'. In so doing, Koizumi seems to have succeeded in cultivating his popular support to an unprecedented level. His approval rating has risen to around 70 percent, the highest historical level ever. Most political analysts interpret the victory of the LDP in the summer 2001 Upper House elections as a clear mandate for the Prime Minister's reform programme.

In the meantime, the end of the information technology (IT) boom in the U.S. casts a dark shadow on the world's IT industry. The unexpectedly swift recovery of the Asian economies in the years immediately following the 1997–99 financial crisis was largely the result of their spectacular success in exporting IT-related products to the U.S. as well as to Japan (Kaiser, Kirton, and Daniels 2000; Kirton and von Furstenberg 2001). Does this imply that the regions could suffer more than other regions from an economic downturn in the U.S.? If so, it is natural to question how much of a threat to the economic and financial stability of the Asian region exists. It is worthwhile to consider whether the region's economies have learned enough from the Asian financial crisis so as to be better prepared for any future shocks.

This chapter explores two closely related issues at the centre of how the G7 and the International Monetary Fund's (IMF) global financial governance affect Asia and, in particular, Japan, and how Asia and Japan in turn affect the G7 and the IMF. The first issue is the character of Prime Minister Koizumi's reform initiative and its implications for the Japanese economy. The second is the Japanese approach to the global effort to build a more enduring, and effective, international financial architecture. Without a doubt, this approach is closely associated with what has emerged from a set of proposals and actions that the Japanese government made since the eruption of the Asian financial crisis in 1997 (Watanabe 1999; Kiuchi 2000; Katada 2001; Ito 2001).[1]

Along these lines, it will be argued that Koizumi is currently the best hope for restructuring Japan's financial sector and economy as a whole, even if its immediate outlook remains uncertain. While his weakness is a lack of support among LDP senior politicians, his strength lies in an extraordinarily high approval rate among the public, who yearn for a break from the past. It will be further argued that, having recognised that Japan is limited in how it can contribute to the rest of Asia through its own economic stimulation, the country is firmly committed to rebuilding the region's financial markets and regaining the confidence of the international investor community. Japan's efforts to demonstrate the new elements in the Asian financial crisis of 1997–99 resulted in some desirable developments in global efforts toward building a new international financial architecture. Furthermore, Japan is trying hard to create a network of assistance and consultation so as to secure the health of the region's financial markets.

The Japanese Recovery in Decline

It is still fair to claim that the Japanese economy is the most vulnerable among the three major economic regions of the world. Most Japanese financial institutions release their mid-year revisions of economic forecasts every June. The picture they painted in June 2001 was not particularly bright. The average growth projections for 2001 and 2002 were 0.1 percent and 0.8 percent respectively, a significant downward revision from 1.0 percent and 2.0 percent in the projections at the beginning of the year. Approximately, one third of forecasters anticipated some economic contraction by the end of 2001.

The progressive loss of momentum in the recovery during the second quarter of 2001 was almost exclusively caused by sharp drops in IT-related exports and investment. This, in turn, was brought about by the economic slowdown in the U.S. In May 2001, Japan's export volume and industrial production indices dropped by 9.7 percent and 3.9 percent compared to a year earlier, while the import volume index rose by 3.6 percent during the same period. Accordingly, most forecasters predicted almost no growth or even a small contraction in businesses' capital expenditures.

Indeed, the immediate future of the Japanese economy still relies on the economic performance of the United States. Consequently, the currency value has been depreciating steadily from 106 yen per U.S. dollar in the spring of 2001 to 125 yen per U.S. dollar by the summer. This depreciation has helped exporters, but could not keep the economy from stumbling. It suggests that, if the dollar were to fall in the near future, it would do so more against the euro than against the yen. By the end of

2001, the sustainability of the current recovery had come under serious question and there was widespread speculation about another round of recession.

Yet it is important to note that there had not yet been a recognisable contraction in consumption. Somehow, the statistical failure to capture any real trend made it difficult to draw a definite conclusion. All told, consumption appeared simply to be flat. Pessimists regarded this as a lack of strength. They argued that ongoing disinflation was eloquent evidence of weak demand.

Optimists, however, believed that consumption was holding up rather well. In their view, a rapidly shifting composition of consumption was deceiving many analysts. For instance, they pointed out that a marked rise in phone bills due to internet use was eating away at spending on traditional items such as clothing and other daily necessities.

In any event, the current economic stagnation did not seem to result from any traceable failure of macroeconomic management.

Policy makers were seized by the notion that the traditional means of economic stimulation may have been exhausted. The Bank of Japan returned to a zero-interest policy, but without any visible result. Liquidity in the financial market showed no discernible increase in subsequent months; nor did outstanding bank loans. The central bank was having some difficulty in finding qualified bills and notes for its money operations. Indeed, the lack of demand for funds was clearly indicated by the slow growth in the supply of money.

While some foreign economists advocated inflation targeting, disinflation continued due to a surge of cheap imports from China, mainly of food and clothing. There was even a hint that the only remaining way for the Bank of Japan to increase its money supply would be to buy dollar bills and notes. This would be highly controversial. It would not be accepted easily by the U.S., as it would dramatically weaken the yen against the dollar. In any case, it was highly unlikely that the central bank would choose this path.

Moreover, it became increasingly apparent that public works projects involved much wasted money and were failing to induce private investment. It could perhaps be argued that another round of spending increases should not be categorically excluded from the government's toolbox, particularly as a means of crisis management. Nonetheless, a blind expansion in public expenditures might lead to a steep rise in long bond yields, which could seriously erode investment aspirations by businesses.

It is often noted that public works projects as a proportion of gross domestic product (GDP) in Japan is exceptionally high at 6 to 8 percent compared to 3 to 4 percent in other industrialised economies. Japanese citizens have come to realise that public works projects benefit only a small fraction of vested interest groups in rural areas rather than a large segment of the economy. For this reason, as well as from the viewpoint of fairness, increases in public spending visibly lost political support.

The Koizumi Reform Initiative

Against this background, Koizumi changed the focus of economic policy debate almost entirely from short-term macro-management to structural reform. He was successfully able to sell long-term optimism to the nation, as was illustrated by his exceptionally high approval rating and his victory in the Upper House elections in the summer of 2001.

Public Sector Structural Reform

Koizumi's reform initiative is essentially a public sector reform effort. The key idea is to make the public sector lean and efficient in order to maximise private sector dynamism as a means for resurrecting the economy. It is not limited to fiscal reform, although the rationalisation of fiscal spending is an important element of the package. It is expected to cover not only the budgets of central and local governments but also all kinds of public agencies and enterprises. Koizumi intends to carve out an appropriate, more modest place for public sector institutions in the economy.

In particular, he emphasises overhauling the Fiscal Investment and Loan Program (FILP) and the sweeping privatisation of public and quasi-public institutions that operate under it. Koizumi has long been known to advocate privatisation of the Postal Saving Institute, which solicits savings from the public at large and funds the FILP. Under FILP, these savings were deposited with the Fund Trust Bureau of the Ministry of Finance. The ministry, in turn, had long been channelling these funds into a number of other public sector financial institutions and public enterprises. In this regard, FILP was often called Japan's second budget.

Among the public sector banks, recipient institutions included the Government Housing Loan Corporation, the Japan Finance Corporation for Small Business, and the Development Bank of Japan. Public corporations included the Housing and Urban Development Corporation and the Japan Highway Public Corporation. FILP also financed such special national accounts as the special accounts for airport development and the national forest service, and it financed local governments directly. Many of these institutions have now been consolidated and renamed.

By the middle of the 1990s, outstanding FILP funds reached the enormous size of 350 trillion yen, or 70 percent of Japan's GDP. The programme's annual budget approached 20 percent of the central government's budget. This expansion of public institutions fostered the development of powerful vested interest groups through procurement processes among politicians, government bureaucrats, and businesses. Consequently, a sizeable portion of Japan's markets became grossly distorted, due to attempts by these interests to keep private sector businesses off their privileged domains and due to their doubtful pricing and cost-accounting behaviour.

The privatisation of public institutions under FILP is a critical ingredient of Koizumi's initiative. It is one that seems to enjoy the almost unanimous endorsement of private sector economists in Japan. Deregulation efforts in the past had always been compromised, allowing public enterprises to preserve their predominant turf. As a result, there was an incessant expansion of public enterprises that reached the point where they choked off the entrepreneurship of private businesses. Economists agree that Koizumi has put forth the proper structural policy, for the first time in many years.

It is also true, however, that structural reform is not an easy task. It is especially difficult for the president of the LDP, which has long been known as the guardian of vested interest groups. Fortunately, the LDP now appears to be acutely aware that maintaining the *status quo* will no longer be tolerated by voters. The LDP thus finally became desperate enough to choose an unconventional leader who intends to destroy the old system. Nonetheless, the Koizumi reform efforts can be expected to meet with persistent resistance from inside and outside the LDP. It remains to be seen how skilfully the Prime Minister will be able to devise action plans and implement them in the months and years ahead.

Bad Bank Loans

Another pressing task confronting Koizumi is to fix the problem of nonperforming loans at the banks. He has not been very eloquent on this front. Some critics, domestic and abroad alike, complain that he talks a lot but has no action plan. Meanwhile, market anxiety persists so that the Nikkei 225 dropped from 14 000 yen immediately after Koizumi came to power to a summertime low of 12 000 yen, which is generally regarded as the panic point. This criticism, however, while partly true, is somewhat misplaced.

The assumption that nonperforming loans are what prevent banks from financing good business projects is basically wrong. Money is abundant. Most of the banks are weary of the continuous inflow of deposits, but their efforts to steer their depositors toward other savings instruments are proving unsuccessful. In fact, only a small fraction of applicants for new loans are creditworthy. Thus, the lending spread is exceptionally thin by international standards, and no sign of improvement is in sight. Money is chasing borrowers with good prospects, but cannot find very many.

A clue to this paradox lies in the fact that Japan is still the largest capital exporter in the world. And Japanese surplus savings are not yet ready to go abroad, or do so only reluctantly. Capital flight seldom happens, in spite of some of the considerable interest rate differentials that exist between domestic and overseas markets. The only effective way to reduce the gap in Japan's investment and savings seems to be to increase investment opportunities.

In this respect, Japan will have to wait for a series of deregulation and privatisation initiatives to expand business frontiers for private businesses. Such initiatives are especially relevant to the effort to capitalise on the opportunities offered by IT and the new economy. A case in point is how to transform National Telephone and Telegraph, a national monopoly, from being an obstacle to developing IT ventures into a stimulant.

However, Japan's banking sector still has a significant problem with nonperforming loans. It is now clear that the recapitalisation programme of the past was not sufficient. The risk of financial market instability, especially when the economic downturn is much more severe than expected, cannot easily be erased. Adoption of the current price accounting rule for tradable securities in 2001 effectively reduced the banks' ability to window-dress their balance sheets. The drop in stock prices that summer also aggravated the problem.

It is also true, however, that the issue of nonperforming loans is much less serious than it was in 1997 and 1998. Since so many fluid factors affect the size of those loans, it is difficult to agree on the exact figure. One credible estimate suggests that an eventual loss from the bursting of Japan's financial bubble could reach 100 trillion yen, of which more than 70 trillion have been already written off by the banks. It is possible that the banks could have dealt with the problem of nonperforming loans within three or four years, as indicated by the Financial Services Agency.

One related problem that often goes unnoticed is that when banks write off nonperforming loans there is a painful restructuring of borrowers. This restructuring is not confined to big businesses in construction, real estate, and retail; it also involves many of Japan's small businesses. Many will have to cease operations altogether, so unemployment could rise significantly. The subsequent deflationary impact could be unbearable for the economy. Some private sector economists predict that corporate restructuring could add at least 1.4 percent to the current unemployment rate of 4.9 percent, which is the highest level in Japan's history.

True, one can argue that corporate restructuring is inevitable and already overdue. However, any government is obliged to try to engineer a soft landing. A hard landing is, after all, a consequence of desperate actions and cannot be a goal for any sensible manager. By the end of the summer of 2001, the ministers of the Financial Services Agency and Ministry of Finance had worked out an action plan. It remains to be seen if their efforts will be able to increase market confidence.

All told, Japan's economic prospects depend upon two things. The first is how Koizumi will manage the process of restructuring banks' balance sheets as well as those of problem companies so as to minimise any disruption to the rest of the economy. The second is how he will proceed with his public sector reform in the face of resistance and how he will encourage businesses and consumers to remain optimistic.

The Slowdown in the Asian Economies

The second key issue is the prospect for the rest of the Asian economies and the Japanese role in the region. Unfortunately, the region still cannot expect the Japanese economy to serve as an effective replacement for their U.S. markets as the U.S. appetite for their exports diminishes.

The unexpectedly swift Asian recovery in 1999 and 2000 has now been replaced by a slowdown in the region's economies. Many economists had been caught by surprise by that rebound. Some went so far as to claim that the region's economies were devastated beyond repair by the financial crisis of 1997–99. The structural problem, they maintained, was so deeply rooted in corrupt social systems as well as a lack of an infrastructure for any self-corrective mechanisms that it would take some years to rebuild the foundation for future growth. In addition, most of the banks in some countries appeared insolvent and thus unable to finance any immediate recovery.

Why did the region's economy bounce back so early and so strongly? The answer is that multinational corporations (MNCs), western, Asian, and Japanese ones alike, capitalised on currency depreciation and aggressively integrated Asia into their global supply chains of IT components and equipment. Factories rushed to fulfil the rapidly growing demand for IT-related products in the U.S. and Japan. The necessary financing of the export sector was readily made available by foreign banks and by MNCs through trade credits.

However, Asia's embrace of the new economy (Lawton 2001) turned out to work against the region in 2001. IT products were suddenly trapped in a serious oversupply. As the new economy lost its vigour, it became apparent that the old economy remained battered. The process of rebuilding a healthy financial market and restructuring indigenous corporations seemed to progress slowly. It is now judged to be a long-term exercise to re-establish an institutional foundation that can secure self-sustainable indigenous growth.

This is not to suggest that the current economic slowdown will inevitably lead to another round of crisis in the region. With the possible exception of Indonesia, most observers do not anticipate a crisis comparable to the situation in 1997–99, and the Indonesian problem is very much political in nature. But structural reform remains the prerequisite policy task for most Asian economies; structural reform needs a fresh political consolidation, because reform tends to shake the old social fabric and institutional arrangement. Therefore, it is not surprising that the 2001 economic slowdown was accompanied by various degrees of political instability in the region.

There are other relevant aspects of recent developments in the region. First, the gravity of the problem varies from one country to another. The problem is more serious where the recapitalisation of banks' equity bases has been insufficient, as in Thailand. There, a separate asset management company was established for each of the ailing banks. This fragmented approach toward the problem of nonperforming loans has proven to be ineffective. Moreover, consolidation has made unsatisfactory progress thanks to resistance from powerful business groups that want to stay independent.

At the same time, even when the proper measures, including recapitalisation, were taken to regain the health of the banking sector, the problem did not go away when institutional constraints prevented a wholesale corporate restructuring, as in the case of Korea. The high praise initially given to Korea's sweeping reform policy by the IMF and other members of the international financial community faded away when the government began to appear overwhelmed by the obstacles in the way of a further restructuring of major chaebols, Korea's family-dominated conglomerates.

Generally speaking, political stability and economic resolution do not go hand in hand, as seen in the case of the Philippines. Its political leadership was found to be ineffective and discouraged foreign investors in spite of the fact that the country was hardly hit by the Asian financial crisis and thus kept its macroeconomic balance in better condition than its neighbours did. Furthermore, Indonesia still appears to be the most vulnerable country, still in the midst of political turmoil, which deprives its economy of any chance to engineer a process of recovery.

Secondly, the China factor is looming notably larger. It is still debatable if the yuen's devaluation in 1994 was a prelude to the Asian financial crisis of 1997–99 (Kirton 2001). However, the economic interaction between China and the rest of the region seems to be turning a new page in its history. Structural reform in the rest of the region seems be meeting the challenge of adjusting to the rise of China.

China thus far remains an unconvincing hero of structural reform. However, MNCs, including western, Japanese, and other Asian firms, are keener than ever to extend their production networks into China, which clearly benefits from the global marketplace created by the new economy. China's admission into the World Trade Organization (WTO) will undoubtedly exert a fierce competitive pressure upon neighbouring economies.

The recent acceleration of the drop in Japan's consumer price index has been, to a great extent, caused by imports from China. Vegetables and clothing are being produced in China with extensive technical assistance given by Japanese trading houses and retailers, which in turn import the products and market them successfully. The technology transfer is progressing smoothly and Japanese investors appreciate the quality of Chinese management and labour. It is possible that China's structural reform policy has made the country's management and workers learn enough and increased their understanding of the market.

In any event, Japan considers itself to be obliged to contribute to the region's economic stability. One extreme opinion found among some Japanese economists indicates that a unilateral intervention in currency markets could weaken the yen and help the country's exporters. However, the consensus among opinion leaders does not support that move. This approach is partly due to a conviction that the currency cannot be managed effectively without unexpected side effects and partly due to an awareness that it would exert an adverse pressure on the rest of the region.

Japan's View on Global Efforts to Redesign the International Financial Architecture

There is no doubt that Japan has the largest stake in Asia's well-being. In this regard, it was quite natural that Japan responded most actively to the Asian financial crisis of

1997–99 (Watanabe 1999; Kiuchi 2000; Katada 2001; Ito 2001). To begin with, Japan offered a large amount of liquidity to the troubled countries, under the umbrella of a series of Miyazawa initiatives (led by then Finance Minister Kiichi Miyazawa). Japan's total commitment of funds was reported to be US$80 billion or 2 percent of GDP. This corresponds to 80 percent of the US$100 billion, which deserted the region in 1997. The Japanese contribution was much appreciated by the troubled countries.

In light of the difficulties and complexities of creating a support group for Thailand and Korea on an *ad hoc* basis, Japan considered it necessary to establish a permanent forum or institution that would remain ready to deal with a future potential crisis. Japan therefore proposed the creation of an Asian monetary fund (AMF).

The proposal was quickly withdrawn because of U.S. opposition. The U.S. argued that such an institution would interfere with the discipline intended by IMF conditionality. The Japanese government argued in vain that the AMF could be designed to be compatible with the IMF. The U.S., Japan, and others came up with the Manila Framework, which enhances the IMF's capability to deal effectively with capital account crises in developing countries.

Moreover, the Japanese government played a decisive role in getting Japanese lenders in line in order to assemble a locked-in agreement on their credit facilities to Thai and Korean borrowers. This is one form of what is now called private sector involvement. Such involvement was quite effective in stabilising the financial crisis, because Japanese financial institutions were major lenders in the region with outstanding loans of 14 trillion yen. The subsequent reduction of 30 percent in Japanese banks' lending, mostly short-term lending throughout 1998 and 1999, would have had a much more negative effect without private sector involvement.

Where does Japan stand now? It is not entirely clear, as discussions are held only among a small group of stakeholders, in particular among those in charge at the government and banks. Indeed, the subject of restructuring Japan itself has overwhelmed any other policy discussions, particularly at the highest level. However, in general terms, the Japanese view can be summarised as follows.

First, Japan is more or less content with multinational efforts since the 1999 G7/8 Cologne Summit and the establishment of the Manila Framework to restructure the international financial architecture. At the outset of the financial crisis, Japan was quick to point out to the IMF that the Asian crisis was a capital account crisis and not a traditional current account one. Japan suggested that the IMF was poorly equipped to provide the necessary amount of liquidity, which appeared to be huge. The Japanese finance minister even hinted in a speech at the IMF-World Bank annual meeting that it could be desirable to allow the IMF to borrow in the market for the purpose of enhancing its financing capability. This idea also lay behind the proposal to establish the AMF, which had been envisioned as a way to supplement the IMF's ability to supply liquidity. Using the same reasoning, Japan urged the IMF to increase its quotas, adding that the allocation of additional quotas should reflect the change in the relative economic size of member economies. The implication was that there should be an increase in the Asian share. In addition, Japan took the view that contagion can be stopped only in its early stages with a massive injection of liquidity.

Japan also underlined the fact that the conditionality suitable for a current account crisis is inappropriate for a capital account crisis. Conditionality should be tailored to each specific crisis situation, as one differs from another in nature and complexity. Obviously, to do so requires an intimate knowledge of the troubled economy. Therefore, Japan's finance minister emphasised that the IMF should incorporate local inputs more thoroughly into the process of devising conditionality, and went so far as to hint at setting up a programme committee that would include the recipient country as an official member.

As for a set of precautionary measures, in addition to the due process of introducing a proper infrastructure to secure the banking system, Japan indicated that the monitoring capabilities geared at both borrowers and lenders should be strengthened.

Not all of what Japan suggested met with agreement from other nations. Indeed, many specific suggestions were left unanswered. However, Japan still regards recent developments as the proper absorption of the lessons learned from the Asian financial crisis. For instance, the IMF's reasonably quick reaction to the cases of Argentina and Turkey cases reflects its learning, even if not completely successfully.

From the Japanese viewpoint, the fact that there has been some progress in monitoring highly leveraged institutions is also encouraging. The redistribution of the roles of various international financial institutions (IFIs) in times of crisis is going more or less in the right direction. Japan fully supports the creation and implementation of standards and best practices in the financial services sector, although it stresses the need for the right sequence of steps, according to each particular country. A country cannot be categorised as a developing country if it can manage to install all the necessary soft infrastructure overnight.

In addition, Japan was itself somewhat bewildered by the capital controls that were imposed by Prime Minister Mahathir Mohamad to shield Malaysia's economy from being tossed around by short-term money flows. However, a consensus seems to be emerging that some form of capital control, particularly as regards short-term flows, can be employed effectively to pre-empt a crisis. This action must be regarded as the proper exercise of prudential regulations for the domestic financial market.

Regional Efforts to Strengthen its Financial Market

At the same time, the memory lingers on among Asian nations, including Japan, of how assistance did not come from outside the region automatically or swiftly enough. Some collective mechanism to supplement the global financial architecture would have been highly desirable, even if not in the form of the proposed AMF. In other words, the region is very keen on revisiting the idea of a monetary fund and exploring some practical substitute ideas. China has completely altered its position and has become supportive of such an approach.

Japan acknowledges that it is bound to play a vital role in making any regional mechanism work. Moreover, there seems a solid agreement between Japan and the rest of the region that such a regional mechanism does make sense, as crisis contagion has poignantly illustrated that all Asian countries have a common stake. A collective investor relations policy can be effective, in that the international investment community identifies the Asian economies as one group with its own distinctive economic character.

Nonetheless, developments in this direction do not seem destined to create a new institution in the near future. Instead, various agreements and forums are evolving. One is the Chiang Mai Initiative of May 2000: Japan agreed to enter with other Asian countries into a currency swap–borrowing arrangement to supplement an arrangement set up by the Association of South-East Asian Nations (ASEAN). The Japanese government is now negotiating to complete this arrangement, and seeing to it that these new facilities will be made available only when the troubled countries obtain IMF consent for appropriate corrective economic policy.

Moreover, the Bank of Japan and the Japanese Ministry of Finance are making considerable progress in building up forums as a monitoring and co-ordinating platform. These developments are often neglected but are nevertheless very important. These forums can be expected to begin functioning as a sort of mutual surveillance mechanism for macroeconomic management and credit structure supervision.

In 2000, to follow up on the previous set of Miyazawa initiatives, the second stage was launched, aimed at seeking a structural solution to the Asian financial crisis. The underlying idea was based on the conviction that the crisis was brought about by mismatching financing in terms of both the currency and term structure of external borrowing. Therefore, this new initiative advocates the establishment of external bond markets in the region in order to bring about inflows of long-term capital. This will likely provide the Japanese savings surplus with appropriate outlets in the future.

However, developing a regional external bond market is a rather long-term exercise. It is clearly desirable to replace hot money by long-bond financing, but it is not likely to happen in the immediate future. Japanese institutional investors will not be easily attracted to Asian bonds until the economy is fully out of the woods. In fact, the progress to date seems to be limited to only a few measures. For example, the Japanese government banks have started to guarantee some of the qualified sovereign bonds, and the Japanese government has hosted some regional workshops on the way to move toward the creation of workable bond markets.

Japanese banks, with their enormous domestic problems, have a somewhat diminished role in the rest of the region. They concentrate on serving Japanese MNCs. Statistics show that more than 40 percent of the lending by Japanese banks goes to indigenous firms in the region. Yet these firms are suspected to be associated with the operation of Japanese MNCs, so that lending is made with the tacit backing of those corporations.

This constraint on Japanese banks has kept the important issue of private sector involvement in case of crisis from being fully discussed in Tokyo. Some claim that collective action clauses erode the very essence of readily marketable bonds. Others argue that a prolonged and disorderly disruption in debt service payment is worse than orderly compromise. In any event, bonds are not a predominant instrument for Asian borrowers. Furthermore, Japanese investors' holdings of Latin American and East European bonds are not sizeable. Therefore, Japan has not yet developed a sense that collective action clauses could also be a vital issue for Asia.

If there is any consensus, it is that Japanese lenders do not seem ready to accept detailed universal rules or an unconditional delegation of stewardship to allow the IMF or another institution to declare an economic standstill. The Asian experience reminds Japanese lenders of the danger of a straitjacket approach to crisis management. They appreciate the exercise of identifying fair rules such as accommodating all the potential creditors, but they do not see any need to proceed hastily, because the exercise itself is an excellent preparation for a future crisis.

Conclusion

No resurgence of dynamism in the Japanese economy is yet in sight. The traditional means of stimulating the economy, on both the monetary and the fiscal policy fronts, seem to have been exhausted. The problem of nonperforming loans is still a drag on the economy, although it now appears to be much less serious than it was in 1997–98. In light of the recent economic slowdown in the U.S., one cannot overlook a considerable downside risk for the immediate economic outlook. Japan's contribution to the global economy will stay limited.

One ray of hope, however, has recently emerged. Japan's new prime minister, Junichiro Koizumi, seems determined to push forward a series of long-awaited reform initiatives. Although LDP politics could present a formidable impediment to his efforts, Koizumi enjoys an extraordinarily high approval rate among the general public, who remain disgusted with the old system and cherish his call for reform. It is worthwhile to watch Japan's progress in its restructuring endeavour.

The rest of Asia is also facing a risk of significant economic slowdown. This time around, the end of the IT boom has hit the region's export sector hard. As a result, it has become painfully apparent that the restructuring of the banking and indigenous industrial sectors is still unfinished. Another notable development is China's dramatic rise as an industrial power, which seems to force Asian economies into adjusting their competitiveness.

In the meantime, Japan remains engaged in efforts to strengthen the region's economic foundations, of which a critical element is rebuilding the financial sector. Japan is more or less content with the global efforts to rebuild the international financial architecture, especially as in its view the recent efforts indicate that lessons were properly learnt from the Asian financial crisis of 1997–99.

Moreover, in order to regain the confidence of international investors, Japan is striving to build a network of assistance and consultation with the rest of Asia. It remains to be seen, however, how well prepared Asia is for the future strains in the financial markets.

Note

1   These two issues are very broad and although the following description may appear too sweeping or simplistic on occasion, such a broad overview provides an important context and contribution to a detailed analysis of the specific items.

References

Ito, Kunihiko (2001). 'Japan, the Asian Economy, the International Financial System, and the G8: A Critical Perspective'. In J. J. Kirton and G. M. von Furstenberg, eds., *New Directions in Global Economic Governance: Managing Globalisation in the Twenty-First Century*, pp. 127–142. Ashgate, Aldershot.

Kaiser, Karl, John J. Kirton, and Joseph P. Daniels, eds. (2000). *Shaping a New International Financial System: Challenges of Governance in a Globalizing World*. Ashgate, Aldershot.

Katada, Saori (2001). 'Japan's Approach to Shaping a New International Financial Architecture'. In J. J. Kirton and G. M. von Furstenberg, eds., *New Directions in Global Economic Governance: Managing Globalisation in the Twenty-First Century*, pp. 113–126. Ashgate, Aldershot.

Kirton, John J. (2001). 'The G7/8 and China: Toward a Closer Association'. In J. J. Kirton, J. P. Daniels and A. Freytag, eds., *Guiding Global Order: G8 Governance in the Twenty-First Century*. Ashgate, Aldershot.

Kirton, John J. and George M. von Furstenberg, eds. (2001). *New Directions in Global Economic Governance: Managing Globalisation in the Twenty-First Century*. Ashgate, Aldershot.

Kiuchi, Takashi (2000). 'The Asian Crisis and Its Implications'. In K. Kaiser, J. J. Kirton and J. P. Daniels, eds., *Shaping a New International Financial System: Challenges of Governance in a Globalising World*, pp. 37–46. Ashgate, Aldershot.

Lawton, Thomas (2001). 'The New Global Electronic Economy: The Contribution of the G8 Summit'. In J. J. Kirton and G. M. von Furstenberg, eds., *New Directions in Global Economic Governance: Managing Globalisation in the Twenty-First Century*, pp. 39–60. Ashgate, Aldershot.

Watanabe, Koji (1999). 'Japan's Summit Contributions and Economic Challenges'. In M. R. Hodges, J. J. Kirton and J. P. Daniels, eds., *The G8's Role in the New Millennium*, pp. 95–106. Ashgate, Aldershot.

PART III
ASSEMBLING
A NEW INTERNATIONAL
FINANCIAL ARCHITECTURE

Chapter 6

Problems and Reforms
of the International Monetary System

Dominick Salvatore

There is a great deal of dissatisfaction with the architecture and functioning of the present international monetary system. This dissatisfaction gives rise to persistent calls for reforms. Such calls are most insistent during periods of crisis, such as at the time of the collapse of the Bretton Woods system in the early 1970s, the foreign debt problem of less developed countries (LDCs) in the early 1980s, and the financial crises in emerging markets since the second half of the 1990s. However, reforms are demanded even during periods of relative tranquillity in international financial markets, such as at the beginning of the twenty-first century. Dissatisfaction with the functioning of the current international monetary system arises because of misalignments among the world's leading currencies (the U.S. dollar, the euro, and the yen) and because of the system's inability to prevent or resolve quickly international financial crises in emerging markets. This chapter will briefly review the architecture and shortcomings in the operation of the present international monetary system. It will then examine the two major problems facing the present international monetary system, and evaluate proposals for possible solutions.

The Architecture and Operation of the Today's International Monetary System

The current international monetary system has three main characteristics. First, there is a wide variety of exchange rate arrangements. According to the classification set out by the International Monetary Fund (IMF), at the end of 1999 there were 108 countries with pegged or quasi-pegged exchange rate arrangements or that had adopted a leading currency as their domestic currency; 26 countries had managed flexibility, and another 51 countries (including the United States, Japan, the United Kingdom, Canada, Australia, Sweden, Switzerland, and Mexico, and the 12 countries of the European Monetary System via the euro) had practically full flexibility. This adds up to 185 countries (three more than there are members of the IMF). Although most countries had pegged or quasi-pegged exchange rates, four fifths of world trade in 1999 was conducted by countries that had managed or full exchange rate flexibility so that the international monetary system could be regarded more as a flexible than a fixed exchange rate system.

The second characteristic is that there has been substantial exchange rate variability. This is true whether exchange rates have been nominal or real, bilateral or effective, or short run or long run. The IMF estimated that there was approximately five times more exchange rate variability during the period of flexibility (since 1971) than there had been under the preceding fixed exchange rate or Bretton Woods system. Variability of 2 to 3 percent per day and 20 to 30 percent per year is common under the current system. Such variability is greater than anticipated and does not seem to be declining over time; indeed, it is for the most part unexpected.

The third characteristic is that, contrary to earlier expectations, official intervention in foreign exchange markets (and therefore the need for international reserves) has not diminished significantly under the present flexible exchange rate system compared with the previous fixed exchange rate system. Countries have intervened in foreign exchange markets not only to smooth out day-to-day movements, but also to resist trends, especially during the 1970s and since the mid 1980s (see Salvatore 1994).

Since 1971, there has been far greater macroeconomic instability in the flexible exchange rate system of the leading industrial countries than was the case during the previous fixed exchange rate period or during the Bretton Woods period. The system was jolted by two rounds of large oil price increases (1973–74 and 1979–80), which resulted in double-digit inflation and led to recessions as industrial nations sought to break the inflationary spiral with very tight monetary policies. That period has also seen the rapid growth of the eurodollar market and the liberalisation of capital controls. However, it was the resulting sharp increase in international capital flows, as well as the institutional changes and adjustments following the collapse of the Bretton Woods system in 1971, that was the primary cause of the large macroeconomic instability suffered by the leading industrial countries, rather than the prevailing flexible exchange rates. Moreover, it is now widely agreed that no fixed exchange rate system could have survived the combination of oil shocks, portfolio shifts, and structural and institutional changes that the world faced during the past two decades (see Kenen 1994; Salvatore 1994). It must also be remembered that the current managed exchange rate system was not established deliberately as the result of an international agreement, but was instead forced upon the world by default as the result of the collapse of Bretton Woods because of lack of an adequate adjustment mechanism and dollar overvaluation.

The Problem of Exchange Rate Volatility and Misalignments among the Leading Currencies

There is little disagreement that exchange rates among the world's leading currencies (as well as among most other currencies that are allowed to fluctuate) have exhibited large volatility since the establishment of the current managed exchange rate system. There is also no question that great exchange rate volatility, by adding to transaction costs, has affected the volume and pattern of international trade. These costs, however, are not very large and are not greater than those faced by firms in many other markets, as in the metal and agricultural sectors (Dell'Ariccia 1999). Firms engaged in international trade have also learned how to deal with volatility by pursuing hedging and diversification strategies quickly and at little cost. The IMF (1984) concluded that exchange rate volatility did not seem to have exerted a significantly adverse effect on international trade. Measures could, of course, be devised to reduce volatility, but the costs of such measures would in all likelihood not justify the benefits resulting from them.

Potentially more damaging to the flow of international trade and investments than excessive exchange rate volatility are the wide and persistent exchange rate misalignments. Misalignment refers to the departure of exchange rates from their long-run, competitive equilibrium levels. An overvalued currency has the effect of an export tax and an import subsidy on the country and, as such, reduces that country's international competitiveness position and distorts the pattern of specialisation, trade, and payments. A significant exchange rate misalignment that persists for years could not possibly be hedged away and can impose significant real costs on the economy in the form of unemployment, idle capacity, bankruptcy, and protectionism. A major currency's misalignment has harmful and possibly disruptive effects not only on the country (such as the United States or Japan) or region (such as the euro area) issuing the currency but also on the countries that peg their currencies to it (as evidenced by the problems that Argentina, which has a currency board with the peso rigidly tied to the dollar, faced during the three years to 2002 as a result of the strong dollar and a heavily depreciated real, the currency of Brazil).

The most notorious example of exchange rate misalignment was the overvaluation of the U.S. dollar during the 1980s. According to the Board of Governors of the U.S. Federal Reserve System, from 1980 to its peak in February 1985 the dollar appreciated and was overvalued by about 40 percent on a trade-weighted basis against the currency of the ten largest industrial countries. This meant, for example, that American Caterpillar, the largest producer of large earth-moving equipment in the world, could compete neither on the world market nor in the United States with Komatsu, even though Caterpillar was estimated at the time to be 25 percent more efficient than its fierce Japanese competitor. The large dollar overvaluation contributed significantly to the development of the huge trade deficit sustained by the U.S, during those years and to the equally large combined trade surplus of Japan and Germany. It also led to increasing calls for and actual trade protectionism in the U.S. as the country's efficient firms and industries joined less efficient ones in demanding protection because of their inability to compete with their foreign competitors at home and abroad as a result of the overvalued dollar.

It has been estimated (Council of Economic Advisors 1986, 1987) that the 1985 U.S. trade deficit was US$60 to US$70 billion greater (about twice as large) than it would have been had the dollar remained at its 1980 level, and that this deficit cost about 2 million jobs in the United States. Despite the fact that by the end of 1988 the international value of the dollar was slightly below its 1980–81 level (so that all its overvaluation had been eliminated), large global trade imbalances remained and showed no signs of declining rapidly. Economists have borrowed the term 'hysteresis' from the field of physics to characterise the failure of trade balances to return to their original equilibrium once exchange rate misalignments have been corrected. Other major misalignments of the dollar have occurred since the mid 1990s. This is evidenced by the fact that the U.S. dollar was worth 84.6 yen in June 1995, 140.3 yen in June 1998, 106.1 yen in June 2000, and 121.6 yen in June 2001. Furthermore, there is the overvaluation of the U.S. dollar with respect to the euro (the currency of the twelve members of the euro area), which was in the range of 15 to 20 percent in mid 2001.

What is important to note, however, is that although misaligned exchange rates could be regarded as the immediate cause of prevailing global trade imbalances, they were themselves the result of internal structural disequilibria in the leading countries. These structural disequilibria, and not exchange rate misalignments, were the fundamental cause of the huge global trade imbalances facing most leading industrial countries, and remain so today (see Table 6.1). Specifically, it was the more rapid growth and lower savings rate in the United States than in Japan and Europe during the second half of the 1990s that led to the overvaluation of the dollar and to growing U.S. trade deficits during that period. More rapid growth and very low savings also resulted in huge capital flows from the euro area and Japan to the United States, thus turning the United States into the largest debtor nation in the world.

Blame for the failure to encourage nations to eliminate their internal disequilibria and to promote greater co-ordination of macroeconomic policies among the leading industrial countries can be placed squarely on the international monetary system.

Table 6.1   Trade Imbalances of the Leading Industrial Countries (in billions of U.S. dollars)

Country	1992	1993	1994	1995	1996	1997	1998	1999	2000
U.S.	−94.3	−130.7	−164.1	−171.9	−189.4	−194.7	−244.9	−343.3	−447.1
Japan	124.8	139.4	144.2	131.8	83.6	101.6	122.4	123.3	116.7
Germany	28.2	41.2	50.9	65.1	69.4	70.8	78.9	72.0	–
France	2.4	7.5	7.3	11.0	14.9	26.9	24.9	19.4	3.8
UK	−23.3	−20.0	−16.9	−18.5	−20.2	−19.5	−34.0	−42.4	−43.6
Italy	−0.2	28.9	31.6	38.7	54.1	39.9	36.6	20.4	10.7
Canada	7.4	10.1	14.8	25.9	31.1	17.2	12.8	22.8	36.6

Sources: International Monetary Fund, *International Financial Statistics Yearbook 2000*, and *International Financial Statistics*, June 2001.

To a large extent this failure was due to the very different tradeoffs between inflation and unemployment made by the leading countries. Policy co-ordination under the current system has taken place only occasionally and has been very limited in scope. One such episode was in 1978 when Germany agreed to serve as 'locomotive' to stimulate growth in the world economy. This experiment came to an abrupt end, however, when Germany backtracked, fearing a resurgence of inflation. Another episode of limited policy co-ordination was the Plaza Agreement of September 1985, in which the G5 countries (United States, Japan, Germany, United Kingdom, and France) intervened in foreign exchange markets to induce a gradual depreciation or soft landing of the dollar in eliminating its large overvaluation. Successful international policy co-ordination can also be credited for greatly limiting the damage from the 1987 stock market crash and for preventing the 1994–95 Mexican crisis from spreading or having a lasting damaging effect on other emerging markets. Instances of international macroeconomic policy co-ordination, however, are sporadic and rather limited in scope.

Correcting the Misaligned Problem among the Leading Currencies

Because the misalignment problem among the world's leading currencies resulted primarily from the internal structural imbalances in the United States, the euro area, and Japan, the solution to the problem must be sought internally. As pointed out above, the most serious problem facing the United States is grossly inadequate domestic savings in the face of rapid domestic growth. The rapid growth of the U.S. during the second half of the 1990s (and the expectation of its resumption in 2002) is based on the existence of a more flexible economic structure and the more widespread use and adoption of the information technology (the new economy) than in the euro area or Japan. This led to huge capital inflows into the U.S., an overvalued exchange rate, and huge and growing trade deficits. The medium and long-term solution to this problem is for Europe and Japan to liberalise their economies in order to grow more rapidly (and hence import more from the U.S.) and for the U.S. to adopt policies that stimulate domestic savings. The latter is not easy to do because U.S. consumers and firms have become addicted to living with increasing levels of debt and it is difficult to break the habit. An increase in the U.S. savings rate would reduce the need for capital inflows and would reduce or eliminate the overvaluation of the dollar and, with it, its huge trade deficit. This will take time — years — to achieve and, in any event, the trade deficit responds with a lag that can take as long as two years or more before exchange rate changes, so there is a need for short- to medium-term policies to bridge the gap. These are discussed below.

In Japan, the problem is also structural and mostly of an internal nature and thus requires, for the most part, domestic policies to correct. Specifically, Japan has been in a serious financial and economic crisis for the entire past decade. Domestic deflation rather than international disturbance is the primary cause of the large undervaluation of the yen with respect to the U.S. dollar and thus of the large trade Japanese trade surplus *vis-à-vis* the United States. Japan has three possible policies available to overcome its deflationary problem: it could adopt an even stronger expansionary monetary policy, it could depreciate the yen even further, or it could pursue a much stronger expansionary fiscal policy than it has been willing to consider over the past decade. With interest rates already at or close to zero, however, Japan is in a classic liquidity trap. Firms simply would not borrow and consumers would not spend because of lack of confidence in the future of the Japanese economy. Paul Krugman (2001) has been advocating flooding the market with liquidity to resolve the deflationary problem in Japan. This could help, but no one can be sure; Japan's central bank, the Bank of Japan, has not been willing to take this route, thus far, for fear of failure.

The second choice for Japan would be to encourage the yen to depreciate further, so as to stimulate domestic growth by a further large expansion of its exports. This, however, would further increase Japan's already huge U.S. trade deficit — which the United States is simply unwilling to accept. More importantly, given that the Japanese problem is mostly of internal origin, the correct policy requires an internal stimulus. That is, to solve its deflationary problem Japan requires a much larger fiscal stimulus than it has had. The reason usually given for its reluctance to do so is that Japan already has a huge government debt (112 percent of gross domestic product — the same as Italy) and, with the most rapidly aging population in the world, Japan is not inclined to accept the significant increase in its already huge national debt that a large fiscal stimulus would entail. But the aging of the population and the size of the national debt are long-term problems and require long-term solutions. The recession in Japan, instead, is here and now and requires immediate action and sacrifices. It simply does not make sense for Japan to continue to procrastinate, as it has done during the past decade, hoping that somehow the crisis will go away by itself if it waits long enough.

For the euro area, the situation is different, but even here the chronically weak (and misaligned) euro is primarily the product of internal structural disequilibria. The problems in the euro area are inadequate and slow restructuring of its economy, especially of its labour market, and its inadequate pursuit of the new economy. These elements have kept growth at anaemic levels and kept the rate of unemployment unacceptably high. From 1995 to 1999, the average growth of real gross domestic product (GDP) was 2.2 percent in the euro area as compared to 4.4 percent in the U.S.; if growth resumes in the U.S. in 2002, during the past five years the euro area will have grown more rapidly than the U.S. only in 2001 — and only because its growth rate fell less than in the U.S. rate. The long-term policy for the euro area is thus to speed up the restructuring of its economy, liberalise its labour markets more rapidly, and encourage a faster adoption and spread of information and communications technology (ICT). With more rapid growth at home, there will be less capital outflow to the United States and a stronger euro, thus reducing or eliminating the exchange rate misalignment. Becaused the euro area's problem is mostly structural rather than cyclical in nature, a more expansionary monetary policy on the part of the European Central Bank (ECB) would provide only a limited stimulus to growth. Furthermore, with the precise mandate to target only inflation, the ECB's statutes would have to be changed to permit it to use monetary policy to pursue the additional goals of growth and employment (as the Federal Reserve System does) — which is by no means easy to do because it requires a change in the Maastricht Treaty itself.

International Policy Co-ordination to Correct the Misalignment among the Leading Currencies

Since most of the economic problems facing the United States, the euro area, and Japan are structural and internal rather than cyclical and international in nature, for the most part they require domestic policies to resolve. These policies will take a long time to adopt and produce results, but in the meantime they create international problems (such as grossly misaligned exchange rates and unsustainable trade imbalances) that then have repercussions and magnify domestic problems. There is therefore a need for short- and medium-term international policies to bridge the gap. Such measures could be greater macroeconomic policy co-ordination and intervention in foreign exchange markets on the part of the United States, the euro area, and Japan to steer the exchange rates among their currencies toward their long-term equilibrium level. Of course, it is not precisely known what the equilibrium exchange rates are, but some rough idea (based on purchasing power parity or otherwise) is possible. For example, there is some agreement that the dollar is now overvalued by 15 to 20 percent with respect to both the euro and the yen, so the United States, the euro area, and Japan could co-ordinate their policies and jointly intervene in foreign exchange markets to prod the dollar to move toward rough parity with the euro and the yen.

This is not to suggest a massive intervention in foreign exchange markets and far more formal and extensive macroeconomic policy co-ordination than that proposed by the IMF (1996a), Ronald McKinnon (1988), Ralph Bryant (1995), Kiochi Hamada and Masahiro Kuwai (1997), Helen Milner (1997), or Robert Mundell (2000) — which seem unrealistic to achieve under present conditions (for reasons indicated below). Under McKinnon's proposal, the United States, Germany (now the euro area), and Japan would fix the exchange rate among their currencies at their equilibrium level (determined by purchasing-power parity) and then closely co-ordinate their monetary policies to keep exchange rates fixed. A tendency for the dollar to appreciate *vis-à-vis* the yen would signal that the U.S. should increase the growth rate of its money supply, while Japan should reduce it. The net overall increase in the money supply of the U.S., the euro area, and Japan would then be expanded at a rate consistent with the non-inflationary expansion of the world economy. Mundell goes even further and envisions that, with an even greater inflation convergence than has occurred during the past decade, a monetary union among the U.S. dollar, the euro, and the yen areas (and eventually a single world currency; see Cooper 1984) is possible and would represent an optimal arrangement from the world's point of view.

Kenneth Rogoff (2001) disagrees that a single world currency would be optimal. But even if a monetary union among the U.S., the euro area, and Japan would represent an optimal arrangement, it is very unlikely that it would take place in the foreseeable future, and so the comments that follow refer to only to McKinnon's proposal.

The type of close macroeconomic policy co-ordination proposed by McKinnon is virtually impossible under current conditions. For example, during the 1980s and early 1990s, the United States seemed unable or unwilling to reduce its huge budget deficit substantially and rapidly, Germany was unwilling to stimulate its economy adequately even though it faced a high rate of unemployment, and Japan was very reluctant to use sufficiently expansionary fiscal policies to stimulate its economy and dismantle its protectionist policies to allow many more imports from the U.S. so as to help correct their trade bilateral huge imbalance. As long as the U.S., the euro area, and Japan have different inflation-unemployment tradeoffs, effective and substantial macroeconomic policy co-ordination among them is essentially impossible. In fact, the U.S., the euro area, and Japan consider the ability to choose different tradeoffs to be an important advantage of the current international monetary system over the previous Bretton Woods system.

There are also other more practical obstacles to successful and effective international macroeconomic policy co-ordination. One is the lack of consensus about the functioning of the international monetary system. For example, the Federal Reserve System may consider that a monetary expansion would lead to an expansion of output and employment, while the ECB may maintain that it would result primarily in inflation. Another obstacle arises from the lack of agreement on the precise policy mix required. This disagreement arises from the fact that macro-econometric models give widely differing results with regard to the effect of a given fiscal expansion. There are, therefore, the problems of how to distribute the gains from successful policy co-ordination among the participants and how to spread the cost of negotiating and policing agreements. Empirical research reported by Jeffrey Frankel and Katharine Rockett (1988), Jacob Frenkel, Morris Goldstein, and Paul Masson (1991), and Warwick McKibbin (1997) indicates that countries gain from international policy co-ordination about three quarters of the time but that the welfare gains from co-ordination, when they occur, are not very large. It is possible, however, that the empirical studies conducted thus far have not captured the full benefits from successful international policy co-ordination.

Although formal and extensive macroeconomic policy co-ordination is almost impossible among the U.S., the euro area, and Japan, some informal and weaker form of macroeconomic policy co-ordination, together with co-ordinated periodic (as required) intervention in foreign exchange markets is possible. Indeed, such co-ordination was used in 1985 to lead to a soft landing of the U.S. dollar with the Plaza Agreement, in 1987 to prevent the collapse of the stock markets from creating a world-wide economic slowdown, and in 1995 to check the spread of the Mexican crisis to other emerging markets. The foreign exchange market intervention in favour of the euro in the fall of 2000 was not successful because it was very weak, was undertaken half-heartedly, and was not backed by any clear statements by the participating leading central banks on their strong commitment to support the euro.

In conclusion, the large exchange rate misalignment among the U.S. dollar, the euro, and the yen is primarily the result of internal structural disequilibria in the United States, the euro area, and Japan, and such misalignment requires primarily domestic policies to be changed. A properly functioning international monetary system should be able to pressure the leading countries (for example, through the IMF's annual review of their economies) to correct structural disequilibria as soon as possible and, at the same time, co-ordinate foreign exchange interventions and macroeconomic policies co-ordination sufficiently and as required to overcome the short- and medium-term problems created by large currency misalignments. Such action would avoid distortions in the pattern of specialisation and trade and protectionism. Benign neglect will simply not do, and the adoption of a single world currency is utopian at this time.

International Financial Crises and the Architecture of the Future International Monetary System

The second serious problem facing the present international monetary system is its seeming inability to prevent international financial crises, especially in emerging markets. There have been six such crises since the mid 1990s: Mexico in 1994–95, Southeast Asia in 1997–99, Russia in the summer of 1998, Brazil in 1999, Argentina in 1999–2002, and Turkey in 2001. Although the fundamental problem that led to the crisis point was different in each case, the process was very similar. Each started as a result of a massive withdrawal of short-term liquid funds at the first sign of financial weakness in the country. Foreign investors poured funds into many emerging markets during the early 1990s after these country liberalised their capital markets in order to take advantage of high returns and to diversify their portfolios, but immediately withdrew their funds on a massive scale at the first sign of economic trouble in the country — thereby precipitating the crisis. The danger for the international monetary system is that such crises could spread to the rest of the world, including industrial countries (Salvatore 1999).

A number of measures have been proposed and some steps have already been taken to avoid or minimize such crises in the future and thus greatly strengthen the architecture of the present international monetary system and improve its functioning.

These include increasing transparency in international monetary relations, strengthening banking and financial systems, promoting greater private sector involvement, and providing adequate financial resources to emerging markets to prevent them from being affected by financial crises elsewhere (that is, to avoid contagion; see IMF 1996a, 1996b, 1996c, 1998, 1999a, 1999b; Goldstein and Council on Foreign Relations 1999; Eichengreen 1999; Salvatore 2000; Evans et al. 2000; Kumar, Masson, and Miller 2000; Mussa et al. 2000).

Increased transparency is essential because markets cannot work efficiently without adequate, reliable, and timely information. To this end, the IMF established the Special Data Dissemination Standards (SDDS) in 1996, which have already been accepted by about one quarter of the membership. These are early-warning financial indicators, such as the budget and current account deficit, long-term and short-term foreign debts, and international reserves as percentages of GDP; they serve as possible signals that emerging country or countries might be heading for trouble. It is hoped that foreign investors would take note of the potential problem and avoid pouring excessive funds into the country or countries, thus heading off a crisis. The SDDS has since been supplemented by the Dissemination Standards Bulletin Board, a Web site that provides information concerning countries' economic and financial data systems with more than 40 subscribers, including Hong Kong and China.[1] The IMF has also proposed establishing a clearing house to keep track of all the loans and liquid investments made by foreign banks and other financial institutions in emerging markets. Lack of this information has led to excessive loans and other liquid investments in emerging markets in the past, which have also contributed to crisis situations. In March 1999, the G7 set up the Financial Stability Forum (FSF) for the purpose of identifying gaps in financial regulation and supervision that posed a threat to international financial stability. Three months later, the IMF and the World Bank jointly set up the Financial Sector Assessment Program (FSAP) and the related Financial System Stability Assessments (FSSAs) to identify strengths and vulnerabilities so as to help develop appropriate policy responses. In September 1999, the IMF renamed the Interim Committee as the International Monetary and Financial Committee (IMFC).

The second way to improve the architecture of the international monetary system is to strengthen the banking and financial systems of emerging markets. Weakness in banking systems was common to all emerging markets that were involved in financial crises during the past five years. A weak banking and financial system invites a financial crisis and guarantees its severity. The system can be fortified by improving supervision and prudential standards, and by ensuring that banks meet capital requirements, provide adequately for bad loans, and publish relevant and timely information on their loan activities. Insolvent institutions must be dealt with promptly and effectively. Implementing these policies is difficult, especially when nation's banking and financial system is already in trouble, but a sound financial system is essential for the health and growth of the entire economy. The IMF has been formulating standards or codes of good practice in accounting, auditing, corporate governance, payments and settlements systems, insurance, and banking based on internationally accepted Basle Committee's Core Principles for Effective Banking Supervision (some of which have already been implemented as part of the IMF surveillance function).[2]

The third way to strengthen the international monetary system is to involve the private sector more extensively in sharing the burden of resolving a financial crisis in emerging markets. The private sector can contribute by rolling over and renegotiating loans or by providing new money rather than rushing for the exit, and such involvement could be a precondition for IMF assistance. Lenders would be compelled to take some responsibility for the crisis by having lent too many short-term funds to an emerging market for nonproductive purposes. That is, lenders should 'bail in' rather than be allowed to bail out. This is exactly what happened on 28 January 1998 when the IMF and the governments of rich countries put strong pressure on international banks to reschedule US$24 billion of Korean debt in a plan to replace bank loans with sovereign-guaranteed bonds. A similar strategy was taken in Brazil in early 1999. This, however, was relatively easy to do in Korea and Brazil because the problem there was primarily a crisis of liquidity rather than a much more serious structural problem (which would have raised serious doubts whether lenders would ever be repaid or even receive service payments). The legal framework to compel creditors to accept a Chapter 11–type of arrangement, as it exists in the United States today, does not exist on a global scale and it is not likely to be established soon. A formal change in the wording of bond contracts is also a long way off. Lenders would either charge much higher interest rates to compensate them for the higher risk or avoid lending to an emerging market economy altogether. Yet, the notion of moving toward some kind of debt-restructuring system is receiving a lot of attention at the IMF, the World Bank, and the Bank for International Settlements (BIS). The U.S., the European Union, and Japan have also been grappling with this issue at recent G7/8 meetings. Of course, it should not be easy for an emerging market economy in financial difficulty to declare bankruptcy unilaterally (so as to avoid the problem of moral hazard), but some way of bailing in lenders is clearly necessary to resolve a financial crisis, when one does erupt. In such situations, it should be up to the IMF to certify when an emerging market is sufficiently in trouble to trigger the restructuring mechanism.

One reform introduced by the IMF in April 1999 is the contingent credit line (CCL), which provides strong financial backing to an emerging market before it faces a financial crisis, if there is a danger that it might be dragged into a crisis through no fault of its own. For example, it often happens that international investors are unable to distinguish among emerging markets and withdraw funds from all of them when only one or a few face a crisis. Thus, when the crisis erupted in Russia in the summer of 1998, international investors withdrew funds also from Southeast Asia and Latin America even though conditions in those markets were very different. The CCL, however, is yet to be used. The financial resources to provide large financial assistance to an emerging market at risk of being engulfed by a financial crisis elsewhere were available from the doubling of the amount (to US$46 billion) that the IMF could borrow under the General Arrangements to Borrow (GAB), as called for by the Halifax Summit in 1995, following the 1994–95 Mexican crisis.

In the final analysis, however, it must be realised that even if all the reforms under consideration were adopted, they would not eliminate all future financial crises. All that can hoped for is that these reforms would reduce the frequency and severity of future financial crises. In short, some international financial instability and crises may be the inevitable result of liberalised financial markets and the cost that must be paid in return for the benefits that liberalised financial markets provide to industrial and emerging market economies alike.

Notes

1　The Dissemination Standard Bulletin Board is accessible at <dsbb.imf.org>.
2　The Core Principles for Effective Banking Supervision are available at <www.bis.org/publ/bcbs30a.htm>.

References

Bryant, Ralph C. (1995). *International Coordination of National Stabilization Policies*. Brookings Institution, Washington DC.

Cooper, Richard N. (1984). 'A Monetary System for the Future'. *Foreign Affairs*, Fall.

Council of Economic Advisors (1986). *Economic Report of the President*. Government Printing Office, Washington DC.

Council of Economic Advisors (1987). *Economic Report of the President*. Government Printing Office, Washington DC.

Dell'Ariccia, G. (1999). 'Exchange Rate Fluctuations and Trade Flows: Evidence from the European Union'. *IMF Staff Papers* vol. 46, no. 3 (September/December) <www.imf.org/external/Pubs/FT/staffp/1999/09-99/dellaric.htm> (February 2002).

Eichengreen, Barry J. (1999). *Toward a New International Financial Architecture: A Practical Post-Asia Agenda*. Institute for International Economics, Washington DC.

Evans, Owen, Alfredo M. Leone, Mahinder Gill, et al. (2000). 'Macroprudential Indicators of Financial System Soundness'. Occasional Paper No. 192. International Monetary Fund, Washington DC. <www.imf.org/external/pubs/ft/op/192/index.htm> (February 2002).

Frankel, Jeffrey A. and Katharine Rockett (1988). 'International Macroeconomic Policy Coordination When Policy Makers Do Not Agree on the Model'. *American Economic Review* vol. 78, no. 3, pp. 318–340.

Frenkel, Jacob A., Morris Goldstein, and Paul Masson (1991). 'Characteristics of a Successful Exchange Rate System'. Occasional Paper No. 82. International Monetary Fund, Washington DC.

Goldstein, Morris and Council on Foreign Relations (1999). *Safeguarding Prosperity in a Global Financial System: The Future International Financial Architecture*. Institute for International Economics, Washington DC.

Hamada, Kiochi and Masahiro Kuwai (1997). 'Strategic Approaches to International Policy Coordination: Theoretical Developments'. In M. Fratianni, D. Salvatore and J. von Hagen, eds., *Macroeconomic Policy in Open Economies*. Greenwood Press, Westport, CT.

International Monetary Fund (1984). 'Exchange Rate Volatility and World Trade'. Occasional Paper No. 28. International Monetary Fund, Washington DC.

International Monetary Fund (1996a). 'Interim Committee Report'. Washington DC.

International Monetary Fund (1996b). 'International Capital Markets: Developments, Prospects, and Key Policy Issues'. Washington DC.

International Monetary Fund (1996c). 'Standards for the Dissemination by Countries of Economic and Financial Statistics'. Discussion draft prepared by a staff team. Washington DC.

International Monetary Fund (1998). *International Financial Statistics Yearbook*. International Monetary Fund, Washington DC.

International Monetary Fund (1999a). 'World Economic Outlook, May 1999'. Washington DC.

International Monetary Fund (1999b). 'World Economic Outlook, October 1999'. Washington DC.

Kenen, Peter B., ed. (1994). *Managing the World Economy: Fifty Years after Bretton Woods*. Washington DC, Institute for International Economics.

Krugman, Paul R. (2001). 'Reckonings: Half a Loaf'. *New York Times*, 21 March, p. 23.

Kumar, Manmohan S., Paul R. Masson, and Marcus Miller (2000). 'Global Financial Crises: Institutions and Incentives'. IMF Working Paper No. 00/105. Washington DC. <www.imf.org/external/pubs/ft/wp/2000/wp00105.pdf> (February 2002).

McKibbon, Warwick J. (1997). 'Empirical Evidence on International Economic Policy Coordination'. In M. Fratianni, D. Salvatore and J. von Hagen, eds., *Macroeconomic Policy in Open Economies*. Greenwod Press, Westport, CT.

McKinnon, Ronald I. (1988). 'Monetary and Exchange Rate Policies for International Financial Stability: A Proposal'. *Journal of Economic Perspectives* vol. 2, no. 1 (Winter), pp. 83–103.

Milner, Helen (1997). 'The Political Economy of International Policy Coordination'. In M. Fratianni, D. Salvatore and J. von Hagen, eds., *Macroeconomic Policy in Open Economies*. Greenwood Press, Westport, CT.

Mundell, Robert A. (2000). 'A Reconsideration of the Twentieth Century'. *American Economic Review* vol. 90, no. 3, pp. 327–340.

Mussa, Michael, Paul Masson, Alexander Swoboda, et al. (2000). 'Exchange Rate Regimes in an Increasingly Integrated World Economy'. Occasional Paper No. 193. International Monetary Fund, Washington DC. <www.imf.org/external/pubs/ft/op/193/index.htm> (February 2002).

Rogoff, Kenneth (2001). 'Why Not a Global Currency?' *American Economic Review* vol. 91, no. 2, pp. 243–247.

Salvatore, Dominick (1994). 'The International Monetary System: Past, Present, and Future'. *Fordham Law Review* vol. 62, no. 7, pp. 1975–1988.

Salvatore, Dominick (1999). 'Could the Financial Crisis in East Asia Have Been Predicted?' *Journal of Policy Modeling* vol. 21, no. 3, pp. 341–347.

Salvatore, Dominick (2000). 'The Euro, the Dollar, and the International Monetary System'. *Journal of Policy Modeling* vol. 22, no. 3, pp. 407–415.

Chapter 7

One Region, One Money: The Need for New Directions in Monetary Policies

George M. von Furstenberg

Pressures for currency consolidation arise from several sources related to political liberalisation, economic globalisation, and the revolution in information and communications technology (ICT). Freer cross-border provision of financial services and a changed official attitude to foreign establishment and takeovers have encouraged foreign entry. Many regional and global electronic spot markets and electronic trading platforms set their prices in U.S. dollars or, prospectively, in euros. Multinational corporations (MNCs) consolidate accounts in either or both of these currencies, depending on the principal habitat of major divisions, and expect those who participate in their global or regional supply chains to do the same. Cross-border e-banking, e-investing, and e-commerce of all kinds can compete not only with domestic financial and business establishments but also with local currencies that provide inferior consumption insurance at currency-crisis cycle frequencies, and, at longer frequencies, inadequate intertemporal predictability of purchasing power and other 'real' terms of contract.

This chapter argues, and in small part substantiates, that e-commerce, regional economic integration, and global liberalisation have eroded the monopoly of small currencies in their home markets. These developments now threaten the continued viability of a number of such currencies over the medium run. If technological and market-driven pressures lead to increased use of the internationally dominant currency denomination of a region in a lengthening list of financial, e-commerce, and other activities in a liberalising world, then the question for government policy becomes how to respond to these pressures. What kind of institutional arrangements and international architecture for trade in financial services are most suitable for the prospective environment of a greatly reduced multiplicity of currencies? Even partial currency consolidations, such as those afforded by currency boards, are likely to prove unsustainable in the new environment characterised by a momentum toward regional currency and monetary unions.

The evolution from the original European Economic Community of six countries, which went into effect in 1958, to the consummation of the European Monetary Union (EMU) among twelve countries took 44 years. This leisurely pace was due to appreciation of the monetary requirements of deep economic integration, which grew gradually, as long as the Bretton Woods system provided reasonably fixed exchange rates among the major currencies. Even after the demise of that system in 1973, it still took one or two decades for freedom of capital movement fully to be re-established in most parts of the world. With the phasing out of exchange controls and dual exchange rates in ever more developing countries, the gradual achievement of unrestricted capital-account convertibility made fixed but adjustable exchange rates much more vulnerable to being dislodged until they could no longer be fixed credibly.

There now is widespread agreement that, as between the U.S. dollar, the euro, and the yen, 'realistically, there is no alternative to floating exchange rates among the three major currencies' (Köhler 2001). However, pressures to take new steps to assure irrevocably fixed exchange rates within economic unions have grown. There are those, such as Robert Mundell (International Monetary Fund [IMF] 2001c; Friedman and Mundell 2001), who would like to change this reality gradually, viewing a single world currency as a desirable endpoint in the long run, while others find that 'from an economic point of view, it would be preferable to retain at least, say, three or four currencies' (Rogoff 2001, 246).

For the smaller countries in each region, the questions raised by financial liberalisation are quite different. For them, maintaining separate currencies, and, consequently, exchange rates, became less desirable when exchange rates became a growing source of shocks to the economy and its finances, instead of being serviceable shock absorbers. 'Really I do believe that you cannot have a common market when you have fluctuating exchange rates in an area' Mundell (2000, 164) has said. Abrupt changes in nominal and real exchange rates that reverse themselves only slowly after a currency crisis can drastically change competitive conditions between the members of an economic union and hence of each member with outsiders. Such changes are liable to disturb trade relations, rather than to equilibrate them. The desire to avoid such upsets by using a single money inside economically integrated regions may have contributed to a mutual insurance interest in the EMU. Nevertheless, its adoption owed more to the political logic of shared governance and a common anti-inflationary resolve than to overwhelming pressures in financial markets.

Since about the time of the Maastricht Treaty in 1991, the regulatory protections that had allowed many small currencies and fragmented financial markets to continue have been sterilised. International competition in financial services has been facilitated by the spreading application of the principles of mutual recognition and national treatment. Mutual recognition led to the concept of European 'passports' that allow financial services to be provided unchallenged across the European Union's internal borders, while the widespread adoption of the principle of national treatment gives substance to global access that includes the option of foreign establishment anywhere. Invariably, the strongest competitors in financial services operate in the leading international currencies and crowd out financial business in lesser currencies and the local institutions that provide it.

As a result, in the future, there will be greater urgency to decide whether to hang on to a financially small and purely domestic currency in which less and less business can be conducted cost effectively. The alternative is to try to merge it with some form of regional monetary union while there still is a choice. Even in the western hemisphere, where free trade areas such as the North American Free Trade Agreement (NAFTA) have been formed among countries that have currencies that float against each other, the question of monetary unification may not be put aside much longer. Mercosur's common market arrangement has been all but destroyed in the three years since the Brazilian real was left to float against the Argentinean peso in January 1999.

These internal tensions indicate that under present circumstances, Mundell's dictum is proving true: large exchange rate movements among the partners in an economically integrated region almost inevitably threaten stability and hence the reliability of integration among them. The resulting changes in trade advantage are liable to be viewed politically as disruptive and unfair. Monetary union, whether unilateral — like dollarization — or multilateral — like the EMU — now may be the only reliable way to preclude such disruptions. Indeed, the lack of monetary union may detract from economic union because exchange rate movements give a divisive edge to national borders and national trade interests when currency boundaries are maintained. Monetary union is becoming a less and less optional companion of economic union which gives political definition to an economic region.

Apart from the pressures for currency consolidation that arise from the trade side in economically integrated regions, there are also pressures everywhere that arise simply from currency competition in the financial sector. As Stanley Fischer (2001, 22) has surmised, among developing countries that have moved from fixed but adjustable to managed-floating exchange rates in the past two decades, the emerging trend could well be a move to the hard-peg ends of the spectrum of exchange rate regimes.

The medium-term evolution to monetary unions that appears to be underway does not denationalise or privatise money because the money involved remains a creature of the fiat of a state or group of states. Others have already looked ahead to a more distant future in which privately issued electronic money might no longer need to be convertible into traditional money or supported by legal tender in order to be widely accepted as a means of settlement and store of value; Benjamin Cohen (2000) provides an excellent overview. Money would then exist inside global electronic communications and procurement networks. Financial services likewise would be both product and byproduct of the provision of electronic commerce and communication providers, and dedicated financial intermediaries could be bypassed. As a result, monetary and financial union by government construction could become meaningless. Instead of looking so far ahead to new forms of private denationalised moneys, one can merely note a resurgence of the historical forces of currency substitution among 'official' moneys. These forces are leading to a new wave of currency consolidation across national boundaries.

A Glance at History and Medium-Term Prospects

A brief look both back and ahead suggests that, in matters of currency competition, there may be a return to conditions once common in many parts of the world when good moneys knew no boundaries and bad moneys could not yet be forced on people. Gresham's law could come into operation only when a new form of money was declared legal tender at an overvalued legal exchange rate for money and debt contracts denominated in some older form or substantiation of money.[1]

Over time, many countries sought to strengthen the issuing authority's monopoly power in order to afford effective protection for the national currency. Such action led away from the production of national money in monopolistic competition with other such moneys to positively reserving the domestic market for its use. To assure such exclusivity, use of the domestic currency denomination generally has been required for tax accounting and payments and for tenders on government projects. Additional shelter has been provided by capital controls and by financial regulations that strictly limited the booking of foreign currency assets and liabilities for domestic residents and gave the national denomination exclusive rights in many home-country applications. Having made their economies captive to the local currencies, governments were less constrained to resort to inflationary finance, to routinely abuse seigniorage, and to regiment and stifle the development of the financial system and of financial services provided by the private sector. Conversely, (far) fewer monies than states would mean better monies, as Rudiger Dornbusch (2001) succinctly put it. Therefore, apart from pressures for currency consolidation from trade in economically integrating regions, pressures also arise almost everywhere in the developing world simply from the greater currency competition that is now allowed in the financial sector.

Barriers to currency consolidation have tended to erode over the past two dozen or more years as world-wide internal and external liberalisation has taken hold. As a result, national moneys have been exposed to international competition and had to struggle for survival once again. Brian Doyle (2000), Domenico Nuti (2000, 175), and Benjamin Cohen (2000, 3–4) provide estimates of the extent to which the world's most important currencies, particularly U.S. dollars and Deutschmark (henceforth the euro) were located outside their country of issue. Obstacles to foreign competition have been falling first in developed and then in developing countries as they became integrated into the liberal international trade and investment regime and extended national treatment to foreign suppliers with progressively fewer derogations that soon expired. Freer cross-border provision of financial services and a changed official attitude to foreign establishment and takeovers have encouraged foreign entry. These developments also have opened the door to more widely denominating and trading domestic claims in international denominations for purchase by both foreign and domestic residents.

Moving the Financial Business of Small Countries into the Major Currencies

Providing loan, debt, equity and reinsurance financing in foreign denominations is a business in which foreign providers, domiciled in the country that issues the relevant international currency, tend to have a funding and marketing advantage. Because of this inevitable link to the retention of national ownership and competitive advantage, issues of currency denomination have rarely escaped regulatory and legislative scrutiny, with currency substitution — the domestic use of a foreign money or currency denomination (Cohen 2000, 2) — coming in for particular attention.

Granting market access to both domestic and foreign entrants or potential competitors thus raises the question of whether granting access to foreign-currency denomination of a widening list of financial contracts in the domestic market should follow. Certainly offering to do business in the international currency, whether U.S. dollar, euro, or yen, that is the foreign entrant's domestic issue may be its best competitive weapon. Simply following the principle of national treatment could cramp effective market access by foreign providers if it outlaws this weapon by requiring contracts to be written only in local currency, as is still frequently the case in insurance. If foreign providers are only allowed to compete in the same (domestic) currency vehicles in which their domestic counterparts as market insiders often can do better, giving foreign suppliers national treatment on such a — to them restrictive — standard does not really give them meaningful market access at all. Thus, only the combination of national treatment with market access for business done in any currency and for its fittest providers constitutes the kind of effective liberalisation that will generate pressures for currency consolidation rapidly and on a large scale. As another example, imposing a requirement on all insurance providers in the national market to reinsure with a national reinsurance monopoly or to cede to a financially unstable monopoly part of any nonretention does not, on the face of it, violate national treatment. Nevertheless, effective market access may be denied to highly rated potential competitors if they are subjected to what they consider to be reinsurance requirements of this form.

The prerequisite for liberalised market access, now clearly in view, is that individual and corporate citizens in many small countries will be able to choose to pay in more than one acceptable currency and to incur debts and acquire assets denominated in different currencies. Furthermore, using financial derivatives, they will be able to swap, alter, or hedge their currency exposure increasingly at will. However, they can do so only at considerable cost when their own currency is involved: Risk premiums that are reflected in interest rates and hence cause the forward exchange rates for small currencies to indicate more depreciation than implied by their expected future spot rates add to the cost of hedging. These risk premiums are due mostly to currency risk, in the sense that absent currency risk, very little remains of what had been identified as country risk on contracts denominated in an external reference currency such as U.S. dollar or Deutschmark, as southern members of the euro area now can attest.

It is inconceivable, for instance, that if Mexico were to dollarize completely, it would face premiums as high as the 300 to 340 basis points that were observed on its sovereign dollar borrowing in 2000. This is the yield spread over comparable U.S. treasury bills that have been identified by Mexico's central bank, quite conventionally and yet misleadingly, as pure country risk (Banco de México 2000, 16). Dong Tao and Joseph Lau (1998, 22) report that even in Panama, a fiscally disorderly and often poorly governed country, interest rates 'have remained stable at 0–1.3 percent above LIBOR [the London Interbank Offered Rate] over the past two decades' because it was dollarized. That is much less than what has been charged on sovereign-dollar borrowing by Mexico, even though Mexico for some time now has been fiscally much more virtuous than Panama.

Of course, currency consolidation cannot be a panacea for all of a national government's ills, such as fiscal mismanagement. Some of the worst governments of small dollarized countries may not always face lower dollar borrowing costs than some of the best governments of nondollarized countries, such as Chile. But a bad government credit rating would not need to carry over to the borrowing conditions faced by private enterprises in dollarized developing countries because sovereign borrowing risk may not set the lower limit of the risk premiums charged to borrowers in such countries. With fiscal and monetary policy risks decoupled and intraregional currency risk eliminated, credit to first-rate private obligors can involve less default risk than credit to their fiscally unsound governments.

No doubt sovereign default can still have an adverse effect on the external and internal financial relations of private borrowers. Yet, because a lack of fiscal discipline may ruin the credit rating of the government but not of the entire country, it is perhaps not altogether surprising that an international common currency area is not associated with greater fiscal discipline among the lesser members of the area, as found by Antonio Fatás and Andrew Rose (2001). When the national economic penalty for any lapse in fiscal discipline is lower, there will be less of a deterrent, and mutual supervision and correction, as under the European Union's 1997 Stability and Growth Pact, may have to be added to maintain discipline. Help also may come from financial markets, since any deep monetary and financial union encourages and is predicated on sharing good regulatory and supervisory practices and on adopting advanced risk analysis and transparent risk management systems by all its members. Greater independence and alertness in pricing sovereign risk within any country in turn make it more expensive for government to stray from the path of fiscal sustainability and soundness. The expected net effect on the fiscal self-discipline of members is thus uncertain and not an issue that cuts either for or against monetary union.

Microeconomic Drivers of Currency Consolidation

Given these three macroeconomic points about the relation to monetary union of economic union, currency competition due to effective market access, and fiscal policy, it is important to consider microeconomic factors leading to currency consolidation for developing countries. In Mexico, as in almost all other countries of the western hemisphere farther south, pressures and opportunities for dollarizing more and more of the banking and financial business manifest themselves in several ways. For instance, they are both cause and effect of the widespread takeover of local financial groups by foreign financial conglomerates, particularly those headquartered in the United States. In the end, foreign ownership of banking and finance generally predominates in financially small countries. The insurance subsidiaries in the acquiring U.S. financial groups, such as Travelers in Citigroup, will want to offer the same products through the Mexican branches — in this case, of what until 2001 was Banacci — as they do in the United States. These dollar-denominated products may be far more useful to their Mexican customers than peso-denominated policies in pension, life, and annuity applications as well as in the insurance of industrial property whose replacement cost is more stable and predictable in U.S. dollars than in local currency.

While 'the instability of the insurance sector in emerging market economies can be attributed to a wide range of microeconomic and institutional failings' (International Association of Insurance Supervisors [IAIS] 1997, 5), currency instability surely plays a large role among them. In light of the latest in a number of currency crises, the Turkish lira stands out as an example of the currency substitution dynamics in this regard. If insurance companies licensed to operate in Turkey try to hedge their lira liabilities with lira assets, they will still be subject to exchange risk as asset deflation and currency crisis go hand in hand in emerging markets. Contrary to the representations of the International Association of Insurance Supervisors (p. 13), following the principle of currency matching does not ensure protection from exchange rate risks in such markets because a currency crisis often pulls down the entire economic house. In such conditions, there is not much insurance value that can reliably be offered by the private sector, particularly if there is double-digit inflation or higher to start with.

It would make more sense for Turks to buy their insurance either in U.S. dollars or in euros in Euroland, where many of them work, live, or visit relatives, if they could not obtain policies specified and settling in dollars or euros in Turkey. In terms of the euro portion, which is likely to grow rapidly from 2002 on, this in turn puts pressure on Turkish insurance companies, at least after privatisation, to offer their own euro-denominated life, pension, and annuity policies. Since they are at a reputational disadvantage in doing so, those companies may be tempted to offer higher rates of return in euros than the market would normally support. If the insurance companies are nevertheless successful in offering credible euro-denominated products, it would create a demand and market for euro-denominated Turkish securities. This assumes a normal statistical home bias in the allocation of the investment portfolio by Turkish insurance companies that favour domestic issues in order to exploit their information advantage or insider status. Euroization of other balance sheet positions and contracts might well follow, as one decision about currency choice leads to another.

As these circles of currency substitution widen and interlock across ever more markets and services within a country, the question becomes how many currencies will remain in wide use in arrangements that allow foreign currencies to compete effectively. Will the local currency be among the survivors? Regionally centralising tendencies tend to weigh against such a prospect if the country is financially small to start with and if it lacks a very large internal market in which strong network externalities from the use of the domestic money can still be obtained.

Such hollowing out of these lesser national moneys in a widening range of domestic uses without officially giving up one's own national money leads to hazardous cohabitation. Consider, for instance, an Argentinean bank that has 'hedged' the typically large share of its U.S. dollar–denominated deposit liabilities with dollar assets, including claims on Argentineans who have no substantial dollar receivables. Now assume that there is an overvaluation and default crisis that causes Argentina to abandon one-to-one convertibility of its peso for the U.S. dollar and to impose fiscal austerity at all levels of government. In that case, the school principal of a suburban Buenos Aires school will have a double problem in servicing a dollar-denominated mortgage obligation. That principal's salary, which is set in pesos and depressed by fiscal austerity, will decline just when more pesos are required to service the dollar-denominated debt. Furthermore, asset deflation will tend to reduce the value of the security property even in pesos. Hence, the quality of the bank's claim is reduced, its currency hedge eroded, and its capital adequacy and solvency threatened. New lending will plummet as interest rates surge, private sector defaults rise, and economic activity declines over a broad front, with even export-oriented businesses hamstrung for lack of working capital and credit. A full-blown crisis will be on hand.

International Portfolio Diversification Works Best in Liquid Markets Using the Dominant Currency Denomination

There is a more general point to what was just discussed. Economists have often deduced that, from the point of view of obtaining optimal consumption insurance through portfolio diversification, the investment portfolios of otherwise comparably positioned investors from Canada, France, and Japan should look very much alike. The failure for them to do so, because citizens strongly favour claims on their own country's obligors, has been labelled the 'home bias puzzle' (Lewis 1999). Ricardo

Hausmann et al. (2000, 142–144) have argued that for emerging-market economies, all of which are financially small, there is even an inclination not to risk investing at home from the point of view of consumption insurance. The reason is that in a currency crisis, just when income and output fall and internal and external sources of credit dry up, domestic asset values collapse. The addition of a large negative wealth shock to a negative current-income shock would impart a double blow to consumption for investors at home.

Had these investors instead invested in international foreign-currency claims when the sharp real depreciation of the domestic currency occurred, they would have benefited from the real appreciation of the domestic value of their foreign holdings. This would have reduced, rather than amplified, the blow to consumption from a currency and financial crisis. Hence, to obtain optimal consumption insurance, investors in small emerging-market countries should invest outside their own country and currency to an extent even greater than fitting for the average international investor. When Uruguayans hold 85 percent of their savings in U.S. dollar–denominated accounts in their own country, they are reducing this double exposure to a degree that depends on whether they deposit in domestically owned banks or in local branches of foreign banks.

Even in Uruguay's large neighbour, Argentina, about 50 percent of bank assets are held in foreign-controlled institutions by a variety of measures (IMF 2000, 153). Multinational financial institutions are almost always headquartered in the key-currency countries, which have long led the development of the financial services industry and determined its international co-ordination and supervision. They bring their privileged key-currency connection with them wherever they establish a presence around the world and make that denomination their stock in trade. Cross-border banking via the internet (p. 157) might add to the advantage of the dominant currencies since they yield the widest range of transaction services that are true to the quoted price and match the denomination in which the widest range of financial investments and products are quoted. Cross-border e-banking may therefore compete not only with local banks but also with local currencies.

For banks as well as insurance companies, many of the prudential issues posed by growing foreign ownership are unresolved. On the one hand, developing countries are advised by some to buy, lease, or pay for access to existing securities trading and foreign exchange and payments settlement systems rather than build their own (IMF 2001b, 174) and to rely on external supervision of the financial institutions operating in their countries. The end result of this disenfranchisement could be this:

> As financial services are imported, the need for a domestic safety net and corresponding regulation and supervision declines. As financial services are imported from abroad, the question is raised whether small, undiversified economies should have domestic equity and debt markets — and in the extreme, banking systems (Claessens, Glaessner, and Klingebiel 2000, 6).

Governing Global Finance

On the other hand, Donald Mathieson and Jorges Roldos have pointed out for banks what holds analogously for insurance companies and other major financial institutions and exchanges:

> One of the biggest questions for policymakers is what position parent banks will take if branches (a legal part of the parent bank) or subsidiaries (separately capitalized entities) run into trouble. Indeed, what happens to local banks if their foreign parent bank has problems of its own? These relationships ... have yet to be tested in crises (IMF 2001b, 173).

Because competitive pressures contribute to their health, large international currencies tend to convey other advantages to foreign users over denominating in small currencies. To protect their international standing, pre-eminent currencies and their financial infrastructure must be well managed. Lapses in the sound conduct of monetary and financial policy, as in the United States during much of the 1970s and in Japan since the 1990s, tend to diminish the international role of the respective currency, thereby exerting a powerful disciplining effect in the long run. By contrast, emerging market countries typically have currencies that have unreliable purchasing power. Even in the absence of persistently high inflation, they commonly experience real exchange rates that are both highly variable and prone to drift up between major corrections, not necessarily toward a fixed mean. Hence, denominating annuities and pensions and lump-sum or life insurance settlements of any kind in such currencies would provide far less calculable real-value assurance than denominating in one of the large currencies. The latter are key to international pricing in product and finance markets and reliable stores of value and of future purchasing power over a broad range of goods. The added purchasing-power risk thus detracts from the suitability of small currencies for extended use in intertemporal trades. This contributes to the case for currency consolidation.

International financial derivatives, such as interest and currency swaps, forwards, futures, and options received a big boost from the collapse of the Bretton Woods system. As John Plender (2001) has pointed out, this occurred because the collapse of that system shifted the task of managing currency volatility from the public to the private sector. Regional currency consolidation will lower currency risk in some respects that are important for production and sales organisations and for trade in goods and services in the region. But they will not lower exchange risk between the large currencies, such as dollar, euro, and yen, which account for the bulk of the currencies involved in the construction of international financial derivatives. The U.S. dollar has been most prominent of all on the grounds that the underlying debt and equity claims suitable for listing, securitisation, and exchange trading in international financial markets are themselves commonly denominated in dollars, and to a lesser extent in euro and yen. Countries can use only very few other currency denominations for borrowing in international financial markets. Generally, large risk premiums and illiquidity, reflected in wide bid-ask spreads, discourage denominating in peripheral currencies. Since calculability of risk exposure and a high degree of liquidity of positions taken by major participants, including hedge funds, are essential to the functioning of the market in derivatives, standardisation of a common currency, including through the use of American depository receipts (ADRs), is convenient in many, though not all, applications.

Because arbitrage between the local-currency prices of securities originally issued in domestic markets and the corresponding ADRs or global depository receipts (GDRs) cannot be instantaneous because the supply of ADR or GDR securities is fixed in the short run, the question may be asked which quotation is more authoritative in the sense of being freer of self-correcting error when pricing discrepancies occur. It is conceivable that the prices of major corporations headquartered in the western hemisphere outside the United States are set decisively in New York and then translated back with some local addition of 'noise' into local currency if home listing is maintained. If true, this would mean that the calibration of news and the price-making function have shifted from the home base of operations to the foreign global financial centre and from local currency to U.S. dollars. The variance of exchange-translated security prices in the local market would be greater than that of the corresponding ADRs and this would discourage use of the local market and of its local-currency trading by foreign and domestic residents alike. For this and other reasons, in many emerging-country markets, few equity securities are left to trade. Indeed, on account of illiquidity, high transaction costs, and foreign acquisitions of leading domestic companies soon after they had been publicly listed, equity markets in a number of developing countries are on the brink of extinction. However, domestic debt instruments, in particular government debt claims, continue to be favoured by local pension funds.

The dollar may 'intrude' even into exchange contracts between other currencies. The International Monetary Fund (IMF) (1999, 49) explains, for instance, that nondeliverable foreign exchange forwards (NDFs) in emerging markets tend to be settled in U.S. dollars for the difference between the implied exchange rate on the contract and the prevailing spot rate on the maturity date of the contract. The IMF notes further that net settlement in domestic currency existed in many industrial countries in the 1970s and 1980s prior to the removal of exchange controls. The big currencies thus tend to get bigger when capital controls are removed. Some concrete indications why are presented below, after first offering a puzzle.

A Vignette from Financial Markets

Finding international financial puzzles is a growth industry, but the question here is whether attention to currency denomination can be part of the solution. If two closed global equity funds have essentially the same underlying holdings and quality of management, their percentage discount from net asset value would be expected to be the same in efficient markets regardless of the currency denomination in which they are traded. Why, then, is the mean percentage discount of the 65 U.S. dollar–traded funds, out of a total of 69 world equity funds shown with complete data listed in the *New York Times* on 27 May 2001, 15.37 percent (with a variance of the sample mean of 1.41 percentage point), while the mean percentage discount of the four remaining world equity funds that are traded in Canadian dollars is 35.26 percent (with a variance of the sample mean of 10.60 percentage points)? The t-statistic of 5.74 for testing that the true difference between these mean discounts is 0 is significant at the 1 percent level; the question remains how currency denomination can explain these striking differences. Would shifting the trading basis of the four funds to U.S. dollars, together with suitable global marketing, reduce the discount from 35 percent toward 15 percent?

Two Strikes against Operating in the Currency of a Financially Small Country

If the currency of a financially small country is to serve anyone in terms of welfare, it would have to be the citizens of its own country. However, this fails to happen in emerging market countries, where currency crises, asset-price deflations, and financial and economic meltdowns tend to coincide. One of the greatest current failures of the international financial institutions and of the G7 is their failure to recognise the needless pain and suffering caused by small countries hanging on to a separate currency that is being eroded by market forces and to recommend multilateral alternatives.

This point requires some detail before relevant evidence is introduced. Reacting to three major financial crises in emerging markets since mid 1997, in May 1999 the IMF and the World Bank launched the Financial Sector Assessment Program (FSAP). The programme received a strong endorsement in the report of the G7 finance ministers and central bank governors, 'Strengthening the International Financial System and the Multilateral Development Banks', issued in Rome on 7 July 2001 (see Appendix I). One of the three components that make up the FSAP (see Hilbers 2001) is an assessment of the financial system, including macroeconomic factors, that could affect the performance of the system and conditions in the system that may influence the macroeconomy. This component relates most directly to the Financial System Stability Assessment (FSSA) of individual countries. This assessment is used as part of the annual Article IV consultations held by the IMF with its member countries to review their macroeconomic and exchange rate policies. The FSSA is designed to identify macroeconomic vulnerabilities in which 'macroeconomic indicators associated with financial system soundness (such as volatility in exchange rates and interest rates)' play a part (p. 3). This parenthetical mention of exchange rate volatility appears to refer to a stressful atmospheric condition that requires adjustment rather than to a form of trouble that can be avoided by replacing the local currency fully, and not just in part, with a strong international currency as market forces increasingly demand. The G7 statement issued in Rome similarly promises stepped up efforts 'to reduce volatility and improve the functioning of the international monetary system' (see Appendix I, paragraph 7) without ever hinting that, for many emerging countries, getting rid of their troublesome own currency would contribute importantly to both goals.

In fact, the real interest and exchange rates of financially small countries in a region that retains their own currencies tend to be tossed about like corks in a stormy sea, except that, for real exchange rates, the normal sea level may not be stationary. Tables 7.1 and 7.2 provide the evidence. The statistics shown are sample standard deviations (SSDs) of real interest rates and rates of change in real exchange rates for consumers (indicated by the consumer price index) and producers (indicated by the producer price index). Both tables are organised so that the first two panels in each allow inter-period comparisons and the last two can be used to compare results obtained with alternative data constructs for the entire sample periods. Those periods are from 1978 to 1999 for the year-to-year rate of change in real exchange rates and from 1978 to 1998 for the real interest rate during each year. 'Real' or inflation-adjusted data are constructed with both the consumer price index (CPI) and the producer price index (PPI) but reported for sub-periods only with use of the CPI to avoid clutter.

Table 7.1 shows the SSD of the year-over-year rate of change in the real exchange rates of Canada, Mexico, the United States, and Japan with the U.S. dollar, the Deutschmark (for continental western Europe), and the yen (for parts of Southeast Asia). The last column adds the SSD of the crudely trade-weighted average of these three rates of change, only two of which apply to the United States and Japan. Four major points emerge, as follows.

The SSD of changes in real exchange rates of a country such as Canada (that is, at a similar level of financial development as the region's leader) is two to four times as large as that of key countries in regions other than that of the key country in the same region. For instance, Canada's full-period CPI-based SSD is 4.5 percent with U.S. dollars, compared with 12.6 percent with the Deutschmark and 14.1 percent with yen. The last two percentages are similar to the SSD for U.S. real exchange-rate changes with the Deutschmark and yen. The difference for Mexico is far less pronounced — 18.4 percent with the U.S. dollar compared with 26.5 percent for Deutschmark and 25.2 percent with yen. Nevertheless, there is clearly a regional competition and cohesion effect that keep real exchange rates closer together within the same region than across regions even when exchange rates float between all the countries involved in the comparison.

The SSD of the change in Mexico's real exchange rate with the U.S. dollar and on weighted average is three to five times as great as that of Canada. For instance, using the PPI, for the full period, the SSD of Canada is 3.3 percent with U.S. dollar and 3.5 percent on weighted average including an 80 percent weight on U.S. dollar. The corresponding figures for Mexico are 17.0 and 17.7 percent, according to the last panel of Table 7.1. Hence financially small developing countries exhibit much greater variability in their rates of change in real exchange rates than advanced countries in the same region.

Table 7.1   **Sample Standard Deviation of the Annual Rate of Change in the Real Exchange Rate of Selected Countries Using the Consumer Price Index or the Producer Price Index, 1978–99 and Sub-periods**

	With U.S. dollar	With Deutschmark	With yen	Weighted
1. 1978–1987 Consumer Price Index				
Canadian dollar	0.0380	0.1546	0.1691	0.0445
Mexican peso	0.2098	0.3083	0.3005	0.2183
U.S. dollar	0.0	0.1588	0.1682	0.1555
Japanese yen	0.1407	0.1026	0.0	0.1023
2. 1988–1999 Consumer Price Index				
Canadian dollar	0.0515	0.1037	0.1182	0.0555
Mexican peso	0.1609	0.2272	0.2018	0.1689
U.S. dollar	0.0	0.0834	0.0996	0.0723
Japanese yen	0.1034	0.1121	0.0	0.0987
3. 1978–1999 Consumer Price Index				
Canadian dollar	0.0448	0.1261	0.1408	0.0496
Mexican peso	0.1844	0.2646	0.2521	0.1928
U.S. dollar	0.0	0.1204	0.1328	0.1151
Japanese yen	0.1192	0.1060	0.0	0.0986
4. 1978–1999 Producer Price Index				
Canadian dollar	0.0326	0.1161	0.1071	0.0354
Mexican peso	0.1703	0.2506	0.2127	0.1774
U.S. dollar	0.0	0.1177	0.1086	0.1021
Japanese yen	0.0988	0.0952	0.0	0.0808

Note: Bilateral real average annual exchange rate indexes were constructed from the relevant bilateral exchange rates obtained, directly or through cross rates, from line rf or rh of the International Monetary Fund's monthly publication, *International Financial Statistics* (IFS), using either the consumer price index (IFS line 64) or the producer price index (IFS line 63) ratios for the two countries as noted. The information reported here is the sample standard deviation of the ratio of successive year-average values of the respective bilateral real exchange rate indexes from a mean ratio close to 1. If real exchange rates are nonstationary, it is the standard deviation of step-ahead proportional innovations in their random walk. The sample standard deviation of the weighted exchange rates is obtained for both Canada and Mexico by weighting the bilateral real exchange rate with the U.S. dollar, Europe (Deutschmark), and Southeast Asia (yen) by 80 percent, 10 percent, and 10 percent, respectively, before calculating the standard deviation of this weighted average of three bilateral real exchange rates. For the U.S. and Japan, equal weights are given to the respective two bilateral real exchange rates remaining for them in the present scheme.

Table 7.2 **Sample Standard Deviation of the Gross Annual Average Money-Market Real Interest Rate of Selected Countries Using the Consumer Price Index or the Producer Price Index, 1978–98 and Sub-periods**

	Own	US$/ U.S. investor	Deutschmark/ German investor	Yen/ Japanese investor
1. 1978–1987 Consumer Price Index				
Canadian dollar	0.0260	0.1759	0.2930	0.1690
Mexican peso	0.0458	0.2234	0.3268	0.3056
U.S. dollar	0.0322	0.0322	0.1801	0.1833
Japanese yen	0.0173	0.1857	0.1556	0.0173
2. 1988–1998 Consumer Price Index				
Canadian dollar	0.0158	0.0656	0.1235	0.1406
Mexican peso	0.0678	0.2126	0.2988	0.2819
U.S. dollar	0.0122	0.0122	0.0962	0.1092
Japanese yen	0.0173	0.1047	0.1014	0.0173
3. 1978–1998 Consumer Price Index				
Canadian dollar	0.0211	0.1270	0.2153	0.1521
Mexican peso	0.1037	0.2464	0.3302	0.3209
U.S. dollar	0.0268	0.0268	0.1355	0.1444
Japanese yen	0.0185	0.1496	0.1299	0.0185
4. 1978–1998 Price Price Index				
Canadian dollar	0.0400	0.1282	0.2083	0.1426
Mexican peso	0.1104	0.2477	0.3298	0.3143
U.S. dollar	0.0389	0.0389	0.1318	0.1312
Japanese yen	0.0419	0.1560	0.1301	0.0419

Note: Gross short-term interest rates during each year t, $1+i_t$, with i from the International Monetary Fund's monthly publication, *International Financial Statistics* (IFS), line 60b (federal funds rate) where available and line 60c (treasury bill rate) otherwise, were deflated by price indexes centred at year-ends by taking a geometric average of the price indexes (P) reported for adjoining years. Dividing the gross rate of return in local currency by $(P_{t+1}P_t)^{0.5}/(P_tP_{t-1})^{0.5}$ is equivalent to multiplying by $(P_{t-1}/P_{t+1})^{0.5}$ to obtain $1+r_t$, the real gross rate of return on local currency for investors in their own country. To obtain the equivalent rate for foreign investors, U.S., German, or Japanese, going with their currency into and out of local-currency investments, $(1+i_t)(x_t/x_{t-1})$ is constructed first, where x is the year-end foreign currency price of a unit of local currency from IFS line ae or ag. This result is then multiplied by $(P^*_{t-1}/P^*_{t+1})^{0.5}$ to convert to a real gross rate of return for the foreign investors temporarily investing their currency uncovered in the local market but consuming at home at price level P*. The sample standard deviation of the resulting gross real rates of return here reported is, of course, the same as that of the corresponding net real rates; their distribution is assumed to be stationary.

A comparison of the weighted-average results in the last column of panels 1 and 2 shows that from 1978–1987 to 1988–1999 there was a marked reduction in SSD for Mexico and the United States and a small increase for Canada, with the situation of Japan essentially unchanged.

Because the PPI is more weighted toward tradable goods than the CPI, SSD tends to be appreciably lower for real exchange rates constructed with the PPI than with the CPI.

Table 7.2 shows results that are similar to those in the first two bullets above and quite different for the last two bullets.

Real interest-rate variability is far less for consumers investing and using their own currency in the local economy than for foreigners making uncovered investments in local currency instruments in the local money market hoping to gain purchasing power in the foreign market from which they invest. For instance, a comparison of the entries in the 'Own' column with those in subsequent columns of the third panel shows that adding the exchange risk increases the SSD of the real returns in a country by a factor of between 2 and 10, and less for investors in the same region than across regions. Hence, the regional competition and cohesion effect noted above is evident here also. Developing countries presumably pay for the lower real interest variability on borrowing in their own minor currency at home by accepting a higher average expected real interest rate in that currency compared with borrowing in a major international currency.

The SSD of real interest rates offered by Mexico to its own residents and to foreign investors planning to consume elsewhere is appreciably greater than for rates offered by Canada. Hence, as for changes in real exchange rates, the stability of real returns offered by financially small countries is considerably less than that of highly advanced countries in the same region. For instance, U.S. investors in Mexico face an SSD of 24.6 percentage points if they invest their dollars temporarily in Mexican pesos compared with 12.7 percentage points if temporarily invested in Canadian dollars. Furthermore, Mexicans investing in their own currency have experienced an SSD of 10.4 percentage points compared with 2.1 percentage points for Canadians investing and consuming in Canada (panel 3).

The inter-period comparison offered by the first two panels shows that real interest variability in Canada for both Canadians and roundtrip foreign investors in Canada has fallen dramatically from 1978–1987 to 1988–1999, as the level and variability of inflation in Canada have declined. However, the same cannot be claimed for Mexico during the most recent of the two periods, which was one of economic and financial opening.

Unlike with the rates of change in PPI-based versus CPI-based real exchange rates, the SSD of producer 'Own' real interest rates tends to be significantly greater than of the corresponding consumer interest rates.

Although a comparison of the SSD values shown in Tables 7.1 and 7.2 is revealing in some respects, it leaves out other relevant differences. For instance, variations in producer real interest rates may be especially important for business profits, business investment, asset valuation, the quality of bank claims, and, for all these reasons, the level of general economic activity. In financially small developing countries, real interest rates tend to be driven up by crises, while in advanced countries real interest rates may fall to counter adverse shocks. Consequently, in the former group of countries, real interest rate variability is not only high but also destabilising, while it is both low and potentially stabilising for economic activity in the latter.

Furthermore, nudging the short-term real interest rate down (–), thereby inducing the currency to depreciate (+) gently, may be possible for Canada when a stimulus is needed. However, the frequently abrupt real depreciations (+) in developing countries force real interest rates (+) up concomitantly, changing the direction of causation and the sign of the correlation between the two variables. By contrast, if there is a currency depreciation that is larger than desired in Canada, it may be curtailed by an interest-rate hike to keep monetary conditions unchanged. Real interest rates and changes in real exchange rates should therefore show a more consistently negative correlation in Canada than in Mexico, where the correlation, at least during crises, could well be positive. The full sample weakly confirms the expected difference in pattern. For instance, the correlation of Canada's weighted-average rate of change in the real exchange rate with the change in Canada's own real interest rate is –0.41 and statistically significant at the 10 percent level in the t-distribution with 19 degrees of freedom using the PPI for deflation. The corresponding value for Mexico is essentially zero (–0.06), indicating more episodes in Mexico than in Canada of the real interest rate being pushed up by strong and unintended real depreciation.

All the other adverse results of having a Mexican peso officially floating since the crisis of December 1994, reported by Hausmann et al. (2000), now can be imagined easily. They include monetary outcomes that are pro-cyclical, with real interest rates low in expansions and high in contractions, and exchange rate flexibility that has gone with higher — not lower — instability in interest rates, as well as an absence of functional monetary sovereignty that can be used to manage the floating currency and keep it from crisis. In May 2001, the Banco de México once again lowered interest rates in a futile attempt to discourage excessive capital inflows and overappreciation of the domestic currency. If there is an Argentinean default crisis later in 2001, Mexico's interest rates inevitably will rise thereby haplessly repeating the pattern that led to the currency and financial crisis of December 1994.

Common Currency in E-Trade and E-Commerce

Because of the instability of minor currencies and their comparatively low yield in terms of network externalities, many regional and global electronic spot markets and electronic trading platforms price in U.S. dollars or, prospectively, in euros. It may be instructive to consider a simple example. Certain electronic auctions conducted in Canada are bid in U.S. dollars in order to encourage cross-border participation. One could, of course, reflect on the computer screen, second by second, what the auction price amounts to in Canadian dollars. However, little would be gained by this instant currency conversion. For instance, if the price in U.S. dollars achieved at auction is final and binding, paying with a debit or credit card on a Canadian dollar account could cost an extra 2 percent commission for the exchange conversion. Uncertainty would be added for the Canadian buyer at auction because the exchange rate would be the interbank sell rate that prevailed when the charge is processed by the bank.

Instead of putting up with this cost and uncertainty, the Canadian purchaser could, of course, have a U.S. dollar account with a Canadian bank or in the United States. But if the balance in that account must be maintained by drawing on income earned in Canadian dollars, the problem of uncertain settlement costs does not go away.

Of course, once a problem is seen to be acute, help may be on the way, though such help is never costless or foolproof. Nick Ogden (2001), chief executive officer of WorldPay, described some of the coping mechanisms available to allow buyers in different currency areas to make accurate value-for-money judgements when they are making real-time purchase decisions. Retailers set their prices in their operating currency and these prices are translated into more than 130 currencies by the use of an internet-based system that presents every shopper with a price in their own currency. (Other companies are striving for a nonmonetary Pentecost effect by having users of the internet automatically receive messages posted in one language in their respective tongue.) Consumers pay immediately online through a secure system. Their card account is debited with exactly the amount to which they agreed while retailers are credited immediately in the preferred currency at the exact price set by them. According to Ogden, more sophisticated solutions are emerging by contract with online foreign-exchange specialists. The goal is to be able to quote fixed prices readily on both sides of a foreign currency transaction for a set period of time. This would allow the seller to promote goods and services at fixed prices for foreign buyers while protecting the seller's revenues for the duration of the campaign. Of course, such quotation systems will work only if buyers are unable to engage in currency arbitrage or are prevented from all buying in the currency denomination affording the lowest price once the international price relations posted by the vendor have begun to differ markedly from those implied by the grid of current exchange rates. It thus remains tricky and potentially costly to reconcile a single global market and the desire for nominal-cost certainty with the use of a multiplicity of currencies for market making.

With digital signatures now having legal effect, validity, and enforceability in the United States (see 'Summary of Bills Pertaining to Electronic Signatures and Authentication in the 106th Congress' 2000) and in a growing list of other countries, ordering, shopping, and settling in international money anywhere in the region, indeed in the world, have become increasingly attractive. This, however, creates pressures not just to convert to such money but either to be paid in it or to have payments indexed to it. In business applications, there are even stronger pressures for currency consolidation. Transnational bidding on business that should lead to standing orders is handicapped if persistent exchange rate movements keep interfering with what subcontractors or component suppliers must ask. To avoid the disruption of continuing relationships by exchange rate movements that have eventual results for competitiveness that cannot be hedged, those who seek to be integrated into a region-wide supply chain try to control their costs, from parts to labour, in the same currency in which they must bid.

Should Small Countries Keep Nominal Exchange-Rate Flexibility?

Flexible exchange rates are often advertised as a low-cost and fast-acting compensatory mechanism for countries with nominal rigidities that are subject to either real or nominal shocks. The unspoken assumption, frequently falsified (see, for example, Buiter 1997; Hausmann et al. 2000), is that exchange rates can be counted on to move reliably so as to facilitate efficient adjustment rather than having a disturbing way of their own. Intending more than a facile critique of perfect-foresight models, Willem Buiter gives a sardonic example of the heroic deeds to be accomplished by monetary policy enabled by flexible rates against a supposedly unitary shock:

> There is assumed to be only one kind of shock, a national aggregate supply shock. The national monetary authority is assumed to observe the national supply shock immediately and perfectly. It then sets national monetary policy instantaneously and optimally to cope with this shock. The national authority knows the true structure of the economy and this structure of the economy makes certainty-equivalent strategies optimal (Buiter 1999, 50).

Some Canadian (see Laidler 1999), Chilean, and Mexican (see Schwartz and Torres 2001) economists continue to try to prove that flexible exchange rates work just fine for their countries particularly against well-defined shocks to the relative price of their natural resources. A panel of academics assembled at the IMF Institute has taken stock of the current state of the debate in this regard (see IMF 2001a). But these countries have yet to include complete U.S. dollarization or other forms of monetary union among the alternatives seriously evaluated and considered. In Mexico at least, such a union would preclude the very currency and financial crises from which some advocates of flexible rates erroneously get their asymmetric 'supply shock' observations.

As Guillermo Calvo and Carmen Reinhart (2000) have explained, in many countries there is deep and cogent doubt that floating exchange rates have in fact tended to facilitate adjustment in the goods and factor markets. Small open economies in emerging economies rarely find that when things start to go badly — usually because there is an international-portfolio or private capital-account shock — exchange rate movements quickly reverse the tide and let conditions improve again. Instead, currency crises commonly make things much worse before they start getting better, and, contrary to once popular belief, flexible exchange rates do not preclude such crises.

Even when real exchange rates move in textbook fashion to accommodate the needs of trade balance and national expenditure adjustment, some of the other tacit assumptions that make such movement unequivocally beneficial are less and less likely to be satisfied. One such assumption is that countries are internally homogeneous but internationally heterogeneous in their production structure and shock exposure. Likewise, factor mobility, particularly that of labour, often is assumed to be internally high and internationally low. Mexico's adjustment to the 1999–2000 increase in the price of crude oil shows what can be wrong with these assumptions. The oil price increase and the effect on Mexico's federal budget and current account may have encouraged increased private capital inflows that contributed to an appreciation of the Mexican peso in both nominal and real terms. But only small additional amounts of capital and labour have been attracted to oil and gas exploration and development under the auspices of Petróleos Mexicanos while the real appreciation has slowed the development of the non-oil sector in the country at large.

If small countries were indeed internally homogenous and externally heterogeneous so that they had a specialised nationally integrated production structure for final goods, shocks both to domestic supply conditions and to (mostly) foreign demand for the small country's specialised output could in theory be cushioned and adjustment could be speeded by movement in nominal and real exchange rates. But for many small open economies, this picture of the production structure bears little relation to the reality they confront in a regionalising — and, to a lesser extent, globalising — economic system. Becoming a component part of international, most particularly regional, supply chains means that anything that disrupts this chain from the side of either demand or supply anywhere will be felt everywhere else in the region.

By the same token, if many countries in the region share in the production of final goods, such as automobiles or electronic appliances, through the production or assembly of parts, any shock to aggregate demand for the final good will also affect all who contribute to its supply. Under these conditions, exchange rate movements among the partners in the region cannot be part of efficient adjustment. Hence, in an economically interlocking world little remains of the classical case for flexible exchange rates. Once countries are firmly committed to low inflation and do not cherish the freedom to engage in inflationary experiments, they will benefit further by irrevocably relinquishing the option to change their exchange rate with their hard-currency neighbours. Indeed, currency union would enhance the regional integration process by markedly raising trade and GDP within the union (Frankel and Rose 2000). Even if a common currency 'only' doubles, rather than triples, trade among those who have started to share it, as Volker Nitsch (2001) has claimed, a dense web of intra-industry relations is facilitated by a common currency. The allocation of investment by countries is likely to be more efficient if hedging against exchange rate movements within the region is not a consideration. Robert Devlin et al. (2000, 17) undertook a painstaking review of the literature that generally found no or only moderately adverse effects of exchange rate instability on trade; they emphasised that creating a financially integrated currency union is not at all identical to a simple reduction of exchange rate volatility to zero between the respective countries. It is much more comprehensive and powerful in its integrative effect.

Is a Currency Board Arrangement Sufficient for Currency Consolidation?

A number of business and banking groups seeking some form of monetary union with the United States, for instance in Mexico, recently have come out in favour of a currency board arrangement (CBA) because they view such an arrangement as more acceptable politically than complete dollarization. This section generally argues that currency boards may, or may not, advance the objective of monetary union. All depends on how appropriate the choice of the peg is to the CBA's trade and finance and what better alternatives are available in its economic neighbourhood.

In theory, currency boards have a fixed reserve ratio against high-powered money and a fixed exchange rate with something 'hard' in common with the gold standard. Yet while there were rules of the classical gold standard that were sufficiently widely observed to make the standard credible and speculation generally stabilising (Eichengreen 1994, 43), CBAs now make their own rules. For instance, the CBAs in Argentina and Hong Kong have very little in common in the way they operate, the extent to which they are backed by reserves and constrained by their particular status, and the fluctuations they have experienced in their credibility. As described in John Dodsworth and Dubravko Mihaljek (1997) for instance, there is little that is classical or ruled out in the operation of Hong Kong's currency board since its re-establishment in 1983. Indeed, some of its defences against speculative attack, such as using more than 10 percent of its foreign exchange reserves in August 1998 to discourage short selling by buying shares in the local stock market, have been unprecedented.

Apart from each CBA being *sui generis* and thus in need of detailed individual assessment, there is also the question of the choice of currency peg that is appropriate for each. It is not true that any of the major hard currencies will do equally well for all, and some countries are simply out of reach of any commendable CBA for lack of any hard-currency neighbours in the surrounding economic region. For instance, Hong Kong, Argentina, and Lithuania, all with a U.S. dollar–based currency board, are surrounded (or will be surrounded when the renminbi starts to float against the U.S. dollar) by countries that have real exchange rates that may develop very differently. Because these countries are unduly exposed to foreign-induced misalignment of their trade-weighted exchange rate, the rationale for sticking with their CBA can become doubtful. When such a misalignment becomes acute, as between Argentina and Brazil in the aftermath of Brazil's currency crisis of January 1999 and again in the spring and summer of 2001, risk premiums surge. They may feed on themselves by placing the benefits of maintaining the CBA further in doubt.

CBAs that peg unnaturally to a currency from outside their major trading region are prone to stress. Singapore's switch from a sterling-based currency board in 1967 to the U.S. dollar, although precipitated by the desire to disassociate from the pound's devaluation from US$2.8 to US$2.4, was appropriate to its trade and finance as well. Singapore broadened its exchange rate reference further a few years later when it made the transition to managed floating. By contrast, Lithuania's perverse insistence on maintaining a dollar-based currency board in what is rapidly becoming a sea of euros has been costly. Real GDP fell by more than 4 percent in 1999, and little or no growth has been reported for 2000 as the strength of the dollar against the euro persisted during the year.

Thus although CBAs incorporate a strong policy commitment to fixed exchange rates that is backed up by a high level of international reserves, this commitment may still not be sustainable politically when it is perceived to be harmful to the economy and to its secure integration in the region. 'The attempt to defend the currency may simply cause a meltdown of investment and output, causing corporate bankruptcies and a debt crisis all the same. That is yet another reason to cry for today's Argentina' (Velasco 2001, 24).

Only currency boards linked to the respective key currency within economically and financially heavily integrated and interdependent regions are likely to provide adequate insurance against disruptive changes in real exchange rates with their main trading partner or partners. U.S. dollar–based CBAs with Mexico and Central American and Caribbean countries, and euro-based CBAs in Eastern European countries thus could qualify as useful precursors to more complete and less reversible forms of currency consolidation. Currency boards established in distant outposts far away from the 'peg' country and its currency area, however, represent false starts from the point of view of currency consolidation: they are likely to lead to floating or, eventually, to a monetary union not based on a major international currency in the respective region.

Even a currency board with the dominant currency next door may not survive for long when its financial system is exposed to direct competition from its vastly more experienced neighbour. The strength of trade and finance relations, say, of countries in the vicinity of the United States or of Euroland, makes the almost complete financial integration and interest rate convergence that is available upon formally adopting the U.S. dollar or euro more attractive than staying in the half-way house of a currency board. Hence if currency consolidation is to be allowed, some form of monetary union is the way to achieve it. Whether that union should take the form of unilateral dollarization or of multilateral and co-managed monetary union as in Euroland is another important matter meriting detailed analysis already started elsewhere (von Furstenberg 2000a, 2000b).

Conclusion

Due in part to the liberalisation of international capital flows and, to a lesser extent, of trade in financial services, small open economies now make much more use of foreign money, especially the dominant currency of their region, than international trade analysis and past measures of effective exchange rates have tended to recognise. Some of the proper weighting can be estimated with techniques developed at the U.S. Federal Reserve (see von Furstenberg 2001, 323–324, for a summary and application). Technological developments have also favoured currency consolidation. The native denominations of financially small countries, in particular emerging economies, are therefore at a distinct disadvantage in both spot transactions in the electronic marketplace and in intertemporal trade and insurance. Even direct consumption insurance counsels residents of emerging economies exposed to currency crises to keep away from investing in their own currency at home lest shocks to their income be compounded by shocks to their wealth. Foreign financial institutions from the key-currency countries are the principal suppliers of financial services because conducting business transactions in the key currencies is what the market demands.

Erratic and frequently destabilising exchange rate behaviour and country risk premiums that are due, in good part, to currency risk are the downside to keeping separate currencies in small countries. Doing so is more likely to discourage and disrupt their membership in international supply chains than to promote adjustment to supply shocks. Even CBAs are unlikely to prove a highly durable substitute for the more complete forms of currency consolidation provided by regional monetary union. However, they may lead the way to such union if they are established with a peg to the currency that is most suitable for intense commercial and financial relations with neighbouring countries in the respective region.

As Bernard Hoekman and Carlos Primo Braga (1997) have pointed out, and as devastating currency crises in emerging markets demonstrate every few years, foreign exchange transactions and insurance services, together with other services, are an input to the production of most industries. Such services are directly and indirectly consumed by households. An inefficient domestic currency arrangement detracts from the efficiency that can be achieved by many types of services, including insurance, in the domestic economy. For these reasons, any failings in the monetary and exchange arrangements to which a country may cling can be very costly to the economy as a whole. If currency consolidation holds the promise of alleviating many of these failings it should be encouraged through multilateral agreements so that the deep financial infrastructure required for deep and mutually beneficial integration can be built.

Note

1　Gresham's law holds that if two kinds of money have the same denominational value but different intrinsic values, the one with higher intrinsic value will be hoarded and driven out of circulation by the other.

References

Banco de México (2000). 'Inflation Report'. July-September-October.

Buiter, Willem H. (1997). 'The Economic Case for Monetary Union in the European Union'. *Review of International Economics* vol. 5, no. 4, pp. 10–35.

Buiter, Willem H. (1999). 'Optimal Currency Areas: Why Does the Exchange Rate Regime Matter?' Sixth Royal Bank of Scotland/Scottish Economic Society Annual Lecture, 26 October. Edinburgh.

Calvo, Guillermo A. and Carmen M. Reinhart (2000). 'Fear of Floating'. NBER Working Paper No. 7993, November. <papers.nber.org/papers/W7993> (February 2002).

Claessens, Stijn, Thomas Glaessner, and Daniela Klingebiel (2000). 'Electronic Finance: Reshaping the Financial Landscape around the World'. Financial Sector Discussion Paper No. 4, World Bank, September. Washington DC. <www.worldbank.org/research/interest/ confs/upcoming/papersjuly11/E-finance.pdf> (February 2002).

Cohen, Benjamin (2000). *Life at the Top: International Currencies in the Twenty-First Century*. Essays in International Economics, No. 221. Princeton University, Princeton.

Devlin, Robert et al. (2000). 'Macroeconomic Stability, Trade, and Integration'. Paper presented at a policy forum on Macroeconomic Policy Coordination and Monetary Cooperation in Mercosur, 9 October. Rio de Janeiro.

Dodsworth, John and Dubravko Mihaljek (1997). 'Hong Kong, China: Growth, Structural Change, and Economic Stability during the Transition'. International Monetary Fund Occasional Paper No. 152. International Monetary Fund, Washington DC.

Dornbusch, Rudiger (2001). 'Fewer Monies, Better Monies'. *American Economic Review* vol. 91, no. 2, pp. 238–242.

Doyle, Brian M. (2000). 'Here, Dollars, Dollars...: Estimating Currency Demand and Worldwide Currency Substitution'. Board of Governors of the Federal Reserve System Discussion Paper No. 657, January.

Eichengreen, Barry J. (1994). *International Monetary Arrangements for the 21st Century*. Brookings Institution, Washington DC.

Fatás, Antonio and Andrew K. Rose (2001). 'Do Monetary Handcuffs Restrain Lefiathan? Fiscal Policy in Extreme Exchange Rate Regimes'. Discussion Paper No. 2692. Centre for Economic Policy Research.

Fischer, Stanley (2001). 'Exchange Rate Regimes: Is the Bipolar View Correct?' *Journal of Economic Perspectives* vol. 15, no. 2, pp. 3–24.

Frankel, Jeffrey A. and Andrew K. Rose (2000). 'Estimating the Effect of Currency Unions on Trade and Output'. NBER Working Paper No. W7857, August. <papers.nber.org/papers/ w7857> (February 2002).

Friedman, Milton and Robert A. Mundell (2001). 'One World, One Money?' *Policy Options* vol. 22, no. 4, pp. 10–30.

Hausmann, Ricardo, Michael Gavin, Carmen Pagés-Serra, et al. (2000). 'Financial Turmoil and the Choice of Exchange Rate Regime'. In E. Fernández-Arias and R. Hausmann, eds., *Wanted: World Financial Stability*, pp. 131–164. Inter-American Development Bank, Washington DC.

Hilbers, Paul (2001). 'The IMF/World Bank Financial Assessment Program'. *Economic Perspectives*. February. <www.imf.org/external/np/vc/2001/022301.htm> (February 2002).

Hoekman, Bernard and Carlos Primo Braga (1997). 'Protection and Trade in Services: A Survey'. Discussion Paper No. 1705. Centre for Economic Policy Research.

International Association of Insurance Supervisors (1997). 'Guidance on Insurance Regulation and Supervision for Emerging Market Economies'. <www.iaisweb.org/framesets/pas.html> (February 2002).

International Monetary Fund (1999). 'International Capital Markets: Developments, Prospects, and Key Policy Issues'. <www.imf.org/external/pubs/ft/icm/1999/index.htm> (February 2002).

International Monetary Fund (2000). 'International Capital Markets: Developments, Prospects, and Key Policy Issues'. <www.imf.org/external/pubs/ft/icm/2000/01/eng/index.htm> (February 2002).

International Monetary Fund (2001a). 'Country-Specific Needs Still Dictate Choice of Exchange Rate Regime, Panelists Find'. *IMF Survey* 16 April, pp. 123–126. <www.imf.org/external/pubs/ft/survey/2001/041601.pdf> (February 2002).

International Monetary Fund (2001b). 'Discussants Weigh Impact of Foreign Participation in Financial Systems of Developing Countries'. *IMF Survey* 21 May, pp. 173–174. <www.imf.org/external/pubs/ft/survey/2001/052101.pdf> (February 2002).

International Monetary Fund (2001c). 'Mundell Calls for a Closer Monetary Union as Step toward Single World Currency'. *IMF Survey* 5 March, p. 75. <www.imf.org/external/pubs/ft/survey/2001/030501.pdf> (February 2002).

Köhler, Horst (2001). 'New Challenges for Exchange Rate Policy'. Remarks at the Asia-Europe Meeting of Finance Ministers, 13 January. <www.imf.org/external/np/speeches/2001/011301.htm> (February 2002).

Laidler, D. (1999). 'What Do the Fixers Want to Fix? The Debate about Canada's Exchange Rate Regime'. C.D. Howe Institute.

Lewis, Karen V. (1999). 'Trying to Explain Home Bias in Equities and Consumption'. *Journal of Economic Literature* vol. 37, no. 2, pp. 571–608.

Mundell, Robert A. (2000). 'Exchange Rate Arrangements in Central and Eastern Europe'. In S. Arndt, H. Handler and D. Salvatore, eds., *Eastern Enlargement: The Sooner, the Better?*, pp. 158–165. Austrian Ministry for Economic Affairs and Labour, Vienna.

Nitsch, Volker (2001). 'Honey, I Shrank the Currency Union Effect on Trade'. Draft dated 7 May. Bankgesellschaft Berlin, Germany.

Nuti, Domenico M. (2000). 'The Costs and Benefits of Euro-Isolation in Central-Eastern Europe Before and Instead of EMU Membership'. In S. Arndt, H. Handler and D. Salvatore, eds., *Eastern Enlargement: The Sooner, the Better?*, pp. 171–194. Austrian Ministry for Economic Affairs and Labour, Vienna.

Ogden, Nick (2001). 'Cross Border Security'. *World Finance* spring, pp. 38–39.

Plender, John (2001). 'The Limits of Ingenuity'. *Financial Times*, 17 May, p. 12.

Rogoff, Kenneth (2001). 'Why Not a Global Currency?' *American Economic Review* vol. 91, no. 2, pp. 243–247.

Schwartz, M. J. and A. Torres (2001). 'Long-Term Viability of a Flexible Exchange Rate Regime in Mexico'. Paper prepared at the Banco de México, January.

'Summary of Bills Pertaining to Electronic Signatures and Authentication in the 106th Congress' (2000). *Tech Law Journal* <techlawjournal.com/cong106/digsig/Default.htm> (February 2002).

Tao, Dong and Joseph Lau (1998). 'Dollarisation: An Emergency Exit for Hong Kong?' *Asian Economic Perspective*. Credit Suisse/First Boston. August.

Velasco, A. (2001). 'The Impossible Duo? Globlization and Monetary Independence in Emerging Markets'. Paper prepared for the Brookings Trade Forum, 10–11 May, rev. 20 May. Washington DC.

von Furstenberg, George M. (2000a). 'The Case against U.S. Dollarization'. *Challenge* vol. 43, no. 4, pp. 108–120.

von Furstenberg, George M. (2000b). 'U.S.-Dollarization in Latin America: A Second-Best Monetary Union for Overcoming Regional Currency Risk'. *Economia, Societá, e Istituzioni* vol. 12, no. 3, pp. 281–317.

von Furstenberg, George M. (2001). 'Pressures for Currency Consolidation in Insurance and Finance: Are the Currencies of Financially Small Countries on the Endangered List?' *Journal for Policy Modeling* vol. 23, pp. 321–331.

Chapter 8

International Standards, Crisis Management, and Lenders of Last Resort in the International Financial Architecture

Michele Fratianni and John C. Pattison[1]

The concept of lender of last resort (LOLR) is integrally related to minimum international standards, crisis management, and other facilities in the international financial architecture. In domestic banking, it has a long history and is rooted in the works by Walter Bagehot (1873) and Henry Thornton (1802). Typically, the domestic LOLR provider is a monetary authority that can either create a monetary base or has access to it. Domestic LOLR activity should be distinguished from crisis management (Goodhart 1999; Capie and Wood 1999). The Federal Reserve Bank of New York was a crisis manager in the case of Long-Term Capital Management, but not a domestic LOLR provider. Private lenders provided emergency financing to the hedge fund. There are many other examples.

This chapter focusses on two related international financial activities: emergency official lending and financial crisis management, and their link with financial standards. Lending and crisis management both aim at restoring foreign currency liquidity in a country under stress. This shall be called the first international LOLR. Some authors claim that international LOLR services can only be provided by an institution that can create a monetary base at the world level. Since no international organisation has such powers, it follows that there is no international LOLR (Capie 1998; Capie and Wood 1999). Goodhart (1999), on the other hand, believes that the LOLR function is strictly connected to the ability to sustain financial losses. In this sense, the International Monetary Fund (IMF) is less restricted than national central banks in providing LOLR. The IMF has more capital than any national central bank and its credits enjoy senior ranking. The IMF has reported few losses on its loans in the past. Yet, it faces a critical weakness as a provider of international LOLR: it has no world government to stand behind it. National central banks, however, have national governments that make good on their commitments. While governments have committed to a regime of burden sharing by advancing funds to the IMF (and other multilateral lending institutions), there is no prospect for an open-ended pre-commitment.[2] Similar considerations hold for the European Monetary Union (EMU), where the centralisation of monetary control in the hands of the European Central Bank contrasts with the decentralisation of fiscal responsibilities.

Pessimistic assessments of international LOLR have been voiced by Barry Eichengreen (1999) and Kenneth Rogoff (1999), among others. Yet, substantive amounts of official emergency lending occur. According to Stanley Fischer (1999), the IMF has already evolved into an international LOLR provider, at least since the 1995 Mexican rescue. This role has been enhanced by contingent credit lines (CCLs), which can be used by borrowers under specific circumstances. Reflecting these trends, the Meltzer Commission recommended a slimmer IMF that would concentrate primarily on liquidity crises in emerging market economies (Meltzer 2000). This reformulated institution would provide funds, with some exceptions, only to solvent governments that meet specific pre-qualifications or standards.

While the bulk of attention has been directed at the role of the LOLR for governments, international financial markets and institutions may also require such services. These two issues are closely related, especially when linked by IMF stabilisation programmes. Who is to provide LOLR services to a foreign subsidiary of a bank or to a foreign branch of a bank? Who is to monitor the international interbank market and be accountable for its performance? The state of the art in this area is marred by institutional ambiguities and uncertainty.

As in the domestic case, the international LOLR should be distinguished from crisis management. For example, in 1998, the Bank for International Settlements (BIS) co-ordinated a large facility for the Banco Central do Brasil, supported by 19 central banks with a parallel facility operated by the Bank of Japan. The lending was done by central banks with the BIS acting as a crisis manager. Crisis management has the advantage of activating a large pool of funds through the participation of domestic LOLR providers; its disadvantage lies in the costs of co-ordination.

The chapter is organised into six sections. The second section reviews the practice of domestic LOLR. The third section evaluates the role of a putative international LOLR agency in a world where financial crises are sparked by inadequate levels of foreign reserves as well as by foreign debt highly skewed toward short-term maturities and by currency mismatches. The fourth section considers the institutional aspects of an international LOLR agency. In particular, the question of whether it is better to transform the IMF into an international LOLR agency must be considered, according to the suggestions of the Meltzer Commission, than to assign the role of international crisis manager to this institution. The fifth ection shifts the focus of international LOLR services from governments to international financial institutions. The last section draws conclusions.

Lender of Last Resort in a Domestic Setting

By the management of the monetary base, a central bank can alter the quantity of liquidity in the market. The central bank can also affect the composition of liquidity by lending to a specific institution and offsetting this transaction with an open-market sale of securities. There is some debate whether LOLR applies to injections of liquidity into the market or to compensated liquidity injections to specific institutions (see Goodfriend and King 1988; Capie 1998; Capie and Wood 1999; Jeanne and Wyplosz 2000; Goodhart 1999).

Bagehot (1873) recommended that in order to stem a liquidity crisis a central bank must lend freely, at a penalty rate and against good collateral. These requirements work together. The penalty rate provides a deterrent for solvent institutions to borrow from the central bank's discount window. Collateral provides evidence of solvency, as well as limiting capital losses borne by central banks that at the time were privately owned. But in today's money markets — at least in many of the industrial countries — liquidity needs are met by the interbank market where banks lend and borrow without collateral. This market tends to be 'cheaper' than borrowing at the discount window of the central bank. Thus, a critical question for LOLR provision is whether interbank markets are prone to failures. Two possible reasons of failure are imperfect information and co-ordination failures. With asymmetric information, an individual lender in the interbank market is unable to distinguish illiquid from insolvent borrowers. Another reason for failure occurs if an individual lender in uncertain markets is not sure it can be a borrower in the future; hence, the lender withdraws from placing funds in the market.

Charles Goodhart and Dirk Schoenmaker (1993, 379, see Table 3) provide evidence on domestic LOLR. They find that of a sample of 74 failing banks, 23 did not need external funding, 9 were rescued by other banks, 22 were rescued by the deposit insurance fund, 18 were rescued by government, and 2 were rescued by central banks. Goodhart (1999) interprets the results as follows:

> Unless such problems involve only a small potentiality for loss, so that the CB [central bank] can handle it on its own books, such systemic problems will nowadays require joint management and resolution by the supervisory body, the CB and the government.

Big financial crises require big pockets, which only governments have.

Bagehot (1873) emphasised that central banks should commit to abundant lending at penalty rates. Yet, the practice of domestic LOLR points to the opposite. Today's central banks are reluctant to pre-commit to open-ended LOLR, and when they do intervene many of them do not charge a penalty rate. Central banks prefer to rely on what Curzio Giannini (1999, 14–15) calls constructive ambiguity, a mixture of nonpenalty rates and conditionality imposed on the borrowing institutions. Central bankers believe they can control moral hazard more effectively though constructive ambiguity than through Bagehot rules.

Evidence on interbank markets comes from Craig Furfine (2000), who shows that the U.S. federal funds market was able to handle the flight to liquidity and quality following the 1998 Russian debt default and the Long-Term Capital Management bailout. Christian Upper and Andreas Worms (2001), using a matrix of bilateral interbank data for Germany, show that contagion can only occur if the loss rate on interbank loans exceeds 40 percent. However, these results shed no light on the international interbank market in particular.

In sum, governments are more likely to rescue financial institutions than are central banks. When central banks provide LOLR services, they prefer constructive ambiguity to Bagehot rules. The interbank market, at least the U.S. federal funds market, appears to be resilient in times of liquidity stress, but this is not sufficient to provide comfort on the international interbank market.

International Financial Crises

An international financial crisis occurs when one or more countries run out of foreign-currency liquid assets and are unable to participate in meaningful international financial transactions. Internationally, liquid assets consist of short-term assets denominated in foreign currencies that are traded in international markets without impediments or controls, such as government and corporate securities, foreign currency deposits, access to international credit[3] as well as the standing credit for implementing interest rate hedges to convert the currency of borrowings. International crises encompass both currency and banking crises. George Kaufman (1999, 13–14) provides a typology of the causes of financial crises. These can be created by:

- low liquidity, that is, a low ratio of international reserves to foreign currency liabilities;
- skewed term structure of foreign debt, that is, a high ratio of short-term foreign currency liabilities to total foreign currency liabilities; or
- currency mismatch, that is, an excess of foreign currency liabilities over foreign currency assets.[4]

The early literature on financial crises concentrated almost exclusively on currency crises driven by domestic macroeconomic policies and fundamental domestic economic conditions that were incompatible with the fixed exchange rate regime.[5] The exit of the British pound and the Italian lira from the European Monetary System (EMS) in 1992 shifted the focus to self-fulfilling speculation in order to explain the timing of currency crises. Poor fundamentals were responsible in determining what candidates were prone to speculative attack. The Mexican financial crisis of 1994 and the Asian financial crisis of 1997 raised a new concern, namely the link between financial fragility and currency crisis. In commenting on the Asian crisis, the IMF notes:

> Conventional fiscal imbalances were relatively small, and only in Thailand were significant real exchange rate misalignments evident … [With regard to] the crisis in Indonesia, Korea, and Thailand, all three shared weaknesses in financial systems, stemming from weak

regulation and supervision and (to varying degrees) a history of heavy governmental involvement in credit allocation, including through government guarantees; these were reflected in the misallocation of credit and inflated asset prices (IMF 1999, 33).

The crisis facing the IMF in Indonesia, Korea, and Thailand was quite different from most instances in which IMF provides financial support. The crisis originated mainly in deep-seated vulnerabilities in the financial and non-bank corporate sectors (p. 36).

The Russian financial crisis, on the other hand, was more complex and reflected unrealistic assessments of emerging financial markets, declining oil and commodity prices, and a reduced incentive to solve domestic structural problems.[6] The IMF (1999, 39) launched 'an anticrisis program, which attempted to lengthen the maturity structure of government debt and intensify structural reform'. Financing was made available through several programmes. None of these appeared to be classic liquidity emergencies.

Liquidity Crises

At least two of the many types of liquidity crises should be distinguished. Type 1 illiquidity stems from gridlocks in the infrastructure of the payment, clearing, and settlement mechanisms that, in turn, reduce liquidity in international and systemically important domestic financial markets. This type of illiquidity leads to the failure of solvent institutions because of their inability to settle or hedge transactions. Type 2 illiquidity relates to the lack of liquidity of individual countries, which manifests itself in inadequate levels of reserves.

The size of a country's reserves depends on its exchange rate policy. Flexible exchange rates require minimal foreign reserves; a fixed exchange rate regime requires a significant stock of reserves. If the fixed rate is not in line with fundamentals, the stock of reserves must be larger to account for swings in capital flows. If the fixed rate becomes unrelated to fundamentals, speculative attacks may force the central bank to lose most or all of its foreign reserves and ultimately abandon the peg. Under these circumstances, there would be no point for that country to obtain additional liquidity, for it would lose it in maintaining an unsustainable peg. In the case of Russia, the IMF acknowledged that 'the IMF has established that, after receiving Fund financing, the Central Bank of Russia used an approximately equivalent amount in exchange market intervention to support the rouble' (Dawson 2001).

Type 2 illiquidity crises are analogous to bank panics in domestic LOLR. There is the potential for contagion in addition to an impact on national governments. The IMF (1999, 40) recognised Brazil as an 'official' victim of contagion: 'Brazil was hit hard by contagion from the Russian crisis in August 1998 when international investors again reassessed the risk of their exposure to emerging markets.' The IMF and other lending institutions acted as international LOLRs with respect to Brazil.

Type 1 illiquidity crises have received less attention than Type 2 illiquidity crises.[7] The currency crisis literature — both of the first and second generations — has focussed almost exclusively on Type 2 illiquidity. So has the IMF as the principal sovereign lender.

Both types of illiquidity interact in the world of global financial markets. International financial institutions lend and borrow funds daily in large volumes in multiple currencies. This is the same as the process whereby hundreds of major banks, securities dealers, and, to a lesser extent, insurance companies adjust their cash and maturity positions in domestic money markets in local currencies. Type 2 illiquidity in a specific country is likely to have international ramifications through its impact on domestic and international markets, clearing, and settlement systems (that is, Type 1 illiquidity).

At the end of 1998, the IMF recognised liquidity risk, but attention remained more focussed on international asset market and trading activity than on financial fragility:

> There are likewise significant gaps in the modelling of the nexus of market, credit and liquidity risks, gaps that came into sharp focus during the Asian crises and in the aftermath of the Russian devaluation and moratorium ... in the recent turbulence, market risk itself gave rise to credit and liquidity risk (IMF 1998, 142).

Debt Structure, Moral Hazard, and the International Financial Architecture

The risk of moral hazard affects country borrowers, private lenders, and official financial agencies such as the IMF and World Bank. For Type 2 illiquidity, moral hazard is the consequence of at least three special factors. The first is the sovereign immunity of the borrowing country and its political subdivisions and agencies. Without this immunity, sovereign lending would be equivalent to large corporate credit, which is managed by strict credit-granting criteria, conditions that must be in place prior to advancing the funds, choice of law, dispute resolution mechanisms, loan covenants, insolvency and default provisions, market-clearing interest rates, and other factors. Such provisions, however, do not apply in the same way to borrowers who can avail themselves of protection in law from creditors through sovereign immunity.

The second factor is that official lending is not carried out by arm's-length lenders. Sovereign loans are granted by international financial institutions (IFIs) and central banks, on the basis of political determinants as well as financial ones to IFI members. In a domestic setting, bank regulators and supervisors are alert to the risks of non-arm's-length lending to related and affiliated parties and provide regulations for the associated risks, although this has not been an issue internationally.

The third factor is that IFIs and their members have strong preferences to avoid default. In a world of financial liberalisation, with many lenders and borrowers, defaults are legally complicated and can take many years to resolve. Hence, many policy initiatives aim at eliminating the consequences of default with the result of creating greater moral hazard.

Attempts to reduce moral hazard have focussed on altering the behaviour of borrowers by way of pre-qualification requirements and post-lending conditionality as well as pricing. The behaviour of private sector creditors is subject to other initiatives related to moral hazard, for example, bail-ins and sharing clauses on bond issues. Some policy initiatives, such as lending into arrears by IFIs, are designed in part to prevent some of the consequences of what would become a default combined with cross-default clauses in private loan agreements. But in so doing, such initiatives remove some of the discipline from decisions by borrowers, thereby increasing moral hazard.

The result is a complex web of incentives and disincentives with unintended consequences for moral hazard. Thus, debtor-creditor relationships are at the heart of the international financial architecture in a world of current and capital account liberalisation. Policy recommendations attempt to address these issues individually rather than comprehensively. There is encouragement to sovereign borrowers' moral hazard, where the threat of default is weak. IFIs do not fear default because they have a guarantee from their members, whereas private borrowers do. Consequently, the pressure exerted by lenders on their governments to provide additional official lending and bail-outs does not find an adequate counterweight. Without an expanded *ad hoc* mandate, the roles of some IFIs would have diminished markedly with the move to floating exchange rates. Moral hazard by lenders exists and is important. However, lenders lose, as they did with Russia or with some private sector borrowing losses in Asian countries.

As a result of these matters, the Meltzer Commission recommends that the IMF function as an international LOLR (Meltzer 2000, 8). In the commission's view, IMF lending would be short term, at penalty rates, and conditional on *ex ante* standards of financial soundness, 'except in unusual circumstances, where the crisis poses a threat to the global economy'. The pre-conditions would be monitored by the IMF after the loan was advanced. In a paper prepared for the Meltzer Commission, Michele Fratianni and John Pattison (2000) argue for the use of financial standards as a precondition for access to the international LOLR provision.

Manmohan Kumar, Paul Masson, and Marcus Miller (2000, 12) are critical of the Meltzer proposal because of the effect of pre-qualification in excluding countries from IMF assistance. They suggest that the implementation of the Meltzer proposals would not satisfy the incentive and moral hazard issues, and 'from the perspective of the Report, it appears that LOLR must either stand aside and leave the emerging country to its fate, or it must stand ready to give unconditional support if the crisis poses a systemic threat'. A related issue is whether countries can credibly pre-commit to policies because of political processes and time inconsistency of governments in general.

Pre-qualification, according to these three authors, does not have a mechanism to rein in moral hazard. They propose, instead, a mechanism based on effort monitoring, as implied by IMF conditionality lending. More specifically, they envision a carrot-and-a-stick approach. A country caught in a liquidity crisis, despite having implemented an adjustment policy, would qualify — as a result of this effort — for the carrot in the form of lending. A country caught in a liquidity crisis in the absence of an adjustment policy would qualify for conditionality lending.

Ex post conditionality lending is not superior to *ex ante* international LOLR pre-qualification. The weakness of the pre-qualification proposal is that the international LOLR agency may either lend too much or too little to the nonqualifiers, instigating either moral hazard or welfare losses. The weakness of conditionality lending is that the IMF may be too generous to justify the conditions of its subsequent lending. Furthermore, a country's effort is much more difficult to monitor than defined states of nature. Creative accounting can frustrate the most punctilious auditors. Changes to local bank lending practices, cronyism on the part of the government, and the quality of bank regulation and supervision may not be transparent to outside observers. Effort monitoring, in particular, can be distorted by political motivation. Finally, if effort is primarily observable through its impact on macroeconomic variables, how long will the conditionality agency wait before it concludes that no effort has been exerted? This is particularly problematic given borrowing country membership in the IMF and other political factors.

IMF conditionality has been attacked from opposite sides of the political spectrum. Critics from the left blame the IMF for prescribing a harsh medicine that falls disproportionately on the poor. For them, the cost of conditionality lending is excessively high. Critics from the right blame the IMF for lending too much and at subsidy terms. For them the cost is negative. The middle ground believes that borrowing countries are quite willing to undertake the IMF conditions: those conditions are the result of a negotiation between the borrower and the IMF and are believed to be in the self-interest of the borrower. For them the cost is very close to zero. The costs and domestic effort of conditionality are critical for the carrot-and-stick approach.

While conditionality remains the main staple of IMF lending, the IMF makes available a CCL facility that provides virtually unconditional credit to those countries (in difficulty) that have pre-qualified. James Boughton (2001, ch. 15, 47–48) recounts how IMF staff made similar proposals in the 1980s but were put aside by then Managing Director Jacques de Larosière, presumably because of moral hazard considerations.

The above discussion illustrates some of the contrasts between pre-commitment and conditionality. One objection raised against pre-commitment, noted earlier, is that governments cannot credibly commit to policies because they cannot bind future governments. On the other hand, if fully embraced by the borrowing country, conditionality implies a lowering of the cost of conditionality. In fact, many countries want the discipline of an IMF programme for domestic political reasons. Another factor is that an IMF loan might be perceived by the marketplace as signalling anticipated financial problems with potentially self-fulfilling results.

A private lender does not restrict itself either to conditions set before the loan is granted or to covenants to be monitored after the loan has been granted. Both conditions figure in well-structured loans. The challenge for the IFI is to create and implement a process that embodies desirable credit practices in the context of borrowers that have a low propensity to obey ordinary commercial law and that have lenders in a conflict of interest. It could be argued that in these two circumstances, it is all the more important to establish risk-oriented credit and monitoring standards, which these same countries would require of their commercial banks but not of their IFIs.

Currency Mismatches

Domestically, a liquidity crisis is linked to a mismatch in the maturity structure of assets and liabilities of the financial system. This includes temporary shortages of assets of maturities required to settle transactions, to hedge transactions, to realise a predictable cash value, and, in some countries, to require banks to provide a reserve of liquid government securities. The operational decision underlying domestic LOLR requires the ability to discriminate between illiquidity and insolvency. Olivier Jeanne and Charles Wyplosz (2000, 3) claim that Bagehot rules on LOLR 'provide incomplete guidance as to the optimal lending-in-last-resort policies in the modern international financial environment'. The reason for this conclusion stems from currency mismatches in banks' balance sheets. Notwithstanding that there are sometimes regulations to the contrary, as already pointed out, banks in currency-crisis countries often have an excess of foreign currency liabilities over foreign currency assets matched by an excess of domestic assets over domestic liabilities. An international financial crisis forces domestic financial institutions to exchange domestic assets for foreign assets to cover the currency mismatch. It is this transformation that renders Bagehot rules potentially inoperative.

The Jeanne-Wyplosz model underscores two main points. First, banks' solvency is tightly connected to monetary and exchange rate policy. Solvent banks can become insolvent where the domestic currency depreciates beyond a certain range, where this cannot be hedged, or where counterparties to hedges fail. Second, there are circumstances under which the international LOLR agency may be called to put up a large amount of resources, beyond the reach of existing institutions. However, the model's implications can be considered from an altogether different perspective; namely, what standards must a country follow in order to qualify for international LOLR services? This is the perspective of the Meltzer Commission. In terms of currency mismatch, this is a difficult standard to define. The requirement that a country adhere to balance-sheet hedging is overly simplified in a world of many assets, liabilities, and hedging techniques. Moreover, such a rule would neglect stock-flow issues, for example the uses that borrowed funds are put to, such as the impact on capital in generating export earnings. If complete hedging turns out to be inappropriate as a policy tool or too costly to enforce, an alternative — suggested by Kumar, Masson, and Miller (2000, 17) — would be to insure foreign-currency deposits with the provision that the loans of the international LOLR would be used 'for the exclusive purpose of operating this insurance'.

The International Context of Lending of Last Resort to Governments: Beyond Pre-Commitment and Conditionality

There is no international organisation comparable to a domestic LOLR provider. Stanley Fischer (1999) has argued that the IMF is in fact an international LOLR agency, albeit limited. The Meltzer Commission (2000) would like to transform this *de facto* role into a *de jure* one and at the same time constrain the institution to lend primarily to countries that pre-qualify in terms of adhering to specific financial standards. Kumar, Masson, and Miller (2000) criticise the Meltzer Commission's proposal on the grounds that it would not satisfy the incentive and moral hazard issues. Even within the confines of these authors' model, pre-qualification is not a fundamental flaw of international LOLR, when the alternative is *ex post* conditionality lending. However, neither alternative has optimal properties and both face operational difficulties.

IFIs must use all of the tools at their disposal, particularly because of sovereign immunity and conflict of interest issues. Pre-commitment is similar to conditions that precede the signing of a private loan, while conditionality is similar to loan covenants. Both pre-commitment and conditionality are needed, as are more conditions, such as monitoring. The IMF lends to governments on lower credit standards and without adjusting interest rates for credit risk, as distinct from the Bagehot rules.[8] The IMF lends where the private sector would not. In private lending, the practice is to conduct a credit analysis first on the borrower, then on the industry of the borrower, and finally to assess the country repayment risk. The character of the borrower, his or her honesty, and previous credit history are considered. A loan would then be contemplated in terms of the borrower's capital structure, liquid assets, alternative sources of repayment, and restrictions on the use of the funds in order to protect the lender. In terms of this last condition, covenants and restrictions such as prohibitions on certain uses of funds could be implemented. IFIs are not overly concerned with credit criteria because they do not fear their own failure as institutions; they are guaranteed and they have legal preference in repayment by borrowers.

Documentation requires a legal jurisdiction, such as England or the State of New York, where confidence is high that courts would enforce property rights. The documentation would contain a default clause specifying events that would permit the lender to cease additional loan disbursements or to demand repayment. These specifications allow time for the renegotiation or resolution of the loan and also provide a signal of repayment difficulties. If the sovereign borrower can explain why the event occurred and the lender, after consideration, finds that the event does not imperil the repayment of the loan, the default can be waived. For official international loans, many of these market-related criteria are inoperative. As Allan Meltzer notes (1999, 35), 'Russia does not have the rule of law, private property, a solvent banking system, transparent accounting, or most other requirements for a functioning market system'.[9] In sum, private banks do not make loans when the customer is obviously badly managed, but IFIs do.

IFIs, in particular the IMF, do not follow private sector practices. IMF lending, unlike private lending, is subsidised. The difference between the opportunity cost of lending and the explicit interest rate charged by the IMF, in equilibrium, is equal to the implied cost of the constraints on domestic policies imposed by the IMF on the borrowing country. There would be no IMF lending if the implied cost of the constraints on domestic policies were 'excessive'. Borrowing countries have a choice; when they accept IMF lending with conditionality and then complain about the constraints, they behave contradictorily. The essential policy points with regard to international LOLR are the lack of credit analysis and alternative incentive and disincentive effects of pre-qualification versus conditionality.

Lenders, even IFIs, must consider the possibility of default when they structure a loan. Defaults are complex events because of the large numbers of lenders, cross-default clauses — whereby the default of one loan causes a default on others — and so forth. Lenders are in different positions depending upon how they lend, that is, by way of syndicated loan, by way of international bond issue, or other types of loan facilities. Lee Buchheit (1998, 17) comments:

> A central premise of the 1980s-style debt rescheduling technique was the need to achieve 'equal treatment of creditors' — a goal that required, in practice, prolonged negotiations with the sovereign debtors followed by many months of cajoling or bludgeoning virtually every last creditor to accept the resulting financial package.

Buchheit contrasts this with what he calls the public sector bail-out technique as practised in Mexico in 1995 and in several Asian countries. Multilateral and other funds were provided to reassure investors and encourage private sector lenders to resume lending, therefore avoiding any default and subsequent claims on safety nets.

The solution to international loans under risk of default requires a legal mechanism so that contractual provisions can speed the resolution of these difficulties. The legal and financial position of a country is in limbo while debt renegotiations take place with hundreds of creditors. Furthermore, small investors and creditors cannot afford to commence litigation against sovereign borrowers. Large lenders, such as banks, will not litigate in most cases, as they want an orderly solution that will allow for future business. As Buchheit (1998, 19) puts it, 'When the sting of possible litigation is removed will issuers become more relaxed about defaulting?' Is international LOLR used as a substitute for loan rescheduling? Is it used improperly? Why does official international lending occur despite repeated evidence of the mismanagement of the borrowing economy? How many times does a country need to tap IMF funds before it is considered lending of first resort rather than of last resort? The answers to these questions suggest that both politics and legal issues have encouraged official lending as an alternative to long-term loan solutions, fostering moral hazard behaviour on the part of governments.[10] The issue of moral hazard has been brought to the front stage (Meltzer 1999, 2000; Calomiris and Meltzer 1999). Since 1985, the IMF has lent and organised rescue packages to Mexico, Thailand, Indonesia, Korea, Russia, Brazil, Turkey, and Argentina. Adam Lerrick (2001), an investment banker, comments as follows on the December 2000 loan to Argentina:

> There is a real debate as to whether Argentina is experiencing illiquidity, which is the province of the IMF, or insolvency, which is clearly beyond its mandate … The IMF maintains that a write-down of Argentina's debt is not required. But that's because it knows that a heavy subsidy on new loans from official lenders — which are 7%-10% below true market rates— will provide $1.5-$2.0 billion in each year.

On the basis of these considerations, the Meltzer Commission opted for pre-qualification instead of conditionality lending. Going further and requiring both plus additional requirements are recommended.

International LOLR Agency versus Crisis Manager

Two weaknesses prevent the IMF from becoming a true international LOLR agency. The first is that it can neither create monetary base in any key currency nor use special drawing rights (SDRs), the institution's own 'currency', to buy and sell national currencies (Capie 1998; Capie and Wood 1999). The second is that there is no deep pocket backing the liabilities of the IMF (Goodhart 1999). Nor does the existing incentive structure favour the transformation of the IMF into an international LOLR provider. Governments often use tax revenues to rescue failing banks and must account for their actions at election time. Transfers of tax revenues, actual or expected, to a foreign government or financial institution, when carried out transparently, are more politically costly than transfers to a domestic institution. Consequently, governments have few political or fiscal incentives to rescue foreign governments or financial institutions. If they must intervene to prevent domestic spillovers, they assist institutions over which they exert primary regulatory and supervisory responsibilities (von Hagen and Fratianni 1998, 165; Herring and Litan 1995, 102), and thus justify the transfer of tax revenues. In sum, the logic of national monetary sovereignty and tax revenues works against any prospective transformation of the IMF into a true international LOLR provider. On the other hand, the IMF is a hidden method for governments to lend outside of national budgetary accountabilities.

From a policy perspective, it is much more plausible for the IMF, in conjunction with the BIS, to play separate roles in international crisis management. An early account of crisis manager is described by Capie and Wood (1999, 214–215):

> The UK's 1890 Baring crisis is an excellent example of the Bank of England acting in that role ... There was a fear that if Barings failed, there would be such a run on London that Britain might be forced off the gold standard or, at the least, have to suspend it ... A hurried inspection of Barings suggested that the situation could be saved, but that £10m was needed to finance current and imminent obligations. A consortium was organized, initially with £17m of capital. By November 15, the news had leaked, and there was some switching of bills of exchange into cash. But there was no major panic and no run on London or on sterling. The impact on financial markets was small. Barings was liquidated, and refloated as a limited company with additional capital and new (but still family) management.

A recent example of international crisis management can be gleaned from the description of the 1998 financial assistance package to Brazil (IMF 1998, 15):[11]

> The terms of a $41 billion IMF-led financial assistance package for Brazil, in support of the program of adjustment and structural reform described below, were released on November 13, 1998. Of the total amount, $18.1 billion ... would be provided by the IMF in terms of a three-year Stand-By Arrangement, about $4 billion each from the World Bank and the Inter-American Development Bank, and $14.5 billion from 20 governments channeled through, or provided in collaboration with, the Bank for International Settlements (BIS). The U.S. government is the largest bilateral contributor, with a credit line of $5 billion. There is no explicit contribution from the private sector, since the Brazilian authorities believed it would be most effective to seek the voluntary participation of international banks in a rollover of credit lines once the financial package had been arranged. Initial contacts by the authorities with private banks suggest that banks will hold open their trade and interbank credit lines. The bilateral financing is not guaranteed by any collateral — something that distinguishes the package from the one arranged for Mexico in 1995, where U.S. repayment was guaranteed by oil revenues.

Another example was the $40 billion package organised by the IMF for Argentina in January 2001. Half the sum was provided by private sector lenders.

It has been argued elsewhere that the BIS has a comparative advantage as an international crisis manager (Fratianni and Pattison 2000). The BIS has a long experience in dealing with central banks and co-ordinating their financial activities. During the Bretton Woods regime, the BIS routinely arranged and co-ordinated multiparty swap agreements. Today, the BIS holds some of the central banks' reserve assets, including gold and currencies, and invests them in international bank deposits, treasury bills, and other securities. It also acts as an agent for some international loan issues and a collateral trustee for some international bond issues. The BIS also co-ordinates international loans to national central banks. Finally, and most importantly, the BIS is much more agile and less political than the IMF. Hence, it is in a position of greater independence to implement and monitor lending policies decided by the IMF.

The crisis manager would co-ordinate the international loan facility. The job description of a crisis manager would include due diligence, choice of applicable law, setting an interest rate to clear the market on a risk-adjusted basis, as well as acting as agent for the group of lending institutions co-ordinating the credit conditions of the loan, loan covenants, collateral where applicable, and monitoring. As an agent, the crisis manager would determine appropriate covenants to secure the assets, monitor conditions applying to the loan, such as any collateral, and assess the actions of the borrower to ensure agreement and compliance with loan covenants. As an interest-rate setter, the crisis manager would ask the five most important domestic LOLR providers in the world — the U.S. Federal Reserve, the European Central Bank,[12] the Bank of Japan, the Bank of England, and the Swiss National Bank — whether they would be willing to satisfy the loan request at, say, the London Interbank Offered Rate (LIBOR) plus two percentage points. If that request was not fully met at that rate, the penalty rate would then move up, say, to LIBOR plus three, and so on. While collateral is used infrequently, there are examples of it: for example, in the U.S. loan to Mexico in 1995, Mexico pledged a guarantee based upon oil revenues. With this method, lending governments could determine the cost of the subsidies that they are providing.

The penalty, or risk-adjusted market rate is in contrast with the practice of domestic LOLR reviewed above. The reason is that constructive ambiguity in an international setting is not as likely to work. In a domestic setting, the regulator or central bank can monitor and enforce conditions attached to the LOLR; in an international setting, it cannot. Thus, moral hazard must be curbed to some extent through the interest rate rather than through conditionality after the loan is already granted. To ensure that the loan would not be mispriced, the crisis managers and the international LOLR providers would invite private commercial banks to bid on part of the liquidity loan. To signal that the liquidity loan is not mispriced and yet allow a rapid response, the private quota could be set quite low, say, at 5 to 10 percent of the total loan.

The international LOLR providers would not have to take a vote to extend a credit. They would vote with their loans. An unfilled request would signify either significant concern with repayment, the mispricing of the loan or insufficient guarantees, loan covenants, or collateral, or a combination of reasons inhibiting lenders. An unfilled private quota would signify the presence of a subsidy in the loan. The participation of private lenders makes the proposal market friendly. This proposal would not find favour with sovereign borrowers used to subsidy rates and political influence to achieve financing. Many sovereign borrowers have been long-term borrowers from international financial institutions while at the same time enjoying access to international financial markets on market terms.

It has been argued that there is credit rationing such that private banks would not be willing to charge the market clearing interest rate for the credit quality involved. A counter argument is that this is why the amount required is limited to 5 percent. It is anticipated that there will be enough institutions willing to invest a small part of their assets in a portfolio of higher yielding, higher risk loans. There is ample evidence of this in bank acquisitions of high yield loans and bonds, mezzanine and bridge financings, and some banks that take much larger credit risk on small business portfolios at much higher yields.

Lending of Last Resort to Financial Institutions

While most attention on international LOLR focusses on lending to governments, the important role for domestic and international financial institutions cannot be ignored. Domestic financial institutions may be faced with various kinds of liquidity crises created by stabilisation programmes. This assumes more importance in the context of the Meltzer Commission recommendation that 'eligible member countries must permit, in a phased manner over a period of years, freedom of entry and operation for foreign financial institutions' (Meltzer 2000, 7).

For example, under what circumstances can a German bank in the United States be served by the Federal Reserve discount window, or a French bank by the Bank of England? This issue is also relevant in the European Monetary Union where the rules of access to LOLR facilities remain murky (Goodhart 2000). These questions are more difficult in the emerging market context. In a global system, especially under the conditions set by the Meltzer Commission, is there adequate recourse to a LOLR? While there is concern with the transmission of systemic risk, there is no international agreement on a framework of policies and programmes. The position seems to be that banks and financial markets pose less concern than governments.

Ambiguities and uncertainty are pervasive. One uncertainty lies between foreign bank entities and domestic banks in emerging markets; presumably, the former are subject to safety nets in their home countries. Another is between foreign bank subsidiaries and foreign bank branches. The subsidiaries are subject to safety nets in their host countries, but also have safety nets in their home countries. Branches would depend upon local banking law in the host state. Also, domestic safety nets often insure only domestic currency deposits. Another issue deals with the international LOLR provision for Type 1 illiquidity: how would such loans be made? On which security, home or host country? What central bank or bank supervisor would monitor and be accountable for performance?[13] A fourth uncertainty relates to the international interbank market, where the adjustment for short-term liquidity and maturity imbalances occur. In the latter case, for example, a bank mismatched in the nine-month period might sell six- and twelve-month deposits and buy nine-month deposits. The risk is that both liquidity and maturity mismatching for solvent institutions might require monetary policy intervention in the event of dislocations in some part of the yield curve, especially in the face of a financial crisis. Joseph Bisignano (1999, 39) notes that:

> The international interbank market might be thought of as having a 'precarious credit equilibrium', where at some point lenders may feel they hold potentially legally unenforceable claims, mistrust the quality of public information on the borrower and question the credibility of any government guarantees.

Should market volatility rise, a perfectly hedged position — for example, in foreign exchange options or government bonds — might require greater margin for the hedge, necessitating greater short-term international borrowing and liquidity. In sum, international LOLR services are just as likely to occur in international financial markets as they are in loans to sovereign countries. Yet, the debate over international LOLR accords too little of a role to Type 1 illiquidity issues and financial institutions and markets generally.

Conclusion

Bagehot's domestic LOLR rules are more difficult to apply in open and integrated economies. When applied to banking systems or national economies, solvency is not independent of monetary and exchange rate policy. Hence, the distinction between illiquidity and solvency loses significance. The extension of LOLR to the international economy runs against two limitations: the inability of any international organisation to create a monetary base and the inability of governments to pre-commit resources credibly in order to sustain the activity of the international LOLR agency.

There is no international counterpart to the domestic provider of LOLR. In this light, the recommendation of the Meltzer Commission that the IMF act as an international LOLR to countries that meet specific standards is sensible, but it is incomplete as a solution to all of the moral hazard issues. The weakness of pre-qualification is that the international LOLR agency may either lend too much to the qualifiers or too little to the nonqualifiers, creating either moral hazard or welfare losses. The alternative of IMF *ex post* conditionality lending runs the risk that this agency may be too generous relative to the conditions attached to its lending. Furthermore, country effort is much more difficult to monitor than pre-existing states of nature.

Liquidity is not well understood as an economic, policy, or analytical issue in the international financial architecture. There is a compelling need to separate LOLR into at least two categories: sovereigns and financial markets and institutions. The United Kingdom's House of Commons (1983) reported that debt crises may create a need for LOLR facilities to banks. Domestic liquidity crises could be caused by IMF recommendations and restrictive monetary policy in order to protect a fixed exchange rate. IMF policy recommendations may create precisely the domestic banking or financial crises with which classic domestic LOLR was designed to deal. Furthermore, Type 1 illiquidity crises crises need to be imbedded in the international financial architecture, rather than being dealt with on an *ad hoc* basis, often by the U.S. Federal Reserve System.

There is a need for much greater rigour in official international lending. Official loans are made with much less diligence and care than are private sector loans, notwithstanding the higher risk of sovereign debtors as well as a result of not being arm's-length loans. International agencies may well be lenders of last resort in terms of credit, as they lend on conditions markedly inferior to those of private lenders, to some extent because they do not fear their own insolvency as a result of government guarantees. These conditions distort incentives and create dependency. Greater separation of functions are recommended, as regulators' mandate for commercial financial institutions. The objective should be to separate the prudent management and monitoring of official sovereign loans from the decision to make them. The BIS could play a larger role in this segregation of duties. Another recommendation is a mandatory minimum component of private sector lending of at least 5 percent in order to ensure that pricing, loan covenants, and similar credit standards are set responsibly. This would create the prudent management of these loans, and would allow for greater accountability in the event of default.

Banking standards and adherence to the BIS core principles of banking supervision are minimum steps in domestic financial management, but they are often missing in emerging economies. These standards are very basic and well below the practices of major international financial centres. Nonetheless, they should be required, together with basic accounting principles and equitable insolvency law, as conditions for any *repeated* international financial facilities to a country. As Bisignano (1999, 36) notes, 'Many of the banking crises of recent vintage have had as a contributing factor the absence of sound corporate governance of enterprises and intermediaries, whose components include rigorous accounting, auditing and disclosure requirements and efficient prudential regulations and supervision'. These standards are not complete. There is a need for greater attention to liquidity as discussed above. There is currently little international guidance on liquidity, especially in contrast to capital requirements, while liquidity issues are at the heart of many international financial crises.

The IMF is often the creator and the assessor of some international standards, the collaborator with other IFIs on other standards, the country economic advisor, global crisis manager, co-ordinator, credit analyst, lender, and subsequent monitor for whatever international LOLR occurs. This commingling of responsibilities in one single institution is not desirable. Conflicts of interest are inherent. These wide responsibilities may be consistent with the policy goals, in which case this situation is still not desirable. The IMF should not set international standards, monitor these same standards, and enforce them in lending decisions, especially if the last remain politically determined, while simultaneously advising both sides in these transactions. It is for this reason that the BIS, as distinct from the Basle Committee on Banking Supervision that meets at the BIS, should be a crisis manager.

Notes

1 The authors thank Charles Goodhart and Allan Meltzer for their comments and suggestions.
2 Not only is burden sharing limited, but the actual disbursement of funds also requires formal approval by member governments.
3 This occurs through various sources, such as the stand-by arrangements, extended fund facilities, and supplemental reserve facilities of the IMF, *ad hoc* lending co-ordinated by the BIS, special facilities from central banks and export credit agencies, and interbank lending and 'paid-for' lines of credit provided by private banks.
4 There is some evidence that countries under international stress face rising ratios of foreign currency liabilities to foreign currency assets and short-term foreign liabilities to total foreign liabilities (Kaufman 1999, Tables 5 and 6; Jeanne and Wyplosz 2000, Figure 1). But there is also evidence of countries that, despite high and rising ratios, escape international financial crises.
5 See Olivier Jeanne (2000) for a survey of the literature on currency crises.
6 According to Charles Goodhart (1999), Russia was too nuclear to fail.
7 The BIS (2000, 39) is spearheading work in this direction and has recognised that 'the Asian crisis in 1997, and especially the turbulence in mature markets in autumn 1998, represented a watershed in market liquidity conditions in several segments of global markets'.
8 Olivier Jeanne and Jeromin Zettelmeyer (2000) quantify the direct IMF subsidy by the difference between the special drawing rights (SDR) interest rate (which is a weighted average of the yields on three-month treasury bills of the five participating currencies) and the 'rate of charge' on IMF loans. This differential is fairly small; however, it ignores the default risk. Furthermore, IMF loans have got bigger in the 1990s and the risk of default has risen. The IMF subsidy would be an upper limit of 1 percent of the borrower's gross domestic product (GDP). It should be recalled that IMF debt is senior, and defaults have been miniscule.
9 Similar considerations hold for the Asian currency crisis of 1997. On this point, Joseph Bisignano (1999, 1) notes that 'because of the deficiencies of corporate governance, transparency and less than adequate attention to supervisory oversight, the financial crisis of East Asia is to a degree a case of self-inflicted wounds'.
10 For some commentators, moral hazard is as much an issue with lenders as with borrowers. It would be difficult to explain the IMF loans to Russia and Turkey without considering the political motivation of the U.S. government.
11 This particular credit is of interest in demonstrating not only the types of interlocking credit arrangements, but also the economic context in which it arose. The IMF (1998) points out that, after getting inflation down from 2700 percent to under 3 percent, the fiscal stance was loosened and the requirement for public sector borrowing grew. The IMF pointed out that this growth was because of 'an excessively generous pension system, inflexibility of civil service employment rules, the lack of a hard budget constraint on sub-national governments, and a distorted system of indirect taxation' (p. 114). All this had been known, but Brazil was a long-term client of the IMF.

In the same report, the IMF went on to note that the Brazilian deficits made the country vulnerable to changes in investor sentiment and the resultant capital outflows. The crisis in Russia as well as the Asian crisis led to such portfolio shifts. The Brazilian government tightened fiscal policy and raised interest rates by 20 percent. Monetary policy continued to support a crawling peg declining at 7.5 percent annually against the dollar. Overnight interest rates went to 40 percent. This restrictive policy did not stop capital outflows. As a result, Brazil sought international lending support. But there was no discussion in the IMF document about the impact of the increase in domestic interest rates to 40 percent on the liquidity, solvency, and the functioning of the domestic financial system.

12 More precisely, it is the European System of Central Banks, rather than the European Central Bank, that would be asked to provide LOLR. The Maastricht Treaty does not authorise the European Central Bank to act in this capacity.

13 Some of these issues appear in policy issues of the G10 countries and of the European Monetary Union; see Claudio Borio (2000), Graeme Chaplin, Allison Emblow, and Ian Michael (2000), and Paul Decker (2000).

References

Bagehot, Walter (1873). *Lombard Street: A Description of the Money Market*. Paternoster Library, London.

Bank for International Settlements (2000). 'Market Liquidity and Stress: Selected Issues and Policy Implications'. *BIS Quarterly Review*. November.

Bisignano, Joseph (1999). 'Precarious Credit Equilibria: Reflections on the Asian Financial Crisis'. *BIS Working Papers*, no. 64. <www.bis.org/publ/work64.htm> (February 2002).

Borio, Claudio (2000). 'Market Liquidity and Stress: Selected Issues and Policy Implications'. *BIS Quarterly Review*. November. <www.bis.org/publ/r_qt0011e.pdf> (February 2002).

Boughton, James (2001). *Silent Revolution: The International Monetary Fund, 1979–1989*. International Monetary Fund, Washington DC.

Buchheit, Lee C. (1998). 'Changing Bond Documentation: The Sharing Clause'. *International Financial Law Review*. July.

Calomiris, Charles W. and Allan H. Meltzer (1999). 'Fixing the IMF'. *National Interest*, no. 56 (Summer).

Capie, Forrest M. (1998). 'Can There Be an International Lender-of-Last-Resort?' *International Finance* vol. 1, no. 2, pp. 311–325.

Capie, Forrest M. and Geoffrey E. Wood (1999). 'The IMF as an International Lender of Last Resort'. *Journal of International Banking Regulation* vol. 1, no. 3 (September).

Chaplin, Graeme, Allison Emblow, and Ian Michael (2000). 'Banking System Liquidity: Developments and Issues'. *Financial Stability Review*, no. 9 (December), pp. 93–112. <www.bankofengland.co.uk/fsr/fsr09art2.pdf> (February 2002).

Dawson, Thomas C. (2001). 'Russian Central Bank Met IMF's Goals. Letter to the Editor'. *Financial Times*, 29 March, p. 12.

Decker, Paul (2000). 'The Changing Character of Liquidity and Liquidity Risk Management: A Regulator's Perspective'. Federal Reserve Bank of Chicago, April.

Eichengreen, Barry J. (1999). *Toward a New International Financial Architecture: A Practical Post-Asia Agenda*. Institute for International Economics, Washington DC.

Fischer, Stanley (1999). 'On the Need for an International Lender of Last Resort'. Paper presented at the joint luncheon of the American Economic Association and the American Finance Association, New York, 3 January.

Fratianni, Michele and John C. Pattison (2000). *An Assessment of the Bank for International Settlements*. International Financial Institution Advisory Commission (Melzer Commission), Washington DC.

Furfine, Craig H. (2000). 'Empirical Evidence on the Need for a Lender of Last Resort'. *BIS Working Papers*, no. 88.

Giannini, Curzio (1999). *'Enemy of None but a Common Friend of All'? An International Perspective on the Lender-of-Last-Resort Function*. Princeton University Press, Princeton.

Goodfriend, Marvin and Robert G. King (1988). 'Financial Deregulation, Monetary Policy, and Central Banking'. Working paper 88-1. Federal Reserve Bank of Richmond Economic Review.

Goodhart, Charles A. E. (1999). 'Myths about the Lender of Last Resort'. Henry Thornton Lecture, City University Business School, 17 November.

Goodhart, Charles A. E. (2000). *Which Lender of Last Resort for Europe?* Central Banking Publications Limited, London.

Goodhart, Charles A. E. and Dirk Schoenmaker (1993). 'Institutional Separation between Supervisory and Monetary Agencies'. In F. Bruni, ed., *'Prudential Regulation, Supervison, and Monetary Policy', Giornale Degli Economisti E Annali Di Economia*, pp. 353–440.

Herring, Richard J. and Robert E. Litan (1995). *Financial Regulation in the Global Economy*. Brookings Institution, Washington DC.

House of Commons (United Kingdom) (1983). *International Monetary Arrangements: International Lending by Banks*. Vol. 1, Report, Treasury Civil Service Committee. Her Majesty's Stationery Office, London.

International Monetary Fund (1998). 'World Economic Outlook and International Capital Markets'. <www.imf.org/external/pubs/ft/weo/weo1298/index.htm> (February 2002).

International Monetary Fund (1999). 'IMF Annual Report 1999'. International Monetary Fund, Washington DC.

Jeanne, Olivier (2000). *Currency Crises: A Perspectives on Recent Theoretical Developments*. Special Papers in International Economics. Vol. 20, International Finance Section. Princeton University Press, Princeton.

Jeanne, Olivier and Charles Wyplosz (2000). 'The International Lender of Last Resort: How Large Is Large Enough'. Mimeo.

Jeanne, Olivier and Jeromin Zettelmeyer (2000). 'International Bailouts, Domestic Supervision, and Moral Hazard'. Mimeo.

Kaufman, George G. (1999). 'Banking and Currency Crises and Systemic Risk: A Taxonomy and Review'. Paper presented at the conference on Regulation and Stability in the Banking Sector, De Nederlandse Bank, 3–5 November. Amsterdam.

Kumar, Manmohan S., Paul R. Masson, and Marcus Miller (2000). 'Global Financial Crises: Institutions and Incentives'. IMF Working Paper No. 00/105. Washington DC. <www.imf.org/external/pubs/ft/wp/2000/wp00105.pdf> (February 2002).

Lerrick, Adam (2001). 'When Is a Haircut Not a Haircut? When the IMF Is the Barber'. *Wall Street Journal*, 23 February, p. A15.

Meltzer, Allan H. (1999). 'What's Wrong with the IMF? What Would Be Better?' In W. C. Hunter, G. G. Kaufman and T. H. Krueger, eds., *The Asian Financial Crisis: Origins, Implications, and Solutions*. Kluwer Academic Publishers, Norwell, MA.

Meltzer, Allan H. (2000). *Report of the International Financial Institutions Advisory Commission*. United States Congress, Washington DC. <www.house.gov/jec.imf/meltzer.htm> (February 2002).

Rogoff, Kenneth (1999). 'International Institutions for Reducing Global Financial Instability'. *Journal of Economic Perspectives* vol. 13, pp. 21–42.

Thornton, Henry (1802). *An Enquiry into the Nature and Effects of the Paper Credit of Great Britain*. Hatchard, London.

Upper, Christian and Andreas Worms (2001). 'Estimating Bilateral Exposures in the German Interbank Market: Is There a Danger of Contagion?' Paper presented at the Conference on Bank Structure and Competition, Federal Reserve Bank of Chicago, May. Chicago.

von Hagen, Jürgen and Michele Fratianni (1998). 'Banking Regulation with Variable Geometry'. In B. J. Eichengreen and J. Frieden, eds., *Forging an Integrated Europe*. University of Michigan Press, Ann Arbor.

PART IV
THE NEED FOR NEW DIRECTIONS

Chapter 9

Crisis Prevention and the Role of IMF Conditionality

Giorgio Gomel[1]

The issue of crisis prevention has come powerfully to the fore owing primarily to two aspects of the experience of financial distress of the late 1990s. First, the massive resort to official financing to cope with an emergency in one or more large countries and to design a rescue package raises the question of the adequacy of official reserves in globalised markets. Second, the international community is willing to shoulder the burden of intervention aimed at managing crises that, in many cases, are triggered by structural distortions or errors in economic policy, and that willingness accentuates moral hazard for debtors and creditors alike — so much so that such intervention becomes politically unacceptable. There is a risk of fuelling mismanagement by governments that resort to foreign credit and of fostering superficial evaluations of creditworthiness by the markets and intermediaries that provide finance.

Traditionally, intervention by the International Monetary Fund (IMF) in support of a country suffering from a crisis in balance of payments is accompanied by conditionality; that is, the actual disbursement of funds in successive tranches is conditional upon the country's implementing an economic programme to restore a sustainable macroeconomic equilibrium (Eichengreen 1999).

The crises of the 1990s were marked by a complexity not to be found in the experiences of the preceding decades. There was no lack of traditional macroeconomic imbalances, which tended to concentrate in the external accounts, but these were exacerbated by severe disequilibria in banking and financial systems, bankruptcies, and inefficiency in vast sectors of the corporate system, and inadequacies in the spheres of prudential controls and disclosure requirements.

Hence, the scope of conditionality had to be extended beyond macroeconomic policy to embrace microeconomic measures, the operating rules of markets, and prudential supervision. This broad scope strengthens and even gives pre-eminence to what might be called *ex ante* conditionality, namely, the set of preventive measures aimed at minimising the risk of a crisis. The strategy of prevention thus requires the involvement of a plurality of actors, with appropriate forms of co-ordination.

An overhaul of the IMF's functions has, for some time, been a prominent topic of debate among scholars and policy makers (Summers 1999; Meltzer 2000; Fischer 1999). However, the IMF's central role in supervising the international monetary and financial system and in facilitating co-operation among member countries does not appear to be in question.

The battery of intergovernmental groups working for international economic co-operation has been enhanced of late, particularly with the addition of organisations concerned with prevention. Since 1999, the G20 and the Financial Stability Forum (FSF) have been operating alongside older formations (the G7, G10, and so on). The added political value of these groups consists of the direct involvement of important emerging market countries in defining best practices and rules of conduct that, when applied at the national level, will no longer be viewed as imposed from the outside but as the fruit of common understanding. It can be argued that the ranks of countries participating in new forms of international rule making are growing.

It is now the consensus view that the adoption of disclosure standards, best practices, and codes of conduct in the economic and financial field is necessary, although certainly not sufficient, to ensure financial stability at the international level. In some areas, such as accounting and auditing standards, the private sector can play a significant role and in fact has already done so. But acknowledging that role does not imply any lessening in the importance of the function of multilateral institutions, the IMF first and foremost; only the IMF has the power to legitimate the standards drafted by private organisations and self-regulating bodies to verify that they are actually observed.

The ability of the IMF to enforce the traditional macroeconomic policy conditions on countries requesting financial assistance outstrips its capacity to enforce *ex ante* conditionality. The reasons for this are evident. Compliance with traditional macroeconomic conditions is easily verified: ordinarily, these conditions are translated into monetary, exchange rate, and fiscal policy measures destined to restore a sustainable internal and external balance. Above all, a country's determination to fulfil the conditions is strengthened by the link with the IMF's financial support.

But when a country is not under the gun of a crisis, what will prompt it to alter certain aspects of its economic policy along the lines suggested by the IMF in the course of its normal monitoring of the economies of member countries? How can one verify not so much the introduction of banking regulations, which is simple enough, but the actual application of those regulations? How can one be certain that the information made public, for example, on the balance sheets of banks and nonfinancial firms, is complete and accurate?

A greater diversity of the forms of conditionality (macroeconomic, institutional, *ex post*, and *ex ante*) and an effective system of incentives and penalties must be flanked by an appropriate configuration of the procedures for applying and checking compliance with those forms of conditionality. It is possible to envision a constellation of forces ranging from political pressure by various intergovernmental groupings to 'educational' action on the part of the central banks and supervisors, to oversight and self-regulation of the markets, all the more effective the less exposed they are to moral hazard.

The Debate on Conditionality and Its Structural Components

Conditionality is indeed at the heart of the catalytic role of IMF programmes. It is the combination of a credible adjustment programme and official financing that allows members to regain access to capital markets following a crisis and in due course reduces the need for official support. Official financing is necessary to restore market confidence but on its own would not do the job; it could even be counterproductive if it provided private investors with the necessary resources to flee for the exits, running away from the crisis-stricken country virtually unscathed. Conditionality, when designed in a credible and effective manner, is also essential to the success of the strategy devised by the international community to involve the private sector in managing sovereign financial crises. Concrete results on this matter have been lacking so far, but some progress has been made in identifying the chief ingredients of a solution, namely a combination of firm *ex ante* limits to official financing and the possibility for debtor countries to resort to standstills, namely to suspend debt-service payments if confronted with a crisis, with the approval of the international community.

If the IMF continues to be involved in both crisis prevention and crisis management, then conditionality, including so-called structural conditionality, will continue to be a necessary instrument to regain credibility and access to capital markets (IMF 2001b; Goldstein 2001). Structural conditionality is not a capricious addition to the IMF's policy toolkit, but stems from the many challenges that the organisation has been required to address since the 1980s.

For example, traditional macroeconomic conditionality was deemed to be ineffective because the exclusive focus on short-run aggregate demand management neglected the structural causes of problems with the balance of payments and resulted in excessive hardship on borrowing countries through unduly contractionary fiscal and monetary policies. The argument gained further strength in light of the IMF's increasing involvement in low-income and transitional countries where structural weaknesses were pervasive.

Aggregate demand management largely focusses on the quantity of adjustment, say, a reduction of fiscal imbalances, often at the expense of the quality of adjustment, say the long-term sustainability of public finances. Domestic and international investors, however, increasingly take a long-term view of the problem. Accordingly, they will be wary of supporting a programme that is excessively biased toward short-term, temporary measures and does not address the structural weaknesses in the economy, for instance in the fiscal or the financial sector. The IMF's catalytic role is thus likely to be severely hampered if markets agents are not convinced about the sustainability of the adjustment effort.

IMF-supported programmes have been repeatedly criticised for their failure to allow countries to graduate from IMF support. The inability to graduate from that support is often mentioned as evidence of the failure of conditionality. Structural conditionality helps address this criticism insofar as it contributes to a more permanent resolution of the factors that lie behind the balance of payments need.

In sum, long-term considerations are a critical component of IMF programmes. They are intended to ensure that members are able to address the root causes of their external payments imbalances and thus reassure markets about the long-term nature of the adjustment process. So-called structural conditions will be necessary insofar as they help achieve the objective of a sustained improvement in the balance of payments.

A brief analysis of the question of structural reforms and the core areas of IMF activities is required. Reviews conducted at the IMF indicate that structural conditionality has largely been confined to core areas and that its composition has shifted from an emphasis on trade and exchange rate liberalisation to institutional and financial sector reforms. This shift in turn reflects the increasing importance of financial sector issues in IMF programmes and the fact that early programmes have been relatively successful in achieving progress in reforming the trade and exchange rate systems. In this respect, continuing reliance on IMF support is not necessarily an indication of programme failure and addiction to official financing, but to some extent can be seen as a measure of the success of IMF programmes, with countries moving along the ladder of structural reforms.

Finally, on the concept of ownership, there is one prominent and recurring argument in the debate, namely that the increased scope of conditionality — too many and too detailed conditions — undermines programme ownership and is largely responsible for the unsatisfactory record of programme implementation. This is not a fully convincing argument. First, as the IMF has documented in some of its recent studies, the implementation rate shows no negative correlation with the extent of structural conditionality. Second, the very concept of ownership is fairly elusive. Both theory and experience show that adjustment and, even more so, structural reform create both winners and losers. Ownership is not independent of the identity of the winners and losers and the way their conflicting interests are reconciled through the political process. The creation of a broad political consensus is key to the design and conduct of sound policies. In this endeavour, structural reforms can be of help: particularly when compared to restrictive macroeconomic policy, they may alleviate the distributional tradeoffs by raising economic efficiency and strengthening growth prospects. Moreover, while individual reforms may exacerbate distributional conflicts, a broad-based reform programme may both amplify the efficiency gains and generate a sufficiently large range of winners to muster political support. Overall, therefore, there is little or no reason to argue that an ambitious programme of structural reforms would necessarily undermine programme ownership and implementation. Clearly, the programme must not be perceived as being imposed by an outside agency and the country must not delay its approach to the IMF for too long for the fear of having too many conditions imposed. In normal times, ownership can be created through a patient and gradual process that combines policy advice, technical assistance, and, ultimately, programme conditionality together with financial support. During a crisis, however, there is little time, if at all, to build political support and the need for prompt action will typically take priority over the desire to build a strong constituency in support of the programme. In such situations, structural reforms might be essential to reassure markets as to the long-term sustainability of the adjustment effort.

The Soft Law Approach[2]

In the design of reform of the international financial architecture, the predominant view has been that the process should mostly rest on recommendations, guidelines, or other arrangements of a nonbinding nature, which are internationally agreed but the implementation of which would be in essence left to national authorities, with incentives such as 'peer pressure' or 'market discipline'.

This strategy has been labelled the 'soft law approach', due to the fact that its content has neither the strength of ordinary law nor the weakness of international conventions. As Mario Giovanoli (2000, 33–34) writes:

> With a few exceptions in respect of rules embodied in proper instruments of international law (such as the Articles of Agreement of the IMF), most of the international rules, guidelines, standards and other arrangements governing cross-border financial relations are not of a legally binding nature and are therefore generally referred to as soft law. For instance, the FSF's Web site, which is the most comprehensive compendium of international standards in this field, gives the following definition:
>
>> Standards are codes, guidelines or principles that set out what are widely accepted as good practices. The widespread adoption of high-quality internationally accepted standards, or codes of good practice, can make an important contribution to effective policy-making, well-functioning financial markets and a stronger international financial system ... Adopting internationally accepted standards of financial supervision and regulation will help policy-makers implement policies that promote sound and efficient markets and enhance credibility and investor confidence. Through promoting sound policy-making and orderly and efficient markets, the *voluntary* adoption of standards of good practice will ... help to make the international financial system stronger and more stable.

The soft law approach gained momentum in the official community early in 1999, with the establishment of the FSF, which is a true novelty in the topography of international co-operation. Its mandate is to improve co-ordination and the exchange of information among the various authorities responsible for financial stability; the FSF is also entrusted with assessing the vulnerabilities affecting the international financial system and identifying and overseeing any action needed to address such vulnerabilities. Its composition is peculiar: it comprises representatives of finance ministries, central banks, and regulatory agencies of a number of countries (the G7 plus Australia, the Netherlands, Hong Kong, and Singapore), plus representatives of the international financial institutions and of the main self-regulatory groupings (such as the Basle Committee, the International Organisation of Securities Commissions, and the International Association of Insurance Supervisors).

The soft law strategy that hinges on the FSF is, in essence, a decentralised process based on informal international understandings that are to be implemented at the level of domestic jurisdictions. It has three fundamental components: standards, governance, and incentives.

Standards

The purpose of the FSF in this field is to collect, endorse, and disseminate the activity of standard-setting bodies so as to ensure speedier and fuller compliance. The FSF's first act was the compilation of the comprehensive Compendium of Standards, consisting of some 60 sets of standards relevant to international financial stability. Among these, the FSF has identified twelve sets of standards as key for sound financial systems and that therefore deserve priority implementation. These standards represent minimum requirements for good practice.

The area of standard setting, however, does not exhaust the activities of the FSF. Under the heading of vulnerability, the FSF has so far published three reports, on highly leveraged institutions, capital flows, and offshore financial centres respectively. The latter is of particular importance in this context, because it represents the first attempt of the official community to come to grips with a major gap in the present regulatory setting, namely the existence of financial centres that derive their attractiveness to investors and financial intermediaries from having lower taxes and more lax regulatory requirements. The FSF report included a tripartite list of offshore centres, with individual centres classified according to the quality of their regulatory framework.

Judging the quality of standards is no easy task, since the specificity and degree of precision of international standards varies considerably. In general, they lack the precision required for legal enforceability. Nonetheless, it is important to have countries accept rather general principles. Moreover, it may be easier to have countries adopt international standards if those standards are flexible enough to be adapted to local legal traditions. This can be seen as but one aspect of the 'legitimacy' problem.

There are three dimensions to the problem. One is eminently technical. It is awkward to establish internationally accepted norms or minimum standards given the diversity of legal systems, traditions, and regulatory setups in areas such as bank supervision, securities markets regulation, bankruptcy law, and systems of accounting and auditing. The second one is political. A sovereign state is asked to transpose into its legal practices norms and codes that emanate from forms of international co-operation in which the state may not participate at the cost, in the case of refusing to conform, of being 'punished' by the adverse appraisals and ratings in globalised markets. The third dimensions pertains to the capacity of countries, chiefly emerging market economies, to impose those norms and standards. There may be technical or operational impediments inhibiting their adoption and application.

Governance

For informal co-operation to work, the prescriptions that flow from it must first be perceived as legitimate by their recipients. This perception calls for the inclusion of a large number and variety of countries beyond the original membership limited to the most industrialised nations. However, informal processes, such as the Basle process or the soft law approach now being pursued, rely on consensus. This concern notwithstanding, some expansion in the membership of the main forums was simply inevitable to increase the chances of success of the process. Through enlarged participation, the concern that a particular group of countries wanted to impose its own standards would be mitigated. Thus, the G7 took the initiative of setting up both the FSF and the G20, a new grouping comprising, besides the G7 itself, the main emerging economies.

An appropriate set of arrangements could be as follows. Rule making should remain the responsibility primarily of the specialised self-regulatory organisations: the Basle Committee for banks, the International Organisation of Securities Commissions for securities markets, the International Association for Insurance Supervisors for the insurance industry, and the International Accounting Standards Committee for accounting standards. Effective rule enforcement should be the job of the governments that choose to incorporate the rules into their national legal systems. International institutions would also have a key role to play, particularly the IMF. It can exert strong pressure on countries if the rules and standards are embodied in specific recommendations it endorses, which would give the rules a political legitimacy now lacking insofar as they are the product of bodies made up of members restricted to the most highly developed countries. The IMF could also require that countries observe some standards as an essential element of conditionality; that is, it could link the granting of credit to action on financial structures, markets, and corporate governance. Even when no outlay of financial resources is at issue, the IMF could make the judgement of the observance of international standards part of its ordinary oversight activity. In and of themselves, such public judgements, which are the object of the observance reports already being drafted on an experimental basis, can exert effective market discipline. In the end, the financial markets would presumably punish countries that failed to observe certain minimum standards, lowering their ratings, increasing risk premiums, and hence making credit more costly.

The national supervisory authorities, finally, could supplement such action by making the IMF's judgement on effective observance of the standards a factor in determining (under the Basle Capital Accord) the capital ratios on lending to a country or in allowing access of foreign intermediaries to their own markets.

Incentives

Standards do not have a legal character, being mere recommendations of international bodies. Working through incentives is therefore crucial to ensure their adoption. In principle, there exist two different sets of incentives for countries to adopt standards: those that flow indirectly from market reactions to lack of observance, and those that result directly from the actions of the official community. In a market-led global economy with decentralised governance, one would expect the first set to provide the stronger mechanism. However, the surveys conducted by the FSF's Task Force on Implementation of Standards appeared often to be unfamiliar with many of the existing standards. Where they were familiar, they declared that other considerations, such as political risk and economic fundamentals, be placed above the regulatory/supervisory setup.

Official incentives may be grouped into two categories: peer pressure and financial incentives. Peer pressure is the traditional mechanism through which the Basle process works. More recently, a tougher attitude has prevailed in relation to countries or financial centres that do not conform to internationally accepted codes of good behaviour. Three notable examples are the creation of the Financial Action Task Force by the G7 to combat money laundering in a list of jurisdictions, graded according to their degree of willingness to co-operate with international authorities concerned about money laundering, the list of jurisdictions considered to be tax havens, published by the Organisation for Economic Co-operation and Development (OECD), and the FSF's initiative concerning offshore financial centres. These initiatives, however, are too recent to assess whether they could be sustained in the medium to long term so as to yield their intended fruits.

As to financial incentives, the most obvious is the inclusion of the observance of regulatory and supervisory standards in IMF conditionality. This is something that, to some extent, the IMF already does as described above; in fact, the most recent review conducted by the IMF staff underscores that about a quarter of structural conditions pertain to the financial system (IMF 2001a). In spite of the pressure to which the IMF has been subjected to reduce the scope and weight of structural conditionality in its programmes, this remains an effective instrument.

Notes

1 Opinions expressed are the author's and do not represent the Banca d'Italia.
2 This section draws extensively on Curzio Giannini (2001).

References

Eichengreen, Barry J. (1999). *Toward a New International Financial Architecture: A Practical Post-Asia Agenda*. Institute for International Economics, Washington DC.

Fischer, Stanley (1999). 'On the Need for an International Lender of Last Resort'. Paper presented at the joint luncheon of the American Economic Association and the American Finance Association, New York, 3 January.

Giannini, Curzio (2001). 'Broad in Scope, Soft in Method: International Cooperation and the Quest for Financial Stability in Emerging Markets'. Manuscript, Bank of Italy.

Giovanoli, Mario (2000). 'A New Architecture for the Global Financial Market: Legal Aspects of International Financial Standard Setting'. In M. Giovanoli, ed., *International Monetary Law: Issues for the New Millennium*. Oxford University Press, Oxford.

Goldstein, Morris (2001). 'IMF Structural Conditionality: How Much Is Too Much?' Working Paper No. 01-4, Institute for International Economics. <www.iie.com/catalog/WP/2001/01-4.pdf> (February 2002).

International Monetary Fund (2001a). 'Conditionality in Fund-Supported Programs — Overview'. 20 February. <www.imf.org/external/np/pdr/cond/2001/eng/overview> (February 2002).

International Monetary Fund (2001b). 'Streamlining Structural Conditionality: Review of Initial Experience'. 10 July. <www.imf.org/external/np/pdr/cond/2001/eng/collab/review.htm> (February 2002).

Meltzer, Allan H. (2000). *Report of the International Financial Institutions Advisory Commission*. United States Congress, Washington DC. <www.house.gov/jec.imf/meltzer.htm> (January 2002).

Summers, Lawrence H. (1999). 'The Right Kind of IMF for a Stable Global Financial System'. Remarks to the London School of Business, London. <www.ustreas.gov/press/releases/ps294.htm> (February 2002).

Chapter 10

On Some Unresolved Problems of Monetary Theory and Policy

Paolo Savona

When John Richard Hicks delivered the Edward Shann Lecture at Perth in February 1967, he presented a brilliant overview of the history of monetary thinking. He stated that the theory evolved and matured in close relationship with the development of monetary and financial institutions along with related events. (He coined the term 'credit structure'; see Hicks 1967.) The overview ran from the thinking of David Ricardo — whose quantitative theory presupposed a system of metal currency without a central bank — to John Maynard Keynes, who more than a century later brought economic theory in line with the reality of a system of paper and fiduciary money, and the presence of a central bank and financial speculators.

Not only did Hicks track the development of monetary theory, but he also did it in parallel with the development of real theory (as simplified in the well-known IS-LM model) and thus influenced current thinking. He reached a conclusion widely accepted today: that money is effective in combating an overheated economy, but much less effective in promoting real growth. And, in the same lecture in 1967, he gave Keynes a somewhat tardy recognition in acknowledging that growth can in fact be spurred by fiscal policies, a thesis that has today lost much of the vigour that it enjoyed in the second half of the twentieth century, at least from the spending side.

With all the respect due to this great master, it is only logical to recognise that Hicks's thinking was the product of its epoch and thus of the institutional reality of the times. Since 1967, many innovations have affected the world credit structure (in the sense that Hicks used the term): the development of the market in eurodollars in the 1960s, the decision by the United States that the dollar was no longer convertible into gold and the related switch from fixed to floating exchange rates in the 1970s, the emergence of two other international reserve currencies — the Deutschmark and the yen — in the 1980s, the globalisation of financial markets and the exponential diffusion of 'infomoney' (or e-money) and derivatives, the Asian financial crisis, the new economy, and the birth of the euro (or, if one prefers, the looming disappearance of the German mark) in the 1990s.

Despite these Copernican revolutions, monetary theory (and, as a consequence, the way in which central banks operate) has not changed. This severe lag can have very serious effects, some of which are not yet entirely foreseeable. As a result, new realities are being examined with analytical instruments that are obsolete, and these realities are being managed with antiquated and inadequate techniques.

At the conclusion of his lecture, Hicks warned of an unresolved problem hanging over the international monetary system, pointing out that the stability of credit internationally presupposed the continuous application at the global level of the measures applied domestically for monetary control.

> The remedy, my old nineteenth-century experience would tell us, would be an International Central Bank, an international bank which would underpin the credit structure, but in order to underpin it must have some control over it. That was what Keynes, who understood this international aspect very clearly, wanted to get at Bretton Woods, but all he got was a currency board (for it is little more than a currency board, being so tied up with rules and regulations) — the IMF. That, we are finding — and Mill could have told us, one hundred twenty years ago, that it is what we should find — is not enough. But how should the powers, which governments have been unwilling to entrust to their own central banks (once they have realized what is involved) be entrusted to an international bank? That is the dilemma, the old dilemma, to which we have now come back, on the international plane.
>
> Stated like that, the problem looks insoluble. In such black and white terms, it probably is. But to set rules against no rules is to make too sharp an opposition. Can we find rules that are acceptable to national pride, and to national self-interest, and which yet give scope for some minimum of management — just enough to give the international credit structure the security it so sorely needs? It will be a narrow passage, but one must hope that there will be a way through (Hicks 1967, 138–139).

Thirty-five years have passed since Hicks spoke in Perth. Yet the dilemma persists, now aggravated by dynamic new financial and global developments. This awareness opens up a very broad range of problems, but the analysis in this chapter is limited to only two aspects:
- How to reconcile globalisation with existing monetary policies and the variety of the exchange rate regimes and the predominance of floating rates; and
- How to adapt monetary theory and practice to monetary and financial developments.

Globalisation and Monetary Order

The problem of how to reconcile globalisation with monetary policies can be approached through a practical reference, given the fact that the situation on a theoretical plane is a consequence.

When the European Monetary Union was created by the Maastricht Treaty, its architects realised that it would be impossible to create a single European market if individual member nations retained 15 different currencies linked by flexible exchange rates. Since these decision makers did not feel they could clear this hurdle either by turning to fixed rates or by using a common unit of exchange (the European Currency Unit), they adopted the more extreme solution of making 15 currencies disappear with the creation of a single currency, the euro, under a unified system of national central banks and the birth of a supranational bank, the European Central Bank (ECB) in Frankfurt, which was logically, even if not physically, off-shore. Three countries — Great Britain, Denmark, and Sweden — suspended their adherence to the Maastricht Treaty while maintaining the right to join the system at a later date.

Few would object to the statement that a single market requires the existence of a single currency, or, as a second-best option, the retention of national currencies linked by fixed exchange rates and, as a fundamental prerequisite, the free movement of capital in all forms and in any sort of maturity. In the light of this consideration, the frequent admonitions from the champions of economic liberalism, the United States above all, or from international organisations such as the World Trade Organization (WTO), to respect the rules of the global market ring hollow — and will continue to ring hollow at least until the 'narrow passage' identified by Hicks can be left behind.

In fact, the proper functioning of the global market is impeded by those who oppose any kind of co-ordination of national monetary policies, given that the establishment of a world central bank is, at present, an impractical goal. Instead, they support a regime of exchange rates that, in the way it currently operates, generates values that are at variance with economic fundamentals.

In the lecture he gave when he was awarded the Nobel Prize, Robert Mundell (2000) insisted on a global solution along the lines of the one adopted by the European Union, repeating a number of his well-known convictions but, above all, making it clear that his perceptions are no different from those voiced by Hicks. Like a faithful apostle, Mundell feels the need to preach the pure orthodoxy: a single currency for everyone, and may that be the end of it.

The reasons expressed by the United States in 1971 for starting to dismantle the existing system of exchange rates are now familiar: The Bretton Woods agreement was based on a paradox, attributed to the economist Robert Triffin, whereby the dollar's convertibility into gold at a fixed price would function only if no one tried to convert dollars into gold (in other words it would not function), and the U.S. government wanted to protect itself from the effects of malgovernment (not simply monetary and fiscal mismanagement) by interrupting the transmission of those bad policies into its domestic economy.

Underlying the Nixon administration's decision to break with Bretton Woods was the premise that flexible exchange rates would adjust external imbalances more smoothly. The new system certainly resolved Triffin's paradox and it did protect the U.S. economy from contamination, but the theoretical expectations of how flexible rates would function did not materialise in practice. The imbalances tended to develop in the opposite direction from the one observers had expected.

Today, only the protective effect for the strongest currencies remains operational. But what does that really amount to? The Deutschmark has disappeared. The Japanese yen has weakened. Thus, the U.S. dollar remains (and rightly so, but that is not the problem) the only currency to benefit from flexible exchange rates, becoming the source of the malfunctioning of the credit structure in the global market.

Countries must either agree to dollarize the global market officially — a far from outlandish idea since it is in fact already dollarized — or must find a way to co-ordinate national monetary policies closely enough to simulate the situation that appears most favourable in terms of logic.

As Hicks warned, in an age less complicated than the one at present, it will be a narrow passage, but one must hope that there will be a way through.

Adapting Monetary Theory and Practice to Monetary and Financial Developments

With regard to the problem of bringing monetary theory and practice in line with the evolution of the credit structure over the past quarter century, it is useful to remember that there are two ways of analysing how well the credit structure is functioning (always using the term as Hicks used it).

The first is the analysis elaborated by Milton Friedman and Anna Schwartz (1963), which calculates monetary base in terms of the quantity of money being created. The second, re-elaborated by James Tobin (1961; 1965), examines the various items (assets and liabilities) in the balance sheets of the economy (households and firms) to identify the degree of substitution among them.

Concentrating on the first of these analytical methods, that of monetary base, research undertaken by Paolo Savona, Aurelio Maccario, and Chiara Oldani (2000) with the support of the Guido Carli Association, showed a clear relationship between the different types of derivatives contracts that are analogous to the demand for money for speculative motives. In other words, both are related to interest rates. If the theories elaborated by Keynes and successive economists still have some usefulness in clarifying the effects of the speculative demand for money on the financial mechanism (and the real one as well, although this will become more clear in the discussion of the Tobin model), it follows that derivatives are a form of money, or quasi-money, and that they should be calculated in the targets set by central banks.

This conclusion is admittedly difficult to apply in practical terms. Instead of trying to find a solution to the problem, central banks have reacted by denying that the problem exists at all. (There are some notable exceptions within the Bank of Italy.) At the practical level are two factors. The first is that, in order to reduce the opportunity cost of holding money (which comes under the category of luxury goods), the treasurers of banks and firms prefer to shift operations into derivatives, which allows them to call in money as they need it, keeping their current demand near zero. The second is the use of vast amounts of quasi-money for speculative purposes, because the operator can put up only a fraction of the total value and the trades themselves are carried out at a very low cost.

The consequence of all these operations has brought about the paradox identified by Keynes (before modern derivatives even existed), namely the paradox of liquidity: everyone feels liquid but the market itself is not. And the consequence of the paradox is that central banks, when faced by systemic crises brought on by excessive speculation, become lenders of last resort, responding on demand to the market's need for a monetary base. The example of Long-Term Capital Management in the U.S. is a textbook case.

For these and for other reasons, money, whether it can be spent immediately (that is, classified by the central banks as M1) or includes short-term assets (that is, M2), has lost its importance in current monetary management (but not in analytical models). This is at least the case for those who care to see, rather than those who deny they have seen anything at all. The existence of derivatives and of infomoney has blurred the very definition of money. Only a few central banks (among them, alas, the ECB) continue to believe that pursuing objectives based on the orthodox content of monetary targets (M1, M2, M3, etc.) can enable them to carry out their responsibility for controlling the quantity of money — a responsibility that has been placed in their care by democratic governments that, unfortunately, also seem unaware how profoundly monetary and financial realities have changed.

The New Frontiers of Monetary Theory and Policy

There is good reason to believe that Alan Greenspan's success in managing the U.S. economy — that has been his achievement — was due to his close attention to portfolio equilibrium *à la* Tobin, whether through a deliberate choice or through a pragmatic sensitivity to the moods of the domestic U.S. market.

Bank deposits have become much less attractive to savers, as have government and state bonds, because of their low yields and also because of the declining interest on the part of the issuers — a number of factors have been at work here — so that the attention of market operators has focussed on stocks and on real investments. As a result, economic theory and practice have again had to face the eternal question of how the effects of changes in the credit structure are transmitted to the real economy. The market has reproposed the question in the most simplified form possible — the choice between possessing capital directly or in its various financial expressions — but behind this simplicity a far more complicated mechanism is at work in transmitting those effects. Compared to the past, there is now a vast quantity of derivatives together with a range of options provided by information technology. Both these factors very significantly affect the rate of substitution between monetary and financial assets. Both make it much harder to decode the workings of what has been called the 'black box'.

In the light of this reality, monetary policy is now burdened with the portfolio changes among assets that influence growth and inflation, either because central bankers believe such an ambition is possible, or because governments demand it of them. In this context, derivatives, even before they became relevant as quasi-money, are important because they influence the rate of substitution among assets and liabilities, a reality that cannot leave central banks indifferent. Credit structures and central bank policies are determined to an ever-growing extent by the presence of derivatives.

Monetary authorities have already gone down in flames on the exchange markets in fighting primitive forms of derivatives. When faced with more sophisticated forms, they fled to their home bases after battles conducted with obsolete instruments produced at the national level. They are therefore wary of fighting new battles on a wider and more dangerous front, and this diffidence has even led them to deny the usefulness of studying what to do and how to do it. The best among them realise that the challenge must be met, but they are reluctant to commit themselves. It was no coincidence that Alan Greenspan floated a very radical remark during a meeting with U.S. stock market executives: I wonder, he said, if the central banks will not have to be responsible for the way stock markets behave. The notion was so revolutionary that he immediately quipped that he would much rather be the one who asks the question than the one who has to answer it.

Who should try to answer the question, if not economists?

At the 1999 G8 Cologne Summit, the leaders expressed concern over the way the global credit structure was developing. They called on their distinguished experts to analyse the problem and to propose solutions for a new international financial architecture. This mandate, however, was given to the very same people who are responsible for the current situation (mainly officials from their ministries of finance and central banks). Not surprisingly, their conclusion was that the international financial architecture only needs to reinforce its two existing main pillars: the necessity for each country to put its own house in order, and the increased vigilance of intermediaries.

The facts are that the world credit structure has fundamentally changed (with a particular role performed by derivatives), the market has taken control of the creation of the world's money supply, expropriating the sovereignty of national institutions, and flexible exchange rates damage the unity and the efficiency of the global market. These facts are implicitly considered by the experts of the new international financial architecture as world phenomena that can be governed at home and with a better vigilance on the part of the 'sheriffs of credit'. It is strange that all these radical developments (which could one day spin out of control) have not changed the theory and practice of monetary control, which remain as they were when John Richard Hicks gave his lecture in 1967. It seems even more strange that some authorities consider positive these barely regulated developments.

References

Friedman, Milton and Anna Schwartz (1963). *A Monetary History of the United States, 1867–1960*. Princeton University Press, Princeton.

Hicks, John Richard (1967). 'Monetary Theory and History: An Attempt at Perspective'. In J. R. Hicks, ed., *Critical Essays in Monetary Theory*, pp. 155–173. Clarendon Press, Oxford.

Mundell, Robert A. (2000). 'A Reconsideration of the Twentieth Century'. *American Economic Review* vol. 90, no. 3, pp. 327–340.

Savona, Paolo, Aurelio Maccario, and Chiara Oldani (2000). 'On Monetary Analysis of Derivatives'. In P. Savona, ed., *The New Architecture of the International Monetary System*, pp. 149–175. Kluwer Academic Publishers, Boston.

Tobin, James (1961). 'Money, Capital, and Other Stores of Value'. *American Economic Review* vol. 51, no. 2, pp. 26–37.

Tobin, James (1965). 'The Monetary Interpretation of History (A Review Article)'. *American Economic Review* vol. 55, no. 3, pp. 464–485.

Chapter 11

Britain, Europe, and North America

Alan M. Rugman and Alina Kudina[1]

In the June 2001 British general election, Tony Blair's Labour government was returned to power for another five years. The big issue for Prime Minister Blair is when to call a referendum on Britain joining the European single currency, the euro. On 1 January 2002, France, Germany, Italy, Spain, Belgium, and the other twelve members of the European Currency Union stopped using their sovereign currencies for personal transactions. Instead, they now use the common euro. Since 1 January 1999, companies and governments have been using the euro and there has been a centralised monetary policy from the Frankfurt-based European Central Bank (ECB).

Should Britain join the euro countries, give up the pound, sacrifice its monetary policy, and further increase its integration in Europe? While this is a political issue as well as an economic one, what do the data indicate about British interdependence with the rest of the EU? Briefly, the empirical evidence reviewed in this chapter is that British/North American economic links are just as strong as British/European links. A slim majority of British trade is with Europe, but only a minority of British foreign direct investment (FDI) is with Europe. In fact, more than 60 percent of FDI is elsewhere, with nearly 50 percent in North America. The United States is the largest single foreign investor in Britain, holding 40 percent of the inward stock.

Currently, 70 percent of British voters reject British membership of the euro. They think that Britain is better off outside Euroland. London is a leading world financial centre and Britain holds a global, rather than a regional, business position. The economic data indicate that Britain needs to consider institutional arrangements to govern and foster its economic interdependence with North America, as well as its economic relations with the EU.

The issue of Britain and the euro cannot be analysed properly, however, unless the economic background of globalisation is properly understood. As argued by Alan Rugman (2000), the world, in fact, is not global, but rather is dominated by the 'triad' of North America, the EU, and Japan. In many ways, the G7 is really a G3 of the United States, the EU (including Britain, France, Germany, and Italy as part of that large 15-member state block), and Japan, which still has the largest economy in Asia. These three economic blocks have been developing in different ways, but they still dominate the world economy. It is important to review the evidence on this.

The Evidence on Triad Economic Activities

The reality of triad-based regional economic activity (and the regional nature of the production processes of multinational enterprises) is supported by the evidence. The aggregate economic data on trade and FDI reveal the lack of globalisation and the importance of regional-triad production. Trade data (reported in Rugman 2000) confirm that most economic activity is triad-based. The triad made 57.3 percent of world exports in 1996, and 56.5 percent of imports. Exports and imports to the non-triad areas were about 43 percent of the world total. Most of the world's trade is controlled by the triad. According to data for 1997, the triad's exports total US$4200.9 billion, with the majority of the EU exports of US$2092.3 being internal, as will be shown below. The EU exports only 7.6 percent of its total to the United States (US$158.1 billion), while the United States exports 20.5 percent of its total to the EU (US$140.8 billion) and 9.5 percent to Japan (US$65.6 billion). Japan exports 28 percent of its total to the United States (US$118.4 billion) and 15.6 percent to the EU (US $65.7 billion).

The core triad members can be expanded if Canada and Mexico are added to the United States, which is what the North American Free Trade Agreement (NAFTA) produces, and if a group of countries is constituted for 'Asia'. This group consists mainly of Japan, Australia, New Zealand, China, Taiwan, Hong Kong, India, Indonesia, Malaysia, the Philippines, Singapore, and Thailand, as well as smaller Asian Pacific economies. This expansion gives us the 'broad' triad. Figure 11.1 confirms that the world's trade is controlled by the triad, using NAFTA and Asia rather than the United States and Japan. According to data for 1997, the triad's exports total US$4145.8 billion, with 60.6 percent of the EU exports of US$2092.3 being internal, at US$1268.5 billion. The EU exports only 8.7 percent to NAFTA (US$182.1 billion) and 9.4 percent to Asia (US$197.6 billion). NAFTA exports 15.4 percent of its total to the European Union (US$155.3 billion) and 22.4 percent to Asia (US$226.0 billion). Asia exports 21.1 percent of its total to NAFTA (US$220.0 billion) and 14.7 percent to the European Union (US$153.3 billion).

In summary, the extent of the intra-EU exports is 60.6 percent. For NAFTA, internal trade is 49.1 percent and for Asia it is 53.1 percent. The majority of world trade in each triad is within the internal markets of the triad, and most of the rest is among themselves.

There is also abundant evidence that FDI is dominated by the triad. The latest available aggregate data on stocks of FDI to the triad is for 1997, and is published by the United Nations Conference on Trade and Development (UNCTAD) (1999) in *World Investment Report 1999*. This specialised United Nations agency has been responsible for gathering data on FDI and making policy recommendations, based on economic analysis, for the last 20 years. It was once based in New York but moved to Geneva in the early 1990s.

Figure 11.2 reveals the dominance of the core triad members as sources of FDI. These data report the aggregate stocks of FDI, that is they reveal the historical value and wealth of foreign subsidiaries to the home country. They do not represent an annual flow of FDI.

By 1997, the EU was the largest engine of FDI, with an aggregate outward stock of US$1309 billion. The outward stock of the United States (leaving aside its NAFTA partners for a moment) was US$861 billion. Japan's outward stock was US$272 billion. The combined value of the core triad members is US$2442 billion, which is 71 percent of the world's total stock of FDI in 1997 of US$3473 billion.

The most important number in Figure 11.2 is that for internal EU FDI: US$513 billion. This is a larger number than for any single inter-triad stock of FDI. It shows that 40.5 percent of all EU FDI is internal.

The data in Figure 11.2 yield several important insights (all data are in US$ billion). The total stock of outward FDI in the triad amounts to the sum of internal figures in the boxes, that is, 2442. The total amount of inter-triad outward FDI stock is the sum of the six arrows between the three triad boxes, that is, 858. The difference is the stock of outward FDI in the triad that is both internal triad FDI and FDI by the triad to the rest of the world; these two amounts total 1584. That is 64 percent of the total

Figure 11.1   Exports in the Broad Triad

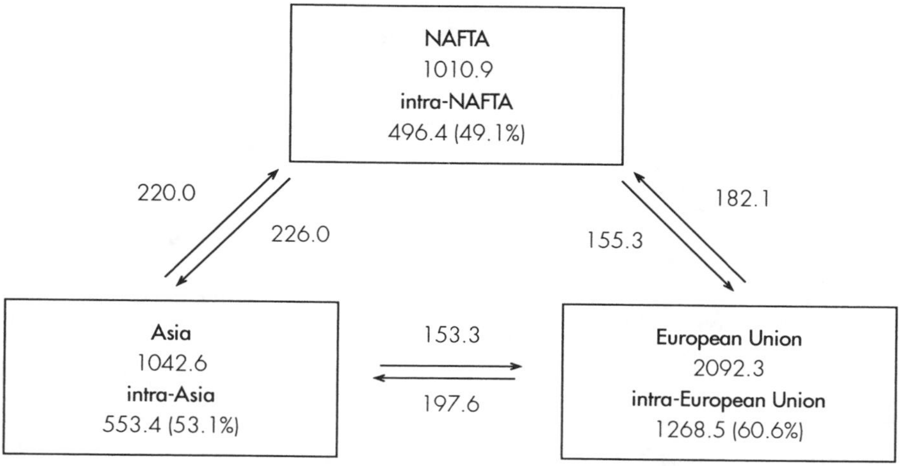

Note: Data are for 1997, in US$ billion.

Source: International Monetary Fund, Direction of Trade Statistics, 1999.

outward stocks of the triad. The total world stock of outward FDI for 1997 (not reported in Figure 11.2) is 3473. The total triad stock of non–inter-triad FDI is 1584. This is 45 percent of the world's stock.

The total triad FDI is 2442 (consisting of the inter-triad FDI stock of 858 plus the non–inter-triad FDI stock of 1584), which is 71 percent of the world's total stock of outward FDI. The amount of FDI originating in the non-triad countries is equal to the world stock (of 3423) less the triad stock (of 2442), which is 981, or 27 percent of the world's total.

When the two NAFTA partners are added to the U.S. stock of outward FDI, the NAFTA total increases to 999.1, as shown in Figure 11.2. The amount of internal-triad FDI in Figure 11.2 is very large, since the internal EU FDI stock alone is 513. The amount for North America is 196 and the amount for Asia is 91.2. Thus the internal FDI stock in NAFTA is 20 percent of its total, while for Asia it is 33.5 percent.

From these observations, one can conclude that the triad dominates FDI, and that as much as 40 percent of FDI is internal to each triad rather than inter-triad. Inter-triad FDI, however, is very large, particularly between the EU and the United States, and only a quarter of the world's FDI is not controlled by the triad.

Figure 11.2   Total Outward FDI Stocks in the Core Triad

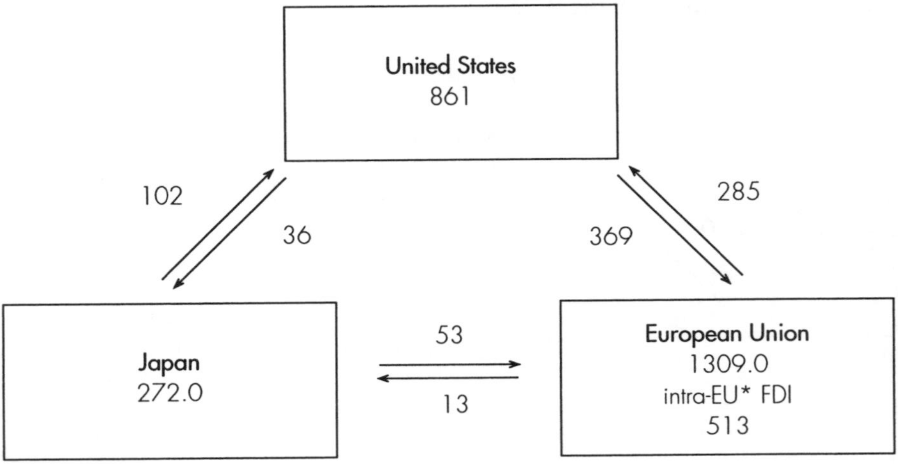

Notes: Data are for 1997, in US$ billion. *Data are for 1996.

Sources: United Nations 1999; Organisation for Economic Co-operation and Development 1998.

The data for the three-partner NAFTA and for the broad Asian triad, based on Japan, basically confirm the analysis of the EU given so far. Data for Japanese exports and imports show that in 1998 about 40 percent of Japan's exports and 52 percent of its imports were intra-regional to Asia and Oceania. About 36 percent of Japanese exports went to North America and 27 percent of imports came from there. Finally, 18 percent of Japan's exports went to the EU compared with 14 percent of Japan's imports from there (Rugman 2000).

Trade Data for Britain

It is widely believed that Britain is economically integrated with the rest of Europe. The evidence used mainly consists of trade data. Indeed, in 1999, nearly 59 percent of UK exports went to the other 14 member states of the EU. But this figure has declined from a high of 60.5 percent in 1991, and was running at about 53 percent for most of the 1990s. In contrast, in 1999, only 14.7 percent of UK exports went to the United States, up from 10.9 percent in 1991, and around 12 percent for most of the 1990s. These data are reported in Table 11.1. Data for UK imports by major regions are reported in Table 11.2, and show a similar pattern to the export data.

**Table 11.1   UK Exports by Region, 1991–99
(percentage of total exports)**

	1991	1993	1995	1997	1999
Europe	69.7	58.2	59.8	61.9	64.1
EU	60.5	52.1	53.9	52.7	58.7
North America	12.8	14.8	13.6	13.6	16.8
U.S.	10.9	12.9	12.2	12.2	14.7
Asia	10.6	2.3	13	13.1	8.5
Japan	2.2	2.2	2.5	2.6	2.0
Other Countries	6.9	14.8	13.6	14.0	10.5
World Total	100.0	100.0	100.0	100.0	100.0

Note: Total Europe includes EU and other Western Europe (Norway, Switzerland, Turkey, Iceland) plus Poland, Czech Republic and Hungary.
Total Asia include Japan, South Korea, Indonesia, Brunei, China, Hong Kong, India, Malaysia, Pakistan, Philippines, Singapore, Taiwan and Thailand.

Source: UK Office for National Statistics for 1999 data.

Foreign Direct Investment Data for Britain

Over the last 40 years, there has been a rise in the number of multinational corporations (MNCs) and the global spread of FDI has expanded. Today, world business is dominated by the largest 500 MNCs in the world, virtually all of them from the triad of the United States, EU, and Japan. These corporations account for more than 90 percent of the world stock of FDI and, themselves, do more than half of the world's trade, often intra-firm (Rugman 2000).

British economic integration with Europe is much less striking when one considers FDI data. Indeed, British FDI in North America has increased remarkably in recent years.

In terms of UK outward stocks of FDI, in 1999 there was 45.4 percent in North America but only 35.5 percent in the EU, down from 42.2 percent in 1997. The recent dramatic increase in British FDI in North America is reported in Table 11.3.

In 1999, only 45.6 percent of the total stock of FDI in the UK came from the EU. The largest single foreign investor in the UK was the United States, accounting for 40 percent. The total FDI from North America (given that Canada is a large investor in the UK) was 42.6 percent. These data are reported in Table 11.4.

In other words, Britain's inward stock of FDI is split between the EU and North America. The North American ownership of Britain's assets range from Ford UK to the *Daily Telegraph*. Surely, the UK government should be doing just as much to

Table 11.2 UK Imports by Region, 1991–99 (percentage of total exports)

	1991	1993	1995	1997	1999
Europe	62.6	62.6	63.8	61.1	60.4
EU	57.3	55.0	56.8	54.4	53.9
North America	13.5	13.3	13.5	14.9	14.6
U.S.	11.7	11.7	11.9	13.3	12.7
Asia	13.3	15.6	15.2	14.0	16.9
Japan	5.5	6.0	5.6	4.9	4.8
Other Countries	10.5	8.5	7.6	10.0	8.1
World Total	100.0	100.0	100.0	100.0	100.0

Notes: Total Europe includes EU and other Western Europe (Norway, Switzerland, Turkey, Iceland) plus Poland, Czech Republic and Hungary.

Total Asia include Japan, South Korea, Indonesia, Brunei, China, Hong Kong, India, Malaysia, Pakistan, Philippines, Singapore, Taiwan and Thailand.

Source: UK Office for National Statistics for 1999 data.

safeguard the jobs and related businesses that depend upon North America as upon the EU? A trade and investment pact with North America is needed. This could be as an associate member of NAFTA, or of the Free Trade Agreement of the Americas, if the latter is successfully negotiated by 2005. This does not require that the UK join NAFTA, but that a separate agreement be concluded. The UK needs tariff-free access to North American markets. The North Americans need long-run national treatment safeguards for their FDI in the UK.

Table 11.3   UK, Outward Stocks of Foreign Direct Investment (percentage of total investment)

	1995	1996	1997	1998	1999
Europe	38.9	45.0	45.5	40.4	39.9
EU	37.0	43.1	42.2	33.3	35.5
North America	34.5	27.9	30.3	43.2	45.4
U.S.	31.6	25.3	27.1	41.2	43.8
Asia	9.2	10.2	8.9	6.4	6.0
Japan	1.2	1.3	0.7	0.6	0.9
World Total	100.0	100.0	100.0	100.0	100.0

Source: Office for National Statistics, ONS Overseas Direct Investment Inquiries, Bank of England, London.

Table 11.4   UK, Inward Stocks of Foreign Direct Investment (percentage of total investment)

	1995	1996	1997	1998	1999
Europe	40.5	41.5	37.9	36.6	50.0
EU	33.7	32.5	29.4	26.6	45.6
North America*	44.8	44.2	48.6	51.2	42.6
U.S.	42.8	41.6	45.9	49.2	39.6
Asia	6.2	6.0	6.0	5.1	2.2
Japan	4.3	4.4	4.3	3.6	1.4
World Total	100.0	100.0	100.0	100.0	100.0

* North America includes the USA and Canada

Source: Office for National Statistics, ONS Overseas Direct Investment Inquiries, Bank of England, London.

This affiliation with North America would be incompatible with the UK joining the euro and remaining as a full member state of the EU. But Britain could retain its economic affiliation with Europe through a free-trade agreement. The UK could revert to being a member of the European Economic Area (EEA). The former seven members of European Free Trade Agreement include the UK, Austria, Sweden, and Finland, which have now all joined the EU. But Norway remains a member of the EEA. As such, Norway has full tariff-free access to the EU and also benefits from national treatment for investment.

If the UK keeps an economic affiliation with the EU, through its membership in the EEA, then there is little or no economic cost in leaving the EU. But there are major political benefits. Britain need not join the single currency, adopt a common social policy, or accept judicial rulings from the European Court of Justice. With a free trade agreement, instead of a common market link with the EU, British sovereignty is retained at no economic cost.

It is acknowledged that the UK needs to retain a strong economic linkage with Europe. This is especially important for British inward investment (Table 11.4), which focusses less on North America than does British outward investment (Table 11.3).

Recent Direct Investment

The stock of British FDI in the United States nearly doubled in 1998 and almost tripled in 1999 as compared to the 1997 level, as shown in Table 11.5. It went up by GBP 62 699 million to the level of GBP 121 782 million in 1998 and by GBP 63 581 million to the level of GBP 185 363 million in 1999. Major acquisition of U.S. companies by

Table 11.5   UK, Outward Stocks of Foreign Direct Investment (GBP, million)

	1995	1996	1997	1998	1999
Europe	76 434	87 582	99 263	119 547	169 002
EU	72 808	83 902	92 072	98 564	150 158
North America	67 904	54 286	66 158	127 704	192 085
U.S.	62 159	49 170	59 083	121 782	185 363
Asia	18 038	19 916	19 389	18 863	25 319
Japan	2397	2437	1605	1716	3679
World Total	196 687	194 601	218 162	295 716	423 343

Source: Office for National Statistics, ONS Overseas Direct Investment Inquiries, Bank of England, London.

British companies in 1998 included British Petroleum's purchase of Amoco for US$48.2 billion and in 1999 Vodafone's purchase of Air Touch for US$60.3 billion.

Over the same period of 1997 to 1998, the EU received only an increase of GBP 6492 million (or 10.4 percent of the U.S. stock change). Thus, in 1998 the level of British outward investment in the EU stood at GBP 98 564 million. However, in 1999 British companies became much more proactive in their attitude toward investing in the EU countries. As a result, the UK FDI stock in the EU was augmented by GBP 51 594 million to the level of GBP 150 158 as of the end of 1999. For example, the British Zeneca group bought Sweden's Astra for US$34.6 billion in 1999. Nevertheless, the EU share still constitutes only 35.5 percent of the total outward FDI stock, whereas the U.S. part amounts to 43.8 percent of the total. Therefore, the importance of the United States as an economic partner for the UK is more than evident.

The data on the level of the UK inward direct investment show a somewhat different pattern. As shown in Table 11.6, while the stock of the U.S. inward direct investment in the UK was rather more stable in recent years, it surged by GBP 14 314 million (26 percent) in 1997 and by GBP 20 071 million (29 percent) in 1998. Although Wal-Mart bought ASDA for US$10.8 billion the stock of U.S. FDI in Britain actually declined in 1999. In contrast, while the level of EU inward investment in the UK was stagnating between 1995 and 1998, it recorded a huge two-fold leap in 1999, when it went up by GBP 54 906 million to the level of GBP 103 695 million. In 1999, for example, Germany's Mannesmann purchased Orange for US$32 billion and Deutsche Telecom acquired One 2 One for US$13.6 billion.

Table 11.6 UK, Inward Stocks of Foreign Direct Investment (GBP, million)

	1995	1996	1997	1998	1999
Europe	52 144	55 856	58 037	67 241	113 741
EU	43 493	43 774	44 927	48 789	103 695
North America*	57 781	59 473	74 399	93 970	96 832
U.S.	55 129	55 956	70 270	90 341	90 155
Asia	7934	8072	9166	9289	4893
Japan	5542	5888	6562	6624	3145
World Total	128 885	134 654	152 956	183 544	227 433

* North America includes the U.S. and Canada.

Source: Office for National Statistics, ONS Overseas Direct Investment Inquiries, Bank of England, London.

In contrast, data from the U.S. Department of Commerce demonstrate a smoother pattern of the investment activity of British companies in the United States. According to the Department of Commerce, the stock of the UK investment in the United States grew by US$12 282 million (or 9.3 percent) in 1998 and US$39 980 million (or 27.9 percent) in 1999 (see Table 11.7).

Conclusion

These data suggest that the UK must have two economic relationships: one with Europe and one with North America. This is possible with two free-strade and investment agreements. The current Blairite one-dimensional focus on European integration presents major political and social pitfalls for the UK. While most British trade is with the EU, only a minor amount of both inward and outward FDI stocks is with the EU; as much, or more, is with North America. As a consequence, Britain needs to revert to balanced economic diplomacy within a triad/regional world economic system.

Note

1   Research assistance has been provided by Cecilia Brain.

Table 11.7   United States: Direct Investment Position Data (USD, million)

	1995	1996	1997	1998	1999
Foreign Direct Investment Position in the US on a Historical Cost Basis					
All countries	53 553	598 021	681 842	778 418	965 632
Europe	332 374	370 843	428 721	518 576	670 030
UK	116 272	121 582	130 883	143 165	183 145
U.S. Direct Investment Position Abroad on a Historical Cost Basis					
All countries	699 015	795 195	871 316	1 000 703	1 130 789
Europe	344 596	389 378	425 139	518 433	588 341
UK	106 332	134 559	154 462	183 035	212 007

Source: U.S. Department of Commerce, Bureau of Economic Analysis.

References

Organisation for Economic Co-operation and Development (1998). *International Direction of Trade Statistics*. Organisation for Economic Co-operation and Development, Paris.

Rugman, Alan M. (2000). *The End of Globalization*. Random House, London.

United Nations Conference on Trade and Development (1999). 'World Investment Review 1999'. United Nations Conference on Trade and Development, Geneva.

ANALYTICAL APPENDICES

Appendix A

Impressions of the Genoa Summit, 20–22 July 2001

Nicholas Bayne

The Genoa Summit was the target of violent riots, which left one dead, more than 200 injured and $40 million of damage. The riots obsessed the media, who claimed the G8 leaders themselves achieved little and that summits in this form could not survive. But although preoccupied with the causes and consequences of the riots, the leaders in fact launched some important initiatives. If these are fully implemented — a big if — Genoa may prove one of the most influential summits.

Only G8 heads of state and government came to Genoa 2001, maintaining the practice begun at Birmingham 1998. G7 finance ministers had met on 7 July and G8 foreign ministers on 18–19 July, both in Rome. They issued reports and conclusions (see Documentary Appendices), considered further below. At Genoa itself, the G7 leaders met on the first afternoon and issued a statement. They were then joined by Russian president Vladimir Putin and United Nations secretary general Kofi Annan for the announcement of the Global Fund to Fight AIDS, Tuberculosis, and Malaria. At dinner, the G8 met leaders from developing countries, mainly from Africa, and the heads of other international institutions, including the World Health Organization (WHO), the World Bank, and the World Trade Organization (WTO). The main G8 agenda occupied the second day, with the issue of the usual communiqué.

Although Italian prime minister Silvio Berlusconi was new in office, he had chaired a summit before — at Naples in 1994. He wisely kept on the sherpa team that had been responsible for the preparations under his predecessor Giuliano Amato. The Italian presidency strove to maintain continuity with the previous year's Okinawa Summit and to limit the Genoa agenda to three precise themes — poverty reduction, the global environment, and conflict prevention. This enabled the documents issued by the leaders to be kept commendably short: a G8 communiqué of 3300 words on five pages, a G7 statement of 1800 words on six pages, and four more statements of a page apiece. The full Summit documentation, however, is much more copious: three reports from G7 finance ministers, four statements from G8 foreign ministers, texts on the new Global Health Fund, and reports from the task forces on information technology (the Dot Force) and renewable energy.

This was the first G8 summit for U.S. president George W. Bush and Japanese prime minister Junichiro Koizumi. Although he clashed with Jacques Chirac at times, Bush found the Summit a useful platform for putting his views across, probably more useful than he had expected. His frank and open manner seemed to have gone over well. Koizumi too proved a livelier summit participant than most Japanese leaders. Tony Blair for the United Kingdom and Jean Chrétien for Canada had both been recently re-elected. Blair was very active, especially on Africa, and worked well with Bush. Chrétien attracted interest because of what Canada would be doing at the following year's summit. Chirac was outspoken and individualistic, as usual, and Germany's Gerhard Schroeder Germany made little obvious impact. The European Commission's Romano Prodi seemed in shock because of the riots, while Guy Verhofstadt, prime minister of Belgium and president of the European Union, was talkative but inexperienced.

The Violent Demonstrations

The policy discussions were inevitably distracted by the riots in the streets. Genoa was an awkward city for security. The G8 delegations and media were isolated in the 'Red Zone' around the port, many being lodged on board ship. A wider 'Yellow Zone' was meant to keep protestors at a safe distance. A massive police presence, ugly physical barriers, deserted streets, and boarded-up shops made Genoa look like a city under siege, even before the riots began.

Large crowds of demonstrators — estimated at anything between 70 000 and 200 000 — descended on Genoa and were lodged in tented camps around the city. The great majority were peaceful demonstrators, lobbying on issues such as debt forgiveness, action on AIDS, or the environment. But there were substantial numbers of obstructive protesters, trying, for example, to break police cordons by force of numbers, and of destructive activists, seeking violent confrontation with the police. On the first day, one protester was killed during ugly clashes with the police. Confrontation continued in central Genoa on the second day, with cars burnt and shops sacked and looted, although elsewhere some mass demonstrations passed peacefully. At midnight on that day, the police raided, without a warrant, the headquarters of the Global Social Forum, the Italian umbrella body for peaceful protest groups. They claimed to have found members of the anarchist Black Block being sheltered there, well as illegal arms.

The violence was roundly condemned, however, by responsible international nongovernmental organisations (NGOs), such as Drop the Debt and Médecins Sans Frontières. They realised that confrontational protests could never influence G8 decisions in the way the peaceful marches of Jubilee 2000 had done at Birmingham 1998 and Cologne 1999.

The leaders were shocked by the violence and issued a statement regretting the death. They closed ranks in insisting that violent riots must not prevent them from meeting. But some — including Berlusconi — were uneasy that the leaders of eight rich countries seemed isolated in an ivory tower. The leaders spent several sessions discussing ideas to make the summits more acceptable and less a focus for protest. This included ideas such as:

- choosing more suitable sites for summits. (Chrétien said the 2002 Summit would be at Kananaskis, a small resort in the Canadian Rockies.)
- reducing the number of participants. (The U.S. brought 900 people, the UK only 27; Chrétien said that next year accommodation at Kananaskis would limit national delegations to 30.)
- greater effort to consult civil society groups in the summit preparatory process. The Italians had started well in consulting international NGOs, but got sidetracked into dealing with Italian groups only.
- more systematic involvement of non-G8 countries. The G8 foreign ministers in Rome spoke of creating a 'forum' for regular contact with developing countries.

As this account will show, non-G8 countries and NGOs have already become deeply involved in summit preparations and follow-up.

Issues at the Genoa Summit

The G7 Meeting and Statement

The two main issues discussed by the G7 leaders, before Putin arrived, were the world economy and Africa, in preparation for their meeting with African leaders over dinner. The G7 statement covers economic prospects, a new trade round, strengthening the financial system and debt relief, plus a sentence welcoming the closure of the Chernobyl nuclear power plant. Some of these issues, however, were not actually discussed until the following day.

Economic Prospects. Following previous practice, the finance ministers had not issued a statement on economic prospects from their pre-Summit meeting, but had briefed the press in surprisingly optimistic terms. Since then, Alan Greenspan had said the U.S. economy had touched bottom, but was not yet recovering, and the crisis had deepened in Argentina. Even so, the leaders expressed confidence in a future recovery and support for Koizumi's strategy in Japan. Berlusconi, as G8 chair, had received a letter from President Fernando de la Rua about the measures taken in Argentina. Berlusconi and Chirac both said publicly that a reply was sent promising that the G8 would provide more help if these measures did not work. However, the wording of the G7 statement is more guarded.

Trade and the World Trade Organization. The G7 statement contained a strong passage in which the heads 'engage personally and jointly in the launch of a new ambitious Round' in the WTO. The statement responded well to the concerns of developing countries, but avoided any impression of the G7 dictating to them. There was no reference to contentious agenda items such as labour standards or antidumping

— these were left for future negotiation in Geneva. The statement helpfully associated Japan and Canada with the U.S.-EU agreement achieved at the Gothenburg European Council. Unlike previous summits' treatment of a new trade round, Genoa reflected a new transatlantic rapport, achieved by EU commissioner Pascal Lamy and U.S. trade representative Robert Zoellick. This commitment on a new WTO round was one of the most important results of the Genoa Summit.

Strengthening the Financial System. The statement endorsed two reports issued by the finance ministers, one mainly on the multilateral development banks (MDBs) and the other on abuses of the financial system.

- The report on MDBs wanted the banks to focus on poverty reduction — not defined in detail — and to tighten up their management procedures. The tone was rather paternalistic toward developing countries. The report did not endorse Bush's latest proposal for converting World Bank loans into grants, made after the G7 finance ministers had met. The Genoa statement made a noncommittal reference to this, but the other G7 members had considerable reservations.
- The report on abuses recorded action over the previous year in money laundering, offshore financial centres (OFCs), and tax havens. There had been progress on money laundering since the Financial Action Task Force (FATF) named 15 jurisdictions in June 2000 as 'non-co-operating'. Four were taken off this list and eight others had improved significantly. But three countries, including Russia, remained vulnerable to counter-measures later in that year, and six more countries had come onto the list. The message on tax havens was much weaker than a year earlier, partly because of protests from the targeted countries but mainly because of American pressure.

Debt Relief. The G7 statement endorsed the findings of a third finance ministers report, called 'Debt Relief and Beyond'. It gave an update on the Enhanced HIPC Initiative in the previous year, noting that 23 countries had reached 'decision point' (as against only nine by Okinawa), leading to overall debt relief of £53 billion. It then dealt with some unfinished business: getting the best use of resources saved by debt relief; helping conflict countries to get into the programme; ensuring debt relief is sustained, leading to a 'lasting exit'; and getting other creditors to match what the G7 have done. There was no extension of debt relief itself, so that campaigners for complete debt forgiveness or the reduction of debt to the International Monetary Fund (IMF) and the World Bank (such as Drop the Debt) were clearly disappointed. But they could take some comfort from the fact that this remained an active G7 concern.

The Global Fund to Fight AIDS, Tuberculosis, and Malaria

Berlusconi and Annan, in the presence of the other G8 leaders, announced the formation of the Global Health Fund, with pledges from the G8 countries of US$1.3 billion (plus US$0.5 billion from other sources). Annan welcomed this initiative, as 'a very good beginning', although he added that 'much, much more is needed' and recalled the UN estimate of US$7–10 billion extra spending per year. But while Annan spoke only of AIDS and implied UN ownership of the fund, the earlier tension between UN and G8 plans was eased at Genoa, so that the two approaches were now tied together.

The G8, as their communiqué makes clear, intended to cover AIDS, malaria, and tuberculosis, as forecast at Okinawa 2000. They envisaged management by a board of donor and beneficiary countries and 'specialised organisations' (which would involve the WHO and the World Bank as well as the UN). The G8 were actively seeking contributions from the private sector and the involvement of NGOs at local level; private firms and nonprofit bodies would be involved in the fund's management as nonvoting members of the board. The sensitive issues of pharmaceutical patents and pricing were treated by seeking the co-operation of firms in the industry and by invoking the flexibility provided in the WTO's agreement on trade-related aspects of intellectual property (TRIPs).

Most comment from NGOs criticised the amounts as too small in light of the size of the AIDS epidemic. Some of this criticism seemed wide of the mark. This fund was not designed to meet all the needs of the AIDS crisis. It would provide extra financing to be integrated into national health plans, for which recipient countries remained responsible. It was intended to be in operation by the end of 2001. There must be limits to the amount of extra money the target countries could absorb early on; the aim was also to tie the fund's spending to clear output targets. The main weakness in the G8 position was that their pledges looked like one-time contributions, without any assurance of continuity of funding. But Bush and Blair, among others, indicated that they would be ready to provide more once the fund was in operation.

The Outreach Dinner and the Genoa Plan for Africa

The leaders had a working dinner on Friday with five African presidents (Algeria, Mali, Nigeria, Senegal, and South Africa), representatives from El Salvador and Bangladesh, and the heads of the UN, the Food and Agriculture Organization (FAO), the WHO, the WTO, and the World Bank. The discussion concentrated on Africa and especially the G8 response to the plan for the revival of Africa presented by Senegal and South Africa. This plan, called the New African Initiative, represented a fusion of the Millennium Africa Plan, promoted by Thali Mbeki of South Africa, with proposals launched by Senegal, the whole being backed by the African Union (the successor to the Organization for African Unity). The essential feature of this African plan was its focus on the responsibility of the African countries to put their own house in order, if they hope to attract support from the G8 and other sources of outside help.

The exchanges led to the issue of a short statement on the Genoa Plan for Africa. This was a very important initiative, which, thanks to the direct contacts of the G8 with the African leaders, went much further than expected. It welcomed the African commitments as 'the basis for a new intensive partnership between Africa and the developed world'. It promised help from the G8 both in conflict prevention in Africa and in a wide range of development activities, including health and education, information and communications technology (ICT), private investment, and international trade. Each G8 member would designate a personal representative to prepare an action plan, under Canadian leadership, for approval at the Summit in 2002. Blair publicly called it a Marshall Plan for Africa.

This initiative confronted the problems in that part of the world that has gained least from globalisation. It linked in well with other parts of the G7/8 agenda, both under poverty reduction and conflict prevention. It was a rare example of the summit finding synergy between the economic and political strands of its agenda. It reflected the new interest of the G8 leaders in outreach, as suitable for a globalising world and a response to criticisms of exclusiveness. However, as always, the test of this initiative will lie in the implementation, on both the G8 and the African side. There was much exhortation to international institutions, but no new G8 commitments, for example of aid funds or trade access. The G8 also added another wing to the G8 bureaucratic architecture, despite their claim to want things kept simple.

The G8 Meetings and Communiqué: Economic Issues

The G8 spent a full day of meetings on their economic agenda, taking political issues over lunch and the future of summitry over dinner. Except where their communiqué confirmed commitments already made, for example in health, its content was rather disappointing. The greater part of the G8 communiqué was devoted to poverty reduction. It was supported by the report from the G7 finance ministers entitled 'Debt Relief and Beyond'. This covered trade, investment, health, and education, following the lines of the preparatory document of the Italian presidency.

Trade and the Poorest Countries. Two brief paragraphs in the G8 communiqué, on trade access and capacity building, were expanded in the finance ministers report. The finance ministers admitted that the poorest countries had lost market share, especially because they faced high tariffs for their main exports. As compared with the promises made at Okinawa, however, the actual commitments on market access were uneven. The EU's Anything But Arms initiative was a real advance. But the U.S. had not moved beyond measures adopted in early 2000 (and initiated back in 1997), while the Japanese and Canadian schemes omitted many products of greatest interest to the poorest countries. Pledges to do better in future thus rang rather hollow. Similarly, the passages on capacity building were short on commitments on what more the G8 would do themselves, as opposed to co-ordinating existing actions and encouraging others.

Other Issues in Poverty Reduction. The passage on investment was largely exhortation to other international institutions; health is treated above. However, education had a bit more substance. The G8 renewed their commitment to helping to meet international educational targets, but could not find an obvious focus for their actions, as they had in health. They therefore created a task force of officials to work on this over the next year. Chrétien announced his wish to focus on education at the 2002 Summit. There was also a useful cross-reference to the Dot Force report (see below) and an acceptance (by the finance ministers) that 'additional resources should be provided'.

There was some discussion of expanding aid volumes, with Berlusconi and Prodi invoking the target of giving 0.7 percent of gross national product in aid. But this did not feature in the communiqué, which spoke only of 'strengthening and enhancing effectiveness' of aid.

Information and Communications Technology and the Dot Force. The most impressive document issued at the Summit was the first report of the Digital Opportunity Task Force (the Dot Force) established at Okinawa to help poor countries benefit from ICT. This was remarkable both for process and substance. It was produced by a group combining governments of both G8 and developing countries, international institutions, private firms, and NGOs. Many of the members turned up to present the report and conveyed an impressive sense of common purpose. The report focussed on nine clear and sensible action points, including the following:

• Countries should develop national e-strategies, with help to make them compatible.
• Access to ICT should be made easier and cheaper.
• ICT should be used in education at all levels, as well as health care and the fight against AIDS.
• ICT business activity should be encouraged.
• There should be special efforts to help the poorest countries and encourage local applications.

The report contained no estimates of resources needed. The Dot Force members justified this by saying that their task was to devise the policy environment, within which resources could be deployed. But the World Bank described its current ICT-related lending, and the Canadian chair of the Dot Force for next year stressed that the next report would focus on implementation.

This report was a considerable achievement, in the face of great initial scepticism. The G8 communiqué endorsed the report and renewed the Dot Force's mandate. Hardly any leader drew attention to the Dot Force and its work in press briefings, which suggested some doubt about their personal commitment to it. However, it received favourable comment in the leaders' own meetings, as evidence of continuing interest, so that the prospects for the harder task of implementation remained favourable.

Renewable Energy. The G8 Renewable Energy Task Force had a similar wide composition to the Dot Force and its report (which was circulated but not presented) had the same objective of creating the right policy environment. However, the communiqué did no more than thank the participants for their work, without taking a position on it, remitting further action to G8 energy ministers. This was because of U.S. opposition: the U.S. feared the report would inhibit their national energy strategy. However, the work is not lost, being remitted to G8 energy ministers.

Environment. The main issue was climate change and the Kyoto protocol. All could agree, including Bush, on the need to reduce greenhouse gas emissions and to take action to bring this about. References in the communiqué to flexibility of policy and co-operation on research looked like moves toward the U.S. position. The U.S. had indicated that it was working on alternative approaches to the Kyoto protocol, but these would not be ready until the next Conference of the Parties to the climate change convention (COP7), in Morocco in 2002. The communiqué implied U.S. readiness to involve others in this process, so that Genoa marked a modest advance over what was discussed between the EU and U.S. at Gothenburg. The Summit was also useful in persuading Japan, Canada, and Russia to join the agreement being worked out at COP6 at Bonn, even though the U.S. stood aside from the progress made there.

Biotechnology and Food Safety. A brief discussion produced the usual uneasy truce between those who rely on science and the partisans of the precautionary principle. Blair said the former view prevailed, Prodi said the latter did, and a close reading of paragraph 30 in the communiqué shows that both views are well recorded. There was a slight advance as compared with Okinawa, in that France and other Europeans were readier to give weight to scientific evidence, but the U.S. remained sceptical about the precautionary approach. An earlier passage in the communiqué (paragraph 20) noted the potential value of biotechnology for agriculture in poor countries.

The G8 Meetings and Statements: Political Issues

Outside Africa, political issues had low priority at the Summit. They did not feature in the main G8 communiqué, but were dealt with in separate statements on the Middle East and regional issues. These in turn related to the conclusions issued by the G8 foreign ministers in Rome on 19 July, who also disposed of eleven other regional issues. On the Middle East, the heads briefly confirmed the foreign ministers' unanimous view that the Mitchell Plan was the only way forward and that outside monitoring, as proposed by the EU, could be helpful. The short statement on regional issues covered Macedonia and the Korean peninsula, seeking peace and reconciliation in both.

Conflict Prevention and Africa. Conflict prevention was a lead subject for the Italian presidency, which sought agreement to extend the process begun by G8 foreign ministers at Berlin in 1999 and at Miyazaki in 2000. The foreign ministers at Rome endorsed progress reports on small arms, diamonds, children in conflict, civilian policing, and conflict and development, and added two new items — on women in conflict and the private sector. In fact, both the ministers and the leaders seemed more interested in specific cases of conflict, especially in Africa, than in the general concept of conflict prevention, which was not discussed at the Summit. But on balance the Italians should be well pleased with the conflict prevention component of the Genoa Plan for Africa.

Disarmament. A long statement by the G8 foreign ministers in Rome avoided open disagreement on missile defence, while Colin Powell (U.S.) and Igor Ivanov (Russia) were at pains to show that they could work together well on other things. At Genoa, Putin (against the advice of his officials) decided not to raise the subject among the G8 leaders, so that disarmament is not mentioned in their documents. Instead, Putin used the Summit as the occasion for a fruitful bilateral with Bush, which suggested a deal might be struck linking missile defence with the reduction of nuclear weapons.

Assessment

Most of the media comment from Genoa reacted to the riots by advocating changes in the style and process of summitry. But that is not really the solution to making the G8 summits more publicly acceptable. Summits will instead be judged by the quality of the agreements reached. In that respect, the Genoa Summit provides an excellent example of the strengths and weaknesses of the G7/8 process, in conditions of advancing globalisation.

The Summit concentrated on issues relating to developing countries, especially the poorest. This focus on poor developing countries was fully justified: That was where the main problems of globalisation arise, as well as the worst suffering from conflict and natural disasters. The Italian choice of topics, especially poverty reduction and conflict prevention, also allowed good continuity between the Japanese and Italian presidencies. Two of the main achievements of Genoa — the Global Health Fund and the Dot Force report — built on foundations laid at Okinawa the year before. Although Okinawa proved less productive in other areas, that justified a grading of B for the 2001 Summit.

The Genoa Plan for Africa was the greatest innovation from the Summit. This was the first time the G8 had entered into a specific partnership with a group of non-G8 countries (the only parallel is the G7's commitment to Russia in the early 1990s). It provided an opportunity to integrate the political and the economic agenda, where the summits had seldom managed to achieve their potential. There were strong links with many other topics handled by the G7/8, including debt relief, trade access, ICT, health, and education. The comparison with the Marshall Plan was apt, because the African states, like the postwar European countries, were prepared to take 'ownership' of their efforts to achieve political and economic revival.

Genoa also showed how far the G7/8 had moved in the previous two years to involve both private firms and nonprofit bodies in summit preparation and follow-up.

This was most vivid in the Global Health Fund and the reports from the Dot Force and the Renewable Energy Task Force. But in almost every other economic topic, greater participation of civil society was sought. This also applied in the political agenda, for example in the two new topics of women and the private sector added to conflict prevention. There was a striking contrast between the full involvement of many NGOs in the G8's work and the violent riots on the streets.

The G8 leaders have begun to accommodate these new actors since they began meeting on their own at Birmingham in 1998. But at the same time the official apparatus of G7/8 ministerial and official bodies continues to grow; Genoa added new official groups on Africa and education, a meeting of energy ministers, and a conference on climate change. This gives an impression of a proliferating bureaucracy stifling the summit, which even affects some of the leaders, who nostalgically hanker after a much simpler format. In fact, the leaders need to give the same freedom of action to the subordinate groups as they have taken for themselves, only giving personal attention to key initiatives like the Dot Force.

The G7 and G8 agreed in Genoa on some major initiatives designed to help poor countries. They also reached a vital and very welcome consensus on a new trade round, which resolved differences among themselves, as well as showing sensitivity toward developing countries. But in other areas, for example in climate change or food safety, Genoa had less success in resolving internal G8 divergences. It is important not to weaken this capacity, which is one of the main justifications for the summits.

The most important test for Genoa, and for the G8 process generally, is whether the promises made are honoured. The recent record shows that the leaders are good innovators but poor implementers. Genoa will be judged on whether its main commitments bear fruit:

- Whether the Doha WTO meeting in November will launch a new trade round or, like Seattle, fail because of differences among the G7.
- Whether the Dot Force would maintain its good progress over its second year. Implementation is harder than policy formulation, so that the backing of the G8 leaders will still be needed.
- Whether the Global Health Fund can mobilise enough resources not only to get started but also to maintain operations, on a scale sufficient to roll back the incidence of AIDS, malaria, and tuberculosis.
- Whether the Genoa Plan for Africa really proves to be a new Marshall Plan; this will involve not only commitment from the African leaders but much more generous help from G8 members and others.

Full implementation of these undertakings would put Genoa very high on the summit grading scale. But will it happen? Will the G8 learn from its past mistakes? In the early 1990s, the G7 leaders similarly 'engaged personally and jointly' to complete the Uruguay Round of trade negotiations in three successive years, only to fail because of disputes over agriculture. The Denver Summit of 1997 also raised expectations on Africa, which were not fulfilled. In general, the Genoa documents set out clear diagnoses of the problems addressed. But often the G7/8 response is not to take new policy measures or to provide new resources, but only to intensify existing actions or to co-ordinate them better.

As they prepare for Kanasaskis 2002, the Canadians would do well to give as much attention to the G8 meeting its current commitments as to new initiatives, for example in education. The G8 now works much more closely with other governments, private business and civil society — that is one consequence of globalisation. But as a result its performance record comes under closer scrutiny. It is the failure to keep the promises made that most frustrates campaigning NGOs and helps to turn peaceful demonstrators into obstructive protestors, easily tempted into violent behaviour.

G7 Finance Ministers Meeting, Rome, 7 July 2001: Performance Assessment

George M. von Furstenberg

The G7 finance ministers met in Rome on 7 July 2001, to prepare for the 20–22 July Genoa G8 Summit. The longest serving member was Paul Martin of Canada, while Paul O'Neill of the United States, Masajuro Shiokawa of Japan, and Giulio Tremonti of Italy were new to the group. Hans Eichel of Germany, Gordon Brown of the United Kingdom, and Laurent Fabius of France were the remaining members.

The ministers issued a 30-paragraph statement (see Appendix H), the main provisions of which appear below. Its main recommendations are reflected in the section on 'Strengthening the International Financial System' of the leaders' much shorter G7 Statement issued at Genoa on 20 July 2001 (see Appendix J). Included here also is also a summary of the statement on the world economy that was contained only in the G7 Statement because it provides needed background to the finance ministers' concerns.

After summarising, this report briefly comments on the achievements and omissions of the finance ministers' statement in addressing international economic and financial issues. These issues are reduced growth in the world economy, taking continuing steps to strengthen the international financial infrastructure, and the multilateral development banks.

Lower Growth in the World Economy

1. The G7 statement noted a slowing of economic growth ranging from sharp (United States) to moderate (United Kingdom) even though growth remained positive in all G7 countries except Japan. In spite of this growth recession, the G7 felt that the continuation of structural reforms and watchful waiting were all that was called for at present. There was confidence that 'sound economic policies and fundamentals provide a solid foundation for stronger growth'.

2. High and volatile oil prices were a matter of continuing concern clouding the world economic outlook. Furthermore, the recent crisis in Turkey and the latent crisis in Argentina were casting a shadow.

Steps to Strengthen the International Financial Infrastructure

1. *Private Sector Involvement in Crisis Prevention and Resolution.* Such involvement is to be further encouraged through measures ranging from increased information sharing between countries and their private creditors to the adoption of collective action clauses in loan covenants so as to permit creditor committees to accept, by qualified majority, reschedulings, writedowns, or other work-out plans that are applicable to all creditors. The purpose is to reduce moral hazard by lenders without encouraging default by borrowers.

2. *Surveillance and Implementation of Standards and Codes.* The preparation of country-specific inventories of measures is important to prepare for compliance with internationally accepted codes and standards guiding the transparent operation, constitution, and supervision of the different lines of the financial business in developing countries. Since 1999, this activity has become part of the comprehensive Financial Sector Assessment Program (FSAP) conducted by the International Monetary Fund (IMF) and the World Bank with a growing list of countries. The G7 finance ministers reaffirmed their commitment to promote the implementation and surveillance of internationally agreed codes and standards, in particular the twelve key standards identified, for instance, for banking, insurance, and securities markets, by the Financial Stability Forum (FSF) co-ordinated by the Bank for International Settlements (BIS). Given that large parts of banking and insurance are effectively bankrupt in many developing countries, the gradual implementation of the standards and codes, including their capital requirments, might eventually reduce financial fragility.

3. *Opening Access to the Capital Market.* This section of the finance ministers' statement harks back explicitly to the 'Report on Strengthening the International Financial Architecture' submitted to the Cologne Summit in 1999. It recognises foreign direct investment (FDI) and productive use of equity flows and borrowed resources as hallmarks of countries that have successfully integrated into the world economy. It also recognises that opening up access to the capital market is a complex process that can benefit from policy advice and from technical and financial assistance. Nevertheless, it concludes that excessive capital flow volatility can not feasibly or effectively be addressed by a Tobin tax on financial transactions. The goal of launching a new trade round at the fourth ministerial of the World Trade Organization (WTO) in Qatar in November 2001 would also promote open access to markets, including the capital market and its services.

The Multilateral Development Banks

1. Multilateral development banks (MDBs), such as the World Bank and its affiliates and the regional development banks, are to place increased stress on helping

countries organise themselves for poverty reduction in the context of a comprehensive development framework and of country-owned development stratgies such as those developed in their poverty reduction strategy papers (PRSPs). Investment in human resources through the increased provision of health and education services are central to that strategy.

2.   The MDBs are to work jointly with each other with the help of memorandums of understanding between the World Bank and the regional development banks because such co-ordination is crucial to improving efficiency at the institutional level. Good governance is to be promoted by strengthening public sector management, accountability, and anticorruption measures in all countries.

Overall Evaluation

The finance ministers revisited many of the issues that had been covered extensively already at the 1999 Cologne Summit without breaking appreciable new ground in either the analysis of the causes of financial instability, such as most recently experienced in Turkey and Argentina, or in the preventive measures suggested. In particular, nothing new appears to have been learned about the appropriate exchange rate system and the reduced number of currencies that can safely survive in liberalised financial and investment markets. The comments here will elaborate on this point.

The finance ministers, like the IMF whose approach they endorse, did not focus on the root cause of international financial instability in emerging countries, which lies in their increasing exposure to currency competition and the resulting instability of their exchange rate and financial sector. If the currency of a financially small country is to serve anyone in a legitimate welfare sense, it would have to be the citizens of its own country. This, however, it fails to do in emerging market countries where currency crises, asset-price deflations, and financial and economic meltdown tend to co-incide. One of the greatest current failings of the international financial institutions and of the G8 is their failure publicly to recognise the needless pain and suffering caused by small countries hanging on to a separate currency that is being eroded by market forces and to recommend multilateral alternatives.

This point should be made some detail. Reacting to three major financial crises in emerging markets since mid 1997, the IMF and the World Bank in May 1999 launched the FSAP. The programme received a strong endorsement in the report of the G7 finance ministers and central bank governors on 'Strengthening the International Financial System and the Multilateral Development Banks' that was issued in Rome on 7 July 2001 (see Appendix I). One of three components of the FSAP is an assessment of the financial system, including macroeconomic factors, that could affect the performance of the system and conditions in the system that could affect the macroeconomy. This component relates most directly to the Financial System Stability Assessment (FSSA) of individual countries. The FSSA is used as part of the annual

Article IV consultations that the IMF holds with its member countries to review their macroeconomic and exchange rate policies. The FSSA is designed to identify macroeconomic vulnerabilities in which macroeconomic indicators associated with financial system soundness (such as volatility in exchange rates and interest rates) play a part. This parenthetical mention of exchange rate volatility appears to refer to a stressful atmospheric condition that requires adjustment rather than to a form of trouble that can be avoided by replacing the local currency fully, and not just in part, with a strong international currency as market forces increasingly demand. The G7 statement issued in Rome similarly promises stepped up efforts 'to reduce volatility and improve the functioning of the international monetary system' (point 7) without ever hinting that, for many emerging countries, getting rid of their troublesome own currency would contribute importantly to both goals. As dollarization of the western hemisphere south of the United States progresses and as Euroland is acquiring a halo of euroizing countries, how to prepare for mutually beneficial multilateral forms of monetary union may have to become a subject at future finance ministers meetings and G8 summits, although it is unlikely to receive an official welcome in Canada in 2002.

Appendix C

The G7/8 Commitments Report 2000

John J. Kirton, Ella Kokotsis, and Diana Juricevic

The 2000 G7/8 Summit held in Okinawa proved to be a most productive meeting, judged by the number and range of identifiable, specific, future-oriented commitments issued by the leaders in their concluding, comprehensive G7 and G8 communiqués.

Together the five documents issued by the leaders at Okinawa offered 169 such commitments.

Of these, 12 came in the G7 communique, 97 in the G8 communique, 54 in the G8's separate Okinawa Charter on Global Information Society, and 6 in the G8 Statement on Regional Issues. The fifth document issued by the leaders, the G8 Statement on the Korean peninsula, contained no commitments.

The commitments were distributed across 18 issue areas, as indicated in Table C.1.

The number of commitments by issue area in the two main G7 and G8 communiques suggests that the Okinawa Summit had as its main focus and legacy co-operative achievements in the areas of crime and drugs, development, and health (particularly infectious disease). Combining the last two areas, it was thus genuinely a 'development' oriented summit.

The 54 commitments in the Okinawa Charter on Global Information Society, especially when combined with the three commitments on information and comunications technology (ICT) in the G8 communiqué, suggest it was also the first G7 'digital summit'. Yet the heavy emphasis in this separate charter on 'Bridging the Digital Divide', led by the eleven commitments specifically under this heading, suggests that development was a primary focus and one well integrated into and supported by the second major theme.

The 14 commitments in the G8 communiqué on conflict prevention, disarmament, nonproliferation, arms control, and terrorism, together with the six commitments in the Statement on Regional Security, suggest that the Okinawa was also genuinely a political-security summit, with its total of 20 commitments in this realm. Its commitments on regional security embraced equally the three regions of the Middle East, the Balkans, and Africa. Perhaps due to the sensitivities of Japan's regional neighbours, no commitments were made on the Korean peninsula, either in these documents or in the separate statement issued on this subject.

It is difficult to assess whether the 2000 Okinawa G7/8 Summit was more productive than G7/8 summits in earlier years, as a similarly comprehensive assessment of commitments has not been conducted for those earlier years. However, a partial estimate is available by comparing those issue areas where commitment data in the main G7 and

Table C.1   G7/8 2000 Commitments

G7 Communiqué	*12*
International Financial Architecture	3
Enhanced HIPC Initiative	4
Abuse of Global Financial System	3
Nuclear Safety/Ukraine	2
G8 Communiqué	*97*
World Economy	1
Information and Communications Technology	3
Development	15
Debt	5
Health	15
Trade	4
Cultural Diversity	2
Crime and Drugs	18
Ageing	6
Biotechnology/Food Safety	3
Human Genome/Environment	11
Conflict Prevention	3
Disarmament, Nonproliferation, Arms Control	7
Terrorism	4
Okinawa Charter on Global Information Society	*54*
Introduction	1
Seizing Digital Opportunities	14
Bridging the Digital Divide	11
The Way Forward	7
Fostering Policy, Regulatory and Network Readiness	6
Improving Connectivity and Access, Lowering Cost	7
Building Human Capacity	5
Encouraging Participation in Global E-Commerce Nets	3
G8 Statement on Regional Issues	*6*
Middle East Peace Process	2
Balkans	2
Africa	2

G8 communiqués, produced by the same methodology, do exist. These data exist in earlier work by Ella Kokotsis (1999). This work has shown that the summits from 1989 to 1995 produced a yearly average of 4.8 commitments on climate change, 2.1 in biodiversity, 1.6 on developing country debt (from 1988 to 1995), and 3.5 on assistance to Russia (from 1990 to 1995). A comparison of similar issue areas at Okinawa suggests that the G7/8 in 2000 was considerably more productive on developing country debt, much less productive on assistance to Russia (where the economy was then doing relatively well), and somewhat less productive on climate change and biodiversity. This confirms the development focus of Okinawa. Given the variable pattern and limited number of issue areas for comparison, it is not possible to offer a definite conclusion about how productive Okinawa was in an overall sense compared to previous summits. However, Appendix D suggests it was highly productive.

Tables C.2a and C.2b list the precise commitments identified. The method and coding instructions for identifying individual commitments is available on the G8 Information Centre at <www.g8.utoronto.ca>. Note that commitments that contain sub-headings with further commitments are counted separately, with one number assigned to the main heading and a separate number for each of the individual commitments listed below.

Ranking Commitments by Ambition-Significance

In order to secure a more refined understanding of how productive the Okinawa Summit was as a decisional forum in the particular sense of 'co-operation', as measured by specific future-oriented commitments, it is important to assess not just the overall number, but the ambition and significance of each individual commitment the summit generated.

Led by Diana Juricevic, the G8 Research Group is devising a scale to rank commitments according to their level of ambition-significance. Outlined below is the evolving framework for ranking commitments according to their level of ambition-significance. An 'ambitious' commitment is one that clearly identifies a goal, clearly identifies measures to attain that goal, and clearly identifies a target date at which time that goal is to be completed. A 'significant' commitment is one that is timely, novel, and has appropriate scope. A commitment that is both 'ambitious' and 'significant' satisfies the above six criteria. The ambition-significance ranking is scored out of a possible 6 points corresponding to the six criteria. A score of 6 entails both a high level of ambition and a high level of significance. A score of 3 entails a high level of ambition but has no level of significance. A score of 0 entails no level of ambition and no level of significance.

The coding manual for assessing the ambition-significance of each individual commitment is presented immediately below.

A. Ambition

1. Does the commitment identify a *goal*?
   Yes = 1 point
   No = 0 points
2. Does the commitment identify *measures* to attain the goal?
   Yes = 1 point
   No = 0 points
3. Does the commitment identify a *target date* by which time the goal is to be completed?
   Yes = 1 point
   No = 0 points

B. Significance

4. Timeliness*
   Is the purpose of the commitment to respond to a current crisis?
   Is the purpose of the commitment to prevent/address a future crisis/issue?
   (1 point)
5. Scope*
   Is the commitment directed only at G8 countries?
   Is the commitment directed at countries outside G8 membership?
   (1 point)
6. Novelty*
   Is the commitment referring to an issue that was addressed at previous summits?
   Is the commitment referring to an issue that has not been addressed at previous summits?
   (1 point)

   * Note that the scoring criteria for (4), (5), and (6) is specific to the particular commitment to be ranked. Take the issue of 'Scope', for example. At times it is appropriate for a particular commitment to be directed only at G8 countries (in this case, a score of 1 would be allocated), while at others it is appropriate for the commitment to be directed outside G8 membership (in this case, a score of 1 would be allocated). Every effort has been taken by the Research Group to minimise the measurement error associated with this ranking process, including the implementation of a two-stage verification process to ensure that, if there is a bias in the ranking, this bias is applied consistently across all commitments and across all issue areas.

   Taken together these criteria suggest that each individual commitment, and through normal or weighted averages an entire summit, can be judged as follows:

Ambition-Significance Ranking
0 = No Ambition, No Significance
1 = Low Ambition, No Significance
2 = Moderate Ambition, No Significance
3 = High Ambition, No Significance
4 = High Ambition, Low Significance
5 = High Ambition, Moderate Significance
6 = High Ambition, High Significance

Before applying this framework to the entire set of 169 commitments identified above, it must be noted that ranking commitments by ambition-significance is an arduous task containing several methodological challenges. In this exercise the G8 Research Group is attempting to quantify an essentially qualitative enterprise. Every attempt has been made to reduce the level of measurement error and simultaneity bias. Nevertheless, these two problems still exist. As a result, there tends to be a systematic overstatement of the level of ambition-significance for each commitment as well as a systematic overstatement of the level of compliance. Given the fact that the Research Group has been examining this issue from a political science perspective and not from an economics perspective, no regressions have been employed and the corresponding economic techniques to correct for simultaneity bias have not been used.

With these caveats, the ambition-significance framework specified above has been applied, on a trial basis, to the 12 commitments in the G7 communiqué and to the 97 commitments in the G8 communiqué, as noted above. For this exercise, however, the individual sub-commitments listed above have been amalgamated into a single commitment, thus reducing the overall number of commitments from 109 (12+97) to 82 (12+70). (This comes from the consolidation in the G8 communiqué of commitments in Development from 15 to 8, Health from 15 to 4, Crime and Drugs from 18 to 14, and Ageing from 6 to 1.)

The results are listed in Table C.2.

The average scores, arranged by issue area, by communiqué, and overall, are listed in Table C.3.

These figures indicate that the Okinawa Summit, with an average score of 2.8 by equally weighted issue areas, or 2.69 by individual commitments, came close to the midpoint of the scale of 0 to 6 for assessing the ambition-significance of a summit's commitments. These scores are consistent with qualitative judgements, issued at the immediate conclusion of the Summit, that Okinawa was a summit of 'solid achievement' (Kirton 2000), or one deserving a grade of B (see Appendix A).

It is notable that both the G7 and G8 summits score in this midpoint range. While the G8 scores slightly higher on the measure of equally weighted issue areas, the variation

Table C.2a   Commitments Ranked by Ambition-Significance:
G7 Communiqué 2000

	Goal	Measure	Target Date	Novelty Timeliness	Scope	Content	Total (Score=6)
International Financial Architecture							
7	1	0	0	0	1	0	**2**
8(a)	1	0	0	0	1	0	**2**
8(b)	1	1	0	0	1	1	**4**
HIPC							
20(a)	1	0	0	0	1	1	**3**
20(b)	1	1	0	0	0	0	**2**
22	1	1	0	0	1	1	**4**
23	1	0	0	1	0	0	**2**
Global Financial System							
26(a)	1	0	0	0	0	0	**1**
26(b)	1	1	0	1	0	1	**4**
26(c)	1	0	0	1	0	1	**3**
Nuclear Safety							
29	1	1	0	0	0	0	**2**
30	1	1	0	0	0	0	**2**

Table C.2b   Commitments Ranked by Ambition-Significance:
G8 Communiqué 2000

	Goal	Measure	Target Date	Novelty Timeliness	Scope	Content	Total (Score=6)
World Economy							
9	1	0	0	0	0	0	**1**
IT							
11	1	0	0	1	0	0	**2**
12(a)	1	1	0	1	0	0	**3**
12(b)	1	1	1	1	1	0	**5**
Development							
13	1	0	1	1	0	0	**3**
15	1	0	0	1	1	0	**3**
17	1	0	0	0	0	0	**1**

19	1	1	1	1	1	1	**6**
20(a)	1	1	0	1	0	0	**3**
20(b)	1	0	1	1	0	0	**3**
20(c)	1	1	1	0	1	1	**5**
20(d)	1	1	0	0	0	0	**2**
Debt							
24(a)	1	0	0	0	1	0	**2**
24(b)	1	1	0	0	1	0	**3**
24(c)	1	1	1	0	1	1	**5**
24(d)	1	1	0	0	0	0	**2**
25	1	0	0	1	0	0	**2**
Health							
29	1	1	1	1	1	1	**6**
30	1	1	1	1	1	1	**6**
31(a)	1	1	1	1	0	0	**4**
31(b)	1	0	1	1	1	1	**5**
Trade							
35	1	0	0	0	0	0	**1**
36(a)	1	0	0	0	0	0	**1**
36(b)	1	0	1	0	1	0	**3**
38	1	0	0	0	0	0	**1**
Cultural Diversity							
41	1	1	0	1	0	1	**4**
42	1	1	1	1	0	1	**5**
Crime and Drugs							
43(a)	1	1	1	1	0	1	**5**
43(b)	1	0	1	0	1	0	**3**
43(c)	1	0	0	0	0	0	**1**
44	1	1	0	0	0	0	**2**
45(a)	1	0	0	1	0	0	**2**
45(b)	1	0	0	0	1	0	**2**
45(c)	1	0	0	1	0	0	**2**
45(d)	1	1	1	1	0	0	**4**
46	1	0	0	1	0	0	**2**
47(a)	1	0	0	0	0	0	**1**
47(b)	1	0	0	0	1	0	**2**
47(c)	1	1	0	0	0	0	**2**

49	1	0	0	1	0	0	**2**
50	1	0	0	0	0	0	**1**

Ageing

52	1	1	0	1	0	1	**4**

Life Science

55	1	0	0	1	1	0	**3**
58	1	1	0	1	0	1	**4**
59	1	0	0	1	1	0	**3**

Human Genome

62(a)	1	0	0	1	0	0	**2**
62(b)	1	0	0	1	0	0	**2**
63	1	0	0	1	1	0	**3**
64	1	0	0	0	0	0	**1**
65(a)	1	0	1	1	0	0	**3**
65(b)	1	1	1	1	0	0	**4**
66	1	0	0	0	1	0	**2**
67	1	0	0	0	0	0	**1**
68	1	1	1	0	0	0	**3**
69(a)	1	0	0	0	1	0	**2**
69(b)	1	0	0	0	0	0	**1**

Conflict Prevention

73(a)	1	0	0	1	0	0	**2**
73(b)	1	1	0	1	1	0	**4**
73(c)	1	0	0	1	0	0	**2**

Arms Control

74(a)	1	1	0	0	0	0	**2**
74(b)	1	0	0	0	0	0	**1**
77(a)	1	1	1	1	0	0	**4**
77(b)	1	0	0	0	1	0	**2**
78(a)	1	0	0	0	0	0	**1**
78(b)	1	1	0	0	0	0	**2**
78(c)	1	0	1	1	0	1	**4**

Terrorism

79(a)	1	0	0	1	0	0	**2**
79(b)	1	1	0	1	0	0	**3**
80	1	1	0	0	0	0	**2**
81	1	0	0	0	0	0	**1**

Table C.3   The 2000 Okinawa G7/8 Commitments Ranked by Average Ambition-Significance

G7 Communiqué

International Financial Architecture	2.67
HIPC	2.75
Global Financial System	2.67
Nuclear Safety	2.00
Average by Equally Weighted Issue Area	*2.52*
Average by Individual Commitments (N12)	*2.60*

G8 Communiqué

World Economy	1.00
Information Technology	3.33
Development	3.25
Debt	2.80
Health	5.25
Trade	1.50
Cultural Diversity	4.50
Crime and Drugs	2.21
Ageing	4.00
Life Science	3.33
Human Genome	2.18
Conflict Prevention	2.67
Arms Control	2.29
Terrorism	2.00
Average by Equally Weighted Issue Area	*2.88*
Average by Individual Commitments (N70)	*2.69*

Average of G7+G8 by Equally Weighted Issue Areas (N18)	*2.80*
Average of G7+G8 by Individual Commitments (N82)	*2.67*

is sufficiently slight to make interpretations based on this difference hazardous. The pattern does suggest, however, that the presence of Russia may marginally help and at a minimum does not harm G7/8 performance (although the different set of issue areas dealt with in each forum is the critical factor). This suggestion is reinforced by a direct G7 versus G8 comparison in those issue areas (the G7's HIPC versus the G8's debt, the G7's nuclear safety versus the G8's arms control) that are to some degree similar. By this standard only the G8's low score on 'World Economy' supports the case for caution in allowing Russia more of a place in the G7's economic/financial domain.

As suggested by Table C.4 (which combines the G7 and G8 issues areas in a single scaled ranked by their ambition-significance score), there is a wide variation by issue area in the performance of the summit.

Table C.4   G7/8 2000 Issue Areas Ranked by Ambition-Significance of Commitments

Health	5.25
Cultural Diversity	4.50
Ageing	4.00
Information Technology	3.33
Life Science	3.33
Development	3.25
Debt	2.80
Average by Equally Weighted Issue Areas	*2.80*
HIPC (G7)	2.75
Conflict Prevention	2.67
International Financial Architecture (G7)	2.67
Global Financial System (G7)	2.67
Average by Individual Commitments	*2.67*
Arms Control	2.29
Crime and Drugs	2.21
Human Genome	2.18
Terrorism	2.00
Nuclear Safety (G7)	2.00
Trade	1.50
World Economy	1.00

There are several striking patterns in this data. First, issue areas from the G8, rather than from the G7 tend to dominate the list. In fact, no issue area from the G7 ranked above the overall average by equally weighted issue areas. This suggests that the innovative dynamism of the G7/8 system has passed decisively from the G7 to the G8.

Second, the highest scoring issue areas are those that are relatively new to the G7/8 agenda, and in at least one case (cultural diversity) entirely new. Leading the list are health, cultural diversity, ageing, information technology, and life science, followed by development, debt, and HIPC. This suggests that Okinawa was indeed a development summit, as its producers had planned. But in some ways the competing theme of information technology did take precedence in the end (especially if one adds the results of the commitments in the separate Okinawa Charter on Information Technology not included in this analysis). Even more importantly, Okinawa was marked by its domestic intrusiveness, through its ambitious and significant commitment in areas long the preserve of domestic politics, and ones where often state-provincial and local governments as well as national ones have significant responsibilities. Above all, Okinawa should be remembered by this calculus as a social policy summit.

This premium on innovation is also evident in the political-security domain. Here conflict prevention ranks first as the most ambitious-significant issue area. More venerable subjects, even those featured at recent summits, such as arms control, crime and drugs, terrorism, and nuclear safety, rank well down on the list. (The regional security commitments issued in a separate declaration are not included in this analysis.) The low ranking of nuclear safety is somewhat of a surprise, given how large the 1999 criticality accident at Tokaimura loomed in Japanese political life.

Also noteworthy is the low ranking for those issue areas where the G7/8, and especially Japanese-hosted G7's have traditionally excelled. Standing out here is trade, whose very low score confirms the harsh judgement of informed observers about the Okinawa Summit's performance in this domain (Bayne 2001, Ullrich 2001). Moreover the low score for 'world economy', delivered by a G8 that was about to go into sharply slower growth in the coming months, and at a summit hosted in a long stagnant Japan suggests that complacency rather than prescience and prevention was the dominant approach.

At first glance, this overall pattern lends support to those who criticise the summit for its episodic focus on an ever-changing array of issues, rather than praise it for its persistent iteration on the most difficult but central issues in the world (Bayne 1999). Yet the solid scores on development, debt and HIPC, and the international financial architecture and the global financial system belie this criticism. They suggest a good balance between the new and the old. While Okinawa was thus at its most productive as an agenda-setting summit for the new century, it also 'hung in there' (Bayne 2000) to make progress on some persistent problems left over from the old one.

References

Bayne, Nicholas (1999). 'Continuity and Leadership in an Age of Globalisation'. In M. R. Hodges, J. J. Kirton and J. P. Daniels, eds., *The G8's Role in the New Millennium*, pp. 21–44. Ashgate, Aldershot.

Bayne, Nicholas (2000). *Hanging in There: The G7 and G8 Summit in Maturity and Renewal.* Ashgate, Aldershot.

Bayne, Nicholas (2001). 'Managing Globalisation and the New Economy: The Contribution of the G8 Summit'. In J. J. Kirton and G. M. von Furstenberg, eds., *New Directions in Global Economic Governance: Managing Globalisation in the Twenty-First Century*, pp. 171–188. Ashgate, Aldershot.

Kirton, John J. (2000). 'Preliminary Personal Assessment of the Kyushu-Okinawa Summit'. 23 July. <www.g7.utoronto.ca/g7/evaluations/2000okinawa/kirtonassesment.htm> (February 2002).

Kokotsis, Eleanore (1999). *Keeping International Commitments: Compliance, Credibility, and the G7, 1988–1995.* Garland, New York.

Ullrich, Heidi K. (2001). 'Stimulating Trade Liberalisation after Seattle: G7/8 Leadership in Global Governance'. In J. J. Kirton and G. M. von Furstenberg, eds., *New Directions in Global Economic Governance: Creating International Order for the Twenty-First Century*, pp. 219–240. Ashgate, Aldershot.

Appendix D

G7/8 Commitments and Their Significance

John J. Kirton, Ella Kokotsis, and Diana Juricevic

	1975	1979	1980	1981	1982	1986	1987	1988	1989	1993	1994	1995	1996	2000	2001
Total Leaders' Commitments															
Total Commitments	37	34	55	40	65	39	54	27	61	29	51	76	125	169	58
G7 Declarations	23			31	30			16	38		27	59	58	12	10
														(43%)	(40%)
G8 Declarations	NA			NA	NA			NA	NA		NA	NA	NA	97	43
														(45%)	
Political Declarations	–				–			7	–	5	–	–	49	54	
Chairs' Political Summaries			–	2				4			12	19			
Other Declarations	14			7	35		–	–	23		–	–	18		
Total Leaders' Commitments by Issue Area															
World Economy	10	1	5	5	13	9	11	1	1	4		4	19	1	1
Financial System	5		4		6			4	2					6	5
Microeconomics									3				12		
Employment	–			–	35		6	–	–	2	12	3	7	–	1
Education				–				–						–	7
Ageing			–			–						1		6	
ICT				–	–			–	–		–	–	3	57	3

	1975	1979	1980	1981	1982	1986	1987	1988	1989	1993	1994	1995	1996	2000	2001
Trade	–	3	6	6	–	4	9	6	6	1	5	9		4	2
Development	4	6	6	10	4	7	4	3	2	6	4	7	21	15	12
Debt Relief/HIPC	–		–	–				2	2	5		5		9	7
Health	–							–					3	15	3
Energy	1	21	25	8	2			–	–	–	–	–	–	–	–
Environment	–						3	–	11	3	5	5	7	11	9
Biotech/Food Safety							1							3	2
Nuclear/Ukraine	–					1		–	–		7	3	5	2	–
Cultural Diversity														2	–
Refugees		3		1											
Human Rights	–							–	3			2	5	–	–
East-West Relations	3			2	4	4	5	4	9	8					
Transition Economies	–							–	–			1	1		
Multilateral Inst.	–							–	–			19	4		
Crime and Drugs	–						2	1	11		3	3	14	18	2
Terrorism	–		5	7		14	13	2	9			2	7	4	–
Arms Control	–			–				–	–			4	4	7	–
Regional Issues	–			1				–	–			4	4	–	2 (33%)
Middle East	–				1			4	–			1	–	2	–
Africa	–			–				–	–			1		2	2 (75%)
Asia Pacific	–		4					–	2			1	–	–	–
Europe	–			–	–			4	2			1	9	2	–
Conflict Prevention	–							–				4	–	3	–

Notes: A dash (–) indicates the subject was discussed but no commitment was made. Figures in brackets are significance scores.

DOCUMENTARY APPENDICES

Appendix E

Statement of G7 Finance Ministers and Central Bank Governors

Palermo, 17 February 2001

1. We, the Finance Ministers of the G7 countries, the Central Bank Governors of Canada, Japan, the United States, and the United Kingdom, the President of the Euro-group, and the President of the European Central Bank, met today in Palermo with the Managing Director of the International Monetary Fund to review recent developments in the world economy. We, the Finance Ministers and Central Bank Governors of the G7 also discussed the progress made towards strengthening the international financial architecture, in particular by laying plans for the reform of Multilateral Development Banks, the implementation of the HIPC Initiative and ways to proceed beyond debt relief, including for the preparation for the Genova Summit. We also met with the Finance Minister and the Central Bank Governor of Russia and with Representatives of the European Commission to discuss recent developments of the Russian economy.

Developments in the World Economy

2. Although global growth this year is likely to be somewhat slower than we expected when we last met, the basic factors that have supported sustained growth in many of the major industrial economies remain in place. We agreed on the need for both macroeconomic and structural policies in all our countries to support growth. In this context, lower energy prices and stable oil markets are important.
3. We reemphasized our commitment to foster conditions for sustainable growth worldwide. In this context, we stressed the importance of continued cooperation among the G7 countries. More specifically:
   - In the United States, economic growth has slowed, though economic fundamentals remain strong. Monetary and fiscal policies should aim at supporting sustained growth, while preserving budgetary restraint and price stability and increasing national saving over the medium term.
   - In the United Kingdom and Canada, growth remains healthy and unemployment is low, with some signs of a temporary slowing in economic growth. Policies should continue to sustain growth and employment over the medium term, while meeting inflation targets.
   - In the euro area growth prospects remain favourable, thanks to strong domestic demand. Policies should be directed at enhancing growth potential, through

continued coordinated reform efforts aimed at increasing product and labour market efficiency. Tax reforms are being implemented while pursuing fiscal consolidation. In view of Europe's aging population, budgets and social security systems need to be further strengthened.

- In Japan, while a modest recovery is expected, prices continue to decline and downside risks remain. In this context, monetary policy should continue to ensure that liquidity is provided in ample terms. Efforts to strengthen the financial sector should be enhanced.

Exchange Rates

4. We discussed developments in our exchange and financial markets. We reiterated our view that exchange rates among major currencies should reflect economic fundamentals. We will continue to monitor developments closely and to cooperate in exchange markets as appropriate.

Emerging Market Economies

5. After two years of strong recovery, the outlook for emerging market economies has become more mixed. We welcome the substantial progress achieved in emerging Asia to reduce vulnerabilities, including the improvement of the external debt structure in the crisis-affected countries, and the adoption of more sustainable exchange rate regimes. To secure future growth, it is important to pursue necessary reforms of the financial and corporate sectors. In Latin America, sound macroeconomic and structural policies are needed to help reduce vulnerabilities. In all emerging market economies, we stress the importance of further intensifying efforts to implement internationally agreed standards and codes. The pace of reforms should not be relaxed.

Russia

6. We welcome the recent improvements in the macroeconomic and balance of payments situation of the Russian economy. We strongly urge the Russian authorities to step up the process of economic reforms and meet in full their financial obligations in order to restore promptly normal relations with the

international financial community. While some elements of the comprehensive tax reform package have been adopted, critical challenges remain, such as enforcing the rule of law, attacking nonpayments and barter, strengthening the banking system, improving corporate governance, and fighting money laundering. On the latter, we urge the Russian authorities to move quickly to remedy the deficiencies identified by the FATF in June 2000. We call upon the Russian authorities, as they address the difficult and complex process of economic transition, to implement a credible programme of reform, and create the essential market institutions and infrastructure for sound growth. In this context, we encourage the Russian authorities to continue to work with the IMF and World Bank.

HIPC and Development Beyond Debt Relief

7. We noted with satisfaction that the implementation of the enhanced HIPC (Heavily Indebted Poor Countries) Initiative has already enabled 22 countries to reach the Decision Point. These countries are now receiving significant debt relief. We are committed to helping them implement their poverty reduction strategies and thereby reach their Completion Points. This will lead to $34 billion of debt relief under HIPC, reducing the debt of these countries on average by two thirds. We noted that most of the eligible countries that have not yet reached the Decision Point are currently in, or just emerging from, conflict. We call on these countries to reach a peaceful resolution of their problems, and we intend to help them in their reconstruction efforts.

8. We urge all creditors to participate fully in providing on a timely basis their share of debt reduction under the enhanced HIPC Initiative. The G7 governments have gone beyond the HIPC targets and agreed to commit to provide 100 percent debt reduction on ODA and eligible commercial credits for countries qualifying for HIPC debt reduction. We urge other bilateral creditors to take similar action.

9. We consider that debt reduction is only one element of a broader, more ambitious strategy for poverty reduction, based on three pillars. First, action is needed to launch a new multilateral trade round and to open further markets to exports from the poorest countries. Second, a more favourable environment for attracting private investment needs to be created in the poorest countries. Third, within country-owned poverty-reduction strategies, resources need to be channelled, in a more efficient and coordinated way, to the social sector, as we work towards the objectives contained in the 2015 International Development Goals (IDG).

Strengthening the International Financial Architecture, Including Reform of the Multilateral Development Banks

10. We noted the progress made to reinforce the international financial system. We look forward to further progress on prioritization of IMF conditionality, implementation of the internationally agreed codes and standards, crisis prevention, private sector involvement, and financial liberalization. We note the need for further discussion on quotas at the IMF Board.

11. We also discussed the main features of the reform of the MDBs, following on the recommendations contained in the Fukuoka report of July 2000. The MDBs have made considerable progress on internal and policy reforms in recent years, but more can be done to focus their action on poverty reduction, consistent with the IDG. Key principles of the reform are: greater selectivity in setting priorities, focus on the needs of the poorest, effective and transparent internal governance, and improving development impact.

12. To this end, MDBs should:
    - further improve and strengthen accountability and transparency, including through the establishment or the reinforcement of central control mechanisms to ensure compliance with agreed policies and safeguards;
    - enhance substantially coordination and interaction among themselves and with other development actors;
    - ensure full and timely disclosure of all program and policy documents;
    - undertake expeditiously a comprehensive review of pricing policies;
    - integrate due diligence and fiduciary diagnostics into country assistance strategies and in decisions on the choice of lending instruments.

    In our view, selectivity in setting priorities and improving development impact require particular attention to: appropriate provision of global public goods, good governance, private sector development in lower income countries, and financial sector development, including fighting financial abuse. We look forward to intensifying our dialogue with the MDBs to this end and to reviewing progress at the Spring meetings.

Action against the Abuses of the Global Financial System

13. Following our report to the Okinawa Summit and the Heads' recommendations we note the positive evolution of the dialogue with the countries involved. The Financial Action Task Force (FATF) has recently reported the significant progress made by most of the fifteen non-co-operative countries and territories (NCCTs) listed in June 2000. Seven countries have already enacted most, if not all, of the legislation needed to fight money laundering effectively. We encourage those

jurisdictions to demonstrate their willingness and ability to implement these reforms, so that they can be de-listed at the earliest possible time. To this end, we remain committed to continuing dialogue with the identified countries, and to provide technical assistance where possible. However, we reaffirm our commitment, where dialogue has failed to generate adequate progress, to implement coordinated countermeasures that may be recommended by the FATF at its meeting in June 2001. We urge the International Financial Institutions, in particular the International Monetary Fund and the World Bank, to help NCCTs implement the relevant international anti-money laundering standards (the FATF 40 Recommendations), as appropriate, through technical assistance, programme design and policy dialogue.

14. We reaffirm our support for the efforts of OECD to address harmful tax practices. We encourage the OECD to continue its efforts. We encourage the efforts of the OECD member countries to meet their commitments. We welcome the cooperative dialogue which has been established with countries and jurisdictions outside the OECD area. We welcome the new commitments made by some jurisdictions to eliminate their harmful tax practices by end of 2005. We encourage others to make early commitments, so that as few jurisdictions as possible are included in the list of uncooperative tax havens which we look forward to examining at the Genova Summit. We encourage all OECD governments to consider offering, under the auspices of the OECD and other international organizations, technical assistance to cooperating jurisdictions, if needed to comply with their commitments.

15. We welcome the intent of certain OFCs to improve supervisory, regulatory, co-operation and information exchange policies and practices and encourage OFCs to disclose assessment findings, including those done by the IMF, as a means of demonstrating compliance with and progress in meeting international standards in these areas. We ask the FSF to monitor the implementation of its recommendations and to consider means of recognising progress being made by certain OFCs and recommend any future action, if necessary.

Appendix F

Statement of G7 Finance Ministers and Central Bank Governors on Turkey

19 March 2001

We welcome the announcement of the Turkish authorities on the framework for a strong new economic reform programme, supported by the IMF and the World Bank.

The programme will rightly focus on achieving low inflation and sustainable public finances through sound fiscal and monetary policies, supported by vigorous implementation of structural reform. We particularly welcome the comprehensive and urgent plans in the programme to tackle the problems of the banking sector, in co-operation with the World Bank and the IMF.

Long-term political commitment by the Turkish authorities to rigorous implementation of their programme remains absolutely critical to its success, and we will maintain our support for these efforts. A return of market confidence and the continuous engagement of the private sector are also critical for the Turkish economic recovery.

Appendix G

Statement of G7 Finance Ministers and Central Bank Governors

Washington, 28 April 2001

1. We met today to discuss recent developments in the world economy, strengthening the international financial system, the reform of the multilateral development banks and measures to meet the challenges of international development. We also met with the Finance Minister and the Deputy Central Bank Governor of Russia and with representatives of the European Commission to discuss recent developments in the Russian economy.

Developments in the G7 Economies

2. Although global growth has slowed over the past year, the foundations for economic expansion are sound. In fact, the prospects for improving the world standard of living are compelling. We are all dedicated to the proposition that it is in the interest of the world economy for each of our economies to grow closer to their potential. We agreed that we should be vigilant and forward-looking in maintaining and implementing polices that promote strong productivity growth, including sound macroeconomic policy, structural reform and international economic cooperation. We will work together to achieve the goal of free trade. We recognize that lower energy prices and stable oil markets are important.
    *   In the United States, growth has slowed sharply. However, long-term economic fundamentals — productivity gains and factor market flexibility — remain strong. Monetary policy should continue to be aimed at contributing to sustained growth and maintaining price stability. Fiscal policy should also be targeted at bolstering long-term fundamentals.
    *   Growth in Canada has also slowed; in the United Kingdom the slowdown appears to be only moderate. In both countries, unemployment and inflation remain low. Policies should continue to support the foundations for sustained growth and employment over the medium term, while meeting inflation targets.
    *   In the euro area, growth prospects have moderated, though remaining favorable. Policies should continue to emphasize strengthening potential growth and lowering unemployment through further structural reforms that increase the efficient operation of labor and product markets. Fiscal policy should aim to improve economic efficiency, notably through tax reform, while preserving the pace of the consolidation of public finances.

- In Japan, economic activity has weakened, and prices continue to decline. Against this background, monetary policy should continue to provide ample liquidity until consumer price inflation stays at or above zero. Vigorous implementation of financial and corporate sector reforms is needed in order to support medium-term recovery.

Exchange Rates

3.   We discussed developments in our exchange and financial markets. We reiterated our view that exchange rates among major currencies should reflect economic fundamentals. We will continue to monitor developments closely and to cooperate in exchange markets as appropriate.

Broader Global Economic Developments

4.   The slowing in the pace of global economic activity has also affected the prospects for growth in the emerging market and developing economies. In Asia, on the whole, after two years of strong growth, there are clear signs of a slowdown. Throughout the region, the implementation of structural reforms will be crucial to fostering strong, sustained growth. In Latin America, where growth also has slowed, structural measures are needed to raise productivity growth, and further fiscal consolidation is required to reduce financing requirements. In central and eastern Europe, reforms undertaken during the past few years have contributed to recent strong growth; fiscal consolidation and further structural reforms are needed to maintain performance. In Africa, although growth continues to rise, per capita incomes remain very low. Implementation of credible macroeconomic and structural adjustment remains a prerequisite for strong growth and broad-based poverty reduction.

5.   We agree that free trade is an important driver of economic growth. Open markets can increase efficiency and productivity, thereby promoting development and poverty reduction in all countries. We strongly support efforts to launch a new WTO round this year, to reduce trade barriers in both industrialized and developing countries. We also welcome industrialized country initiatives which, by providing improved market access for exports from the poorest countries, will facilitate their integration into the world economy. It would be appropriate for the IMF and World Bank to reflect on ways and means to facilitate trade liberalization.

Turkey

6. We welcome Turkey's strong economic reform program as a basis for Turkey to reach agreement with the IMF on a package that merits the continued support of the international community's public and private sectors. We look forward to Turkey's rigorous implementation of all these necessary measures. In this context, we welcome the decision of the IMF and the World Bank to provide additional assistance for the program.

Russia

7. We welcome the continued growth of the Russian economy and encourage the Russian authorities to step up the pace of economic reforms that are necessary for sound and sustainable economic development. Russia needs to take steps to create an economic environment conducive to investment, both foreign and domestic, such as enforcing the rule of law, promoting the free flow of information, attacking nonpayments and barter, strengthening the banking system, and improving corporate governance. We urge the Russian authorities to draw on the expertise of the IMF and World Bank in addressing these issues. We welcome the ratification by the Duma of the Strasbourg anti-money laundering convention and urge the Russian authorities to move quickly to remedy the deficiencies identified by the Financial Action Task Force (FATF) in June 2000, in particular by passing a comprehensive anti-money laundering law. These steps would help facilitate Russia's integration with the global economic system.

Crisis Prevention, Crisis Resolution, and the IMF

8. We stress that strong and effective crisis prevention is a top priority. Both the IMF and individual countries should play key roles in this effort. Learning from previous experience, and with a view to forestalling crises, we resolve to monitor economic and financial developments more closely and to encourage early action to correct policies. In this context, we underscore the following:
    *   Enhanced IMF surveillance is at the heart of crisis prevention. As part of this effort, the Fund should accelerate its work in developing and publishing indicators of national balance sheet and liquidity risk. The Fund should also further its work in building up and publishing macro-prudential indictors for the financial sector.

- We believe that implementation of internationally agreed standards and codes offers countries the opportunity to strengthen their basic infrastructure for growth and stability and to provide information to markets in a way that reinforces these goals. In this context, we encourage all countries to intensify their efforts, recognizing their different stages of development and institutional capacities, to meet international codes and standards and to publish their Reports on the Observance of Standards and Codes (ROSCs).
- We stress the importance of the joint IMF and World Bank effort to assess the strength of financial sectors through the Financial Sector Assessment Program (FSAP). We welcome the increased use of FSAPs and ROSCs as essential instruments to detect countries' vulnerabilities and the future, mutually agreed integration of such assessments in the IMF's surveillance. We welcome the agreement that countries should have the option of releasing a summary of Fund/Bank assessments. We call on the IFIs to support countries in their efforts to strengthen their domestic financial sectors and to pursue capital account liberalization, in order to mobilize capital both from domestic and international markets.
- The IMF needs to sharpen its focus on financial markets and their implications for the sustainability of capital flows. In this context, we welcome the creation of the IMF's International Capital Markets Department and the Capital Markets Consultative Group.

9. More broadly, we urge the IMF itself, as well as member countries, to continue in the drive toward greater transparency and accountability.

10. We also welcome the ongoing work to review conditions attached to IMF lending. This review should be aimed at: reinforcing the public integrity of the IMF; ensuring that all IMF programs meet high-quality standards; helping countries take ownership of programs that achieve meaningful results; and addressing the macroeconomically relevant structural challenges confronting economies. As part of this review, it is also critical that progress be made in strengthening Fund-Bank collaboration so that countries' needs are effectively addressed.

11. Work is underway in several other areas in the IMF. We note the progress made to establish an operational framework for private sector involvement in crisis resolution. We call on the IMF to expedite its program of work on private sector involvement and agree on the importance of taking future decisions in a way that is consistent with such a framework. We note the need for further discussion on quotas at the IMF Executive Board.

Reform of the Multilateral Development Banks

12. Since we met in Palermo, we have intensified our dialogue with the MDBs and held informal consultations with other shareholders. A report on MDB reform will be released at the G7 Finance Ministers' meeting in Rome on July 7, for submission to the Genoa Summit.

13. We reaffirm our strong commitment to strengthen the MDB system. MDBs must continue to play a crucial role in supporting economic development and should ensure that their operations to reduce poverty in developing countries concentrate on enhancing productivity growth and raising income per capita. Towards these ends, they should adopt a more selective approach that sharpens the focus and improves the effectiveness of their operations. We agree that the MDBs' attention should focus on the following areas for immediate action:

    * Strengthening consistency and coordination among MDBs, in particular with respect to the substance and timing of MDB Country Strategies and their linkage to country-owned development strategies such as Poverty Reduction Strategy Papers. It is critical that MDBs harmonize at the highest appropriate standard operational procedures, policies and safeguards.
    * Improving internal governance, in particular by ensuring wide public consultation and debate through the publication of draft and final key institutional policy and strategy documents, including Country Strategies, and strengthening accountability and transparency in the budgetary process.
    * Promoting effective public sector management in borrowing countries, in particular by strengthening analytical and diagnostic work and improving country capacity on fiduciary and safeguard policies.

14. We agree that the MDBs have an important role to play in combating poverty in Middle Income Countries (MICs), and welcome the ongoing debate in the World Bank to further refine this role. In this context, we also agree that the MDBs should expeditiously conduct a review of their lending instruments and pricing policies with a view to enhancing the development impact of scarce MDB resources. We commend the Bank for its efforts to redesign its role in its ordinary lending programs but note that the proposed approach needs further study, particularly with regard to the policy environment, institutional capacity, and accountability of both borrowers and the Bank. We agree that the Bank and its shareholders should consider in the period ahead the scope and modalities of the Bank's proposed shift to programmatic lending. We urge the World Bank and, where appropriate, the other MDBs to continue their work to refine this approach in the next few months.

15. We note the ongoing discussions on the increased use of grants within IDA-13 and encourage the World Bank to carefully explore the related financial implications and practical implementation issues. We welcome consideration of measures to improve IDA's effectiveness, including strengthening the PRSP-led approach.

HIPC and Development Beyond Debt Relief

16. We reviewed the implementation of the Enhanced HIPC Initiative. Twenty-two countries are already receiving interim debt relief under the initiative, which is designed to provide long-term debt sustainability. We urge the other eligible countries, including those in, or emerging from, conflict, to take the necessary steps to focus on poverty reduction and growth and benefit from this important international program. We again urge other bilateral creditors to join with the G7 and other governments in providing 100% cancellation of all eligible debt.

17. We underscore that debt reduction is only one aspect of development and must be complemented by strong reform programs in order to secure its true benefits. In this context, we urge countries receiving HIPC debt relief, working in cooperation with the IFIs, to strengthen the quality of poverty reduction strategies, to enhance their ability to track and monitor the savings from debt relief and to focus these savings on priority investments, such as education and health, and to adopt and implement high quality reforms.

18. We look forward to further discussions on moving beyond debt relief in preparation for the Genoa Summit. In this context, we underscore the importance of focusing on steps to increase opportunities for trade, foster more favorable environments for attracting private investment and promote efficient and coordinated investment in the social sector, as we work toward the International Development Goals. In particular, we will work constructively with others on a health initiative to tackle the infectious diseases of tuberculosis, malaria and HIV/AIDS.

Action Against the Abuses of the Global Financial System

19. We reaffirm our support for all the objectives of the multilateral effort to fight against abuse of the global financial system. We express our support for the ongoing work of FATF, and we welcome the significant progress made by most of the 15 jurisdictions listed by FATF as non-cooperative countries and territories (NCCTs) in June 2000 towards addressing the deficiencies in their anti-money laundering systems. We encourage those jurisdictions to implement needed reforms. We note our continued commitment to maintain a dialogue with these countries, to provide training and technical assistance, to delist those making

adequate progress, and to implement coordinated measures as may be recommended by FATF against those NCCTs where dialogue has failed to generate sufficient progress. In addition, we welcome the FATF decision to undertake a review of its 40 recommendations to strengthen the international money laundering standard. We also welcome the IMF and World Bank Boards' recent decisions to recognize the FATF 40 Recommendations as the appropriate international standard for combating money laundering and encourage the Fund and the Bank, working in collaboration with FATF, to incorporate the relevant FATF 40 Recommendations into a ROSC module as soon as possible.

Appendix H

Fighting the Abuses of the Global Financial System: Report of G7 Finance Ministers and Central Bank Governors

Rome, 7 July 2001

A. Introduction

1. Last year in Okinawa, G7 Leaders endorsed our report on Actions Against Abuse of the Global Financial System. In particular, our report recommended that Governments intensify their cooperation and strengthen international frameworks to effectively combat money laundering and harmful tax practices, and to improve the observance of international standards and good governance. We asked for better coordination of efforts under way in various international fora and for expeditious follow-up actions and stressed the need for open dialogue and the provision of technical assistance where necessary to help countries meet international standards. We also underlined the need to promote international cooperation between law enforcement and tax and regulatory authorities in the fight against financial crime and abuse.
2. Significant progress has been achieved during the past year, and we recommend the following actions to continue the international fight against financial abuse in the year ahead.

B. Money Laundering

3. Last year the Financial Action Task Force (FATF) listed 15 jurisdictions as Non-cooperative countries and territories (NCCTs), and we issued coordinated advisories to encourage our domestic financial institutions to pay special attention to transactions with entities located in NCCTs.
4. We note that the situation has improved markedly. We welcome the progress in enacting legislation and enhancing practices in the Bahamas, the Cayman Islands, Liechtenstein and Panama, while noting the need for continuous attention to several implementation aspects. We note the FATF's decision to de-list these jurisdictions. We will rescind or revise our advisories. We recommend that the FATF, in connection with the relevant FATF-style regional bodies, continue to monitor these jurisdictions' implementation.

5. However challenges remain:
   - The FATF concluded that Nauru, the Philippines and Russia have failed to make adequate progress. We will implement coordinated countermeasures against these jurisdictions later this fall if they have not enacted significant reforms by then, as recommended by FATF.
   - Another eight jurisdictions (Cook Islands, Dominica, Israel, Lebanon, Marshall Islands, Niue, St. Kitts and Nevis and St. Vincent and the Grenadines) have made some progress, though not sufficient to bring their legislation to the required standard or to complete the implementation of legislative reforms. We call on those jurisdictions to take the necessary measures so that they can be de-listed as soon as possible.
   - Finally, Egypt, Guatemala, Hungary, Indonesia, Myanmar and Nigeria have been added by the FATF to the NCCTs list. We urge these jurisdictions to quickly correct identified deficiencies in their anti-money laundering regimes.
6. We welcome the FATF's decision to continue to monitor the progress of all jurisdictions on the NCCTs list. We recommend that, should those jurisdictions fail to sustain their efforts, the FATF should consider additional actions. We will maintain ongoing dialogue with, and provide technical assistance, as appropriate, to, jurisdictions willing and committed to strengthening their anti-money laundering efforts.
7. Evolving money laundering trends and experience over recent years indicate the need to strengthen anti-money laundering standards. We welcome the process of revising the FATF 40 Recommendations (FATF 40), which should lead to an updated set of standards. We call on the FATF, as an international standard-setting organization, to ensure that the revision process is open, transparent and consultative. In particular this should include dialogue with FATF style bodies, IFIs and other relevant international organisations, non-FATF members and private sector experts.
8. We note that important progress has been made on four issues identified in our Fukuoka report as vital to combat money laundering:
   - Gatekeepers: the 1999 G8 Moscow Ministerial Conference on Combating Transnational Organized Crime recognized the need to involve professionals such as lawyers and accountants in the fight against money laundering; since then this issue has been discussed extensively, taking into account differences in national legal systems. We will continue to consider appropriate solutions. In this respect, we note the recent Canadian legislation and the proposed EU directive. We will also continue our efforts to define appropriate solutions and urge the FATF to consider such issues in the context of reviewing the FATF 40.
   - International Payments System: we welcome the clarification by the Committee on Payment and Settlement Systems of the G10 central banks that technical issues are not an obstacle to including originator identification in international

wire transfers. We commit to including this information in our systems and urge the FATF to seek a similar result during its revisions of the FATF 40.

- Corporate vehicles: we underscore our continued concern that corporate vehicles, under certain conditions, can be misused for money laundering and other illegal purposes. We welcome the OECD's report on corporate vehicles, which suggests a menu of possible options to address this matter. National authorities should be able to obtain and share information on the beneficial ownership and control of corporate vehicles established in their own jurisdictions for the purpose of investigating illicit activities and fulfilling their regulatory/ supervisory functions, in accordance with legal frameworks. We welcome the FATF intention to set appropriate standards to combat the misuse of corporate vehicles.
- Stolen assets: We express our concern about money laundering of illegal proceeds derived from theft and diversion of public assets and corruption by government officials. Our experts have begun to review and discuss best practices with regard to identification, tracing and restoration to the rightful owner of foreign stolen assets. We urge broader and enhanced international cooperation on this matter.

C. Offshore Financial Centres

9. Last year the Financial Stability Forum (FSF) published a report with recommendations for improving supervisory and regulatory systems and co-operation practices in all OFCs. This report was followed by an assessment of OFCs' adherence to relevant international standards and then grouped these OFCs by the perceived quality of their supervision, regulation and co-operation. In some OFCs, financial regulation and supervision were considered to be weak, potentially increasing the vulnerability of the global financial system. In some cases weaknesses extended to corporate vehicles.

10. We note that the FSF's publication of the OFC Report and grouping has successfully induced many OFCs to initiate positive action. We welcome the legislative steps initiated by some OFCs as well as their efforts to build up supervisory resources and enhance the reporting of financial data and we encourage them to adhere to relevant international standards, in particular to those relating to (i) cross-border co-operation and information sharing, (ii) essential supervisory powers and practices, and (iii) customer identification and record keeping.

11. In its report, the FSF recommended that the IMF put in place a process for assessing adherence to standards in OFCs. We welcome the IMF's decision to implement these recommendations and note that its initiative, covering both financial sector supervision and statistics, is under way. We welcome the decision by several

OFCs to work closely with the Fund and observe that the initiative has already led them to review their practices.

12. National authorities, standard-setting bodies and other international financial institutions are supporting the IMF's assessment program, making available resources to assist OFCs in implementation, and providing training opportunities. We note however that many OFCs, while committed to concrete action, do not possess sufficient resources to carry out the needed improvements. We will continue our efforts to supply technical expertise, both bilaterally and through multilateral channels.

13. Last year in Fukuoka we welcomed the identification by the FSF of priority jurisdictions that were perceived not to meet international standards for financial supervision and regulation adequately. We urged the IMF to conduct quickly a specific assessment of these offshore financial centers. We expect the IMF to provide an extensive report to the September meeting of the FSF, spelling out the number of jurisdictions assessed to date and summarizing the results of those assessments. We welcome the Forum's decision to take stock of the IMF's assessment exercise and request the Forum to prepare for our September 2001 meeting a report on progress in implementing its recommendations and options for any future action.

D. Tax

Harmful Tax Practices

14. We welcome the report of the Committee on Fiscal Affairs of the OECD on the harmful tax practices project and affirm our support for the work, with its recent developments, aimed at addressing such practices in OECD Member countries, non-OECD economies and tax haven jurisdictions. We look forward to the publication of the OECD 2001 progress report.

15. We note that the project does not seek to dictate to any country what its tax rates should be, or how its tax system should be structured. By providing a co-operative framework within which countries can work together to eliminate harmful tax practices, the work seeks to preserve the effective fiscal sovereignty of all States and to encourage an environment in which fair tax competition can take place. It will also contribute to reduce the scope of financial crime.

16. We note that the ongoing work by the OECD has led thus far to commitments by 10 tax haven jurisdictions to eliminate their harmful tax practices by the end of 2005, and that other jurisdictions listed as tax havens in the June 2000 OECD Report are engaged in a continuing dialogue with the OECD. We also note that

the OECD envisages to extend to 30th November 2001 the time for making commitments. We encourage remaining jurisdictions to commit by that date to transparency and effective information exchange, and to work in a co-operative dialogue with the OECD. We would also welcome the removal by tax havens of other practices to the extent that they inhibit fair tax competition.

17. We also note the developments with respect to the timing of a potential framework of co-ordinated defensive measures, which would apply to jurisdictions outside the OECD no earlier than it would apply to OECD Member countries. However we acknowledge that the adoption of defensive measures is at the discretion of individual countries.

18. We note the continuing commitment by the OECD Members to eliminate their harmful tax practices by April 2003 and we urge the OECD to develop the guidance needed to assist OECD Member countries in determining whether preferential regimes are harmful.

19. We ask the OECD to continue to monitor the effective implementation of commitments.

20. We note the fruitful dialogue that has started with non-OECD economies on their experiences with harmful tax practices and look forward to its continuation. The project would be enhanced as countries outside the OECD associate themselves with the work and we urge them to do so.

21. We recognize that jurisdictions may require technical assistance in implementing the commitments undertaken, notably in the field of exchange of information, and we therefore ask OECD Member countries, IFIs and others to consider providing such assistance as appropriate in developing their programs.

Electronic Commerce

22. We welcome the progress made by the OECD on addressing electronic commerce taxation issues and we note in particular the considerable progress that has been achieved since our Fukuoka Report of last year on specific issues relating to direct and indirect taxation, as well as on the tax administration challenges and opportunities.

23. We also note that Tax Administrations of OECD and non-OECD countries gathered recently in Montreal, and that the validity of the Taxation Framework Conditions, that were agreed in Ottawa in 1998 by OECD countries, has gained considerable endorsement.

24. We encourage a continued fruitful dialogue between OECD and non-OECD governments and business.

25. We urge the OECD to continue working towards implementation of the Ottawa Taxation Framework Conditions in particular with respect to consumption tax aspects.

E. Role of the International Financial Institutions

26. The IFIs have an important role to play in the protection of the integrity of the international financial system against abuse. Strengthening a country's capacity to combat money laundering is an integral part of that agenda.

27. We welcome the IMF and World Bank Boards' recent decisions to recognize the FATF 40 Recommendations as the appropriate international standard for combating money laundering. We underscore our call on the IFIs, working in collaboration with FATF, to incorporate the relevant FATF 40 Recommendations into a Report on Observance of Standards and Codes module on money laundering as soon as possible.

28. We welcome the decision by the Fund and the Bank to include evaluation of anti-money laundering measures in their assessment and surveillance of financial sectors, including in Financial Sector Assessment Programs.

29. As part of the enhanced focus on anti-money laundering, we welcome the MDBs increased due diligence relating to transactions and dealings with entities located in NCCTs.

30. We urge the IFIs to support with technical assistance jurisdictions committed to strengthening their institutional capacity and to correcting deficiencies in their anti-money laundering regimes. We encourage the Regional and Sub Regional Multilateral Development Banks to continue incorporating anti-money laundering efforts into their dialogue and programs with their members. The results should be incorporated in the Joint Report on the Implementation of Codes and Standards we have asked the MDBs to prepare by the end of the year.

Appendix I

Strengthening the International Financial System and the Multilateral Development Banks

Report of G7 Finance Ministers and Central Bank Governors
Rome, 7 July 2001

A. Introduction

1. The international financial system is central to the functioning of the global economy. It provides a framework that facilitates the exchange of goods, services and capital, and that sustains sound economic growth. A central objective for us, the Finance Ministers of G7 countries, is to foster the continuing development of the conditions necessary for financial and economic stability, which in turn are essential if the benefits of global economic integration are to be sustainable and broadly shared.

2. The financial crises in emerging market countries over the past decade have underscored both the costs of financial instability and the speed with which problems in one country can spread to others. Finding ways to limit the occurrence of financial crises, and the severity of those that do occur, has been central to our work agenda in recent years.

3. We identified, at the time of the Cologne Summit, in June 1999, a number of proposals aimed at promoting stability of the international financial system and improving its capacity to withstand the challenges of future crises, including reforming the Bretton Woods institutions, and adopting the appropriate policies to reduce systemic risks.

4. Last year in Fukuoka, we reviewed the major steps taken to further the principles and recommendations outlined in Cologne, in particular efforts by many developing countries to promote financial stability, including the adoption of appropriate foreign exchange regimes and of internationally agreed standards and codes, and the strengthening of domestic financial sectors. We also discussed improvements of the governance and efficacy of activities of the International Financial Institutions (IFIs) including the progress by the International Monetary Fund (IMF) in the assessment of standards and codes, the involvement of the private sector in the prevention and resolution of financial crises, and the enhancement of transparency and accountability in all areas of IFIs operation.

5. In Fukuoka we agreed to continue our efforts to strengthen the international financial architecture by focusing on the reform of the IMF and of the Multilateral

Development Banks (MDBs), on responses to the challenges posed by Highly Leveraged Institutions (HLIs), Offshore Financial Centers (OFCs) and cross-border capital movements, and on regional cooperation.

6. Since last year, substantial progress has been achieved in a number of key areas:
    a. A major review of IMF lending facilities has been completed, to enable a more efficient use of resources and to enhance the catalytic role of official financing. The reform of the IMF contingent credit line facility is aimed in particular at strengthening the Fund's role in crisis prevention.
    b. The IMF has undertaken important initiatives to strengthen financial sector surveillance. We welcome, in particular, the recent establishment of the International Capital Markets Department, and of the Capital Markets Consultative Group to develop a constructive dialogue with the private sector.
    c. The IMF has resolved to put crisis prevention at the heart of its activities, and to intensify its efforts in developing vulnerability indicators and an early warning system. We also appreciate the ongoing work to prioritize and focus conditionality and enhance countries' ownership.
    d. The Fund and the World Bank (WB) have considerably intensified their efforts to increase collaboration in the financial sector. In particular, we stress the importance of the joint IMF and WB efforts to assess the strength of the financial sector through the Financial Sector Assessment Program (FSAP) and welcome the increased use of FSAP and ROSC (Report on the Observance of Standards and Codes) as essential instruments to identify countries' vulnerabilities.
    e. The Fund and the Bank have also started collaborating in the poorest countries to fight poverty and make progress towards the international development goals.
    f. We welcome the progress that has been made at the IMF in making operational a framework for private sector involvement, with a view to reinforce market discipline and provide orderly adjustment.
    g. Significant measures to enhance the transparency and accountability of the Bretton Woods institutions have been put in place. In particular, an independent Evaluation Office (EVO) has been established at the IMF, and will help the Fund to increase the effectiveness of its work and enhance accountability. We look forward to its future work. We also note the need for further discussion on quotas at the IMF Executive Board.

7. Against this background, we reaffirm our commitment to step up our efforts to reduce volatility and improve the functioning of the international financial system. In this respect, we will continue to foster international consensus and action on: strengthening transparency in both the public and private sector; improving prudential regulation and supervision and fighting against abuses of the international financial system; implementing the strategy laid down last year by the International Monetary and Financial Committee (IMFC) for preventing and managing financial crises, including through private sector involvement.

8. Strong and effective crisis prevention and resolution remains a top priority in our agenda and substantial work remains to be done to further strengthen the international financial system. In this respect, this report focuses on private sector involvement, on the implementation of internationally agreed standards and codes, and on the process of opening access to international capital markets.

9. The report also addresses the reform of the MDBs to make their activities more selective and focused on poverty eradication, an issue which was raised last year in Fukuoka.

10. We will work in cooperation with the other members of the international community to ensure the implementation of these measures.

B. Private Sector Involvement in Crisis Prevention and Resolution

11. Private sector involvement in the prevention and resolution of financial crises is an integral part of our efforts to strengthen the international financial architecture. While the IMF has an essential role to play, official resources are limited in relation to private financial flows. The engagement of private investors is thus essential for the resolution of payments imbalances in crises and for the restoration of medium-term sustainability. To strengthen market discipline and promote a stable flow of finance to emerging markets, the official sector needs to avoid creating expectations that private creditors and investors will be protected from losses. At the same time we reaffirm that our aim in crisis management is not to encourage default, but rather to promote agreement between debtors and creditors on cooperative, voluntary steps to help the debtor overcome its payments difficulties.

12. We welcome the progress that has been made recently to involve the private sector in the resolution of financial crises and underscore the need for further progress. We agree on the need for further efforts to implement a range of measures, in particular:
    - we stress the importance of information sharing and enhancing the dialogue between countries and their private creditors, both during normal periods and when addressing emerging pressures in the external account. We encourage countries to establish mechanisms to support a dialogue with creditors and call on the Fund to support this process;
    - we also agree on the importance of collective action clauses to facilitate orderly crisis resolution. The IFIs should encourage the use of such clauses through their operations.

13. We welcome the agreement by the IMF to take forward further work on the framework for private sector involvement with a view to achieving greater clarity, taking into account the need for operational flexibility. In particular, further efforts are needed to:

- review the requirements and procedures used to determine access to IMF financing, including clarifying and strengthening them as necessary in order to reinforce the exceptional character of large official rescue packages. Exceptional financing, through any IMF facility, requires extensive justification. For instance, there should be evidence that the country has experienced a sudden, disruptive loss of confidence; that an early correction of difficulties is expected; and that there is a risk of contagion that could pose a wider threat to the stability of the international financial system. It should also take into account efforts by the debtor country to secure participation by private investors;
- enhance the analytical basis for the Fund's assessment of a country's financial position. Programmes should include thorough analysis of the country's medium-term debt and balance of payments profile, and prospects for regaining market access. To this end, the Fund should also provide detailed information and programme assumptions about sources of private financing and reinforce the monitoring and assessment, as appropriate of private flows during programme implementation;
- review the experience with the Fund's policy for lending into arrears;
- strengthen the relationship and increase coordination between the IMF and the Paris Club in the process of assessing the level and scope of participation of private creditors in debt restructuring cases, especially concerning comparability of treatment; and
- ensure that all programmes are subject to transparent ex-post monitoring and evaluation, with a view to assess the involvement of the private sector against the assumptions made in the programme.

14. We will review progress on this issue early next year.

C. Surveillance and Implementation of Standards and Codes

15. We reaffirm our commitment to promote the implementation and surveillance of internationally agreed codes and standards, in particular the 12 key standards identified by the Financial Stability Forum (FSF). Their implementation is in the economic interest of all countries, and ownership is an important element in this process. We welcome the contributions of the many different actors, including the IMF, the WB and the FSF, in making it possible for countries to implement codes and standards and in assessing their compliance. These efforts should be continued and coordination among the relevant institutions (IFIs and standard-setting bodies) strengthened to ensure that all inputs are effectively integrated.

16. We underscore the importance of continuing to identify market and official incentives to encourage compliance with international codes and standards as well as the need to continue raising market awareness of the significance of codes

and standards and their relevance to private sector pricing and allocation decisions. In this respect, we welcome the ongoing work of the FSF working group on incentives and call on the IMF to continue analyzing the benefits associated with implementing codes and standards.

17. Technical assistance and support is crucial to ensure that no country is left behind in the global effort to raise standards. We welcome the important contribution of the IMF, the WB and national authorities toward addressing resource constraints to implementing standards by providing advice and assistance. The IFIs should catalogue and assess these technical assistance resources and demands to ensure that support is channelled effectively. We agree to make every effort, working together with the IFIs, the FSF and the international regulatory and supervisory bodies, to consider ways to supplement the amount of human, technical and financial resources available to assist countries to implement codes and standards. In this respect, we welcome the commitments that have been made so far. We also welcome the work of the G20 in promoting dialogue on the importance of codes and standards, the appropriate pace of implementation, as well as technical assistance.

18. Significant progress has been made in producing assessments of countries' observance of international codes and standards. IMF-led ROSCs and the joint IMF-WB FSAPs should continue to be the principal and permanent tools for providing independent, authoritative and consistent assessments of individual countries' compliance with codes and standards. We welcome the fact that 133 ROSC modules have now been prepared for 47 countries and that around 52 countries have now completed or committed to undertake an FSAP. Given the importance of enhanced disclosure and transparency in international surveillance, we are encouraged by the fact that 93 ROSC modules have now been published and urge all countries that complete ROSC modules to consider publishing them.

19. We look forward to further participation in ROSC and FSAP initiatives by a range of industrial and developing countries, including G7 countries. In this respect we welcome the commitments made by the Finance Ministers and Central Bank Governors of the G20 to undertake the completion of ROSCs and FSAPs and to promote wider public articulation of commitments to adopt key standards and action plans for compliance.

20. Authoritative information on observance of codes and standards should be fully integrated into enhanced IMF surveillance under Article IV, increasing its effectiveness as a tool for crisis prevention. This is a critical step, and the IMF should work expeditiously to implement it. The work being taken forward in the Fund on the modalities for using codes and standards information to guide and inform surveillance is an important step in this direction and we encourage its early completion.

21. Work to assess compliance with, and to implement, codes and standards needs to take full account of each country's unique development and reform priorities and

institutional characteristics. We agree that countries and the Fund should continue to work, together with standard-setters as appropriate, to set priorities and establish action plans for compliance, within the framework of individual economic reform programs. The existing process for assessing compliance, which allows for progressive implementation of key codes and standards according to country-specific economic circumstances, provides an appropriate mechanism for facilitating prioritization.

22. Since combating money laundering is central to protecting the stability and integrity of the international financial system, we welcome the decision of the IMF and WB to recognize the Financial Action Task Force (FATF) 40 Recommendations as the appropriate international standard for anti money laundering and call on the IFIs, working in collaboration with the FATF, to incorporate the relevant FATF 40 Recommendations into a ROSC module on money laundering as soon as possible.

D. Opening Access to Capital Markets

23. In the Report on Strengthening the International Financial Architecture submitted to the Cologne Summit in 1999, we encouraged the IMF to continue its work on the appropriate pace and sequencing of capital account liberalization. In Fukuoka we re-stated the importance of well-sequenced capital account liberalization, and the need for countries to adopt appropriate macroeconomic, structural and domestic prudential and financial policies. This year, in our report to the Genoa Summit, we propose concrete measures to progress in this direction.

24. Mobilizing capital, both domestic and international, is essential for growth. Foreign direct investment (FDI) and productive use of equity flows and borrowed resources are hallmarks of countries that have successfully integrated into the world economy. Capital account liberalization offers the prospect of considerable benefits to emerging market economies, but also poses policy challenges. Countries that wish to pursue the opportunities offered by international capital markets should be encouraged to do so, and should also upgrade their capacity to manage the risks associated with a more open capital account, including the potential volatility of short-term capital flows.

25. Capital account liberalization is an important component of the broader process of financial liberalization. In this context, capital account liberalization should be undertaken as part of an integrated strategy comprising a stable macroeconomic environment (including a sustainable exchange rate policy), a strong prudential framework in the financial sector (including the adoption of relevant standards and codes), appropriate monitoring of statistical data, sound risk and liquidity management practices both in the public and private sectors, and complementary

structural (including social sector) reforms, to ensure that liberalization does not create new areas of vulnerability.

26. Opening access to capital market is a complex process that cannot be addressed by a standardized, one-size-fits-all approach. The goal of the international community should be to help countries adopt the appropriate policies towards gaining sustained access to global capital markets, while the final responsibility for adopting those policies rests with individual countries.

27. We call on the Bretton Woods institutions to provide support and expertise to countries seeking access to international capital markets. In order to address effectively these issues, the IFIs may rely on a broad range of tools, including:

    a. Policy advice. We welcome the IMF's efforts to provide policy advice on financial sector and capital market issues through the Article IV surveillance process. We encourage the Fund to continue these efforts. We also stress the importance of building on past experience: the country studies that are being undertaken by the G20 should provide important information for countries that are in the process of developing their own strategy towards capital account liberalization. We welcome the recent establishment of the International Capital Markets Department within the IMF. It should enable the Fund to play a leading role in assisting member countries to adopt policies that help them gain or expand access to international capital markets, in close collaboration with the WB and regional development banks.

    b. Technical assistance. We encourage the IFIs to further co-ordinate and extend technical assistance on liberalization-related topics, including deepening and broadening domestic financial markets, managing public assets and liabilities, and building capacity to manage the risks associated with capital flows. In this respect, the ROSC and FSAP could provide a useful platform for identifying potential problems, prioritizing and organizing technical assistance and coordinating with other donors.

    c. Financial assistance. The WB should strengthen its assistance to countries committed to reform their domestic financial system, including through a Financial Sector Adjustment Loan (FSAL). The IMF should stand ready to support programs which include financial sector reforms relevant to the objectives of the Fund, and which can lay the foundations for successful capital account liberalization.

28. We emphasize the contribution of FDI to economic growth and recognize that it is intrinsically more stable than portfolio and lending flows. We agree that the lack of a proper investment environment, due in particular to weak governance as well as to political and economic uncertainty, is one of the deterrents to foreign capital accumulation and needs to be addressed. The sequencing of reform and liberalization should thus give priority to creating a transparent and solid framework for attracting FDI and harnessing its

developmental advantages. In this respect, the credibility of host countries' commitment to liberalization could greatly benefit from the development and implementation of policies promoting non-discriminatory practices, transparency and investor protection. At the multilateral level, a stable and non-discriminatory investment regime could be brought about and maintained through the establishment of a high-standards framework of investment rules. To this end we encourage further work in relevant international institutions, on ways to enhance the predictability and stability of investment regimes in support of liberalization and sustainable development.

29. Competitive and healthy financial markets are essential to build confidence and induce long-term investment. In this respect, financial services liberalization relying on sound prudential regulation is of prime importance in strengthening financial sector efficiency and soundness. We recognize the value of binding commitment to financial services liberalization within the multilateral framework of the GATS. We encourage WTO members to move ahead with progressive financial services liberalization in future negotiations.

30. Concerns for excessive capital flow volatility experienced in the 1990s have revived public interest in restrictions of international capital flows, e.g., in the form of a Tobin tax on international currency transactions. Support for such types of transaction tax generally rests on the belief that it can promote greater financial stability. Several difficulties prevent such a proposal from being a workable tool:

    a. By tightening market liquidity, the tax may actually increase, rather than reduce, volatility.

    b. Even a high level of taxation is unlikely to constitute a credible deterrent to sudden capital outflows in the face of expectations of large devaluations.

    c. It is impossible to differentiate between speculative capital movements and other flows, including short-term trade financing. Hence, the Tobin tax would entail significant distortions in international capital flows, leading to lower rates of capital formation and growth.

    d. Since it is prone to avoidance and is unlikely to be globally enforced, the Tobin tax could cause capital flows to be directed to less regulated institutions and jurisdictions, thus adding to the instability in the international financial system.

31. The pursuit of further trade liberalization in the context of a broad-based new WTO round of trade negotiations can also contribute to strengthen markets and improve growth prospects, particularly in the developing world. Protectionist and trade-distorting policies must be resisted as they would only accentuate economic and financial uncertainties. We welcome the opportunity of the meeting in Qatar next November to launch a new WTO round, and we emphasize the importance of multilateral trade liberalization for sustainable development of the world economy.

E. The Multilateral Development Banks (MDBs)[1]

32. The Multilateral Development Banks are an essential component of the development architecture and have an important role to play in ensuring that the benefits of increasing global prosperity are shared by all countries. In our report for the Okinawa Summit (Fukuoka Report, July 2000), we underscored the importance of strengthening the Multilateral Development Banks to best adapt them to the new challenges. We are committed to moving ahead with this agenda. We stressed that 'accelerating poverty reduction in developing countries must be the core role of the Multilateral Development Banks (MDBs). An increased focus on poverty reduction should underpin all aspects of the MDBs' work, including in programs of policy reform, investment projects and capacity building'. We also underscored that 'economic growth is the primary determinant of a country's ability to raise incomes and reduce poverty and inequality'.

33. The MDBs must continue to play a crucial role in combating poverty and supporting equitable and sustainable economic development. Their operations should concentrate on core social and human investment (in particular health and education), enhancing productivity growth and raising income per capita. It is therefore paramount to ensure that the MDBs are fully equipped to effectively fulfil their institutional mandate in a continuously changing international environment. Hence, we have a strong interest in further strengthening MDBs' development impact and their capacity to effectively meet new challenges. Selectivity, accountability and a focus on results are key principles. Important progress has been made by the MDBs over the last few years in sharpening their focus on poverty reduction, improving their effectiveness in supporting development and achieving results, and making their internal governance more accountable and transparent. Work is underway in all these areas at each MDB. We are committed to work with these institutions and the other shareholders to build on these efforts.

34. In order to maximize their development impact it is crucial that the MDBs concentrate on the basic development priorities that they can best achieve, and work collaboratively among themselves and with other donors to ensure a development framework that is consistent and efficient. This is essential to avoid waste or dilute the impact of scarce development funds. A more selective approach needs to be adopted by the MDBs on the basis of their respective comparative advantages and by better developing synergies and complementarities. They have recently taken important steps in this direction, especially at the country level, in the context of the Comprehensive Development Framework (CDF) and in the context of country-owned development strategies, such as Poverty Reduction Strategy Papers (PRSPs). More could be achieved at the institutional level through an ex ante sharing of tasks in specific areas.

35. We reaffirm that the MDB reform should focus on the following management and operational areas: coordination, internal governance, good governance in borrower countries, pricing issues, global public goods and financial sector reform. The recommendations of this Report are addressed to all the MDBs. At the same time, we recognise that differences in mandate, role and progress already achieved in the different institutions imply that the priorities for reform may differ.[2] However, the adoption of best practice everywhere should be the rule.

36. MDB Management has been kept informed of the contents of this report and kept abreast of its development through an open and frank dialogue. We have also held informal consultations with the other MDB shareholders and NGOs/civil society in order to explain the objectives and the contents of the reform effort.

37. Coordination — Improving coordination among MDBs, at the country and institutional level, is essential in order to achieve a more selective approach to development issues, while promoting greater complementarity and avoiding undue overlapping or duplication of efforts. Positive developments at the country level through the establishment of PRSP and CDF processes increases the momentum for pursuing further progress. In this regard we ask the MDBs to:
    - strengthen the links between their Country Strategies and country-owned poverty reduction and development strategies under CDF principles to ensure a consistent development framework;
    - ensure greater coordination and consistency in substance and timing among their Country Strategies for the same country;
    - report to their own Boards by Spring 2002 on the progress towards the alignment of country strategies, indicating when a full alignment will be achieved.

    Memoranda of Understanding between the World Bank and the Regional Development Banks (RDBs) are a crucial tool to improve collaboration and efficiency at the institutional level. To this end it is paramount to:
    - further strengthen such agreements by identifying the relevant comparative advantages and the Institutions that will coordinate or take the lead in specific areas or sectors;
    - conduct periodic independent reviews of the effectiveness in the implementation of the Memoranda of Understanding. The goal would be to continuously identify areas for further improvement, particularly on issues of selectivity and comparative advantages, justify any overlap, and regularly update such Memoranda.

    Closer coordination can also be achieved by pursuing harmonization, wherever possible, at the highest appropriate standards, of the key operational policies and procedures, fiduciary and environmental safeguards, financial management and procurement rules among the MDBs. It is therefore vital, as stated by the Development Committee in April 2001, to prioritise and accelerate the harmonization process.

- A progress report on harmonization of procurement and financial management will be prepared by the World Bank, in consultation with the other MDBs, for the Development Committee in Fall 2001. We propose that the MDBs build on this by agreeing on an Action Plan indicating the steps needed to pursue the objective of harmonization. This Action Plan could be a part of the MDBs' contribution to the ongoing OECD/DAC process of harmonization.

38. Internal governance — Enhancing internal governance, accountability and transparency is crucial to enable the MDBs to strengthen their role in the fight against poverty and retain institutional credibility. Over the last few years, significant progress towards greater transparency and openness has been made. However, there is still scope for further improvement. To this end, we call upon the MDBs to:

- strengthen project design and evaluation, to attain clear development goals and objectives and measurement of development effectiveness and results; ensure that all Evaluation Departments also report directly to the Board. The MDBs should consider the preparation of periodic reports on development/ transition effectiveness to be submitted to Governors;
- establish or improve existing mechanisms, fully independent from staff responsible for project preparation, to ensure compliance of project proposals with policies and procedures prior to submission to the Board. We look forward to an assessment of the measures taken so far and further proposals being presented by the World Bank and by the RDBs by Spring 2002;
- strengthen or establish inspection mechanisms reporting directly to the Board;
- adopt a more open policy on information disclosure by making draft and final key policy and strategy documents available to the public;
- as a matter of operational urgency, establishing a more transparent budget process, by better linking institutional priorities, as agreed upon by shareholders, to the resources allocated in the budget;
- reviewing their internal organisation and take concrete steps to improve their operational effectiveness. In particular, we encourage the World Bank to continue evaluating its internal organisational structure in order to address critical aspects. We look forward to the results of the reorganisation efforts being conducted by the African Development Bank and the Asian Development Bank.

39. Good governance — Good governance is a broad concept, which entails several crucial areas, such as legal and regulatory framework, judicial systems, etc. Over the last few years, the MDBs have put good governance on the top of their agenda and have committed themselves to mainstream it in all their activities. Although the specific nature of governance issues may vary from country to country, strengthening public sector management, accountability and anti-corruption measures should be priorities in all countries. Strengthening public expenditure

and budget management, and improving promotion and enforcement of safeguard and fiduciary policies in recipient countries should be the MDBs' principal goals. Adjustment and programmatic lending approaches particularly require sound, acceptable and reliable public expenditure management.

We agreed that the MDBs should:

- include in every Country Strategy a review of the country's governance (issues, progress made, reforms underway, commitment to reform and poverty reduction, etc.) with particular focus on public sector management, accountability and anti-corruption measures;
- produce an Action Plan, by Spring 2002, identifying capacity-building needs in the area of public sector management in borrowing countries and assessing their in-house capacity in this field and possible actions to upgrade it, while taking into account the work of other development institutions;
- strengthen analytical and diagnostic work on fiduciary and safeguard policies, developing common methodologies and carry out joint assessments where possible.

40. Lending Instruments and Pricing review — The need for the MDBs to focus on operations targeted at poverty reduction, to be selective in countries with access to private capital, and to enhance the development impact of the resources available, calls for a thorough review of the MDBs' lending instruments and pricing policies. The MDBs are invited to assess whether there is scope for rationalising and streamlining existing instruments within and across the MDBs, especially in the area of adjustment lending and guarantees, to achieve greater coherence and consistency, and to avoid price competition. Pricing reviews — to be undertaken by all the MDBs — should take into account the feasibility, and related financial implications and implementation issues, of price differentiation by instrument, the development impact, and stage of borrower development. They should also take into account the issue of conditionalities across the MDBs. Ongoing work on a comprehensive and new approach to Middle Income Countries (MICs) needs to address the pricing issue, with a view to enhancing the development impact of MDB lending.

We note the current discussions at the Asian Development Bank on the introduction of more favourable terms on Ordinary Capital Resources (OCR) loans targeted to poverty. We also note the ongoing review exercise on IDA pricing, including the increased use of grants within IDA-13, and encourage the World Bank to carefully explore the related financial implications and practical implementation issues.

- The comprehensive review of lending instruments and pricing — to be carried out in the aforesaid terms, and covering all the MDBs — should be completed by the 2002 Spring Meetings of the World Bank.
- As part of this process we note that the World Bank has started working on a comprehensive pricing and instruments review, on which it will report to the

Board by the end of 2001. We encourage the early completion of this exercise so that relevant decisions can be taken before the next Spring Meetings.

41. Provision of Global Public Goods (GPGs) — Some development issues both benefit and require the participation of the entire global community. GPGs have a strong impact on development and poverty reduction. In becoming more involved in the provision of GPGs, the MDBs' main priorities should be fighting infectious diseases, promoting environmental improvement, facilitating trade and supporting financial stability. Each MDB should:

- define more explicitly its role in the provision of these GPGs on the basis of its comparative advantages and effective capacity. Each MDB's activity in these fields should be grounded in its core business and country work. The MDBs should work in close collaboration with other UN Agencies, bilateral donors and civil societies, exploiting synergies and effective partnerships. The World Bank should generally play a more active and a coordinating role — vis-à-vis the RDBs — given its global mandate;
- show how its engagement in the provision of these GPGs is reflected in its budget allocation and identify the most appropriate modalities for GPG financing.

We ask the World Bank in collaboration with the RDBs to prepare a report on these issues by the end of 2001.

42. Financial sector reform — Strong, transparent and well functioning financial sectors are an essential condition for development. The MDBs have an important role to play in helping borrowing countries strengthen their financial sector consistently with their in-house expertise and comparative advantages in this field. The World Bank, where appropriate, should continue developing an active role operating in closest partnership with the RDBs. We welcome efforts to enhance the collaboration between the IMF and the World Bank in supporting financial sector reform in developing countries. In particular, we call on the MDBs to:

- ensure that by the end of 2002 all Country Strategies incorporate financial sector issues;
- play a more proactive role in assisting borrowers, especially low-income countries, in developing institutional capacity and appropriate strategies to meet international codes and standards, including FATF anti-money laundering standards. A joint MDB report, including an Action Plan, on their role in supporting implementation of codes and standards, should be prepared by the end of 2001;
- increase their due diligence relating to transactions and dealings with entities located in Non Cooperative Countries and Territories.

43. Our meeting with the MDBs' Presidents is a tangible expression of our commitment to work with MDB Management and other shareholders to continue strengthening the development effectiveness of these important institutions on

the basis of these recommendations. We welcome the proposal made by the MDBs' Presidents that a senior MDB liaison group will monitor progress on these issues and regularly report to the respective Heads and Executive Boards.

44. We will review the progress made for the 2002 Summit in Canada.

Notes

1 MDBs are taken to cover the World Bank Group and the following Regional Development Banks (RDBs): the Inter-American Development Bank, the Asian Development Bank, the African Development Bank, the European Bank for Reconstruction and Development. The conclusions of this report are also relevant for many of the Sub-Regional Development Banks.
2 This is specially true for the European Bank for Reconstruction and Development (EBRD), in light of its special focus on the private sector and its transition mandate.

Appendix J

G7 Statement

Genova, 20 July 2001

1. We, the Heads of State and Government of the G7 countries and the Representatives of the European Union, met today in Genova to address current challenges in world macroeconomic trends and to bolster efforts aimed at promoting growth and stability, and at improving the efficiency of the international financial system.

World Economy

2. While the global economy has slowed more than expected over the past year, sound economic policies and fundamentals provide a solid foundation for stronger growth. We will remain vigilant and forward looking in implementing measures, as necessary, to ensure that our economies move towards a more sustained pattern of growth, in line with their potential. We pledge to pursue policies that will contribute to global growth by enhancing strong productivity growth in a sound macroeconomic environment, through structural reform, free trade and strengthened international economic co-operation.
   - In the United States, while growth has slowed sharply, long-term trends remain favourable. Markets are dynamic and flexible, and both monetary and fiscal policies are being actively employed to support recovery, while maintaining price stability. The recently enacted tax cuts should bolster growth.
   - In Canada, tax cuts and monetary conditions are supporting growth while structural policies should continue to be aimed at increasing productivity. In the United Kingdom, where the slowdown appears moderate, policies should continue to strengthen the foundations for sustained growth and employment over the medium term, and meet the inflation target.
   - In the euro area, although economic activity has weakened, growth prospects remain favourable. Tax cuts, as well as structural reforms aimed at further increasing employment, should continue to support sustainable non-inflationary growth. The steady implementation of economic reforms will contribute to further raising the potential for growth.
   - In Japan, economic activity has further weakened, and prices continue to decline. Against this background, monetary policy should keep providing ample liquidity. Vigorous implementation of financial and corporate sector reforms is

needed to lay the foundation for stronger economic growth over the medium term. We welcome the recently announced reform initiatives, which will contribute to this end.

3. Emerging market economies are unevenly affected by global economic developments. Growth rates in some countries have slowed towards a more sustainable rate, while in others they have decelerated sharply. We welcome the progress achieved in many countries in increasing their resilience against potential crises and the steps taken over the last year to strengthen the international financial system to better prevent crises. However, recent developments in emerging markets point to the need for further progress in reinforcing domestic financial systems and the underlying fiscal positions. Recent measures taken in Argentina and Turkey represent positive steps in this direction. We commend these efforts and encourage the continued implementation of their reform programs in close collaboration with the IMF and other relevant international financial institutions.

4. High and volatile oil prices are a concern for the world economy, in particular for the most vulnerable developing countries. Increased and diversified energy supplies, improved energy efficiency, expanded infrastructure and stable oil markets are important objectives. Oil producing and oil consuming countries should remain in close contact.

5. In addition to the policies we are pursuing in our own economies, we agreed today that co-operation on three further elements is important to a strengthened global economy:
    *   the launch of a new trade Round;
    *   action to enhance the stability and integrity of the international financial system;
    *   actions to ensure that the poorest countries are not left behind, including the implementation of the Heavily Indebted Poor Countries (HIPC) Initiative.

Launching a New Trade Round

6. Sustained economic growth world-wide requires a renewed commitment to free trade. Opening markets globally and strengthening the World Trade Organization (WTO) as the bedrock of the multilateral trading system is therefore an economic imperative. It is for this reason that we pledge today to engage personally and jointly in the launch of a new ambitious Round of global trade negotiations at the Fourth WTO Ministerial Conference in Doha, Qatar, this November.

7. We are committed to working with developing countries, including the least developed, to ensure that the new Round addresses their priorities through improved market access and sounder, more transparent trade rules. We recognise that there are legitimate concerns in implementing the Uruguay Round Agreements. We welcome the steady progress made so far on implementation

issues and are ready to examine ways to make further progress in connection with the launch of a new Round. Capacity building is essential to integrate developing countries into the trading system, and we are intensifying our efforts to assist in this area, including with international institutions.

8. In the interests of all, the new Round should be based on a balanced agenda, while clarifying, strengthening and extending multilateral rules. An improved dispute settlement mechanism is central to this effort. Increased transparency in the WTO itself is also important to strengthen confidence in the global trading system. The WTO should continue to respond to the legitimate expectations of civil society, and ensure that the new Round supports sustainable development.

9. We recognise the importance of expanding WTO membership on meaningful economic terms. We welcome the fact that negotiations with China are now almost completed and that progress is being made towards Russia's accession. We shall strongly support other applicants in their efforts to meet the conditions for an early membership, with a view to making the WTO a truly universal organisation.

Strengthening the International Financial System

10. Increasing global growth and prosperity depends crucially on a sound and stable international financial system. We are united in our determination to continue to strengthen it to prevent financial crises, to limit the impact of those that inevitably do occur, and to tackle financial abuses.

11. Since the Okinawa Summit a number of important steps have been taken, including: measures to increase the effectiveness of crisis prevention by reinforcing the International Monetary Fund (IMF) surveillance and encouraging the implementation of the key international codes and standards; involving the private sector in crisis prevention and resolution; streamlining and reforming IMF lending facilities; and enhancing IMF transparency and accountability. These efforts should be maintained.

12. Looking forward, we endorse our Finance Ministers' recommendations for action to further strengthen the international financial system and their commitment to foster international consensus in this endeavour. In particular, the international financial institutions and the G7 countries should stand ready to help countries adopt the policies required to ensure sustained access to capital markets. We also support our Finance Ministers' suggestions to further develop the framework for private sector involvement.

13. The Multilateral Development Banks (MDBs) have a central role to play in combating poverty by promoting productivity growth and supporting equitable and sustainable economic development, thus contributing to the achievement of the 2015 International Development Goals. To this end, we welcome and endorse

our Finance Ministers' recommendations for reforming the MDBs and sharpening their focus on core social and human investments, in particular health and education. We encourage the MDBs to continue to evaluate their internal structure in order to enhance their operational effectiveness. We attach particular importance to:

- strengthening co-ordination among MDBs;
- enhancing their internal governance, accountability and transparency;
- reviewing their pricing policies with a view to enhancing the development impact of the resources available;
- promoting good governance in borrowing countries.

We call on MDBs to provide support for global public goods, such as fighting infectious diseases, facilitating trade, fostering financial stability and protecting the environment. We support a meaningful replenishment of IDA and, in that context, we will explore the increased use of grants for priority social investments, such as education and health.

14. We reaffirm our support for the multilateral effort against abuses of the global financial system and endorse our Finance Ministers' recommendations to address this challenge. We welcome the efforts several jurisdictions are making to address weaknesses in their anti money laundering regimes. We endorse the recent Financial Action Task Force decisions de-listing four jurisdictions and recommending the adoption of additional counter-measures against the most uncooperative ones if they do not take appropriate action by September 30, 2001. The International Financial Institutions have an important role in helping jurisdictions improve their anti money laundering regimes and we urge them to step up their efforts in this regard. We encourage progress in assessing adherence to supervisory and regulatory standards in Offshore Financial Centres. We look forward to the 2001 OECD progress report on harmful tax practices and support the work, as envisaged by our Finance Ministers, aimed at addressing such practices. We ask our Finance Ministers for further work in these areas.

HIPC

15. The Enhanced HIPC Initiative we launched in Cologne aims to increase growth, reduce poverty and provide a lasting exit from unsustainable debt, by reducing debt on the basis of strengthened policy reforms. We welcome the important progress that has been achieved in implementing the Initiative. At Okinawa nine countries had qualified for debt relief. Now, twenty-three countries (Benin, Bolivia, Burkina Faso, Cameroon, Chad, The Gambia, Guinea, Guinea Bissau, Guyana, Honduras, Madagascar, Malawi, Mali, Mauritania, Mozambique, Nicaragua, Niger, Rwanda, Sao Tomé and Principe, Senegal, Tanzania, Uganda and Zambia) are benefiting from the Initiative, with an overall amount of debt relief of over

$53 billion, out of an initial stock of debt of $74 billion. This will significantly reduce their debt service, thus freeing resources for social sector expenditure, in particular education and health.

16. We have all agreed as a minimum to provide 100% debt reduction of official development assistance (ODA) and eligible commercial claims for qualifying HIPC countries. We urge those countries that have not already done so to take similar steps, and we underline the need for the active and full participation of all bilateral creditors in providing timely debt relief to HIPCs.

17. We encourage HIPCs that have not yet reached their decision point to quickly undertake the necessary economic and social reforms, including the development of a strategy for overall poverty reduction in co-operation with the World Bank and the IMF. Economic, structural, and social reforms, improved governance, and a strengthened ability to track poverty-reducing expenditures are necessary to ensure the maximum benefit of debt relief. In particular, we call upon those countries involved in military conflicts to lay down their arms, and implement the necessary reforms. We confirm our willingness to help them take measures needed to come forward to debt relief. We pledge to continue working together to ensure that the benefits of debt relief are targeted to assist the poor and most vulnerable.

Nuclear Safety

18. We welcome Ukraine's permanent closure of the Chernobyl Nuclear Power Plant on 15 December 2000, which was a vital accomplishment in support of nuclear safety.

Appendix K

Statement of G7 Finance Ministers on IMF-Argentina Talks

19 August 2001

We welcome the progress that has been made in ongoing discussions between the IMF and Argentina. We are optimistic about the prospects for agreement on a program that will help Argentina return to sustainable economic growth.

Appendix L

Statement of G7 Ministers of Finance

25 September 2001

We held a conference call today to discuss the economic and financial situation in our countries and our common cause in strengthening the international fight against the financing of terrorism. For the US economy, we reported that the events of September 11 will delay the recovery that was underway. However, our economic policies and fundamentals remain strong and we expect a near-term return to sustained economic growth and stable financial markets.

Since the attacks, we have all shared our national action plans to block the assets of terrorists and their associates. We will integrate these action plans and pursue a comprehensive strategy to disrupt terrorist funding around the world. We welcome the actions taken by other countries in recent days and call on all nations of the world to cooperate in this endeavor. In particular, we stressed the importance of more vigorously implementing UN sanctions on terrorist financing and we called on the Financial Action Task Force to encompass terrorist financing into its activities. We will meet in the United States in early October to review economic developments and ensure that no stone goes unturned in our mutual efforts to wage a successful global campaign against the financing of terrorism.

Appendix M

G7 Finance Ministers and Central Bank Governors Statement on Terrorism

6 October 2001

We met today to discuss international efforts to combat the financing of terrorism and to address the impact of last month's terrorist attacks on the global economy.

We stand united in our commitment to vigorously track down and intercept the assets of terrorists and to pursue the individuals and countries suspected of financing terrorists. We will implement UN sanctions to block terrorist assets. We are encouraged by the number of countries throughout the world that have already joined in international action to wage a successful fight against the financing of terrorism. We appreciate their efforts. We welcome the decision by the Financial Action Task Force to hold an extraordinary plenary session in Washington on October 29 and 30 to expand its mandate to combat terrorist financing. We will work together to implement our Action Plan which we release today.

Last month's terrorist attacks could delay the resumption of strong growth in our economies. Decisive action has already been taken to support a robust recovery. Notwithstanding remaining short-term uncertainties, we are confident about our future prospects. We are strongly committed to bringing forward needed measures to increase economic growth and preserve the health of our financial markets. We will continue to monitor exchange markets closely and cooperate as appropriate.

Emerging market and developing economies have felt the effects of the slowdown in our economies and could be affected by uncertainty following last month's terrorist attacks. The prospects of the poorest countries could be damaged, and we will take the necessary steps to mitigate these impacts. Those countries adversely impacted by recent developments should also create the conditions for strong economic growth and sustained private capital flows, and the international financial institutions stand ready to assist.

We also discussed the opportunities flowing from greater interactions and linkages among the world's people. We agreed that greater global economic integration brings large benefits. Key to raising living standards and reducing poverty is increasing productivity growth and raising the rate of potential growth. We will do so by promoting free trade and regulatory reform, strengthened capital markets, and enhanced educational opportunity. We thus reaffirm our support for the launch of a new Round of trade negotiations at the upcoming WTO Ministerial.

Greater economic integration brings with it new challenges, requiring increased international cooperation to support sound governance and strong institutions. We will continue to take steps to address dislocations associated with economic adjustment and work to ensure that all can benefit from integration, including through well-targeted and well-coordinated development assistance, effective implementation of the HIPC Initiative, and poverty reduction strategies.

We welcome Russia's continued economic growth, progress on reform, and ratification of new anti-money laundering legislation. We look forward to additional progress in the financial sector and to an improved investment climate to help sustain growth throughout Russia.

Action Plan to Combat the Financing of Terrorism

We, the G7 Finance Ministers, have developed an integrated, comprehensive Action Plan to block the assets of terrorists and their associates. We pledge to work together to deliver real results in combating the scourge of the financing of terrorism.

More vigorous implementation of international sanctions is critical to cut off the financing of terrorism. We are implementing UNSCR [United Nations Security Council Resolution] 1333 and UNSCR 1373, which call on all States to freeze the funds and financial assets not only of the terrorist Usama bin Laden and his associates, but terrorists all over the world. Each of us will ratify the UN Convention on the Suppression of Terrorist Financing as soon as possible. We will work within our Governments to consider additional measures and share lists of terrorists as necessary to ensure that the entire network of terrorist financing is addressed.

The Financial Action Task Force (FATF) should play a vital role in fighting the financing of terrorism. At its extraordinary plenary meeting in Washington DC, FATF should focus on specific measures to combat terrorist financing, including:

- Issuing special FATF recommendations and revising the FATF 40 Recommendations to take into account the need to fight terrorist financing, including through increased transparency;
- Issuing special guidance for financial institutions on practices associated with the financing of terrorism that warrant further action on the part of affected institutions;
- Developing a process to identify jurisdictions that facilitate terrorist financing, and making recommendations for actions to achieve cooperation from such countries.

Enhanced sharing of information among financial intelligence units (FIUs) is also critical to cut off the flow of resources to terrorist organizations and their associates.

We call on all countries to establish functional FIUs as soon as possible. The G7 countries will all join the Egmont Group, which promotes cooperation between national FIUs, and turn around information sharing requests as expeditiously as possible. We also call on the Egmont Group to enhance cooperation among its members, to improve its information exchange with the FIUs in other countries, and to exchange information regarding terrorist financing. We encourage all countries to establish a terrorist asset-tracking center or similar mechanism and to share that information on a cross-border basis.

Financial supervisors and regulators around the world will need to redouble their efforts to strengthen their financial sectors to ensure that they are not abused by terrorists. We welcome the guidance by the Basel Committee on Banking Supervision on customer identification to stop the abuse of the financial system by terrorists and urge that it be incorporated into banks' internal safeguards. We urge the International Monetary Fund to accelerate its efforts, in close relation with the Financial Stability Forum, to assess the adequacy of supervision in offshore financial centers and provide the necessary technical assistance to strengthen their integrity.

We ask all governments to join us in denying terrorists access to the resources that are needed to carry out evil acts.

Appendix N

Meeting of G20 Finance Ministers and Central Bank Governors

Ottawa, 16–17 November 2001

G20 Finance Ministers and Central Bank Governors

We, the Finance Ministers and Central Bank Governors of the G20, held our third meeting today in Ottawa, Ontario, Canada against the backdrop of a global economic slowdown whose effects have been exacerbated by the tragic events of September 11th, 2001.

The barbarous attacks on the United States were attacks on all of us intended to shake global economic confidence and security. We will ensure that these efforts fail.

We are committed to combating terrorism by cutting off its financial sources. There should be no safe havens for the financing of terrorism. To this end, we have agreed on an Action Plan to deny terrorists and their associates access to our financial systems. We call on other countries to take similar steps.

We are confident that the attacks of September 11 will not undermine our future economic prospects. We have taken policy actions to maintain liquidity and stabilize markets. We stand ready to take additional actions as necessary. These measures will provide the foundation for an early resumption of growth without undermining our future economic prospects. We agreed that heightened security measures should be implemented in a manner that facilitates the cross-border flow of legitimate trade in goods and services. We reaffirm our commitment to free trade and open international markets as a key source of global prosperity. In this context, we welcome the Doha Development Agenda agreed to at the WTO Ministerial Conference launch of a new WTO trade round and commit to work together to achieve multilateral trade liberalisation that accelerates progress against poverty and promotes growth.

The reduction of capital flows to emerging markets underscores the need for sound policies to provide and to maintain a positive investment environment in member countries. We remain committed to this endeavour. Adopting the best practices embodied in international standards and codes also will help support strong, stable growth and reduce the risk of future financial crises. A majority of G20 members have already participated, on a voluntary basis, in assessments under one or both of the IMF/World Bank-led Financial Sector Assessment Program (FSAP) and Reports on Observances with Standards and Codes (ROSCs) consistent with our undertaking at our inaugural meeting in Berlin in December 1999. We will continue to promote adoption of international standards and codes for transparency, macroeconomic policy, sound financial sector regulation and corporate governance in consultation as appropriate with relevant international bodies and with the private sector, and thereby strengthen the integrity of the international financial system. We will continue our work on appropriate exchange rate regimes, prudent liability management, and orderly liberalization of the capital account. These efforts reduce susceptibility to financial crises.

Borrowing countries, creditors and the international community have a common interest in efficient and well-functioning international capital markets. We would welcome the earliest possible resolution of Argentina's debt problem. We recognize that lenders are increasingly differentiating between different international borrowers, be they private or sovereign. Good communication between borrowers and their creditors can play an important role in sustaining capital flows to emerging markets. Building on the recent G-20 Roundtable with private sector representatives on promoting efficient international capital markets, we have asked our Deputies to report to our next meeting on improving the way financial crises are resolved, taking into account the lessons learned from experience in emerging markets. A common objective is to reduce uncertainty and ensure the sustainability of capital flows to emerging markets.

We recognize that the world's poorest and most vulnerable are facing acute challenges in the midst of the global economic slowdown, in particular the increased uncertainty resulting from the terrorist attacks. We look forward to participating constructively in the International Monetary and Finance Committee and Development Committee meetings with a view to ensuring that appropriate international support is available to complement the sound national policies needed to generate economic recovery in those countries most affected.

Building on our discussion at our last meeting in Montreal, we reviewed our experiences in responding to the challenges of globalization. We agreed that greater economic integration has led to demonstrable improvements in living standards for the vast majority of our citizens. The G20 and other countries that have integrated into the global system have in general made significant progress in raising real incomes and reducing poverty. But globalization also poses a number of challenges and risks, which call for enhanced international co-operation. We recognise the need to work with the international financial institutions and World Trade Organization to ensure that the benefits of globalisation are shared by all, including the poorest countries. To obtain the full benefits of globalization, our governments have a critical role in creating well-developed domestic institutions, good governance and sound domestic macroeconomic, social, and structural policies. As reflected in the Montreal Consensus, by sustaining such policies we ensure that our economies are better able to maximize the contribution of open markets to growth, equity, and well-being for all our peoples.

We accepted the generous invitation of India's Finance Minister Sinha to hold our 2002 meeting in New Delhi.

G20 Action Plan on Terrorist Financing

We, the Finance Ministers and Central Bank Governors of the G20, in the name of global peace and security, are determined to stop the financing of terrorism. The fight against terrorist financing is a shared responsibility of the G20 and the broader international community. We have therefore adopted today a comprehensive Action Plan of multilateral cooperation to deny terrorists and their associates access to, or use of, our financial systems, and to stop abuse of informal banking networks.

We will implement quickly and decisively measures that the United Nations have identified as essential to combating terrorist financing. We will block terrorists' access to our financial system. We will work with the International Financial Institutions (IFIs), the Financial Action Task Force on Money Laundering (FATF), the Financial Stability Forum (FSF) and other relevant international bodies to prevent abuses to the financial system and threats to its integrity through the promotion of international standards relevant to terrorist financing, money laundering and financial sector regulation and supervision. We welcome the conclusions of the recent FATF extraordinary plenary on terrorist financing. Above all, we will enhance our ability to share information domestically and internationally as a vital component in the fight against terrorism.

We encourage all nations to join the international effort to choke off the financing of terrorism. Where a country's willingness outstrips its ability to act in concert with us, we will provide technical assistance in accordance with this Action Plan.

In pursuing these commitments, we have agreed to the following concrete steps:

Freezing Terrorist Assets

- Each G20 member will implement the relevant UN Security Council Resolutions, particularly UNSCR 1373, to stop the financing of terrorism.
- To this end, each G20 member will, within its jurisdiction, freeze the assets of terrorists and their associates and close their access to the international financial system.
- Each G20 member will, consistent with its laws, make public the lists of terrorists whose assets are subject to freezing, and the amount of assets frozen, if any.

Implementation of International Standards

- Each G20 member will ratify and implement the UN Convention for the Suppression of the Financing of Terrorism as soon as possible.
- Each G20 member will ratify the UN Convention against Transnational Organized Crime.
- We will work co-operatively and in collaboration with the International Monetary Fund (IMF) and World Bank, FATF, FSF, Basle Committee of Banking Supervisors

(BCBS), and other relevant international bodies to promote the adoption, implementation, and assessment of international standards to combat the abuses of the financial system, including in respect of terrorist financing, financial regulation, and money laundering. We welcome FATF's offer to work collaboratively with us in implementing eight special recommendations on terrorist financing.

International Cooperation: Exchange of Information and Outreach

- We will enhance our cooperation on the international exchange of information, including regarding actions taken under UN resolutions. G20 member countries will promptly implement such measures as are necessary to facilitate this exchange.
- Each G20 member will establish promptly, or maintain, a Financial Intelligence Unit and will take steps to enhance information sharing among them, including through promoting universal participation in the Egmont Group of such units.
- We will promote the fight against terrorist financing within our respective regions, and will ask other countries to join this Action Plan.
- An important element of this effort is the work of the regional FATF-style anti-money laundering bodies. Accordingly, the G20 calls on these regional bodies to meet promptly and to expand their mandates to include terrorist financing.

Technical Assistance

- We are committed to providing, where possible, technical assistance to countries that need help in developing and implementing necessary laws, regulations and policies to combat terrorist financing and money laundering.
- We call on the International Monetary Fund, the World Bank, and other multilateral and regional organizations to provide technical assistance, including by expanding existing programs and training centres.

Compliance and Reporting

- To promote implementation and compliance with international standards, and to share information regarding our respective laws, regulations, and best practices to address terrorist financing, we will support the activities of the UN Counter-Terrorism Committee. We will also actively support surveillance and voluntary self-assessment through the IFIs, FATF and relevant international bodies.
- We will respond positively to the FATF's invitation to participate in a self-assessment of the eight special recommendations on terrorist financing.
- We encourage the FSF to undertake work respecting the actions of financial sector regulators in the fight against terrorism at its next meeting.

- We will ensure that our financial institutions and citizens comply with measures to combat the financing of terrorism and other financial crimes, and will assist them to do so, including through informing financial institutions of their obligations and new developments.
- We urge the regional FATF-style bodies to actively contribute to the FATF's worldwide self-assessment program.
- We will review our progress on this action plan at our next Ministerial meeting.

Bibliography

Alden, Edward (2001). 'Textile Industry Threat to Bush'. *Financial Times*, 6 August, p. 2.

Amato, Giuliano (2001). 'The Challenges of Global Governance'. *Politica Internazionale* vol. 29 (January-April), pp. 31–35.

Attali, Jacques (1995). *Verbatim III*. Fayard, Paris.

Bagehot, Walter (1873). *Lombard Street: A Description of the Money Market*. Paternoster Library, London.

Banco de México (2000). 'Inflation Report'. July-September-October.

Bank for International Settlements (2000). 'Market Liquidity and Stress: Selected Issues and Policy Implications'. *BIS Quarterly Review*. November.

Barro, Robert J. (1995). 'Inflation and Economic Growth'. *Bank of England Quarterly Bulletin* vol. 35, pp. 166–175.

'Basel Postponed' (2001). *Economist*, 30 June, p. 83–84.

Bayne, Nicholas (1998). 'Britain, the G8, and the Commonwealth: Lessons of the Birmingham Summit'. *Round Table* vol. 348, no. 445–457.

Bayne, Nicholas (1999). 'Continuity and Leadership in an Age of Globalisation'. In M. R. Hodges, J. J. Kirton and J. P. Daniels, eds., *The G8's Role in the New Millennium*, pp. 21–44. Ashgate, Aldershot.

Bayne, Nicholas (2000). 'The G7 Summit's Contribution: Past, Present, and Prospective'. In K. Kaiser, J. J. Kirton and J. P. Daniels, eds., *Shaping a New International Financial System: Challenges of Governance in a Globalizing World*, pp. 19–35. Ashgate, Aldershot.

Bayne, Nicholas (2000). *Hanging in There: The G7 and G8 Summit in Maturity and Renewal*. Ashgate, Aldershot.

Bayne, Nicholas (2001). 'The G7 and Multilateral Trade Liberalisation: Past Performance, Future Challenges'. In J. J. Kirton and G. M. von Furstenberg, eds., *New Directions in Global Economic Governance: Managing Globalisation in the Twenty-First Century*, pp. 23–38. Ashgate, Aldershot.

Bayne, Nicholas (2001). 'Managing Globalisation and the New Economy: The Contribution of the G8 Summit'. In J. J. Kirton and G. M. von Furstenberg, eds., *New Directions in Global Economic Governance: Managing Globalisation in the Twenty-First Century*, pp. 171–188. Ashgate, Aldershot.

Bayne, Nicholas (2001). 'Reforming the International Financial Architecture: The G7 Summit's Success and Shortcomings'. Paper presented at the Assembling a New International Financial Architecture: The Deeper Challenges, LUISS University, 17 July. Rome.

Bergsten, C. Fred (1997). 'Open Regionalism'. *World Economy* vol. 20, pp. 545–565.

Bergsten, C. Fred and C. Randall Henning (1996). *Global Economic Leadership and the Group of Seven*. Institute for International Economics, Washington DC.

Birdsall, Nancy and Augusta de la Torre (2001). 'Washington Contentious'. *Politica Internazionale* vol. 29 (January-April), pp. 97–104.

Bisignano, Joseph (1999). 'Precarious Credit Equilibria: Reflections on the Asian Financial Crisis'. *BIS Working Papers*, no. 64. <www.bis.org/publ/work64.htm> (February 2002).

Blitz, James and Stephen Fidler (2001). 'G7 Leaders Seem Upbeat on Economy'. *Financial Times*, 21 July.

Borio, Claudio (2000). 'Market Liquidity and Stress: Selected Issues and Policy Implications'. *BIS Quarterly Review*. November. <www.bis.org/publ/r_qt0011e.pdf> (February 2002).

Boughton, James (2001). *Silent Revolution: The International Monetary Fund, 1979–1989*. International Monetary Fund, Washington DC.

Bryant, Ralph C. (1995). *International Coordination of National Stabilization Policies*. Brookings Institution, Washington DC.

Buchheit, Lee C. (1998). 'Changing Bond Documentation: The Sharing Clause'. *International Financial Law Review*. July.

Buiter, Willem H. (1997). 'The Economic Case for Monetary Union in the European Union'. *Review of International Economics* vol. 5, no. 4, pp. 10–35.

Buiter, Willem H. (1999). 'Optimal Currency Areas: Why Does the Exchange Rate Regime Matter?' Sixth Royal Bank of Scotland/Scottish Economic Society Annual Lecture, 26 October. Edinburgh.

Calomiris, Charles W. and Allan H. Meltzer (1999). 'Fixing the IMF'. *National Interest*, no. 56 (Summer).

Calvo, Guillermo A. and Carmen M. Reinhart (2000). 'Fear of Floating'. NBER Working Paper No. 7993, November. <papers.nber.org/papers/W7993> (February 2002).

Camdessus, Michel and James D. Wolfensohn (1998). 'The Bretton Woods Institutions: Responding to the Asian Crisis'. In M. Fraser, ed., *The G8 and the World Economy*. Strategems Publishing Ltd., London.

Capie, Forrest M. (1998). 'Can There Be an International Lender-of-Last-Resort?' *International Finance* vol. 1, no. 2, pp. 311–325.

Capie, Forrest M. and Geoffrey E. Wood (1999). 'The IMF as an International Lender of Last Resort'. *Journal of International Banking Regulation* vol. 1, no. 3 (September).

Cerny, Philip G. (1995). 'Globalization and the Changing Logic of Collective Action'. *International Organisation* vol. 49, no. 4, pp. 595–625.

Chaplin, Graeme, Allison Emblow, and Ian Michael (2000). 'Banking System Liquidity: Developments and Issues'. *Financial Stability Review*, no. 9 (December), pp. 93–112. <www.bankofengland.co.uk/fsr/fsr09art2.pdf> (February 2002).

Claessens, Stijn, Thomas Glaessner, and Daniela Klingebiel (2000). 'Electronic Finance: Reshaping the Financial Landscape around the World'. Financial Sector Discussion Paper No. 4, The World Bank, September. Washington DC. <www.worldbank.org/research/interest/confs/upcoming/papersjuly11/E-finance.pdf> (February 2002).

Cohen, Benjamin (2000). *Life at the Top: International Currencies in the Twenty-First Century*. Essays in International Economics, No. 221. Princeton University, Princeton.

Collier, Paul and David Dollar (2001). *Globalization, Growth, and Poverty: Building an Inclusive World Economy*. World Bank and Oxford University Press, Washington DC and New York.

Cooper, Richard N. (1984). 'A Monetary System for the Future'. *Foreign Affairs* Fall.

Cooper, Richard N. (1995). 'Reform of Multilateral Financial Institutions'. In S. Ostry and G. R. Winham, eds., *The Halifax G7 Summit: Issues on the Table*. Centre for Policy Studies, Dalhousie University, Halifax.

Council of Economic Advisors (1986). *Economic Report of the President*. Government Printing Office, Washington DC.

Council of Economic Advisors (1987). *Economic Report of the President*. Government Printing Office, Washington DC.

Curzon-Price, Victoria (2000). 'Seattle Virus: A Mutant Form of Protection'. In K. R. Leube, ed., *Vordenker einer neuen Wirtschaftspolitik, Festschrift für Christian Watrin*, pp. 43–53. Frankfurter Allgemeine Buch, Frankfurt.

Dawson, Thomas C. (2001). 'Russian Central Bank Met IMF's Goals. Letter to the Editor'. *Financial Times*, 29 March, p. 12.

Decker, Paul (2000). 'The Changing Character of Liquidity and Liquidity Risk Management: A Regulator's Perspective'. Federal Reserve Bank of Chicago, April.

Dell'Ariccia, G. (1999). 'Exchange Rate Fluctuations and Trade Flows: Evidence from the European Union'. *IMF Staff Papers* vol. 46, no. 3 (September/December) <www.imf.org/external/Pubs/FT/staffp/1999/09-99/dellaric.htm> (February 2002).

Devlin, Robert et al. (2000). 'Macroeconomic Stability, Trade, and Integration'. Paper presented at a policy forum on Macroeconomic Policy Coordination and Monetary Cooperation in Mercosur, 9 October. Rio de Janeiro.

Dluhosch, Barbara (2001). 'The G7 and the Debt of the Poorest'. In J. J. Kirton, J. P. Daniels and A. Freytag, eds., *Guiding Global Order: G8 Governance in the Twenty-First Century*, pp. 79–92. Ashgate, Aldershot.

Dodsworth, John and Dubravko Mihaljek (1997). 'Hong Kong, China: Growth, Structural Change, and Economic Stability during the Transition'. International Monetary Fund Occasional Paper No. 152. International Monetary Fund, Washington DC.

Donges, Juergen B., Andreas Freytag, and Ralf Zimmermann (1997). 'TAFTA: Assuring Its Compatability with Global Free Trade'. *The World Economy* vol. 20, pp. 597–583.

Dornbusch, Rudiger (2001). 'Fewer Monies, Better Monies'. *American Economic Review* vol. 91, no. 2, pp. 238–242.

Doyle, Brian M. (2000). 'Here, Dollars, Dollars...: Estimating Currency Demand and Worldwide Currency Substitution'. Board of Governors of the Federal Reserve System Discussion Paper No. 657, January.

Eichengreen, Barry J. (1994). *International Monetary Arrangements for the 21st Century*. Brookings Institution, Washington DC.

Eichengreen, Barry J. (1999). *Toward a New International Financial Architecture: A Practical Post-Asia Agenda*. Institute for International Economics, Washington DC.

Evans, H. P. (1999). 'Debt Relief for the Poorest Countries: Why Did It Take So Long?' *Development Policy Review* vol. 17, no. 3, pp. 267–279.

Evans, Owen, Alfredo M. Leone, Mahinder Gill, et al. (2000). 'Macroprudential Indicators of Financial System Soundness'. Occasional Paper No. 192. International Monetary Fund, Washington DC. <www.imf.org/external/pubs/ft/op/192/index.htm> (February 2002).

Fatás, Antonio and Andrew K. Rose (2001). 'Do Monetary Handcuffs Restrain Lefiathan? Fiscal Policy in Extreme Exchange Rate Regimes'. Discussion Paper No. 2692. Centre for Economic Policy Research.

Feldstein, Martin (1998). 'Refocusing the IMF'. *Foreign Affairs* vol. 77, no. 2, pp. 20–33.

Fischer, Stanley (1997). 'IMF: The Right Stuff'. *Financial Times*, 16 December.

Fischer, Stanley (1998). 'In Defense of the IMF'. *Foreign Affairs* vol. 77, no. 4, pp. 103–106.

Fischer, Stanley (1999). 'On the Need for an International Lender of Last Resort'. Paper presented at the joint luncheon of the American Economic Association and the American Finance Association, New York, 3 January.

Fischer, Stanley (2001). 'Exchange Rate Regimes: Is the Bipolar View Correct?' *Journal of Economic Perspectives* vol. 15, no. 2, pp. 3–24.

Franchini-Sherifis, Rosella and Valerio Astraldi (2001). *The G7/G8: From Rambouillet to Genoa*. Franco Angelo, Milan.

Frankel, Jeffrey A. and Katharine Rockett (1988). 'International Macroeconomic Policy Coordination When Policy Makers Do Not Agree on the Model'. *American Economic Review* vol. 78, no. 3, pp. 318–340.

Frankel, Jeffrey A. and Andrew K. Rose (2000). 'Estimating the Effect of Currency Unions on Trade and Output'. NBER Working Paper No. W7857, August. <papers.nber.org/papers/w7857> (February 2002).

Fratianni, Michele and John C. Pattison (2000). *An Assessment of the Bank for International Settlements*. International Financial Institution Advisory Commission (Melzer Commission), Washington DC.

Fratianni, Michele and John C. Pattison (2001). 'International Lender of Last Resort: A Concept in Search of a Meaning'. Paper presented at the Assembling a New International Financial Architecture: The Deeper Challenges, LUISS University, 17 July. Rome.

Fratianni, Michele and John C. Pattison (2001). 'International Organisations in a World of Regional Trade Agreements: Lessons from Club Theory'. *World Economy* vol. 24, no. 3 (March), pp. 333–358.

Fratianni, Michele, Dominick Salvatore, and Paolo Savona, eds. (1999). *Ideas for the Future of the International Monetary System.* Kluwer Academic Publishers, Boston.

Frenkel, Jacob A., Morris Goldstein, and Paul Masson (1991). 'Characteristics of a Successful Exchange Rate System'. Occasional Paper No. 82. International Monetary Fund, Washington DC.

Freytag, Andreas (2000). 'Was ist wirklich neu an der New Economy?' *Zeitschrift für Wirtschaftspolitik* vol. 49, pp. 303–312.

Freytag, Andreas and Stefan Mai (2001). 'Does E-Commerce Demand International Policy Co-ordination? Some Reflections on the Okinawa Charter on the Global Information Society'. Paper presented at the Annual Public Choice Society Meeting, 9–11 March. San Antonio.

Friedman, Milton and Robert A. Mundell (2001). 'One World, One Money?' *Policy Options* vol. 22, no. 4, pp. 10–30.

Friedman, Milton and Anna Schwartz (1963). *A Monetary History of the United States, 1867–1960.* Princeton University Press, Princeton.

Funabashi, Yoichi (1987). *Managing the Dollar: From the Plaza to the Louvre.* Institute for International Economics, Washington DC.

Furfine, Craig H. (2000). 'Empirical Evidence on the Need for a Lender of Last Resort'. *BIS Working Papers*, no. 88.

G8 (2000). 'Okinawa Charter on Global Information Society'. Okinawa, 22 July. <www.library.utoronto.ca/g7/summit/2000okinawa/gis.htm> (February 2002).

G8 (2001). 'Digital Opportunities for All: Meeting the Challenge. Report of the Digital Opportunity Task Force (Dot Force) Including a Proposal for a Genoa Plan of Action'. 11 May, Genoa. <www.g7.utoronto.ca/g7/summit/2001genoa/dotforce1.html> (February 2002).

Gardner, Hall and Radoslava Stefanova, eds. (2001). *The New Transatlantic Agenda: Facing the Challenges of Global Governance.* Ashgate, Aldershot.

German Council of Economic Advisors (2000). 'Chancen auf einen höheren Wachstumspfad'. Annual Report 2000/2001, Metzler-Poeschel, Stuttgart.

Giannini, Curzio (1999). *'Enemy of None but a Common Friend of All'? An International Perspective on the Lender-of-Last-Resort Function.* Princeton University Press, Princeton.

Giannini, Curzio (2001). 'Broad in Scope, Soft in Method: International Cooperation and the Quest for Financial Stability in Emerging Markets'. Manuscript, Bank of Italy.

Giersch, Herbert (1979). 'Aspects of Growth, Structural Change, and Employment: A Schumpeterian Perspective'. *Weltwirtschaftliches Archiv* vol. 115, pp. 629–652.

Gill, Stephen, ed. (1993). *Gramsci, Historical Materialism, and International Relations.* Cambridge University Press, Cambridge.

Giovanoli, Mario (2000). 'A New Architecture for the Global Financial Market: Legal Aspects of International Financial Standard Setting'. In M. Giovanoli, ed., *International Monetary Law: Issues for the New Millennium.* Oxford University Press, Oxford.

Goldstein, Morris (2001). 'IMF Structural Conditionality: How Much Is Too Much?' Working Paper No. 01-4, Institute for International Economics. <www.iie.com/catalog/WP/2001/01-4.pdf> (February 2002).

Goldstein, Morris and Council on Foreign Relations (1999). *Safeguarding Prosperity in a Global Financial System: The Future International Financial Architecture.* Institute for International Economics, Washington DC.

Goodfriend, Marvin and Robert G. King (1988). 'Financial Deregulation, Monetary Policy, and Central Banking'. Working paper 88-1. Federal Reserve Bank of Richmond Economic Review.

Goodhart, Charles A. E. (1999). 'Myths about the Lender of Last Resort'. Henry Thornton Lecture, City University Business School, 17 November.

Goodhart, Charles A. E. (2000). *Which Lender of Last Resort for Europe?* Central Banking Publications Limited, London.

Goodhart, Charles A. E. and Dirk Schoenmaker (1993). 'Institutional Separation between Supervisory and Monetary Agencies'. In F. Bruni, ed., *'Prudential Regulation, Supervison, and Monetary Policy', Giornale Degli Economisti E Annali Di Economia*, pp. 353–440.

Haggard, Stephen (2000). *The Political Economy of the Asian Financial Crisis.* Institute for International Economics, Washington DC.

Hale, David (2001). 'Have Hedge Funds Become an Agent of Monetary Policy?'. Zurich Financial Services, 13 June.

Hamada, Kiochi and Masahiro Kuwai (1997). 'Strategic Approaches to International Policy Coordination: Theoretical Developments'. In M. Fratianni, D. Salvatore and J. von Hagen, eds., *Macroeconomic Policy in Open Economies.* Greenwood Press, Westport, CT.

Hausmann, Ricardo, Michael Gavin, Carmen Pagés-Serra, et al. (2000). 'Financial Turmoil and the Choice of Exchange Rate Regime'. In E. Fernández-Arias and R. Hausmann, eds., *Wanted: World Financial Stability*, pp. 131–164. Inter-American Development Bank, Washington DC.

Herring, Richard J. and Robert E. Litan (1995). *Financial Regulation in the Global Economy.* Brookings Institution, Washington DC.

Hicks, John Richard (1967). 'Monetary Theory and History: An Attempt at Perspective'. In J. R. Hicks, ed., *Critical Essays in Monetary Theory*, pp. 155–173. Clarendon Press, Oxford.

Hiemenz, Ulrich (2001). 'Internet, E-Commerce, and Asian Development'. Mimeo. Organisation for Economic Co-operation and Development, Paris.

Hilbers, Paul (2001). 'The IMF/World Bank Financial Assessment Program'. *Economic Perspectives*. February. <www.imf.org/external/np/vc/2001/022301.htm> (February 2002).

Hodges, Michael R., John J. Kirton, and Joseph P. Daniels, eds. (1999). *The G8's Role in the New Millennium*. Ashgate, Aldershot.

Hoekman, Bernard and Carlos Primo Braga (1997). 'Protection and Trade in Services: A Survey'. Discussion Paper No. 1705. Centre for Economic Policy Research.

Holman, Michael and Quentin Peel (1999). 'Too Much to Bear'. *Financial Times*, 12 June.

House of Commons (United Kingdom) (1983). *International Monetary Arrangements: International Lending by Banks*. Vol. 1, Report, Treasury Civil Service Committee. Her Majesty's Stationery Office, London.

International Association of Insurance Supervisors (1997). 'Guidance on Insurance Regulation and Supervision for Emerging Market Economies'. <www.iaisweb.org/framesets/pas.html> (February 2002).

International Monetary Fund (1984). 'Exchange Rate Volatility and World Trade'. Occasional Paper No. 28. International Monetary Fund, Washington DC.

International Monetary Fund (1996). 'Interim Committee Report'. Washington DC.

International Monetary Fund (1996). 'International Capital Markets: Developments, Prospects, and Key Policy Issues'. Washington DC.

International Monetary Fund (1996). 'Standards for the Dissemination by Countries of Economic and Financial Statistics'. Discussion draft prepared by a staff team. Washington DC.

International Monetary Fund (1998). *International Financial Statistics Yearbook*. International Monetary Fund, Washington DC.

International Monetary Fund (1998). 'World Economic Outlook and International Capital Markets'. <www.imf.org/external/pubs/ft/weo/weo1298/index.htm> (February 2002).

International Monetary Fund (1999). 'IMF Annual Report 1999'. International Monetary Fund, Washington DC.

International Monetary Fund (1999). 'International Capital Markets: Developments, Prospects, and Key Policy Issues'. <www.imf.org/external/pubs/ft/icm/1999/index.htm> (February 2002).

International Monetary Fund (1999). 'World Economic Outlook, May 1999'. Washington DC.

International Monetary Fund (1999). 'World Economic Outlook, October 1999'. Washington DC.

International Monetary Fund (2000). 'International Capital Markets: Developments, Prospects, and Key Policy Issues'. <www.imf.org/external/pubs/ft/icm/2000/01/eng/index.htm> (February 2002).

International Monetary Fund (2001). 'Conditionality in Fund-Supported Programs — Overview'. 20 February. <www.imf.org/external/np/pdr/cond/2001/eng/overview> (February 2002).

International Monetary Fund (2001). 'Country-Specific Needs Still Dictate Choice of Exchange Rate Regime, Panelists Find'. *IMF Survey* 16 April, pp. 123–126. <www.imf.org/external/pubs/ft/survey/2001/041601.pdf> (February 2002).

International Monetary Fund (2001). 'Debt Relief under the Heavily Indebted Poor Countries (HIPC) Initiative. A Factsheet'. <www.imf.org/external/np/exr/facts/hipc.htm> (February 2002).

International Monetary Fund (2001). 'Discussants Weigh Impact of Foreign Participation in Financial Systems of Developing Countries'. *IMF Survey* 21 May, pp. 173–174. <www.imf.org/external/pubs/ft/survey/2001/052101.pdf> (February 2002).

International Monetary Fund (2001). 'Mundell Calls for a Closer Monetary Union as Step toward Single World Currency'. *IMF Survey* 5 March, p. 75. <www.imf.org/external/pubs/ft/survey/2001/030501.pdf> (February 2002).

International Monetary Fund (2001). 'Streamlining Structural Conditionality: Review of Initial Experience'. 10 July. <www.imf.org/external/np/pdr/cond/2001/eng/collab/review.htm> (February 2002).

Ito, Kunihiko (2001). 'Japan, the Asian Economy, the International Financial System, and the G8: A Critical Perspective'. In J. J. Kirton and G. M. von Furstenberg, eds., *New Directions in Global Economic Governance: Managing Globalisation in the Twenty-First Century*, pp. 127–142. Ashgate, Aldershot.

Jeanne, Olivier (2000). *Currency Crises: A Perspectives on Recent Theoretical Developments*. Special Papers in International Economics. Vol. 20, International Finance Section. Princeton University Press, Princeton.

Jeanne, Olivier and Charles Wyplosz (2000). 'The International Lender of Last Resort: How Large Is Large Enough'. Mimeo.

Jeanne, Olivier and Jeromin Zettelmeyer (2000). 'International Bailouts, Domestic Supervision, and Moral Hazard'. Mimeo.

Kaiser, Karl, John J. Kirton, and Joseph P. Daniels, eds. (2000). *Shaping a New International Financial System: Challenges of Governance in a Globalizing World*. Ashgate, Aldershot.

Katada, Saori (2001). 'Japan's Approach to Shaping a New International Financial Architecture'. In J. J. Kirton and G. M. von Furstenberg, eds., *New Directions in Global Economic Governance: Managing Globalisation in the Twenty-First Century*, pp. 113–126. Ashgate, Aldershot.

Kaufman, George G. (1999). 'Banking and Currency Crises and Systemic Risk: A Taxonomy and Review'. Paper presented at the conference on Regulation and Stability in the Banking Sector, De Nederlandse Bank, 3–5 November. Amsterdam.

Kenen, Peter B., ed. (1994). *Managing the World Economy: Fifty Years after Bretton Woods*. Washington DC, Institute for International Economics.

Kenen, Peter B. (1996). *From Halifax to Lyon: What Has Been Done about Crisis Management?* Essays in International Finance, No. 200. Princeton University Press, Princeton.

Kirton, John J. (1989). 'The Seven Power Summit as an International Concert'. Paper presented at the International Studies Association annual meeting, April. London.

Kirton, John J. (1993). 'The Seven Power Summits as a New Security Institution'. In D. Dewitt, D. Haglund and J. J. Kirton, eds., *Building a New Global Order: Emerging Trends in International Security*, pp. 335–357. Oxford University Press, Toronto.

Kirton, John J. (1995). 'The Diplomacy of Concert: Canada, the G7 and the Halifax Summit'. *Canadian Foreign Policy* vol. 3, no. 1 (Spring), pp. 63–80.

Kirton, John J. (1999). 'Explaining G8 Effectiveness'. In J. J. Kirton and J. P. Daniels, eds., *The G8's Role in the New Millennium*, pp. 45–68. Ashgate, Aldershot.

Kirton, John J. (2000). 'The Dynamics of G7 Leadership in Crisis Response and System Reconstruction'. In K. Kaiser, J. J. Kirton and J. P. Daniels, eds., *Shaping a New International Financial System: Challenges of Governance in a Globalizing World*, pp. 65–94. Ashgate, Aldershot.

Kirton, John J. (2000). 'Preliminary Personal Assessment of the Kyushu-Okinawa Summit'. 23 July. <www.g7.utoronto.ca/g7/evaluations/2000okinawa/kirtonassesment.htm> (February 2002).

Kirton, John J. (2001). 'The G7/8 and China: Toward a Closer Association'. In J. J. Kirton, J. P. Daniels and A. Freytag, eds., *Guiding Global Order: G8 Governance in the Twenty-First Century*. Ashgate, Aldershot.

Kirton, John J. (2001). 'The G20: Representativeness, Effectiveness, and Leadership in Global Governance'. In J. J. Kirton, J. P. Daniels and A. Freytag, eds., *Guiding Global Order: G8 Governance in the Twenty-First Century*, pp. 143–172. Ashgate, Aldershot.

Kirton, John J. (2001). 'Generating Genuine Global Governance: Prospects for the Genoa G8 Summit'. <www.g7.utoronto.ca/g7/evaluations/2001genoa/prospects_kirton.html> (February 2002).

Kirton, John J. (2001). 'Guiding Global Economic Governance: The G20, the G7, and the International Monetary Fund at Century's Dawn'. In J. J. Kirton, J. P. Daniels and A. Freytag, eds., *Guiding Global Order: G7 Governance in the Twenty-First Century*, pp. 143–167. Ashgate, Aldershot.

Kirton, John J. (2001). 'Prospects for the 2001 Genoa G7/G8 Summit'. 15 July, <www.g7.utoronto.ca/g7/evaluations/2001genoa/prospects_kirton.html> (February 2002).

Kirton, John J., Joseph P. Daniels, and Andreas Freytag, eds. (2001). *Guiding Global Order: G8 Governance in the Twenty-First Century*. Ashgate, Aldershot.

Kirton, John J., Joseph P. Daniels, and Andreas Freytag (2001). 'Introduction'. In J. J. Kirton, J. P. Daniels and A. Freytag, eds., *Guiding Global Order: G8 Governance in the Twenty-First Century*, pp. 1–18. Ashgate, Aldershot.

Kirton, John J., Eleanore Kokotsis, and Diana Juricevic (2001). 'G7/G8 Commitments and Their Significance'. 22 July, <www.g7.utoronto.ca/g7/evaluations/2001genoa/genoa_commitments_sum.html> (February 2002).

Kirton, John J., Eleanore Kokotsis, and Diana Juricevic (2001). 'Promises Made, Promises Kept: Commitment and Compliance at the Okinawa 2000 G7/G8 Summit'. Paper prepared for Canada's Department of Foreign Affairs and International Trade.

Kirton, John J. and George M. von Furstenberg, eds. (2001). *New Directions in Global Economic Governance: Managing Globalisation in the Twenty-First Century*. Ashgate, Aldershot.

Kiuchi, Takashi (2000). 'The Asian Crisis and Its Implications'. In K. Kaiser, J. J. Kirton and J. P. Daniels, eds., *Shaping a New International Financial System: Challenges of Governance in a Globalising World*, pp. 37–46. Ashgate, Aldershot.

Kiuchi, Takashi (2001). 'Japan, Asia and the Rebuilding of Financial Sector'. Paper presented at the Assembling a New International Financial Architecture: The Deeper Challenges, LUISS University, 17 July. Rome.

Köhler, Horst (2001). 'New Challenges for Exchange Rate Policy'. Remarks at the Asia-Europe Meeting of Finance Ministers, 13 January. <www.imf.org/external/np/speeches/2001/011301.htm> (February 2002).

Kokotsis, Eleanore (1999). *Keeping International Commitments: Compliance, Credibility, and the G7, 1988–1995*. Garland, New York.

Kokotsis, Ella and Joseph P. Daniels (1999). 'G8 Summits and Compliance'. In M. R. Hodges, J. J. Kirton and J. P. Daniels, eds., *The G8's Role in the New Millennium*, pp. 75–91. Ashgate, Aldershot.

Krugman, Paul R. (2001). 'Reckonings: Half a Loaf'. *New York Times*, 21 March, p. 23.

Kumar, Manmohan S., Paul R. Masson, and Marcus Miller (2000). 'Global Financial Crises: Institutions and Incentives'. IMF Working Paper No. 00/105. Washington DC. <www.imf.org/external/pubs/ft/wp/2000/wp00105.pdf> (February 2002).

Laidler, D. (1999). 'What Do the Fixers Want to Fix? The Debate About Canada's Exchange Rate Regime'. C.D. Howe Institute.

Lawton, Thomas (2001). 'The New Global Electronic Economy: The Contribution of the G8 Summit'. In J. J. Kirton and G. M. von Furstenberg, eds., *New Directions in Global Economic Governance: Managing Globalisation in the Twenty-First Century*, pp. 39–60. Ashgate, Aldershot.

Lerrick, Adam (2001). 'When Is a Haircut Not a Haircut? When the IMF Is the Barber'. *Wall Street Journal*, 23 February, p. A15.

Lewis, Flora (1991–92). 'The G7 1/2 Directorate'. *Foreign Policy* vol. 85, pp. 25–40.

Lewis, Karen V. (1999). 'Trying to Explain Home Bias in Equities and Consumption'. *Journal of Economic Literature* vol. 37, no. 2, pp. 571–608.

Lockwood, Matthew, Emma Donlon, Karen Joyner, et al. (1998). 'Forever in Your Debt? Eight Poor Nations and the G8'. Christian Aid, London. <www.christian-aid.org.uk/indepth/9805fore/forever1.htm> (February 2002).

Mastroeni, Michele (2001). 'Creating Rules for the Global Information Economy: The United States and G8 Leadership'. In J. J. Kirton and G. M. von Furstenberg, eds., *New Directions in Global Economic Governance: Managing Globalisation in the Twenty-First Century*, pp. 61–74. Ashgate, Aldershot.

McKibbon, Warwick J. (1997). 'Empirical Evidence on International Economic Policy Coordination'. In M. Fratianni, D. Salvatore and J. von Hagen, eds., *Macroeconomic Policy in Open Economies*. Greenwod Press, Westport, CT.

McKinnon, Ronald I. (1988). 'Monetary and Exchange Rate Policies for International Financial Stability: A Proposal'. *Journal of Economic Perspectives* vol. 2, no. 1 (Winter), pp. 83–103.

Meltzer, Allan H. (1999). 'What's Wrong with the IMF? What Would Be Better?' In W. C. Hunter, G. G. Kaufman and T. H. Krueger, eds., *The Asian Financial Crisis: Origins, Implications, and Solutions*. Kluwer Academic Publishers, Norwell, MA.

Meltzer, Allan H. (2000). *Report of the International Financial Institutions Advisory Commission*. United States Congress, Washington DC. <www.house.gov/jec.imf/meltzer.htm> (February 2002).

Messerlin, Patrick (1990). 'Anti-Dumping Regulations or Pro-Cartel Laws'. *The World Economy* vol. 13, pp. 465–492.

Milner, Helen (1997). 'The Political Economy of International Policy Coordination'. In M. Fratianni, D. Salvatore and J. von Hagen, eds., *Macroeconomic Policy in Open Economies*. Greenwood Press, Westport, CT.

Mundell, Robert A. (2000). 'A Reconsideration of the Twentieth Century'. *American Economic Review* vol. 90, no. 3, pp. 327–340.

Mundell, Robert A. (2000). 'Exchange Rate Arrangements in Central and Eastern Europe'. In S. Arndt, H. Handler and D. Salvatore, eds., *Eastern Enlargement: The Sooner, the Better?*, pp. 158–165. Austrian Ministry for Economic Affairs and Labour, Vienna.

Mussa, Michael, Paul Masson, Alexander Swoboda, et al. (2000). 'Exchange Rate Regimes in an Increasingly Integrated World Economy'. Occasional Paper No. 193. International Monetary Fund, Washington DC. <www.imf.org/external/pubs/ft/op/193/index.htm> (February 2002).

Naiman, Robert (2001). 'The "Errors" of the International Financial Institutions'. *Politica Internazionale* vol. 29 (January-April), pp. 83–90.

Nitsch, Volker (2001). 'Honey, I Shrank the Currency Union Effect on Trade'. Draft dated 7 May. Bankgesellschaft Berlin, Germany.

Nuti, Domenico M. (2000). 'The Costs and Benefits of Euro-Isolation in Central-Eastern Europe Before and Instead of EMU Membership'. In S. Arndt, H. Handler and D. Salvatore, eds., *Eastern Enlargement: The Sooner, the Better?*, pp. 171–194. Austrian Ministry for Economic Affairs and Labour, Vienna.

Odom, William (1995). 'How to Create a True World Order'. *Orbis* vol. 39, no. 2, pp. 155–172.

Ogden, Nick (2001). 'Cross Border Security'. *World Finance* spring, pp. 38–39.

Organisation for Economic Co-operation and Development (1998). *International Direction of Trade Statistics*. Organisation for Economic Co-operation and Development, Paris.

Organisation for Economic Co-operation and Development (2001). 'Harmful Tax Practices'. <www.oecd.org/daf/fa/harm_tax/harmtax.htm> (February 2002).

Organisation for Economic Co-operation and Development (2001). 'More about the FATF & Its Work'. <www.oecd.org/fatf/AboutFATF_en.htm> (February 2002).

Persaud, Randall B. (2001). 'OECD Curbs on Offshore Financial Centres: A Major Issue for Small States'. *Round Table* vol. 359 (April 2001), pp. 199–211.

Plender, John (2001). 'The Limits of Ingenuity'. *Financial Times*, 17 May, p. 12.

Porter, Tony (2001). 'The Politics of International Financial Standards and Codes'. Paper prepared for the International Studies Association meeting, 26 July. Hong Kong.

Putnam, Robert and Nicholas Bayne (1987). *Hanging Together: Co-operation and Conflict in the Seven-Power Summit*. 2nd ed. Sage Publications, London.

Rogoff, Kenneth (1999). 'International Institutions for Reducing Global Financial Instability'. *Journal of Economic Perspectives* vol. 13, pp. 21–42.

Rogoff, Kenneth (2001). 'Why Not a Global Currency?' *American Economic Review* vol. 91, no. 2, pp. 243–247.

Rugman, Alan M. (2000). *The End of Globalization*. Random House, London.

Sachs, Jeffrey (1997). 'Power Unto Itself'. *Financial Times*, 10 December.

Salvatore, Dominick (1994). 'The International Monetary System: Past, Present, and Future'. *Fordham Law Review* vol. 62, no. 7, pp. 1975–1988.

Salvatore, Dominick (1999). 'Could the Financial Crisis in East Asia Have Been Predicted?' *Journal of Policy Modeling* vol. 21, no. 3, pp. 341–347.

Salvatore, Dominick (2000). 'The Euro, the Dollar, and the International Monetary System'. *Journal of Policy Modeling* vol. 22, no. 3, pp. 407–415.

Savona, Paolo, ed. (2000). *The New Architecture of the International Monetary System*. Kluwer Academic Publishers, Boston.

Savona, Paolo (2001). 'On Some Unresolved Problems of Monetary Theory and Policy'. Paper presented at the Assembling a New International Financial Architecture: The Deeper Challenges, LUISS University, 17 July. Rome.

Savona, Paolo, Aurelio Maccario, and Chiara Oldani (2000). 'On Monetary Analysis of Derivatives'. In P. Savona, ed., *The New Architecture of the International Monetary System*, pp. 149–175. Kluwer Academic Publishers, Boston.

Schroeder, Gerhard (1999). 'Germany's Helping Hand'. *Financial Times*, 21 January.

Schwartz, M. J. and A. Torres (2001). 'Long-Term Viability of a Flexible Exchange Rate Regime in Mexico'. Paper prepared at the Banco de México, January.

Schwegmann, Christoph (2001). 'Modern Concert Diplomacy: The Contact Group and the G7/8 in Crisis Management'. In J. J. Kirton, J. P. Daniels and A. Freytag, eds., *Guiding Global Order: G8 Governance in the Twenty-First Century*. Ashgate, Aldershot.

Simmons, Beth (2000). 'The Legalization of International Monetary Affairs'. J. Goldstein, M. Kahler, R. O. Keohane, A. M. Slaughter, eds., 'Legalization and World Politics,' special issue. *International Organization* vol. 46, pp. 391–425.

Snidal, Duncan (1985). 'The Limits of Hegemonic Stability Theory'. *International Organisation* vol. 39, no. 4 (Autumn), pp. 579–614.

Solow, Robert (2000). 'Umweltpolitik und internationaler Handel'. Otto-von-Guericke Lecture, Otto-von-Guericke-Universität, 24 May. Magdeburg.

Stiroh, Kevin J. (1999). 'Is There a New Economy?' *Challenge* vol. 82, no. 4, pp. 82–101.

'Summary of Bills Pertaining to Electronic Signatures and Authentication in the 106th Congress' (2000). *Tech Law Journal* <techlawjournal.com/cong106/digsig/Default.htm> (February 2002).

Summers, Lawrence H. (1999). 'The Right Kind of IMF for a Stable Global Financial System'. Remarks to the London School of Business, London. <www.ustreas.gov/press/releases/ps294.htm> (February 2002).

Tao, Dong and Joseph Lau (1998). 'Dollarisation: An Emergency Exit for Hong Kong?' *Asian Economic Perspective*. Credit Suisse/First Boston. August.

Theuringer, Martin (2001). 'International Macroeconomic Policy Co-operation in the Era of the Euro'. In J. J. Kirton, J. P. Daniels and A. Freytag, eds., *Guiding Global Order: G8 Governance in the Twenty-First Century*, pp. 173–187. Ashgate, Aldershot.

Thornton, Henry (1802). *An Enquiry into the Nature and Effects of the Paper Credit of Great Britain*. Hatchard, London.

Tobin, James (1961). 'Money, Capital, and Other Stores of Value'. *American Economic Review* vol. 51, no. 2, pp. 26–37.

Tobin, James (1965). 'The Monetary Interpretation of History (A Review Article)'. *American Economic Review* vol. 55, no. 3, pp. 464–485.

Ullrich, Heidi K. (2001). 'Stimulating Trade Liberalisation after Seattle: G7/8 Leadership in Global Governance'. In J. J. Kirton and G. M. von Furstenberg, eds., *New Directions in Global Economic Governance: Creating International Order for the Twenty-First Century*, pp. 219–240. Ashgate, Aldershot.

United Nations Conference on Trade and Development (1999). 'World Investment Review 1999'. United Nations Conference on Trade and Development, Geneva.

Upper, Christian and Andreas Worms (2001). 'Estimating Bilateral Exposures in the German Interbank Market: Is There a Danger of Contagion?' Paper presented at the Conference on Bank Structure and Competition, Federal Reserve Bank of Chicago, May. Chicago.

Velasco, A. (2001). 'The Impossible Duo? Globlization and Monetary Independence in Emerging Markets'. Paper prepared for the Brookings Trade Forum, 10–11 May, rev. 20 May. Washington DC.

von Furstenberg, George M. (2000). 'The Case against U.S. Dollarization'. *Challenge* vol. 43, no. 4, pp. 108–120.

von Furstenberg, George M. (2000). 'Transparentising the Global Money Business'. In K. Kaiser, J. J. Kirton and J. P. Daniels, eds., *Shaping a New International Financial System: Challenges of Governance in a Globalizing World*, pp. 97–111. Ashgate, Aldershot.

von Furstenberg, George M. (2000). 'U.S.-Dollarization in Latin America: A Second-Best Monetary Union for Overcoming Regional Currency Risk'. *Economia, Societá, e Istituzioni* vol. 12, no. 3, pp. 281–317.

von Furstenberg, George M. (2001). 'Assembling a New Financial Architecture: The G7's 2001 Role and Response'. Paper prepared for 'Assembling a New International Financial Architecture: The Deeper Challenges', LUISS University, 17 July. Rome.

von Furstenberg, George M. (2001). 'Pressures for Currency Consolidation in Insurance and Finance: Are the Currencies of Financially Small Countries on the Endangered List?' *Journal for Policy Modeling* vol. 23, pp. 321–331.

von Furstenberg, George M. and Joseph P. Daniels (1992). 'Economic Summit Declarations, 1975–1989: Examining the Written Record of International Cooperation'. *Princeton Studies in International Finance*, no. 72.

von Hagen, Jürgen and Michele Fratianni (1998). 'Banking Regulation with Variable Geometry'. In B. J. Eichengreen and J. Frieden, eds., *Forging an Integrated Europe*. University of Michigan Press, Ann Arbor.

Wallace, William (1984). 'Political Issues at the Summits: A New Concert of Powers?' In C. Merlini, ed., *Economic Summits and Western Decisionmaking*. St. Martin's Press, London.

Watanabe, Koji (1999). 'Japan's Summit Contributions and Economic Challenges'. In M. R. Hodges, J. J. Kirton and J. P. Daniels, eds., *The G8's Role in the New Millennium*, pp. 95–106. Ashgate, Aldershot.

Wechsler, William F. (2001). 'Follow the Money'. *Foreign Affairs* vol. 80, no. 4, pp. 40–57.

Wolf, Martin (1997). 'Same Old IMF Medicine'. *Financial Times*, 8 December.

Index